Currency and Competitiveness in Europe

Edited by

Klaus Liebscher

Governor of the Oesterreichische Nationalbank, Austria

Josef Christl

Member of the Governing Board of the Oesterreichische Nationalbank, Austria

Peter Mooslechner

Director of the Economic Analysis and Research Department at the Oesterreichische Nationalbank, Austria

Doris Ritzberger-Grünwald

Head of Foreign Research at the Oesterreichische Nationalbank, Austria

Edward Elgar

Cheltenham, UK • Northampton, MA, USA

Published by
Edward Elgar Publishing Limited
The Lypiatts
15 Lansdown Road
Cheltenham
Glos GL50 2JA
UK

Edward Elgar Publishing, Inc.
William Pratt House
9 Dewey Court
Northampton
Massachusetts 01060
USA

A catalogue record for this book
is available from the British Library

Library of Congress Control Number: 2008934875

ISBN 978 1 84844 035 7

Printed and bound in Great Britain by MPG Books Ltd, Bodmin, Cornwall

Contents

Contributors

Enrique Alberola, Head of International Economy Division, Banco de España.

Lorenzo Bini Smaghi, Member of the Executive Board, European Central Bank.

Michael C. Bonello, Governor, Central Bank of Malta.

Jan Brůha, Economist, External Economic Relations Division, Czech National Bank.

Josef Christl, Executive Director, Oesterreichische Nationalbank.

Servaas Deroose, Director, Economic and Financial Affairs Directorate General (DG ECFIN), European Commission.

Martin D.D. Evans, Professor of Economics, and Professor of Finance, Department of Economics and McDonough School of Business (MSB), Georgetown University, Washington, DC, and National Bureau of Economic Research (NBER).

Marcel Fratzscher, Senior Adviser, European Central Bank.

Hans Genberg, Executive Director, Research, Hong Kong Monetary Authority.

Áron Gereben, Deputy Head of Financial Analysis, Magyar Nemzeti Bank, Hungary Financial Studies Division.

Deniz Igan, Economist, Research Department, International Monetary Fund.

Graciela Laura Kaminsky, Professor, Economics Department, George Washington University and National Bureau of Economic Research (NBER).

Paul Kutos, Economist, Economic and Financial Affairs Directorate General (DG ECFIN), European Commission.

Klaus Liebscher, Governor, Oesterreichische Nationalbank.

John Lipsky, First Deputy Managing Director, International Monetary Fund.

Ronald MacDonald, Adam Smith Professor of Political Economy, University of Glasgow and Fellow of CESifo research network, Munich.

Peter Mooslechner, Director of the Economic Analysis and Research Department, Oesterreichische Nationalbank.

Athanasios Orphanides, Governor, Central Bank of Cyprus.

Jiří Podpiera, Director of External Economic Relations Division, Czech National Bank.

Doris Ritzberger-Grünwald, Head of the Foreign Research Division, Oesterreichische Nationalbank.

Antonio Scalia, Head of Risk Management Division, Monetary and Foreign Exchange Policy Department, Banca d'Italia.

José María Serena, Economist, International Economy Division, Banco de España.

Ivan Šramko, Governor, Central Bank of Slovakia.

Massimo Suardi, Head of Unit, Economic and Financial Affairs Directorate General (DG ECFIN), European Commission.

John Williamson, Senior Fellow, Peterson Institute, Washington, DC.

Julia Woerz, Economist, Foreign Research Division, Osterreichische Nationalbank; former staff economist, Vienna Institute for International Economic Studies (wiiw).

Preface

Understanding exchange rates is not an easy task. Unforeseen movements in one direction or another have fuelled the perception in economics that exchange rate behaviour is disconnected from macroeconomic fundamentals, at least in the short and medium term. This disconnection leads to a puzzle, or rather three puzzles, regarding exchange rate levels, exchange rate volatility and purchasing power parity. Yet others reject such a perception. To abandon macro fundamentals – they claim – would be like throwing the baby out with the bath water. In their view, even a microstructure approach leaves some role for macro fundamentals.

Currency and Competitiveness in Europe – the title of this book – combines two key economic concepts that have both generated a bulk of literature. Bringing those two terms together, we focus the debate on the real side of the economy. Moreover, we put a regional focus on Central, Eastern and South-Eastern Europe (CESEE), which allows us to include the aspect of transition and convergence. After all, notwithstanding the very different stages of catching up in the region, differing exchange rate regimes and different degrees of openness constitute major elements influencing the competitiveness of those countries, that is, their ability to participate successfully and sustainably on European or global markets.

The book is based on the Conference on European Economic Integration 2007 of the Oesterreichische Nationalbank, which took place on 19 and 20 November in Vienna. The conference explored the links between the external value of currencies and structural developments in the real economy, focusing specifically on the integration process in CESEE. The conference addressed a wide range of issues, including the worldwide current account imbalances; international currency competition; the role, objectives and challenges of regional monetary unions; the competitiveness of catching-up countries and related challenges for monetary policy. While acknowledging that exchange rates are an important indicator in evaluating a country's competitive position, speakers also highlighted the influence of other factors for international competitiveness – like unit labour costs; sectoral and regional trade structures; quality and technological upgrading of production and location factors, such as tax systems.

The majority of catching-up countries exhibit relatively strong exchange rate appreciation, driven by large productivity gains in the tradable sector, as is also evidenced by the Balassa-Samuelson effect on inflation. CESEE member states of the EU are a case in point, as many of them experienced real appreciation coupled with substantial gains in international market shares. It is worth noting that new EU member states, similar to the first and second tier of Asian Tigers, are especially open economies. Their export structure is very much distinguished by trade in goods, as opposed to more advanced economies, which seem to export relatively more services.

As a result, despite currency appreciation, the new EU member states have exhibited a strong economic performance since the mid-1990s. Their growth rates are on average three percentage points higher than those of the euro area, thus keeping the catching-up process alive. Furthermore, the positive relationship between net foreign liabilities and real appreciation in these new EU member states during the convergence process is also worth noting.

Next to external and internal imbalances of CESEE countries, the book tackles also the problem of global imbalances – net deficits or surpluses in trade and investment among major economic regions. In the framework of the IMF's multilateral consultation initiative, five key global players have presented policy plans on their contribution to reducing global imbalances in an orderly fashion. Some of these countries (or economic areas) considered the IMF to have created the right instrument at the right time and developed their plans in the endeavour to face up to their global responsibility. Others see these voluntary plans as being mainly in the countries' own national interests. Still, the crucial question is whether these multilaterally consistent plans will be implemented, in which case the euro area has a lot to gain.

In the wake of financial integration, a large number of developing countries worldwide had deregulated their financial markets and opened up to pro-cyclical capital flows. In those instances where these decisions went hand in hand with the adoption of fixed exchange rate regimes, deregulation often led to booms and busts, dollarization of the economy and portfolio imbalances. More recently, countries have therefore increasingly moved toward more flexible exchange rate regimes. To regain credibility, however, they have had to establish a new anchor, for instance, via inflation targeting. Alternatively, monetary unification similar to Europe's economic and monetary integration (EMU) might be an option for a few countries. However, monetary union is certainly not a remedy that would fix problems immediately. In fact, the experience with EMU shows that it takes more than mere exchange rate fixing to reap the benefits of a common currency.

Positive examples in this respect are Slovenia, but also Cyprus and Malta. At the time of the conference the latter two were on the verge of adopting the euro. But for most of the potential euro area candidates the fundamental challenges prevail. In particular, the following questions arise: can nominal and real convergence take place simultaneously? What are the specific challenges the candidate countries face? And, how can these challenges best be tackled by monetary, fiscal and structural policies? In this respect the Treaty on the European Community not only represents a transparent, rule-based framework, but also offers leeway for the CESEE EU member states in calibrating their convergence paths.

As to their economic development, there is strong evidence that the introduction of the euro has had positive effects on trade, foreign direct investment and financial integration. The evidence of the impact on growth, however, is mixed. Certainly the loss of the exchange rate as a policy instrument may entail some costs. But in general, monetary integration may contribute to growth by enhancing the quality of macroeconomic policies, providing incentives for reforms and mitigating divergences within the monetary union. EMU increases macroeconomic stability by providing a reliable, well-targeted monetary policy.

Overall, the book touches upon the wide range of topical issues that come to the fore when currency matters are combined with competitiveness considerations. We would hope that the findings established and the new questions raised in this book will serve as a valuable source for future research.

Klaus Liebscher
Josef Christl
Peter Mooslechner
Doris Ritzberger-Grünwald

PART I

How currency and competitiveness contribute to growth and stability

1. Competitiveness still has currency

Klaus Liebscher[1]

Currency and competitiveness topics are staple issues in central banking. Currencies are even at the core of central banks' business – given that, as a form of money, currencies facilitate the transfer of goods and services by serving as a means of exchange, enable the storage of wealth and serve as a unit of accounting.

In order to help money accomplish its tasks across national boundaries we need exchange rates – the prices at which currencies can be traded against each other. With respect to exchange rates, three main questions have been debated by academics and central bankers for years: how are they determined? What is their economic impact? How should monetary policy act?

With regard to the drivers of exchange rate changes, we need to understand that the factors influencing both supply and demand forces can be either structural or monetary policy-related:

1. As for long-term structural factors, one usual suspect is the purchasing power parity theory. It states that identical baskets of goods should ultimately cost the same in one currency as in another currency times the exchange rate between these currencies.
2. Another possible long-run factor of real exchange rate movements – that take into account inflation – is the development of overall or relative productivity levels.
3. A more medium-term structural factor is the balance-of-payment model, which holds that a foreign exchange rate in an equilibrium level requires a stable current account balance.
4. From a monetary policy perspective, another, rather short-term explanation is suggested by the so-called uncovered interest rate parity. Under this condition, differences in interest rates between two economies should be equal to the expected change in exchange rates between their currencies.
5. A further element of explanation can be derived from asset market models identifying interconnections between stock, bond and foreign exchange markets.

6. Finally, ever more research is devoted to non-fundamental causes of exchange rate instability. The 'overshooting hypothesis' helps explain why unstable foreign exchange markets can be efficient. Yet, looking at the microstructure of foreign exchange markets, individually rational behaviour might generate complex dynamics in which bubbles and crashes can occur.

So far the debate on determinants of currencies seems to be far from being conclusive. Alan Greenspan[2] once noted that 'forecasting exchange rates has a success rate no better than that of forecasting the outcome of a coin toss'. I wonder whether we can derive valuable insights from hindsight. Getting answers about the consequences of exchange rate movements for the economy seems to be by no means easier. The impact of the exchange rates changes depends on a set of interrelated transmission channels, of which:

1. The trade channel probably is the most obvious way in which currency developments can impact the economy. An appreciation is likely to entail a negative trade balance, as the prices of foreign currency-denominated exports increase while import prices fall.
2. Apart from that, there are financial market channels through which currency movements have an impact on the economy: a trend increase in the exchange rate raises the relative attractiveness of assets denominated in that currency while it results in the loss of value of investment abroad.
3. Currency fluctuations are also transmitted through the consumer prices channel, according to which exchange rate appreciation would lower consumer prices. In this sense the 'strong euro' has cushioned our economies from recent crude oil shocks.
4. Finally, the confidence channel completes the list. However, consumers and firms can react asymmetrically, since appreciation dampens inflation pressure on the one side but challenges the competitiveness of firms on the other.

If exchange rates and their impact on the economy are apparently so difficult to explain, let alone predict, should monetary policy interfere? As for the euro area, the European Central Bank (ECB) has no exchange rate target. A key implication of a flexible exchange rate system is that the external value of the currency is determined by financial markets and hence cannot be an instrument of economic policy. The primary objective of the Eurosystem, that is, of the ECB and the national central banks of the euro area, is to maintain price stability in the medium term. However, when analysing the economic situation and taking monetary policy decisions, the Governing Council of the ECB considers all parameters – including exchange rates – to the extent that it influences risks to price stability. In this respect, excessive exchange rate volatility is not welcome!

Turning from currency issues to competitiveness, I am tempted to use a play on words and ask: does competitiveness still have currency? My answer to this is definitely yes! Competition should not be understood as a zero-sum game, where winners can only gain what losers lose. A competitive environment might lead to a situation where both sides are absolutely better off. More importantly, it is the consumers who are the ultimate beneficiaries of competition. Competition gives incentives for self-improvement and produces excellence. Competitiveness is linked with the creation, diffusion and application of new knowledge, resulting in technological progress. When it comes to the euro area's international competitiveness, I do believe that there is still room for further improvement.

Extensive global imbalances have built up between major economic regions during the last few years. Whatever their presumed causes – either overspending or underinvestment in the USA; or the saving glut in surplus economies, particularly Asian emerging markets and oil exporting countries – current account imbalances have undoubtedly amplified the pressure on currencies, with possible harmful consequences for global financial stability. It is clear that all regions involved have to assume their responsibility for ensuring the sustainability of their external and internal balances, and for enhancing their growth potential. However, for the time being it appears that the euro area takes the major burden of this adjustment process.

The Group of Seven (G7) meeting of Finance Ministers and Central Bank Governors in October 2007, including the President of the ECB, reaffirmed that 'exchange rates should reflect economic fundamentals'. As announced, they, the G7, welcome China's decision to increase the flexibility of its currency, but 'stress its need to allow an accelerated appreciation of its effective exchange rate'.[3] Earlier in October, the Finance Ministers of the Eurogroup noted with great attention that the 'US authorities have reaffirmed that a strong dollar is in the interest of the US economy'[4] and commented that 'the sustainable recovery path' of the Japanese economy should 'be incorporated in the assessment of risks'. Meanwhile 'the euro area is playing its role by implementing structural reforms and contributing to a rebalancing of growth', according to the Eurogroup.

For the first time in its existence the euro area outpaced the United States in terms of economic growth in 2007. The euro area's seasonally adjusted jobless rate came to 6.9 per cent in 2006, thus hitting its lowest level in more than a decade. This drop is not only the result of economic activity. The labour market and welfare reforms of the past few years have also reduced structural unemployment. Since the introduction of the euro in 1999, some 15 million new jobs have been created in the euro area. This is not to depict an unduly positive picture. The inflation rate for October 2007 came to 2.6 per cent after being below the 2 per cent mark for a year. The outlook for price stability over the medium term is subject to upside risks as increased oil, commodity and food prices as well as the favourable labour market situation are likely to make higher wage settlements possible.

Nevertheless, there are signs that the competitive position of the euro area has improved. Since 2002, productivity growth has contributed considerably to falling unit labour costs in the euro area. Also, the shock resilience of the euro area seems to have improved owing to the 'stability architecture' of the Eurosystem. This architecture rests on three pillars: a stability-oriented monetary policy, sustainable public finances and growth- and competition-oriented structural policies. As for the third pillar, the Lisbon strategy adopted in 2000 with the aim of creating a modern and competitive economy seems to be finally bearing fruit.

However, the observed persistent divergences in unit labour cost growth and inflation in a number of euro area countries clearly point to increasing risks of further competitive losses and potentially costly real economic adjustment. Since the single monetary policy cannot address inflation divergences in individual countries, it is evident that structural reforms, wage-setting processes and budgetary policies must contribute to reverse competitiveness losses in individual euro area countries. If the lessons from success stories both within and outside the euro area are applied elsewhere, the euro area as a whole will emerge as a stronger and more dynamic economy.

On 1 January 2008, Cyprus and Malta adopted the euro, having successfully converged with the euro area countries. Looking ahead, the adoption of the euro will allow them to reap all the benefits of the common currency and enhance their integration with all EU partners. Together with Slovenia, they give a positive example for all other new member countries.

For these new member states, it is vital to achieve real growth that permits their income-per-capita levels to approach average EU levels gradually. Therefore, further steps in monetary integration should be geared toward achieving sustainable real and nominal convergence.

Since the speed of further monetary integration must not compromise its quality, decisions have to be taken on a case-by-case basis in accordance with the Treaty establishing the European Community. At the same time, equal treatment for new and established EU member states must be ensured throughout the whole process. I am sure that the participation of the new member countries in the stability architecture of the Eurosystem will make Europe's Economic and Monetary Union (EMU) an even greater success.

To sum it up, price stability is an important contributor to both orderly exchange rate adjustment and the maintenance of economic competitiveness. Taken together these functions may help build confidence – probably the most essential task central banks have.

NOTES

1. Governor of the Oesterreichische Nationalbank, Austria.
2. Remarks by Chairman Alan Greenspan at the European Banking Congress 2004, Frankfurt, Germany; 19 November 2004, panel discussion: Euro in Wider Circles; http://www.federalreserve.gov/boarddocs/Speeches/2004/20041119/default.htm.
3. G7/8 Finance Ministers Meetings, Statement of G7 Finance Ministers and Central Bank Governors, Washington, DC, 19 October 2007; http://www.g8.utoronto.ca/finance/fm071019.htm.
4. Reuters, Eurogroup position for G7 meeting; Monday 8 October 2007; http://www.reuters.com/article/companyNewsAndPR/idUSL0846597920071008.

2. Financial market turbulence and global imbalances

John Lipsky[1]

Achieving the dual goal of sustaining global growth while reducing global imbalances is a central challenge for the International Monetary Fund (IMF), and for its 185 member countries. The existence of record international payments imbalances has been seen by many in recent years as a risk to both global growth and stability. The unexpected post-2001 resilience of the global expansion – and its largely unanticipated ubiquity – has created unprecedented optimism about the prospects for prospective advances in many aspects, including poverty reduction. If strong growth could be sustained, it would help provide the resources for key social goals such as environmental protection, improved medical care and coping with the profound demographic changes that are fast approaching. Thus, the importance of sustaining global growth has become even clearer than in the past. And the prospects of success seem more plausible than at any time in recent decades, following such hopeful developments as the recent gains in real per capita income in sub-Saharan Africa.

Nonetheless, the emergence of record international payments imbalances – even in the context of strong and globally balanced GDP growth – has underscored a key vulnerability of the expansion. These imbalances have reflected – among other things – significant differences in the pace of domestic demand growth between many key economies. The phenomenon often referred to as the 'global saving glut' in fact has been accompanied by weak investment and sluggish consumption gains in many key economies. It has long been recognized that attaining better balance in the strength of domestic demand gains will be needed if the strong global expansion is to be extended in the coming years. In fact, the persistence of large payments imbalances has been seen widely as a sign of the vulnerability of the past few years' exceptionally favourable performance.

Thus, it is not surprising that the financial market turbulence in the summer and fall of 2007 has heightened the unease regarding the near-term outlook. In this context, it is important that policy makers continue to take the steps necessary to underpin the orderly and effective functioning of global financial markets. Moreover, it is necessary to bolster confidence that global markets will continue to offer the unprecedented opportunities for progress that have been seized in recent years by emerging and developing economies. For example, success in the Doha Round of trade negotiations would provide a powerful and positive signal around the world.

2.1 OVERVIEW

This chapter – reflecting conditions prevailing and assessments made in late 2007 – revolves around three key considerations. First, global risks attached to imbalances are being re-evaluated in light of recent financial turmoil and oil price gyrations. A key consideration is whether recent developments, including exchange rate shifts, have been supportive of attaining our dual goals. The IMF's conclusion is that while the latest developments have increased risks, the most likely outcome remains a favourable one – *if* the appropriate policies are implemented, especially in key economies. Second, the appropriate strategy remains the implementation of a credible set of policy measures that will be maintained over the medium term, not an attempt at a short-term fix. Imbalances will decline gradually – but significantly – if the appropriate policies are adopted. Failure to do so will risk more abrupt – and potentially disruptive – adjustment that could threaten the expansion. And finally, an appropriate set of strategies are precisely those embodied in the policy roadmap proposed in the context of the IMF's Multilateral Consultation on Global Imbalances. It is now vital that this agenda be implemented fully, and that the market turbulence in 2007 is not allowed to distort or delay the needed policy adjustments.

2.2 GLOBAL RISKS

With regard to the risks posed by recent developments, it is, first of all, likely that the combination of financial market turbulence and the new rise in oil prices – if sustained – will tend to dampen growth and heighten the downside risks to growth in 2008. While it is still too soon to draw firm conclusions, here is a rough estimation of what the growth outlook might look like if the rise in energy prices observed in 2007 is sustained more or less in line with current futures prices (see Figure 2.1).

The principal point here is straightforward. It has been widely asserted that one of the important aspects of the current environment is that global growth has decoupled from that of the United States, and to an

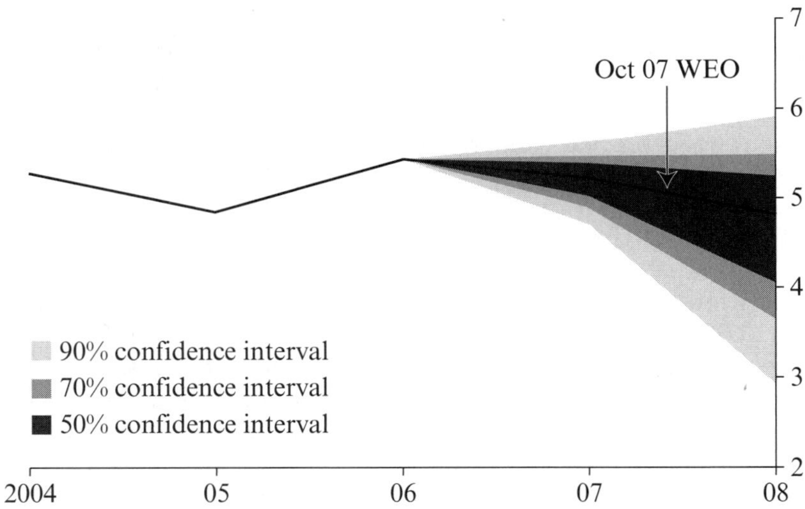

Figure 2.1 *Financial and oil market developments have dampened the growth outlook (per cent)*

important degree, the expansion of the key emerging economies has become independent of that of the industrial economies. However, the latest challenges have been rather broader in nature, affecting virtually all economies.

A new challenge to global growth is the latest rise in oil prices, which touched new all-time highs in dollar terms in 2007 (see Figure 2.2) – despite only minor supply disruptions. Oil demand remains robust – particularly from emerging markets, where in many cases earlier price increases have not been passed through fully or uniformly to consumers. Heightened supply concerns also appear to have played a role in the latest increases. The cumulative evidence of tight supply conditions, a falling dollar and rising geopolitical tensions have played key roles in the recent run-up. Spare production capacity remains appreciably below its historical 'comfort zone'. And this situation is not likely to improve any time soon. With oil market conditions so tight, the recent price rises could persist and it is likely that any significant supply disruption would push prices dramatically higher.

Higher oil prices have important distributional consequences, including for global trade balances. Oil importers – especially, low-income countries – are likely to be hard hit; the impact of the oil price surge in 2007 on trade imbalances could be 2–3 per cent of GDP or more in many countries in sub-Saharan Africa, and, to a lesser extent, in the Caribbean and Central America (see Figure 2.3). For some importers, however, the impact of

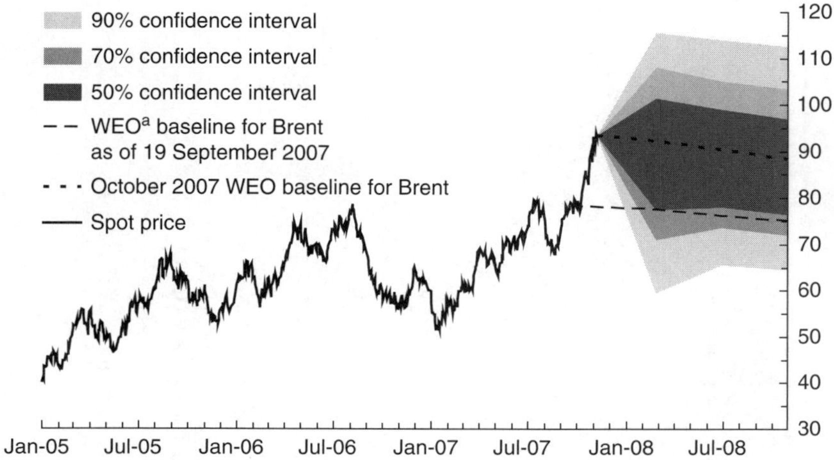

Note: a. World Economic Outlook.

Figure 2.2 Oil prices have reached new highs (Brent; from futures options; as of 9 November 2007; US dollars per barrel)

higher oil prices has been cushioned by dollar depreciation, other commodity price gains or limited pass-through to domestic energy prices facing consumers.

Other factors – such as the weakness in housing markets – could have a broader impact than is often recognized. For example, housing markets in several European countries have weakened, as well as in the United States (see Figure 2.4). Moreover, while it is not always acknowledged, housing valuations and the relative importance of construction activity in the United States are not unusual when seen in a global context.

At the same time, financial market strains are visible in many markets. And the second-round impact of the continued difficulties in interbank funding markets (see Figure 2.5) – exacerbated by doubts about the reliability of valuations on balance sheets; and even by potential worries about the size of excess capital cushions in some financial institutions – does not look like it is going to dissipate quickly.

The impact on credit conditions of recent market strains shows that the risks posed to the expansion by potential pro-cyclical tightening of credit is widely shared, at least in European markets (see Figure 2.6).

In sum, the combination of higher oil prices and financial market strains could slow – at least to some degree – the narrowing of global current account imbalances (see Figure 2.7). Past declines in the dollar have contributed to the US current account deficit moderating faster than expected.

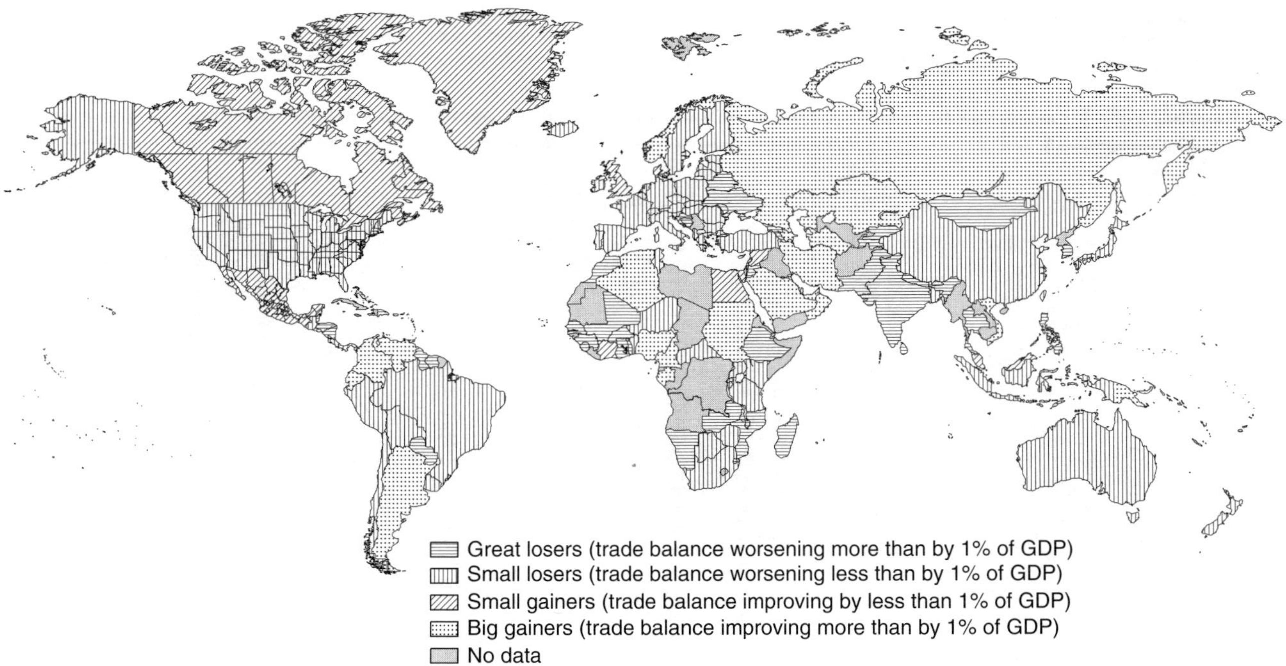

Figure 2.3 First-round impact on trade balance of the oil price surge since early September 2007

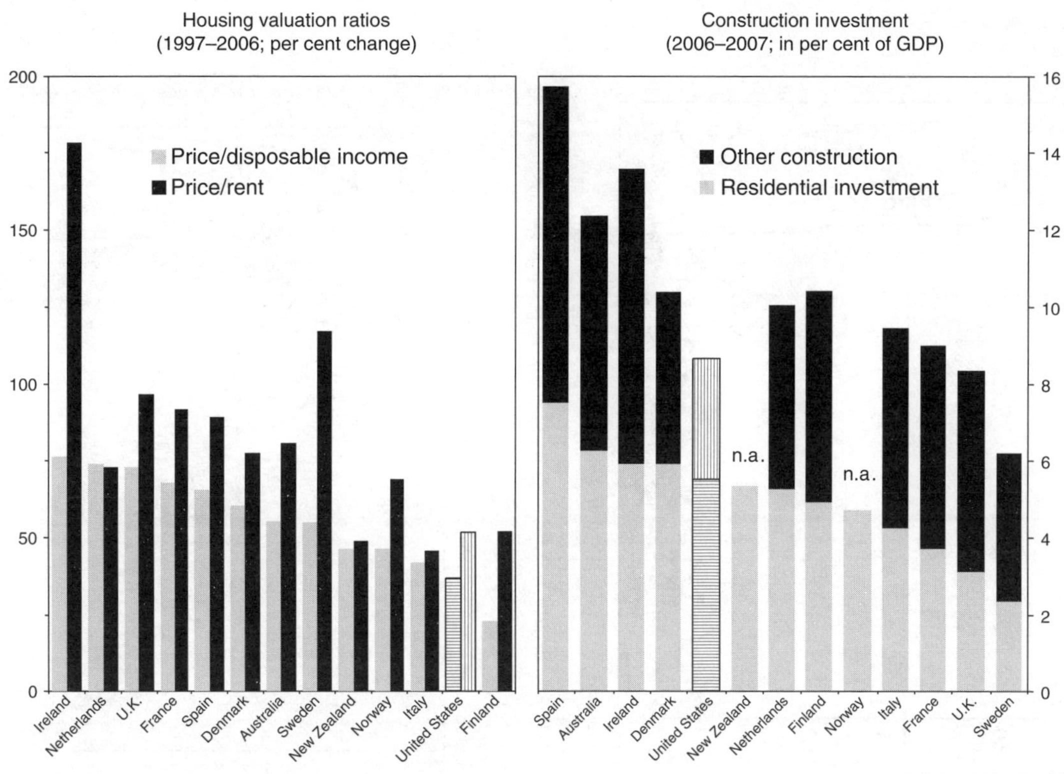

Figure 2.4 Housing-related vulnerabilities elsewhere

(a)

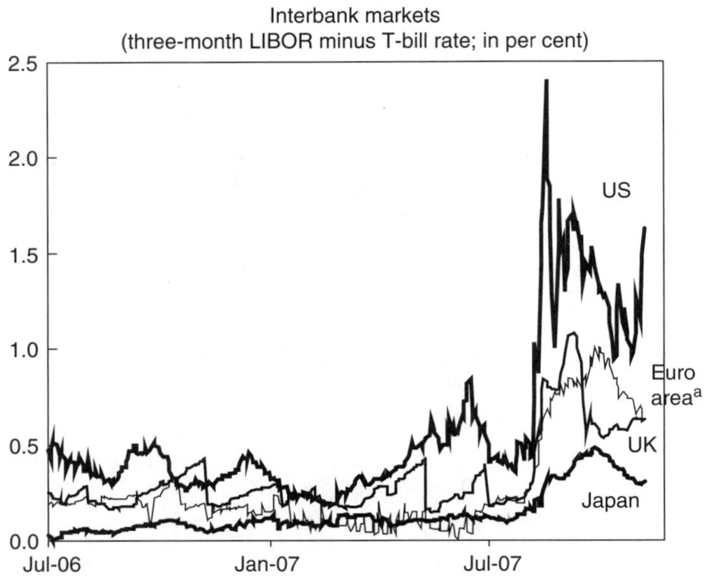

(b)

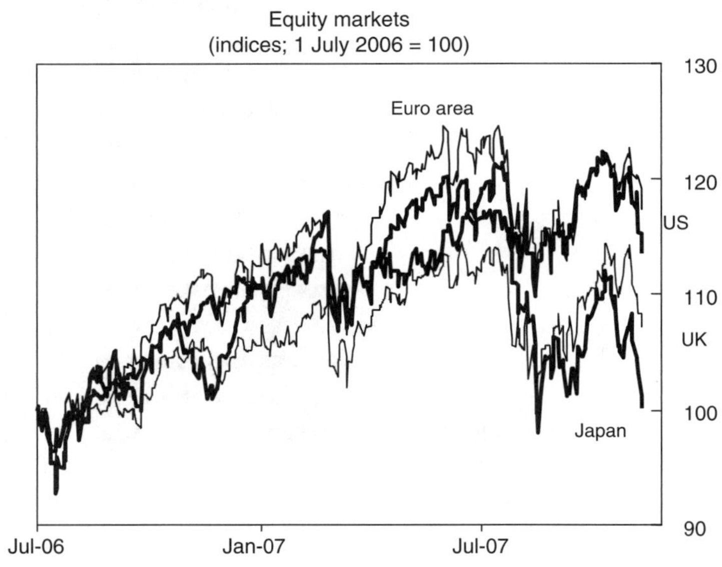

Note: a. Euro LIBOR minus Germany's government bond rate.

Figure 2.5 Financial market strains have entered a 'second phase'

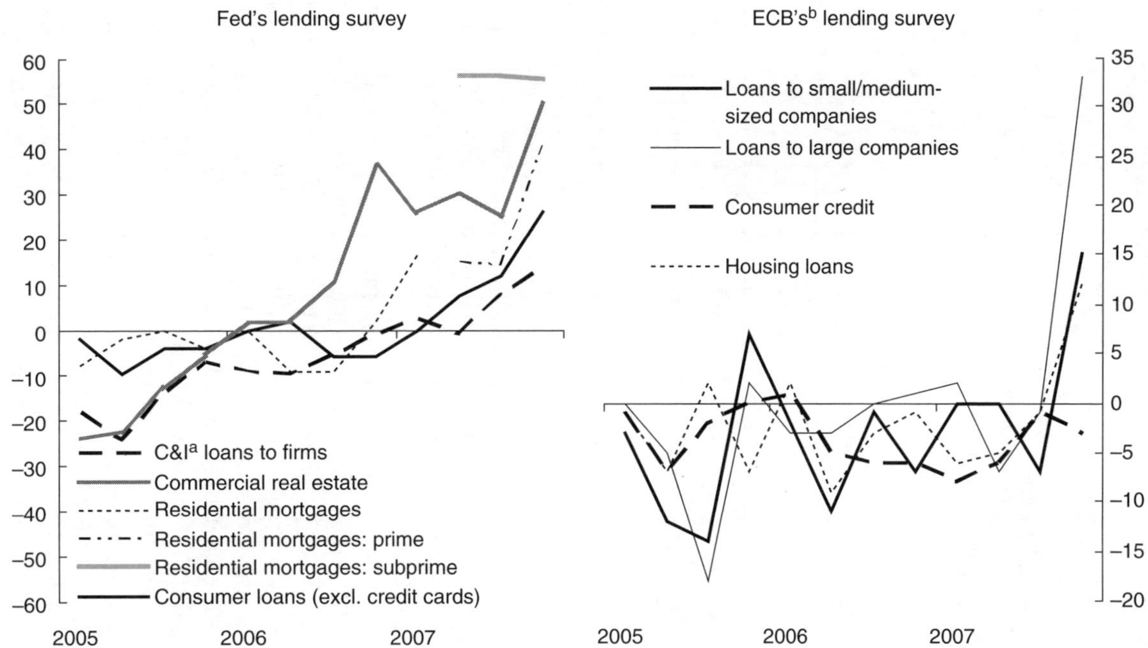

Notes:
a. Commercial and industrial.
b. European Central Bank.
c. Change in the balance of respondents between the 'tightened considerably and tightened somewhat' and the 'eased somewhat and eased considerably'.

Figure 2.6 Bank lending surveys indicate tighter conditions (change in credit standards over past three months; in per cent[c])

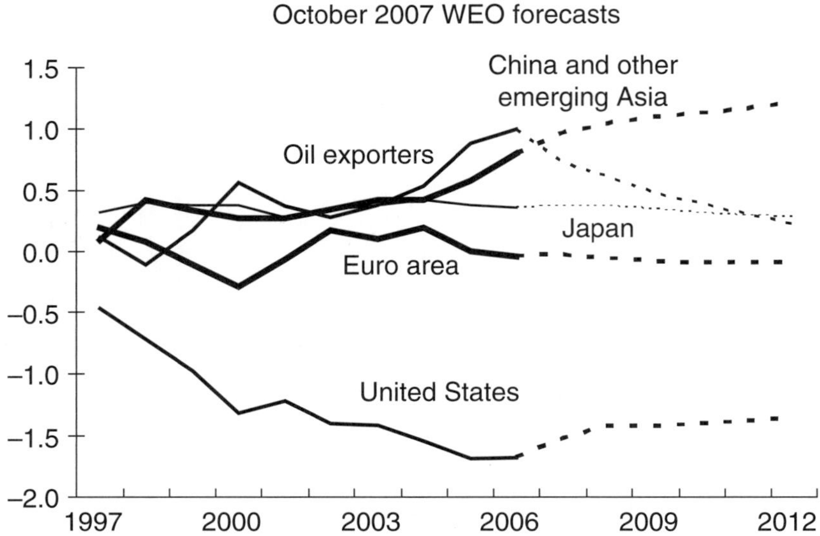

Figure 2.7 Global current account imbalances (per cent of world GDP)

However, the oil trade imbalance is now likely to deteriorate further because of higher oil prices, offsetting some of the reduction in the current account deficit attributable to the dollar depreciation. The expected reduction in oil exporters' surpluses may be less rapid than previously projected – shown here based on the October 2007 World Economic Outlook (where the oil price baseline was about 20 per cent lower than in November 2007, the cut-off date for this chapter).

Recent financial turmoil – particularly the impact on the market for asset-backed securities – raises new questions and requires some rethinking about the financial flows providing the counterpart of global current account imbalances. Up to now, the US current account deficit has been easily financed, but this should not be taken for granted (see Figure 2.8). Financial flows to the United States reflected, in part, the packaging of marketable financial claims in the world's deepest, most liquid and sophisticated financial markets. But doubts have risen about pricing and liquidity in certain key financial markets, and this has already contributed to the recent weakening trend of the US dollar.

Financial turmoil has left a noticeable imprint on US net portfolio inflows, which have been unusually weak since July 2007. This includes reduced foreign purchases of US asset-backed securities – which accounted for somewhere between one-quarter to one-third of recent net financial inflows. The slowdown in these inflows has reflected rising concerns about

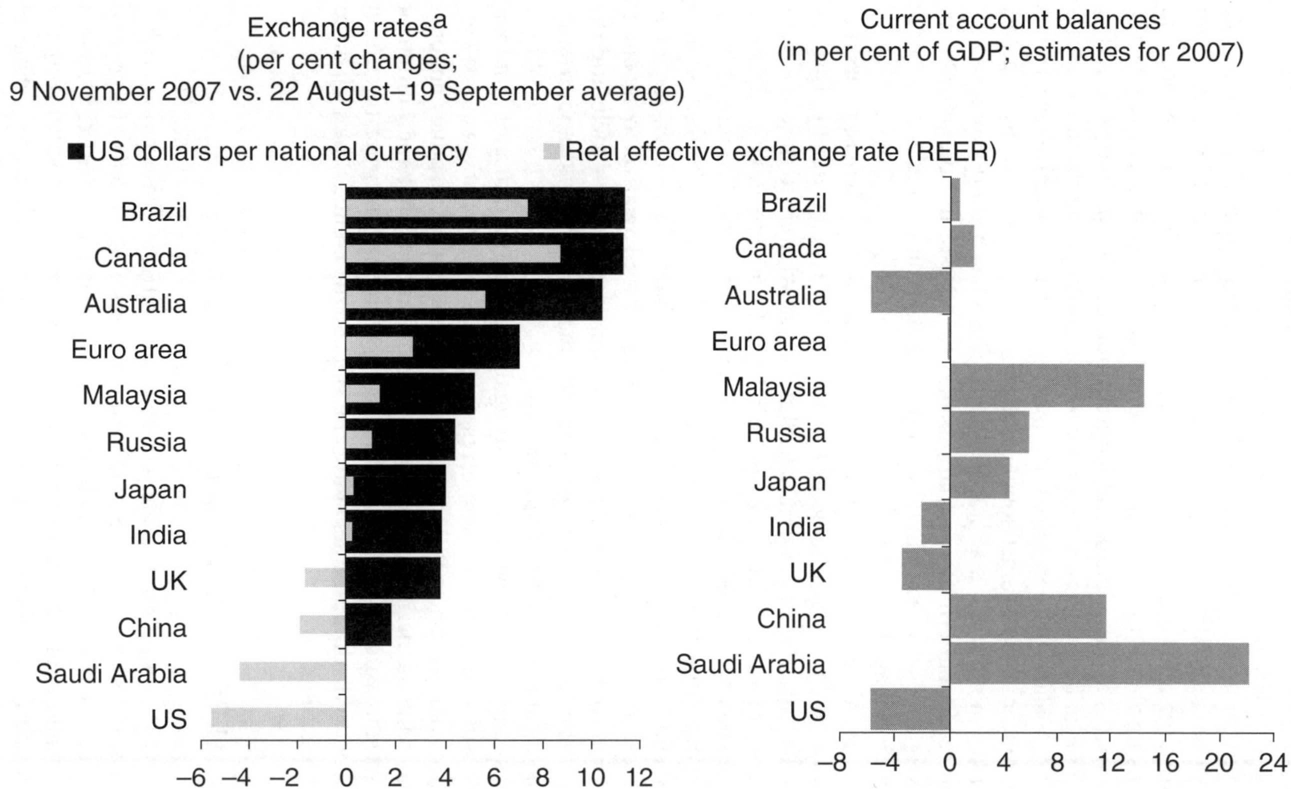

Note: a. Positive numbers denote appreciation of local currency.

Figure 2.8 Exchange rate adjustments not reflecting current account positions the quality of the underlying assets, questions about proper valuation and ratings and illiquidity in some of these markets.

A further weakening of the US dollar could both reflect and contribute to a softening of demand for US assets. The recent pattern of adjustment in exchange rates has not corresponded to the pattern of current account deficits nor has it matched the shifts that were anticipated as likely by the participants in the Multilateral Consultation on Global Imbalances. The dollar's significant depreciation since the turmoil began in the third quarter of 2007 – which has amounted to about 5 per cent in effective terms – has been concentrated against some currencies, with little movement against other key monies. The composition of the shifts has had little direct correlation to the pattern of external imbalances. As a result, the adjustment burdens appear to be falling disproportionately on countries with more flexible exchange rate regimes.

This could be a recipe for fuelling tensions between trading partners that carries added risks, including the threat posed by rising protectionist pressures that could become aggravated if global growth were to slow. It is clear that a set of broad-based and better-balanced fundamental and financial adjustments are needed. The dollar's depreciation so far has moved in an appropriate direction and it has reduced the currency's medium-term misalignment based on the IMF's exchange rate analysis. However, some key surplus economies' currencies remain undervalued relative to medium-term fundamentals, while some more flexible currencies – including the euro – may have strengthened somewhat more than would appear warranted from a medium-term perspective.

To summarize, we need to guard against assuming that global imbalances will take care of themselves smoothly, evenly and in a growth-friendly manner. There is a risk that – barring appropriate policy action – global rebalancing may be weakened or delayed or that the burden of adjustment would not be shared broadly. Moreover, in order to sustain global growth, domestic demand gains outside the United States will need to strengthen.

2.3 APPROPRIATE STRATEGY

What is the appropriate policy strategy to mitigate these global risks? Discussions on how to address global imbalances have tended to follow two separate tracks. The first emphasizes that an imbalance between desired savings and realized investment around the world lies at the heart of the current account imbalances. The second emphasizes the role of exchange rates – particularly those that have remained relatively inflexible in a world of globalized trade and finance – as a key factor behind the evolution and the resolution of the imbalances.

But these two tracks are not mutually exclusive. There is a role for both a rebalancing of saving and investment through macroeconomic policies, as well as a role for exchange rates in safely reducing imbalances in a manner that does not induce unnecessary volatility in output. In fact, these two approaches are mutually reinforcing, as changes in real exchange rates help to achieve the necessary shift in resources between tradable and non-tradable sectors without major disruptions.

A potentially successful three-pronged strategy – in effect the strategy endorsed by the International Monetary and Financial Committee (IMFC) and embedded in the Multilateral Consultation – involves:

- raising US saving;
- raising productivity growth, investment and boosting domestic demand growth in the rest of the world;
- allowing for greater exchange rate flexibility in certain surplus countries.

If progress towards these goals is made in a steady and sustained fashion, global imbalances are likely to be resolved in the desired manner – that is, one that supports global growth while reducing risks.

Let me turn to each of these key strategic components in turn, and identify where further progress is clearly needed. Beginning with industrial countries, the outlook for US private and public saving has improved (see Figure 2.9). After the significant fall in US national saving that began around the mid- to late 1990s, and that played a leading role in the rising US current account deficit after 2000, saving now appears to have stabilized. Given recent developments in US housing and credit markets, the partly wealth-driven decline in household saving rates appears to have bottomed and is set to begin reversing. There are strong reasons to anticipate that US household saving out of current income is going to normalize in the coming years.

The US fiscal deficit has declined significantly – helped by buoyant revenues – although longer-run pressures on public finances remain a concern (see Figure 2.9). Given recent exchange rate trends and the relative balance of risks to demand growth at home and abroad, the US external deficit could be reduced more rapidly than projected. The latest trade data and the positive contribution of net exports to third-quarter growth are evidence in this direction.

In Japan, while the downward trend has eased, investment has yet to recover fully. Investment, which generally declined in advanced economies

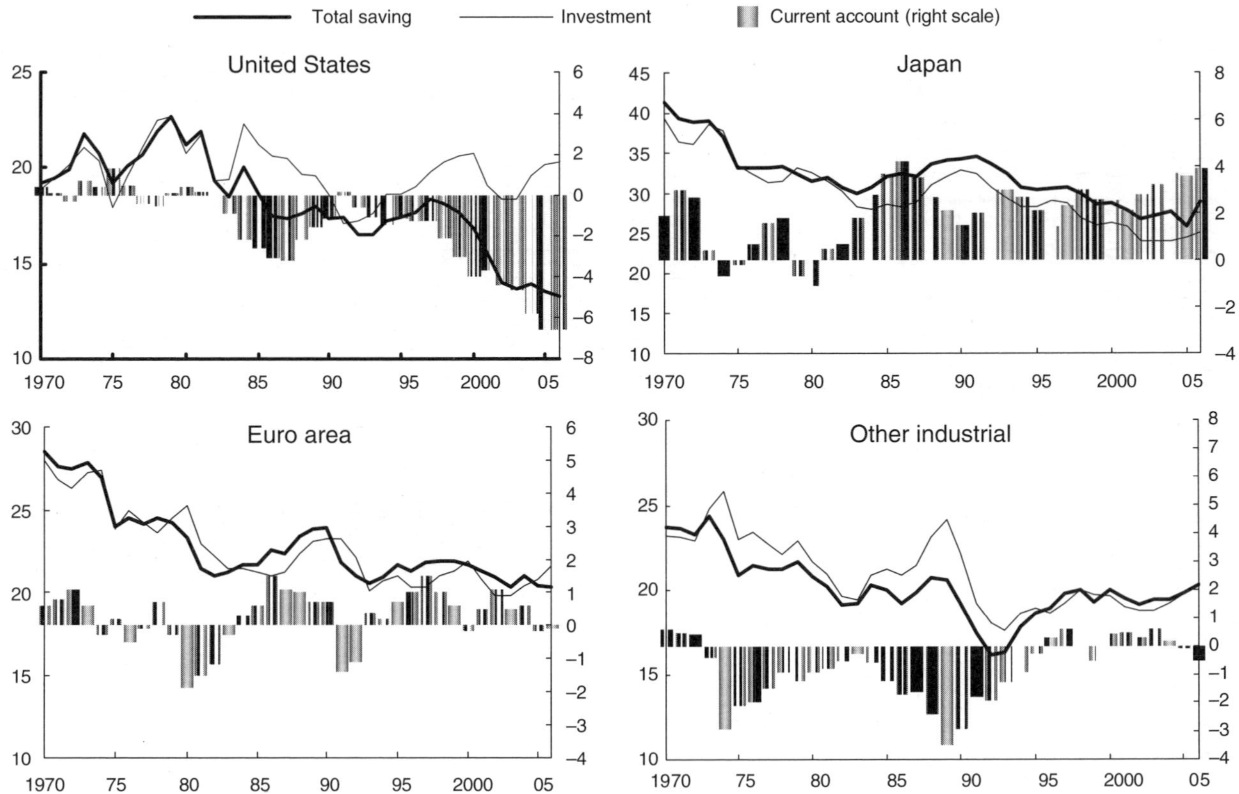

Figure 2.9 US savings has been falling

since the late 1990s and 2000, has broadly returned to prior levels only in 2006, except in Japan. Addressing past excesses, Japanese corporations have reduced debt over a protracted, decade-long de-leveraging process, helped by surging profits, but investment still remains relatively low. The value of the yen and the level of domestic interest rates also remain low by historical standards – amid lingering concerns about the underlying vigour of domestic demand. The underlying strength of productivity, given an ageing workforce, and competition in key sectors, have remained key concerns for the economy.

In the euro area, saving–investment imbalances have been relatively modest, but economic growth and productivity performance have been lacklustre. While growth improved in 2007, structural concerns continue to weigh on longer-term growth prospects.

In emerging markets, saving remains high while investment generally remains sluggish (see Figure 2.10). Saving rates have increased sharply since the beginning of the new millennium in most emerging market regions. In Latin America, the fiscal retrenchment undertaken in the late 1990s, combined with higher commodity revenues, has resulted in higher public saving. Yet investment – both in the public and private sectors – has been sluggish.

Meanwhile, the sharp rise in oil prices and revenues is likely to push saving and current account surpluses higher for oil exporters. So far, oil-producing economies have on average spent 30–40 per cent of their extra oil revenues on increased imports, although there is substantial variation across countries.

In East Asia, while high saving rates have moved essentially sideways, there was an almost uniform drop in investment across the region following the Asian crisis. More recently, there are signs of a gradual investment recovery, and if this were to persist, it would help to alleviate imbalances.

China has seen strong investment, but saving has more than kept pace. Led by rising corporate saving, China's very high domestic saving rate – which reached 53 per cent of GDP in 2006 – continues to produce growing external surpluses despite rapid investment growth.

There has been some progress on improving exchange rate flexibility, but more is needed (see Figure 2.11). The flexibility of the Chinese renminbi against the US dollar, for example, has modestly increased. Since the regime change in mid-2005, the currency has appreciated bilaterally against the dollar, and (surprising to some) to a similar degree as the euro over that period. But as noted previously, the degree of bilateral appreciation has been relatively muted recently since the turmoil in financial markets began in the third quarter of 2007. The renminbi has appreciated by less than 2 per cent against the dollar and has, in fact, depreciated slightly in real effective terms since end-July 2007. Also, the renminbi's real appreciation

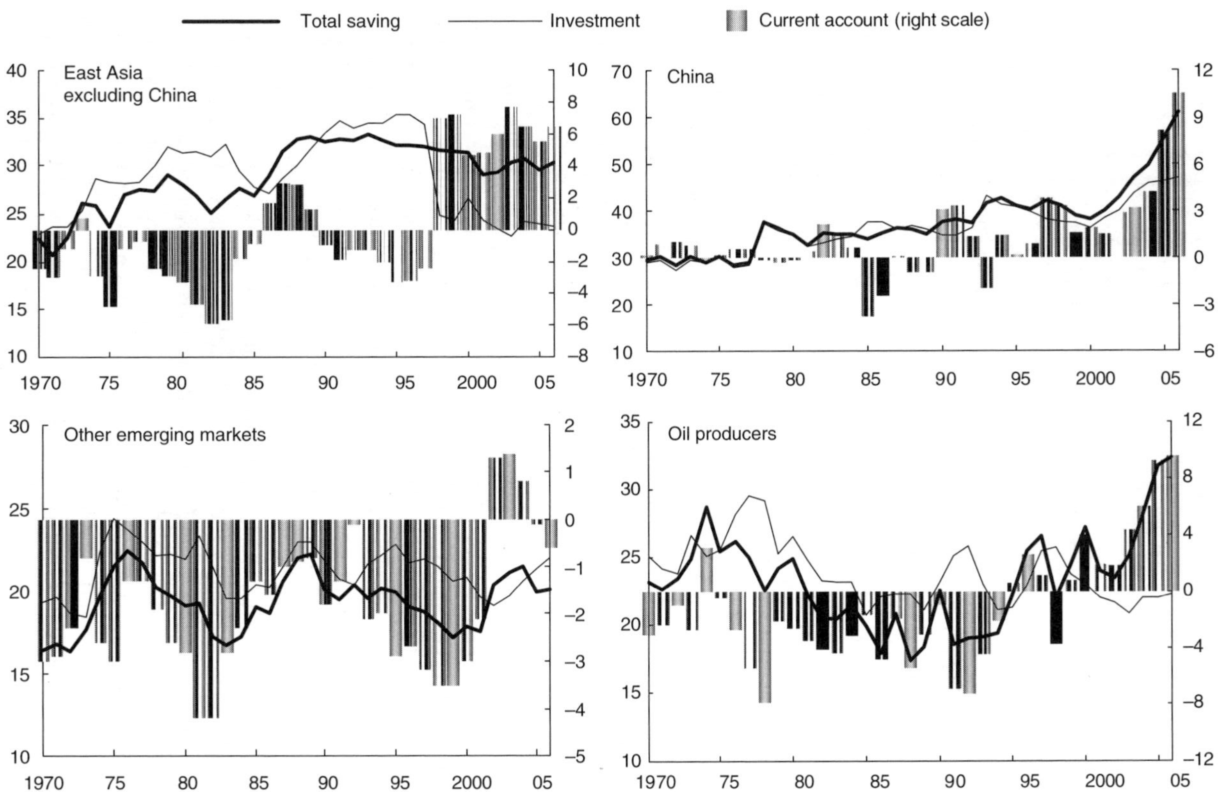

Figure 2.10 *Emerging markets' investment has been sluggish, except in China*

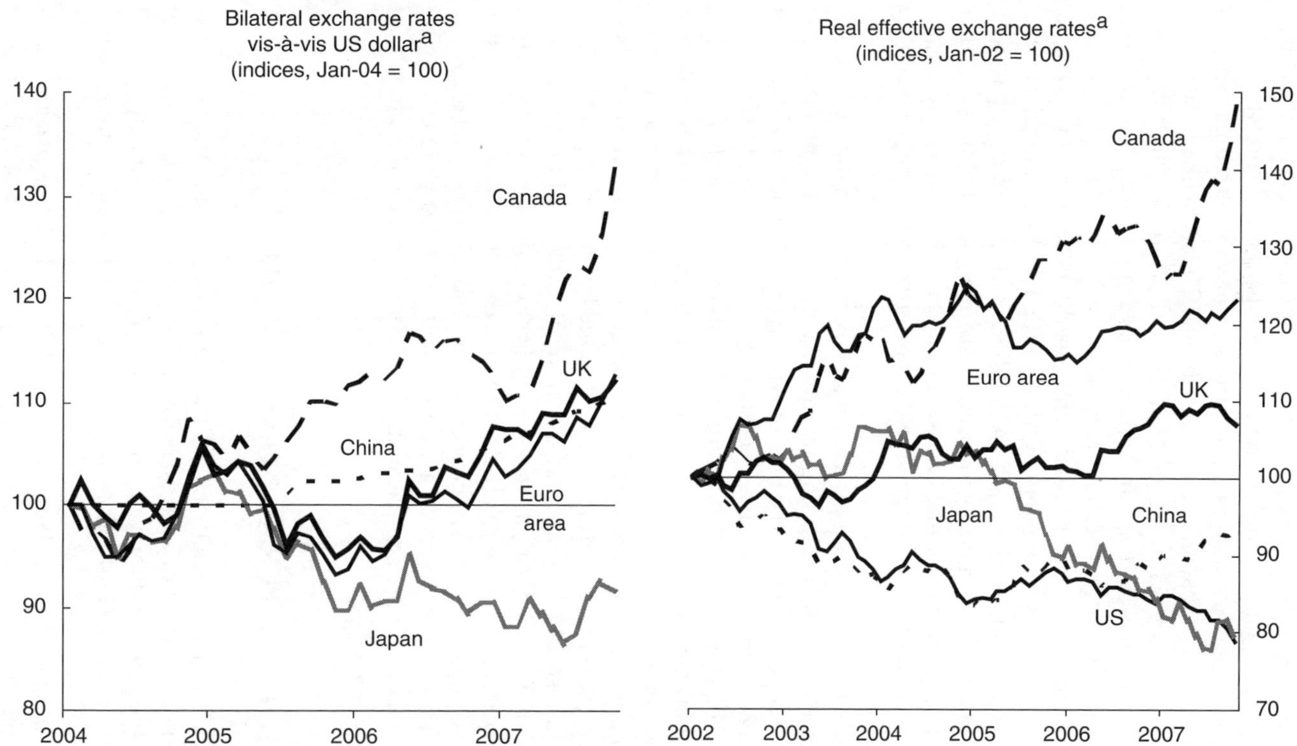

Note: a. Values above 100 denote appreciation.

Figure 2.11 Exchange rate adjustments and flexibility

(about 8.5 per cent between May 2006 and August 2007) has also come through faster domestic inflation, led by surging food prices, and the inability of monetary policy to durably rein in domestic liquidity growth.

The role of the exchange rate and stronger growth in trading partners will be helpful for global rebalancing (see Figure 2.12). Exchange rates have helped in the past with external adjustment. Across countries, IMF research finds that exchange rate depreciations can moderate output losses that occur during current account reversals.

Adjustment of the US external deficit in the late 1980s, for example, involved both a 40 per cent depreciation of the US dollar in real effective terms, and a decline in the US growth differential with trading partners. This adjustment was primarily induced by stronger growth abroad, rather than lower growth in the United States. The large real exchange rate depreciation contributed to the surge in real export growth and helped stabilize economic activity.

What about now? The 16 per cent real effective depreciation of the US dollar since mid-2002 is starting to have an impact on the non-oil trade deficit as a ratio to GDP at the time of writing (end-2007). Consistent with the finding of low pass-through of exchange rate movements to US import prices and high pass-through to import prices abroad, the effect of the dollar depreciation came mainly through a strong acceleration in export volumes. The slower growth of the US economy relative to that of its trading partners also seems to have started having an impact on import volumes in 2006. Of course, these movements tend to be obscured by rising oil prices.

I would also like to point out a feature of today's world that differs significantly from times past. In 1985, 70 per cent of the world's current account surpluses were accounted for by five countries. Today, that same share is accounted for by ten countries, with more diverse exchange rate regimes. This makes the necessary adjustment of exchange rates to bring down imbalances more complicated, both economically and politically. It might also take longer.

2.4 MULTILATERAL CONSULTATIONS

The goal of the IMF's Multilateral Consultation on Global Imbalances has been to meet the dual objectives mentioned at the outset – that is, to help position the global economy on an adjustment path toward a more durable and credible pattern of domestic demand growth while maintaining robust global GDP growth.

The Consultation was launched in mid-2006. The five participants – comprising the euro area, China, Japan, Saudi Arabia and the United

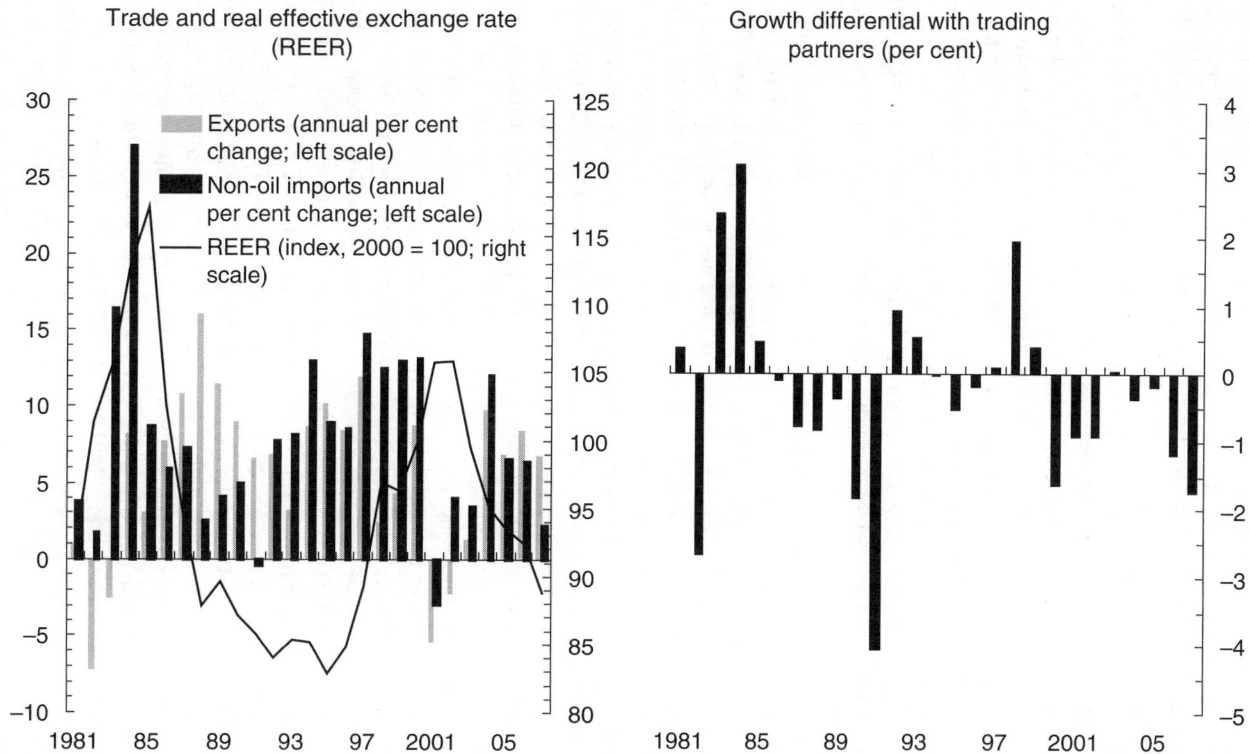

Figure 2.12 Dollar depreciation and growth in trading partners helps global rebalancing

States, together with IMF staff – presented a progress report to the April 2007 meeting of the IMFC. The formal presentations to that meeting were released to the public and they are available on the IMF's website. This includes a joint explanatory note plus the participants' individual policy plans.

This represents a major accomplishment, in that all the participants agreed that bringing down imbalances is a shared responsibility, and that the policy plans submitted by each participant is in line with their own best interests. To achieve a narrowing of imbalances, the policy roadmap that was put forth intended to address the key prongs I discussed earlier to reduce saving–investment imbalances through broad-based adjustment, more flexibly, and in a manner supportive of global growth.

I will very briefly discuss key elements in each participant's plan, and comment on how the IMF staff foresees potential progress and challenges in achieving these plans.

The euro area's plans revolve around sustaining domestic demand growth, which will make a contribution toward improving global performance. The integration and transformation of the euro area (and EU) financial markets will provide a key impetus for improving the efficiency of the area's product and service markets. The renewed Lisbon Agenda reforms are critical to achieving this goal, including through labour market reforms. Consistent with the plans submitted, some progress has already been achieved in the area of financial markets in improving the efficiency of clearing and settlements. Looking ahead, it is important that the resolve to carry on with structural reforms continues, despite clear political pressures that exist to turn back.

China's policy undertakings are structured around three cornerstones and have seen some progress. First, rebalancing growth relatively more toward consumption while slowing investment growth and improving investment efficiency. Second, deepening financial sector reform. And, third, increasing the flexibility of the renminbi. A more effective, market-driven financial system would help to strengthen domestic demand growth, while improving investment efficiency and increasing the usefulness of monetary policy instruments for maintaining macroeconomic balance. Experience has shown that such a sectoral and systemic transition is more easily managed with a flexible exchange rate policy. The announcements of monetary policy measures, and the widening of the daily trading band for the renminbi have been consistent with China's policy plans.

Saudi Arabia's public spending plans in the energy sector and on needed infrastructure and social projects remain on track. The scale of recent revenue increases relative to the size of their economies implies that oil exporters' adjustment will have to be gradual. After all, adjustment must be undertaken in line with absorption capacity. Saudi Arabia is taking a lead in increasing social outlays where returns are high, including on education, health and social safety nets. In addition, Saudi Arabia is implementing ambitious investment plans, including in the hydrocarbon sector. The net effect of these efforts is already impressive.

In Japan, deeper structural reforms are needed to improve growth potential and safeguard living standards, and this would support global growth. The reform priorities are to increase labour market flexibility, promote competition through greater market opening and deepen trade integration. New structural measures will hopefully catalyse and sustain the still-tentative expansion. As consumption spending and investment strengthen, the current account surplus should narrow as a percentage of GDP. Over the longer term, the trend toward a narrowing surplus also will be supported by demographic factors.

Recent progress in these areas has been promising, but the agenda is far from finished. In 2007, we have seen concrete progress on the liberalization of FDI inflows, as well as in advances on job training and placement. However, the areas where progress with respect to its policy plans remains a challenge is in boosting productivity in the anaemic non-tradables sector of its economy.

The linchpin of the US policy statement to the Multilateral Consultation appropriately focuses on raising national saving – both through policy incentives to raise private sector saving, and through plans to eliminate the fiscal deficit (ex-social security) by 2012. There are positive signs of progress. As mentioned above, the current account deficit is shrinking, and 2007 may well mark the first year in 12, that net exports will make a positive contribution to growth. Fiscal balances have also strengthened, in line with the Multilateral Consultation plans, but there are longer-term pressures on public finances, on which there needs to be a stronger political consensus for a solution. The full elimination of the fiscal deficit by 2012 is still going to take some hard work.

Overall, while there has been some progress, much more is needed to achieve full implementation of these policy plans – and, in my view, doing so has become all the more important.

Why is full implementation so instrumental? Will it make a difference? To examine the potential impact of the five participants' Multilateral Consultation policy plans, IMF staff conducted simulations (subject to the usual caveats) using our Global Macroeconomic Model (or GEM). Specifically, we compared the effects of the five policy plans against two alternative scenarios: our baseline scenario was a benign 'no policy adjustment scenario', where all the adjustment in the saving–investment balance is driven by gradual private sector action. As an alternative, we used a

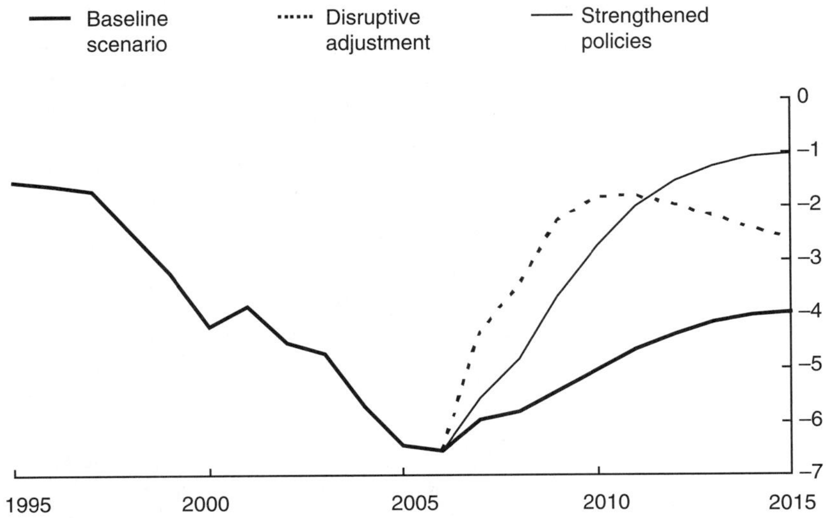

Source: IMF staff estimates.

Figure 2.13 United States: three current account scenarios (per cent of GDP)

'disruptive adjustment scenario', involving a loss of appetite for US assets and a sharp correction in exchange rates, leading to an output contraction. The 'Multilateral Consultation policy adjustment scenario' including the participants' policy plans provided the most stable and enduring adjustment to the US current account deficit.

In terms of the pattern of adjustment in the other participants, this policy adjustment scenario produced a smoother current account normalization in emerging Asia (where the current account surpluses are highest) than the disruptive adjustment scenario, while producing an earlier normalization relative to the baseline scenario (see Figure 2.13).

Turning now to growth, the Multilateral Consultation policy adjustment scenario produces a more gentle slowing of US growth than would a disruptive adjustment, while bringing output back toward the baseline more rapidly. The counterpart to this pattern for emerging Asia is also similar – the gentler slowing of US output growth also cushions the fall in growth, relative to the baseline (see Figure 2.14).

As mentioned above, the roles of Japan and the euro area come out much more clearly in terms of their roles in rebalancing global growth, not so much from current account adjustments. Figure 2.15 shows the changes in output, in the Multilateral Consultation policy adjustment scenario,

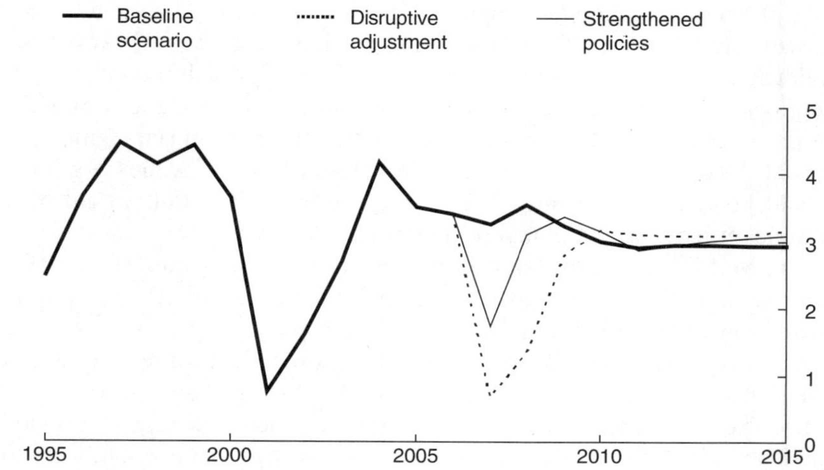

Source: IMF staff estimates.

Figure 2.14 United States: output growth (in per cent)

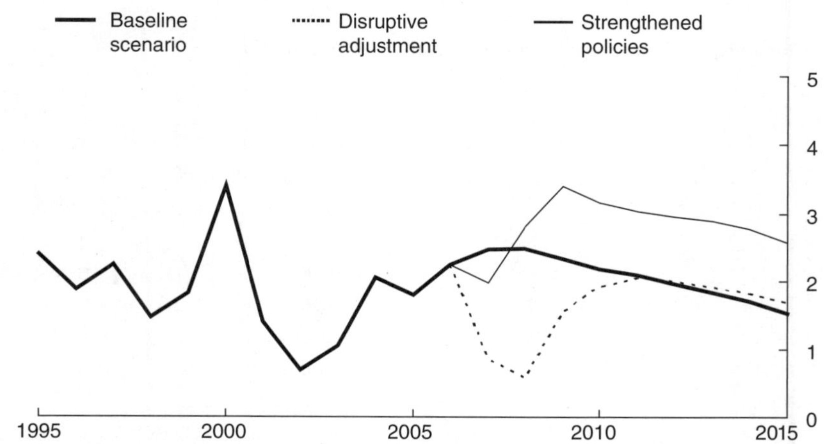

Source: IMF staff estimates.

Figure 2.15 Japan and euro area: output growth (in per cent)

relative to the other two scenarios. Without the policy commitments they have made, the task of preserving global growth while bringing down the imbalances would be considerably more onerous.

We also simulated all the spillover effects of the policy adjustment scenario, and calculated the relative effects of this scenario on global growth over the next six years (see Figure 2.15). Relative to the baseline, global growth would be virtually unchanged in the first three years. However, the following three years generate an increase in global growth rates of 0.6 per cent per year. Moreover, global growth would be better balanced over the medium term. From 2009 onwards, Japan, the euro area and emerging Asia would all grow 1.5–2 per cent more relative to the baseline, while US growth would be virtually unchanged from the baseline. The result would be a significant reduction in global payments imbalances.

The Multilateral Consultation has created a potentially powerful tool for addressing the challenges posed by global imbalances, but the full implementation of these plans is key to achieving the dual goals of bringing down imbalances without sacrificing global growth. In a context of heightened uncertainty and market turmoil, follow-through has gained importance. The Multilateral Consultation was intended precisely to provide guideposts in an uncertain environment, and we hope that it will fully serve that function.

NOTE

1. First Deputy Managing Director, International Monetary Fund.

3. Are global imbalances a problem?

John Williamson[1]

Everyone agrees that the global imbalances are today very large. There is also quite a wide measure of agreement on what would need to be done to rein them in: rebalance world demand by a shift from the United States to East Asia; appreciate most of the currencies of East Asia in effective and bilateral terms and accept bilateral appreciations against the dollar (but not significant – or maybe any – appreciations in effective exchange rates) in the rest of the world. Where there is strong disagreement is on whether it is desirable to take measures designed to secure reasonably prompt adjustment. There is a school of thought that maintains that any cure for the global imbalances would be worse than the disease, and that the best course of action is to do nothing.

While I am not an adherent of this position, I nevertheless believe it to be important to understand the 'do nothing' view, and the dangers that come from allowing it to continue to dominate policy. I also believe that we can learn important lessons about what are and are not real problems by examining the arguments of those who hold this view. That is why it forms the subject of this chapter. I start by laying out a version of the opposing view. I then examine several of its arguments in detail:

- the view that on present trends a gradual adjustment is likely, or else that the market will automatically induce a gradual adjustment in its own good time;
- the view that a deliberate attempt to achieve adjustment would face irreconcilable problems of conflicting national interests;
- the view that the organizational problems of concerting adjustment policies are so formidable as to preclude this solution.

The final section of this chapter shows the basis for believing that a deliberate, concerted adjustment would be less dangerous than the current policy of relying on the market to bring about adjustment in due course.

3.1 THE COOPER VIEW

Richard Cooper (2007) describes at length why the US savings rate may well be under-measured by the conventional national accounts. I suspect that on this the truth lies somewhere between Cooper and convention, but in any event it is not very pertinent to international adjustment since (1) his proposed additions all add equally to savings and investment, and (2) one would need to make analogous additions to the figures for other countries in order to get a correct international comparison. The fact (as he agrees) is that his revised figures do not affect the discrepancy between saving and investment, so they do not address the pertinent question of whether a US current account deficit of over 6 per cent of GDP can be sustained.

The next point he makes is that the actual capital inflow in 2006 was smaller than it would have been if financial markets were fully globalized, in the sense that home bias was everywhere zero. This is because foreign savings (at least when they are measured in a non-Cooperesque way, as he does!) are a much higher proportion of GDP than are US savings, so that if they were invested in proportion to GDP (as he assumes to be implied by the 'no home bias' assumption) there would have been an even larger capital inflow than that recorded. One could argue that the correct test would have been to distribute savings in proportion to investment rather than in proportion to GDP, and that this would have reduced the 'no home bias' inflow to the United States, but it would remain true that the potential capital inflow would have been larger than the actual inflow, which was, of course, sufficient to finance the current account deficit. In any event, I would not challenge Cooper's contention that the United States does not need to fear an imminent end to sufficient availability of foreign savings to finance the deficit.

Cooper also examines demographic developments, noting that population ageing tends to reduce saving but that it cuts investment even more. Since the United States is the only major advanced country that is not ageing, it is to be expected that it will exhibit a relative excess of investment over saving, which can then be expected to result in a current account deficit. Prospective retirees in the rest of the world benefit by being able to make secure, profitable investments. (I agree with this view.)

Cooper also argues that the United States is likely to be able to continue to provide assets on an adequate scale for many years in the future. He points out that the US tendency to hold a much larger proportion of its assets in the form of equity than the proportion of its liabilities that takes the form of equity, both leads to a higher yield on its foreign assets than it has to pay on its liabilities and results in substantial capital gains, especially when the dollar depreciates. But fundamentally he comes back to a 'no home bias' calculation, to show that the proportion of financial assets held by foreigners is still well below what would be needed for foreigners to hold 30 per cent of their assets in the United States. Maybe they do hold assets equal to 89 per cent of GDP, but since financial assets are nearly ten times GDP there is still ample scope for them to hold more. Of course, there is still a lot of home bias in the world, but Cooper's comparisons do show that if we believe globalization is progressively decreasing this bias there is no basis here for assuming that the United States cannot go a lot further into debt.

The last section of Cooper's paper dwells on the difficulties that foreign countries would supposedly face if they had to reduce their surpluses on the requisite scale. They would have to stimulate domestic demand, which he argues would be difficult for export-oriented economies like Japan, Germany and China, since investment would be discouraged by appreciation. There is a widespread desire for fiscal consolidation, which would be an obstacle to raising demand. Use of monetary ease to stimulate consumption would require lower interest rates, which would run counter to the need for currency appreciation. The Lisbon Agenda is focused on greater international competitiveness, not on expanding domestic demand. A Chinese appreciation large enough to eliminate China's current account surplus would still not solve the US problem, while it would threaten Chinese growth since exports have been the driving sector.

On the other hand, if the US deficit is allowed to continue at its current level, or even increase, one would avoid the grave economic consequences of a precipitate dollar devaluation, such as depressing investment outside the United States. Eventually corrective forces will set in, as financial globalization slows and ageing societies cease acquiring new foreign assets and seek to liquidate some existing claims. Then foreign expenditure will rise relative to output and surpluses will decline, perhaps without any need for a dollar depreciation.

3.2 GRADUAL AND AUTOMATIC ADJUSTMENT VERSUS A CRISIS

The 'do nothing' view comes in two versions. One is that a gradual adjustment has already started, for which the prime evidence is the reduction in the US current account deficit as a proportion of GDP. The non-oil deficit has fallen from its peak of 5.1 per cent in 2006 Q3 to its most recent published value of 4 per cent in 2007 Q2. The other version appeals to the fact that a floating exchange rate can depreciate when this is needed to facilitate adjustment, and combines this with an assurance that depreciation will happen in a crisis-free way when foreigners cease to wish to finance the US deficit.

Let us discuss the first version first. The facts are indeed correct: the US current account deficit is now decreasing and foreign demand for US goods is now increasing at a faster rate than domestic US demand, including that for foreign goods. This is highly gratifying, but it is hardly a surprise to anyone who believes that the received theory of what determines the current account is basically right. Growth in the rest of the world has averaged 3.9 per cent since 2006 Q3, against growth of 2.2 per cent in the United States in the same period. Moreover, the dollar has depreciated by 24 per cent (according to the Fed's broad index) since its peak in 2002 Q1 until early November 2007. Of course, that depreciation has been very lopsided, with the euro and most other non-Asian currencies having appreciated strongly (the euro's appreciation against the dollar was over 41 per cent at the time of writing), and most Asian currencies having appreciated rather little in bilateral terms and a number having depreciated in real effective terms. The result has been what we adherents of the derided 'elasticities approach' would have expected, namely a substantially larger decline in the US non-oil current account deficit with the world excluding Asia of USD 28 billion per quarter and a decrease in the deficit with Asian countries of only USD 11 billion.

The critical question is whether this decline in the US deficit marks the start of a trend decline or an interruption of a trend increase. Assuming that US policy continues to react to any sign of increasing unemployment by expansionary macroeconomic policy measures, it seems to me overwhelmingly likely that we are merely witnessing an interruption of the trend increase. I say this because there are three powerful trend factors tending to increase the current account deficit at given pressures of demand and exchange rates:

1. The 'gap factor'. The fact that imports are now over 50 per cent larger than exports means that the trade deficit will increase even with a similar percentage growth rate of exports and imports.
2. The 'Houthakker-Magee' asymmetry in the trade elasticities. If it is true, as Houthakker and Magee (1969) found, that the US income elasticity of demand for imports exceeds the foreign demand elasticity for US exports, then similar growth rates imply trend deterioration in the US current account in the absence of secular real depreciation. Even if, as has been suggested, the finding can be explained away by faster supply-side growth in the economies providing US imports, the fact is that that faster supply-side growth is likely to persist. It is only if the US growth rate is in the future going to be sufficiently below the foreign growth rate that this factor will not come into play.

3. The increase in debt service consequent on an increasing foreign debt. It is, of course, true that so far net debt service has been rather modest, or even negative, mainly because the US has far more of its assets than of its liabilities in the form of equity and therefore gaining the higher returns that equity typically earns. It is also true that part of the return to portfolio equity (and perhaps in practice, though not in theory, of foreign direct investment as well) typically takes the form of capital appreciation that is not recorded in the balance of payments but only in the periodic revaluation of the stock of foreign assets. And it is true that dollar depreciation brings a one-off increase in the net international investment position, because non-equity assets are often denominated in foreign currency while non-equity liabilities are overwhelmingly denominated in dollars. All these factors have helped the United States to delay the ill-consequences of a large foreign debt far longer than many of us realized would be possible, but increasing debts will eventually have the qualitative impact that was expected. And this cannot be evaded in the long run: real devaluation is not compatible with steady state.

The current improvement in the US current account deficit will ameliorate two of these three factors: it will reduce the exports/imports ratio, and it will curb the debt service increase. But no one expects that these changes will push the United States into current account surplus, or even reduce the current account deficit to the level (2.3 per cent of GDP, according to IMF calculations) where the debt/output ratio would stabilize. The expectation has to be that both factors will remain negative for the US current account, merely less negative. Together with the second factor, they will eventually overwhelm the depreciation-caused improvement in the deficit, so an increased deficit will resume without further policy changes.

Adherents of the 'do nothing' view argue that even if an adequate adjustment has not already started it can be relied upon to do so when foreigners decide that they wish to start saving less in order to consume or invest more. Maybe this will involve a dollar depreciation, in which case there is nothing to prevent the dollar responding to market forces, or maybe adjustment will occur with a largely unchanged value of the dollar. In neither case is there a need to worry about the current balance-of-payments deficit.

Since there is no policy that would obstruct a timely dollar depreciation, at least against some currencies, no sensible person can assert that this benign outcome is not conceivable. The danger is that it will be short-circuited by a crisis. By this one is thinking of a rapid depreciation of the dollar against those currencies that float, *accompanied by a loss of confidence that causes falls in consumption and investment and thereby induces a recession*. The fact that this sequence of events has not as yet been triggered by the 2007 financial turmoil is mildly reassuring, but does not justify entirely dismissing the danger. If it materialized, it would be quite likely to trigger a world recession. In the United States, at least the expenditure reduction consequent on the loss of confidence would in due course be offset by the positive expenditure-switching effect of the dollar depreciation. In the rest of the world, the two effects would reinforce one another to magnify recession.

It is important, however, to stress that recession is a danger and not a certainty. Too often the debate is conducted on the assumption that anyone who worries about the US deficit is forecasting that the deficit is definitely unsustainable. That is something we do not, and cannot, know. If the consequences of a continued deficit *may* be a sufficiently grave crisis, that should be motive enough to act.

3.3 ARE THERE CONFLICTING NATIONAL INTERESTS?

The second prong of the 'do nothing' view is the assertion that governments are unlikely to reach agreements to act because of inherent conflicts of national interest. The most powerful version of this view at the moment appears to be that China has a fundamental national interest in maintaining its policy of export-led growth, which implies a large balance-of-trade surplus. China, and a number of other East Asian countries, refuse demands to revalue significantly, since these would threaten to pre-empt their rapid growth and the associated employment creation (see, for example, Dooley, Folkerts-Landau and Garber, 2003).

I see three basic errors in this argument. The first is the association of large current account surpluses with export-led growth. The fact is that the idea of export-led growth was first propagated enthusiastically by Bela Balassa. His example par excellence was the East Asian newly industrialized countries, and then the South East Asian countries of Indonesia, Malaysia and Thailand, long *before* the East Asian crisis of 1997. Yet those countries on average had current account deficits, not surpluses, in their years of rapid growth, as Table 3.1 shows (the countries for which I succeeded in obtaining statistics). What made their growth export-led was that they aimed to resolve their balance-of-payments problems through exporting and not through import substitution. Their success in exporting made them attractive clients for Wall Street to lend to, and this gave them the wherewithal to run import surpluses, which added to their investible funds and thus their growth rates. The consequence was high exports, even higher

Table 3.1 Current account balances of East Asia prior to the 1997 crisis (USD billion)

	1970s	1980s	1990–96
Indonesia	n.a.	−2.7[e]	−4.2
Korea	−1.4[a]	+1.9	−6.9
Malaysia	+0.2[b]	−0.7	−4.0
Singapore	−0.7[c]	−0.1	+4.0
Thailand	−1.1[d]	−1.2	−9.1

Notes:
a. Series starts 1976.
b. Series starts 1974.
c. Series starts 1972.
d. Series starts 1975.
e. Series starts 1981.

Sources: IMF, International Financial Statistics.

imports, high investment and high growth. There was no current account surplus.

The popularity of current account surpluses arose only after the Asian crisis of 1997, initially inspired by a resolve that never again would the countries be thrown on the mercies of the West, which they had found singularly lacking. Growth in due course resumed in those countries, though at the much reduced rate that anyone who thinks growth is in part driven by investment would expect, since the countries had diverted up to 10 per cent of their GDP from investment into net exports.

The second fallacy is the belief that bigger undervaluation is better (for growth). There is good reason for believing that *overvaluation* is damaging for growth, particularly for emerging markets; not only is it easy to think of anecdotal examples of countries in which growth ground to a standstill as they fought to maintain overvalued exchange rates, or to concoct a theory, but there is now solid empirical evidence (Razin and Collins, 1999; Aguirre and Calderón, 2006; Prasad, Rajan and Subramanian, 2007). It is true that there are also two attempts to establish empirically that the bigger the undervaluation, the faster the growth (Bhalla, 2007; Rodrik, 2007), but not all of us find these provide convincing evidence that it is rational policy to run large current account surpluses. And they confront the theoretical obstacle of having to explain why a diversion of resources from investment into the accumulation of low-yielding foreign exchange should lead to growth acceleration. It is fair to say, however, that this subject remains in contention.

The final fallacy, and the one that is most clearly wrong, is the belief that rapid growth in GDP is inevitably associated with fast employment creation. The statistics on China are telling. GDP has certainly grown rapidly, at an average of close to 10 per cent per year for the past ten years, but employment has grown at little over 1 per cent a year. Since this is essentially the rate of growth in the labour force, China's current policy is not succeeding in providing jobs for any significant part of the estimated 250 million surplus workers in the countryside. The reasons are easy to understand. The industry that has grown in recent years is less the labour-intensive part of manufacturing that grew in the early years but rather capital-intensive heavy industry. Moreover, the low price and ready availability of capital have encouraged any given industry to adopt more capital-intensive techniques than it would have done with factor prices that reflected relative scarcities.

Obviously it is of central importance that any curtailment of the incentive to produce exports be accompanied by an increase in demand from other sources. This is the famous rebalancing of global demand; while payments adjustment requires that the United States curtails demand, other countries like China need to expand it, or else we shall have world demand deficiency (recession). In particular, increased Chinese demand will lead to an increase in demand for Chinese non-tradable products. It is a fact that the production of services (which are largely non-tradable) is more labour-intensive than manufacturing. Thus, the supporters of rapid Chinese growth through a highly undervalued exchange rate have it exactly backwards: their strategy is inimical to the rapid absorption of surplus labour into productive modern-sector employment. Payments adjustment pursued with a properly balanced strategy embracing both revaluation and demand rebalancing (that is, expansion in the Chinese case) would increase rather than decrease the absorption of surplus labour.

I would not claim that the case for thinking that payments adjustment to a less unbalanced level would be in the interest of the present surplus countries is as clear for all other countries as it is for China. The most difficult case among the major countries is without doubt Japan. Certainly when Japan was mired in hopeless recession, in the late 1990s and early 2000s, adjustment would have risked imposing a waste of real resources that would have benefited no one. The case is now less clear-cut, given that Japan's real GDP has grown quite rapidly for the last several years, but there is still no scope for a major fiscal expansion in Japan. It seems wrong to absolve Japan of all responsibility for adjustment, but right to allow it a rather less demanding pace of adjustment than other major surplus countries.

Almost all, perhaps all, the oil exporting countries are currently with large current account surpluses; in the case of the Gulf countries in massive surplus. But unless one takes the view that the oil price is near or below its trend path, this seems quite reasonable. If the oil price is abnormally high, they need to save now as part of a strategy to even out their expenditure over the cycle, and in cases of limited domestic investment possibilities they also need to save abroad as part of an optimal accumulation strategy. One may legitimately complain about the lethargic pace of adjustment in most oil exporting countries, which results from the fact that the pace of spending increases only when government spending can be ramped up, but at this stage that leaves little additional scope for deliberately engineering adjustment.

Since Germany is also a major surplus country at the moment, the question is sometimes posed as to whether it too should be expected to implement decisive expansionary actions. My answer to that is in the negative, because payments adjustment generally requires an appropriate combination of exchange rate change and demand change, not just one or the other. (I once quipped that those who believed that adjustment requires just fiscal policy are believers in immaculate adjustment.) And Germany now lacks a separate exchange rate, since it is a part of the euro area. The question that should be asked is whether the euro area as a whole needs payments adjustment, and the answer is no. The German surplus is essentially offset by the Spanish deficit. Imbalances within a monetary area are not phenomena for policy to eliminate.

There is no general proposition according to which surplus countries should be required to adjust simply because they have a surplus. The aim should be to have countries aim for a payments balance that can be expected to enhance their welfare. It is conceivable that welfare maximization would lead to a general desire to avoid deficits, or at least to a net desire for surpluses in the world as a whole. One would normally expect this to be remedied by a lower interest rate, which would stimulate spending and curb saving in many countries. There would only be a problem of global inconsistency if a net desire for surpluses persisted at any positive interest rate. The most likely origin of this problem would be if the oil price were very high and expected to remain high for a long but not indefinite period. Most of the oil exporters would then see a national advantage in saving much of their oil revenue, while most of the oil importers might then wish to shift the deficit on to other countries. (This was in fact the scenario envisaged by the Committee of Twenty after the oil price increase of 1973, though things turned out not to be so drastic.) But at present it is quite unpersuasive to argue that there are not surplus countries that could benefit their citizens by expanding their demand enough to eliminate any question of demand deficiency. It is not in fact difficult to envisage a pattern of global current account imbalances that would be both globally consistent and compatible with a major and sustained cut in the US current account deficit (Williamson, 2007).

3.4 CONCERTING ADJUSTMENT POLICIES

Suppose one agrees that it is a gamble to rely on a continuing US deficit indefinitely, since there is a danger of a collapse of confidence rather than an orderly adjustment at the end of the day. Suppose one agrees also that there are countries that could advantageously – to themselves – move toward a deficit in the current account, and that there is no problem of inconsistency in payments objectives. But there is a third bow to the string of the do nothing school: a belief that it will be impractical to organize a simultaneous policy change on the part of a large number of countries, so that it is preferable to live with what we have at the moment rather than to attempt a concerted adjustment that is doomed to fail.

Let me start by agreeing that it would be possible for half the adjustment to be worse than no change. The matter is no longer quite as clear since there is a chance that the pressure of demand is spontaneously declining, but a few months ago I would certainly have held that a dollar devaluation unaccompanied by contractionary US fiscal policies to make room for an improvement in the balance of payments would simply have led to some combination of higher interest rates and faster inflation. Similarly, a substantial renminbi appreciation without demand expansion would have led to a waste of resources and a tendency toward world recession. It is indeed important that countries implement the whole of the policy package that is being prescribed, not just a half of it.

I also agree that the major institutional form that cooperation has taken in the past, the Group of Seven (G7) countries, is outmoded. It excludes one of the major essential partners in any future adjustment effort, namely China. All the G7 can do about China is lecture it, which it regularly does, but which has proved as ineffective as might have been expected. No proud country like China is going to adjust its policies in response to the calls of a group from which it is excluded.

Nevertheless, we need to recognize that the last Managing Director of the IMF created exactly the right type of group for negotiating these matters. The 'Multilateral Consultation' that he organized under an IMF umbrella contained the right countries (the United States, euro area, China, Japan and Saudi Arabia) in the right context and was given the right agenda. It was expected to report back to the IMF Board, which gave any other interested party the opportunity of participating in a joint policy adjustment. It also gave other countries the opportunity of reacting to the proposals of the inner group, and it offered the opportunity of seeking to organize a wider policy adjustment if that were judged to be necessary. The error was for the Managing Director to declare himself satisfied with the communiqué they produced, which sounded like a typical G7 communiqué in essentially declaring that everything would turn out just fine if only they kept on doing exactly what the participants had been doing all along. The opportunity to negotiate a joint and simultaneous policy change was lost.

3.5 AN ORGANIZED ADJUSTMENT VERSUS LAISSEZ-FAIRE

What is necessary is to create the next Multilateral Consultation with essentially the same group of countries, but with two crucial differences. The first is that the new Managing Director of the IMF must not be so easily satisfied with the outcome. The second difference concerns the US attitude. Rather than taking the position that its role is solely that of demandeur, asking policy adjustments of other countries but taking the view that a fiscal deficit of 1.2 per cent of GDP at the peak of the boom and a belief in a 'strong dollar' with an exchange rate that floats to weak levels entitles it to do nothing further, it needs to show a willingness to make some policy adjustments itself. Between one and four of the other participants in the Multilateral Consultation in fact regarded a tighter US cyclically adjusted fiscal policy as the key policy change required to initiate comprehensive adjustment, and to exclude that policy change from consideration was to doom the negotiations from the start.

If and when the United States shows a willingness to engage in genuine negotiations, the Managing Director should convene a second Multilateral Consultation. The essential nature of the bargain that should be negotiated is clear enough (it was outlined in a workshop held at the Peterson Institute in February 2007). First, it needs to embrace both levels of demand and exchange rates, rather than relying on either one or the other to carry the whole burden of adjustment. Second, unless the repercussions of the financial turbulence are already plunging the world into recession (which is not clear at the time of writing), global demand needs to be broadly unchanged. Demand contractions in some areas (specifically, the United States) need to be offset by demand expansions in other areas (specifically, in East Asia). Third, the exchange rates of some areas – most of the currencies of East Asia, though perhaps not those of Korea and Thailand since their currencies have already appreciated like many non-dollar currencies in other parts of the world – need to appreciate both overall (in effective terms) and bilaterally against the dollar. Fourth, insofar as other non-dollar currencies are managed (and one would expect the merits of using intervention policy, including 'oral intervention', more actively to be a subject for negotiation), they should aim at keeping their effective rates broadly unchanged even though this may entail further bilateral appreciation against the dollar.[2] The time horizon over which these changes are to take place would be a subject for negotiation: if I were a non-East Asian participant I would start off by seeking rather rapid adjustment, but would settle for something that China and Japan felt they could live with, as long as that did not entail waiting for Godot.

Once the outlines of such an agreement had been reached in the Multilateral Consultation exercise, it would be necessary for the participants to negotiate supporting agreements with their peers who are not in the negotiating group. This is really an issue for East Asia, since although it might potentially arise elsewhere (like Europe, the Middle East, or Australia) these areas are not expected to adjust their demand policies and (except for the Middle East) their exchange rates float fairly freely. Presumably one would look to China and Japan to convene a group that would essentially place the East Asian countries in three groups: those that would appreciate along with China and Japan (my candidates would be Hong Kong,[3] Malaysia, Taiwan and Singapore); those that would hold their effective rates broadly constant (Korea, Thailand) and an intermediate group that would depreciate against China but accept an effective appreciation (Indonesia, Philippines). It is, of course, important to realize that for all countries, especially those in the first group, the effective appreciations would be much less than the bilateral appreciations against the dollar precisely because of the simultaneous adjustment of competitor currencies. Changes in demand policies might also be discussed, with countries appreciating in effective terms being expected to offset the deflationary impact of this on the rest of the world by demand expansion, except insofar as they were already suffering from excess demand.

The Multilateral Consultation exercise might also cover some complementary issues. For example, there would be much to be said for establishing some international discipline on what used to be referred to as 'jawboning' and has now been dubbed 'verbal intervention'. These are official expressions of hope about where exchange rates ought to be heading that are presumably intended to influence markets, in the same way that currency intervention is undertaken with the intent of influencing where the exchange rate goes. There is no question that this is not always an effective weapon: to convince oneself of that it is not necessary to think beyond the recent declarations of Secretary Paulson's faith in a strong dollar, after which the dollar proceeded to hit record lows against most non-Asian currencies. At the same time, econometric evidence (Fratzscher, 2004) suggests that verbal intervention sometimes has an effect. It may not be a reliable instrument, but it is a policy instrument, and it needs to be used consciously and with an agreed international objective in mind.

The first principle of rational use of verbal intervention is that governments favour equilibrium exchange rates, rather than always expressing themselves as being in favour of strong or weak rates. Where they wish to see a rate heading depends on where it is relevant to a plausible estimate of equilibrium. It would yield an even greater gain for popular understanding if the press could be persuaded to adopt this position too.

Obviously such a formula is of limited use without an agreed view on equilibrium rates. No one expects governments or the IMF or anyone else to agree exact rates with high margins of precision, but positions of complete agnosticism are equally absurd. Exchange rates that get seriously out of line with fundamentals are recognizable, and they are damaging. No one should be forced to push rates exactly to estimates that will always be rough and uncertain, but there would be advantages in agreeing a pattern of what the official sector believes to be approximate equilibrium rates.

An advantage in the present context is that it would provide a basis for disciplining verbal intervention. Specifically, statements of where a currency ought to be heading would be allowed if they were tending to push a currency toward its equilibrium (measured in effective, not bilateral, terms), but they would be prohibited if they were trying to push a currency away from what had been internationally accepted as a rough estimate of equilibrium. No country would be *forced* to take any exchange rate actions at all, but they could at least be prevented from making situations worse.

A second area where there is scope for the exercise of Multilateral Consultation to yield an outcome that might benefit the world economy concerns the pegging policy of the Gulf oil producers. At present all except Kuwait peg firmly to the dollar, while Kuwait pegs to a basket with a large dollar weight. Intellectually this makes no sense. The United States imports oil, so any systematic variation in its currency or its monetary policy is unlikely to be what oil exporters would find in their national interest. In order to avoid delays while governments change spending in reaction to oil price increases (or decreases, though we have nowadays forgotten that oil prices may sometimes fall) and thus accelerate adjustment, it would make sense for these countries to peg their currencies to a basket that varies along with the price of oil. The most certain and straightforward way of doing this is to peg to a basket that is mainly composed of the major currencies with the balance comprising the price of oil (Setser, 2007).

If the Saudis were persuaded of the virtues of such a change in the Multilateral Consultation, it would then be necessary for them to consult the smaller Gulf countries, in the same way that was earlier outlined for China and its smaller East Asian neighbours.

3.6 CONCLUDING REMARKS

But both verbal intervention and the pegging policy of the Gulf are essentially sideshows. The essence is negotiation of multilateral adjustment as described earlier. Such a negotiation does not seem infeasible, at least with a US willingness to contribute. It presents no obvious dangers: if it runs into the sands, we are no worse off than under the present drift. It is fallacious to argue that we face a problem of irreconcilable national interests. That it would be preferable to present arrangements, which seem to me well-described by the term 'drift', is clear to anyone who accepts that there is a significant probability of the world running into disaster. To repeat, I do not believe that there is a *certainty* of disaster under present trends, but the *likelihood* seems quite high. This is by no means the first time that we have been regaled by assurances that the world has changed and this time it is different, and even if it turns out that these assurances are as misplaced as they have always proved in the past they will doubtless be repeated many times in the future. Maybe one day they will prove true. Let us hope that this is the time, for I confess that I am not optimistic about the prospects of a negotiated adjustment being achieved.

NOTES

1. Senior Fellow, Peterson Institute. Revised version of a keynote lecture delivered to the Conference on Currency and Competitiveness organized by the Oesterreichische Nationalbank in Vienna on 19–20 November 2007. The author expresses his indebtedness to participants in that conference for comments on the previous draft. Copyright Peterson Institute: all rights reserved.
2. At the time of the Peterson Institute workshop in February 2007, the euro stood at about USD 1.30. Our formula at that time was for non-dollar currencies outside of East Asia to seek to hold effective rates broadly constant but to accept bilateral appreciations against the dollar. Since then these currencies have already experienced substantial dollar appreciations but have not as yet had depreciations against the East Asian currencies, so they can now be expected to accept smaller appreciations against the dollar and seek somewhat more competitive effective exchange rates.
3. Yes, that would mean scrapping the currency board. Good riddance: it long ago outlived its usefulness.

REFERENCES

Aguirre, Alvaro and César Calderón (2006), 'The effects of real exchange rate misalignments on economic growth', Santiago: Central Bank of Chile, mimeo.
Bhalla, Surjit (2007), '*There are no growth miracles*', mimeo.
Cooper, Richard N. (2007), 'Living with global imbalances', *Brookings Papers on Economic Activity*, 2.
Dooley, Michael, David Folkerts-Landau and Peter Garber (2003), 'An essay on the revived Bretton Woods system', *NBER Working Paper* No. 9971.
Fratzscher, Marcel (2004), 'Exchange rate policy strategies and foreign exchange interventions in the group of three economies', in C.F. Bergsten and J. Williamson (eds), *Dollar Adjustment: How Far? Against What?*, Washington, DC: Peterson Institute.
Houthakker, Hendrik and Stephen P. Magee (1969), 'Income and price elasticities in world trade', *Review of Economics and Statistics*, **51** (2), 111–25.
Prasad, Eswar, Raghurajan Rajan and Arvind Subramanian (2007), 'Foreign capital and economic growth', *Brookings Papers on Economic Activity*, No. 1.
Razin, Ofair and Susan M. Collins (1999), 'Real exchange-rate misalignments and growth', in A. Razin and E. Sadka (eds), *The Economics of Globalization: Policy Perspectives from Public Economics*, Cambridge: Cambridge University Press.
Rodrik, Dani (2007), 'Is undervaluation good for growth? Theory and evidence', mimeo, http://ksghome.harvard.edu/~drodrik/papers.html.
Setser, Brad (2007), 'The case for exchange rate flexibility in oil-exporting countries', *Policy Brief* No. 07-8, Washington, DC: Peterson Institute.
Williamson, John (2007), 'The target current account outcomes', paper presented to the Bruegel/KIEP/Peterson Institute Workshop on the Global Imbalances in Washington, February.

4. Financial globalization and exchange rate arrangements

Graciela Laura Kaminsky[1]

The crises of the 1990s fuelled a renewed interest in the causes of speculative attacks. Many claim that these crises were of a different nature than the crises of the 1960s and 1970s, arguing that while the latter had been triggered by fiscal and monetary problems, the crises of the 1990s were caused by weaknesses in the banking sector and overall financial fragility.[2] It is further asserted that the financial fragility that preceded these crises was sparked by over-borrowing in international capital markets and the concentration of the debt in foreign currency, with Rodrik (1998) and Eichengreen (1999 and 2005) further concluding that unfettered international capital flows were at the core of these problems. These crises also resuscitated old debates (with new clothes) about the role of exchange rate regimes, with many arguing that fixed exchange rate regimes trigger financial excesses and liability dollarization.[3] This chapter will review the theoretical debate and the empirical evidence on balance sheet problems and their causes.

4.1 FINANCIAL LIBERALIZATION

The crises of the 1990s have claimed many victims: entire banking systems collapsed around the world, roaring growing economies succumbed to their worst recession in modern times and the booming international capital flows of the early 1990s dwindled to a trickle. This is not all. Perhaps the most important casualty of these crises has been the support for domestic and international financial liberalization.

In the aftermath of the Asian crisis, many concluded that globalization had gone too far and had led to extremely erratic capital markets around the world. For example, Joseph Stiglitz (2000) argues for developing countries to put some limits on capital inflows in order to moderate the 'excessive' boom–bust pattern in financial markets. Similarly, Rodrik (1998) rejects capital market liberalization, arguing that there is no evidence that countries with free capital mobility grow faster and indicating that international financial liberalization exposes them to the danger of debilitating crises. Even the International Monetary Fund has joined the group, arguing for the postponement of capital account liberalization until countries make progress in strengthening their financial markets and in improving institutions in general.[4] Moreover, controls on capital outflows, not long ago dismissed as ineffective, are fashionable again. Paul Krugman (1998), for instance, suggests that capital controls may help in managing, at least temporarily, an otherwise disorderly retreat of investors.

The rationale for restricting international capital flows is grounded in the belief that market failures and distortions pervade capital markets around the world. One of the most frequently cited distortions is that of asymmetric information, which is rampant in international capital markets due to geographical and cultural differences that complicate the task of obtaining information. In addition, imperfections in international markets are magnified by the difficulties in enforcing contracts across borders.[5] With imperfect information, investors may overreact to shocks, withdrawing massively from countries at the first signs of economic problems, or become euphoric and pour in capital in quantities beyond those justified by 'good' fundamentals.

The empirical literature on banking crises has also uncovered a link between liberalization of the domestic banking industry and banking crises. For example, Kaminsky and Reinhart (1999) find that the likelihood of banking crises increases by 40 per cent following the deregulation of the domestic banking sector. A variety of models have been proposed to explain this link. For example, Allen and Gale (1999, 2000), Hellman, Murdock and Stiglitz (2000) and Tornell and Westermann (2005), among others, show that financial liberalization leads to risky behaviour by banks. In particular, Hellman et al. (op. cit.) show that financial liberalization fuels competition and reduces bank profits, eroding banks' franchise value, while at the same time allowing banks to take more risk. Since governments cannot commit not to provide bailouts in cases of crises, banks have incentives to gamble for resurrection, reaping the benefits in case of success and passing the losses to the government in times of crises. Moreover, Tornell and Westermann (op. cit.) argue that financial liberalization triggers lending boom–bust cycles in economies with credit restrictions and overall imperfections in financial markets. Allen and Gale (2000) further show that these lending booms can feed into stock market bubbles because agency problems generate an incentive for borrowers to use bank loans to buy risky assets, with these bubbles ending up in banking crises and recessions. Overall, these models rest on the idea that market failures and distortions pervade capital markets and are the sources of the boom–bust patterns.

Other authors, in contrast, highlight the benefits of financial liberalization. They claim that financial liberalization allows capital to move to its most attractive destination, increasing productivity and growth and fostering a better functioning of financial markets. For example, Bekaert, Harvey and Lundblad (2005) find that liberalization leads to a one percentage point increase in annual economic growth as well as to a decline in output volatility. Also, Henry (2000a, 2000b) finds that liberalization triggers an increase in the investment rate and a substantial revaluation of equity prices in a large number of countries. Galindo, Micco and Ordóñez (2002) study whether financial liberalization promotes economic growth by analysing its effect on the cost of external financing to firms. In particular, their hypothesis is that the liberalization of domestic and external financial markets reduces the cost of external corporate funding by reducing the impact of problems associated with moral hazard and adverse selection. From this perspective, the impact of financial development differs according to the needs of particular firms for external funds. Firms that rely more on external funds will be more heavily impacted by financial development than those that require little capital. The results suggest that industries that depend on external finance grow almost one percentage point faster (relative to industries with low external financing dependence) in episodes of globalization compared with episodes of repression. Traditional neoclassical models provide the theoretical support for these findings. In these models, financial liberalization reduces the cost of capital and fuels a significant boom in lending and stock market prices, but does not trigger a financial crash.

However, the evidence on the links between financial liberalization and growth is not conclusive. For example, Edison and Warnock (2003), using data from 57 countries from 1980 to 2000, conclude that there is no robustly significant effect of financial integration on economic growth.[6] Similarly, Kraay (1998), using a sample of 117 countries, finds no effect of financial liberalization on growth or, at best, mixed results.

To reconcile the evidence that globalization is at the heart of financial crises with the hypothesis that international capital markets allow capital to move to its most attractive destination and promote more stable financial markets, Kaminsky and Schmukler (2003) examine the possible time-varying effects of financial liberalization on stock market price cycles. Figure 4.1 reproduces some of the results in that paper. The figure shows the average amplitude of booms and crashes for 14 emerging markets[7] during periods of repression, in the short run following liberalization, and in the long run following liberalization. The evidence in this figure seems to point to excessive cycles, with larger booms followed by larger crashes in the immediate aftermath of financial liberalization. However, liberalization

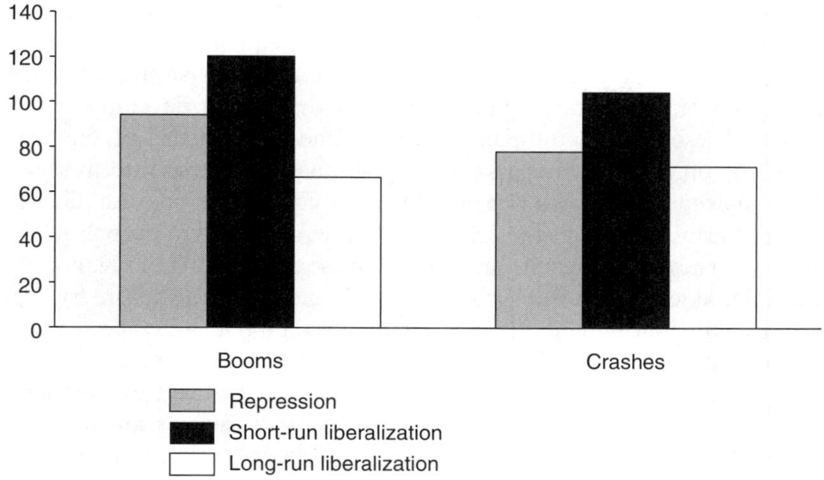

Source: Kaminsky and Schmukler (2003).

Figure 4.1 Average amplitude of booms and crashes in stock prices in 14 emerging markets (in per cent)

does not permanently bring about more volatile financial markets. If liberalization persists, stock markets in emerging countries become more stable.

One possible explanation examined in Kaminsky and Schmukler (ibid.) (using a variety of measures of law and order) is that financial liberalization triggers institutional reforms that make financial markets function better while governments may have few incentives to promote reforms in countries with repressed financial sectors.[8] Interestingly, the evidence for the 14 emerging countries indicates that deregulation indeed precedes institutional reforms. This sequence may also be due to the actions of domestic investors who, having access to international capital markets following deregulation, demand better enforcement rules to continue to invest in domestic financial markets. As suggested by Stulz (1999), the liberalization and gradual integration of emerging markets into international financial markets may help strengthen the domestic financial sector as foreign investors generally have better skills and more information and can thus monitor management in ways that local investors cannot. Liberalization also allows firms to access mature capital markets. Firms listed on foreign stock markets are in the jurisdiction of a superior legal system with higher disclosure standards, which promotes more transparency in the management of the firm and can trigger improvements in corporate governance. Mishkin (2003) also argues that financial liberalization promotes transparency and accountability, reducing adverse selection and moral hazard and alleviating liquidity problems in financial markets.

Loayza and Ranciere (2004) also provide evidence about the time-varying effects of financial liberalization and financial development on growth. These authors estimate transitory and trend effects of financial deepening on growth using a sample of about 80 countries and find that financial deepening, which in general is closely related to financial liberalization, harms growth in the short run but leads to higher growth in the long run. These latest results are closely linked to the results in Kaminsky and Schmukler (2003) and suggest that financial liberalization triggers growth in the long run because it fuels institutional reform.

Gourinchas and Jeanne (2003) also explore this theme and distinguish two classes of benefits of financial globalization. The first category includes benefits in terms of international allocative efficiency, such as consumption smoothing in response to shocks or the possibility of accelerating domestic capital accumulation with the help of foreign capital. The second class of benefits encompasses incentives to implement good policies or reform that are generated by an open capital account. This includes imposing market discipline on domestic macroeconomic policies induced by the threat of capital flight. More broadly, it can also include incentives to reform the domestic economic system in a way that reduces unproductive activities (diversion, rent-seeking) or secures better guarantees of property rights. To examine the relative importance of the benefits of international allocative efficiency, the authors calibrate a simple neoclassical growth model of a small, open, capital-scarce economy with data on post-World War II emerging economies. While they find that financial openness increases domestic welfare by allowing households to smooth consumption and by increasing the possibility of accelerating domestic capital accumulation, they also find that the benefits are not very large when compared with the benefits of alternative policies that reduce domestic distortions or increase domestic productivity.

4.2 EXCHANGE RATE REGIMES

The crises of the 1990s have also stirred the debate on the pros and cons of fixed and flexible exchange rate regimes. While the debate is old, it has acquired a new twist. It does not focus anymore on asymmetric real shocks to determine whether a group of countries belongs to an optimum currency area. The discussion is now centred on the effects of liability dollarization and the moral hazard problem triggered by the exchange rate government guarantees implicit in 'soft' pegs. According to Burnside, Eichenbaum and

Rebelo (2001) and Schneider and Tornell (2004), under fixed exchange rate regimes, firms do not fully internalize their exchange rate risk and will be more likely to engage in balance sheet mismatches than under a floating regime. Even without moral hazard considerations, the exchange rate regime might also affect the currency composition of debt by modifying the relative return volatilities of domestic and foreign currency assets. Ize and Levy Yeyati (2003) show that, in the minimum-variance portfolio equilibrium, financial dollarization is explained by the relative volatilities of inflation and real exchange rates. Since pegs tend to reduce real exchange rate volatility, they also increase dollarization.

Another strand of the literature on exchange rate regimes focuses on the so-called 'fear of floating syndrome'.[9] This view points out that many countries, while claiming to be floaters, actively engage in exchange rate stabilization operations because of worries about the effects of floating when debts are denominated in foreign currencies.

A number of studies have also focused on the two-way causality between portfolio choices and exchange rate policies. For example, Chamon and Hausmann (2002) examine the optimal monetary policy when domestic firms have a large dollar-denominated debt. They point out that when firms expect a policy of stable exchange rates, they will borrow in foreign currency. In this situation, unexpected changes in the real exchange rate can drive the firms into costly bankruptcy. Naturally, fear of bankrupting the firms will lead the monetary authority to peg the currency, validating their expectations. Hence this model can have more than one equilibrium policy. Chang and Velasco (2004) also build a model of a small open economy with incomplete markets in which domestic residents can only borrow nominal bonds denominated in both home and foreign currency. They also assume sticky wages. In this model, flexible exchange rates can stabilize the labour market – as it is emphasized in the traditional literature – but can exacerbate the volatility of domestic consumption, if domestic residents are long in one currency and short in the other, as it is emphasized in the most recent literature. Again, in this model, currency mismatches affect monetary policy as well as monetary policy affects portfolio choices, with this model also delivering multiple equilibria. Importantly, Chang and Velasco (ibid.) show that social welfare would increase if the monetary authority could pre-commit to floating.

Testing the effect of the exchange rate regime on dollarization is problematic due to the two-way causality between exchange rate regimes and dollarization. Iannariello (2005) is the first to examine the two-way causality between exchange rate regimes and dollarization. She examines these links using data for Argentina, Bolivia, Chile, Colombia, Czech Republic, Ecuador, Egypt, Estonia, Hungary, Indonesia, Korea, Malaysia, Mexico,

Nigeria, Peru, Philippines, Poland, South Africa, Thailand, Turkey, Ukraine and Venezuela for the period 1990–2001. Using panel vector autoregressive (VAR) techniques, she finds that a move from a peg to a crawling peg regime leads to a persistent decrease in financial dollarization close to 4 per cent of GDP. She also finds that fluctuations in the index of exchange rate regimes can explain about 50 per cent of the variance in dollarization, suggesting the relevance of this channel.

More recently, Berkmen and Cavallo (2007) also study the two-way causality between exchange rate regimes and dollarization using a panel of industrial and developing countries. To solve the problem of identification, they use the method of 'identification through heteroskedasticity' developed by Rigobon (2003). The study shows that, controlling for endogeneity, countries with aggregate liability dollarization tend to be more actively involved in exchange rate stabilization operations, but it finds mixed results for the reverse causality.[10]

There is also a growing empirical literature that focuses on the determinants and effects of currency mismatches using firm-level data. For example, Martínez and Werner (2002) examine the currency composition of corporate debt in Mexico before the 1994 crisis when Mexico had a fixed exchange rate regime and following the crisis when Mexico allowed the exchange rate to float more freely. They study 318 firms listed in the Mexican Stock Exchange from 1992 to 2000. They find that for the median firm, the exposure to the depreciation risk decreases when floating, with the ratio of dollar debt to exports decreasing from 3.9 in 1994 to 1.6 in 2000.

Cowan, Herrera and Hansen (2005) also look at firm-level data for Chile to identify changes in the level and distribution of dollar debt across two distinct policy regimes. Before 1999, Chile had an exchange rate band and therefore an explicit commitment to exchange rate stability. Since 1999, the Central Bank of Chile has allowed the exchange rate to float freely. This study also finds significant drops in the level of currency exposure after the exchange rate was floated in 1999, suggesting that flexible rates reduce currency exposure by eliminating the implicit exchange rate insurance and forcing firms to internalize exchange rate risk correctly.

Kamil (2006) extends the Martínez and Werner (2002) and Cowan et al. (2005) studies to seven Latin American countries: Argentina, Brazil, Chile, Colombia, Mexico, Peru and Uruguay. This sample includes 2000 firms from 1992 to 2005. Kamil (ibid.) finds that liability dollarization in the less export-oriented firm declines about six percentage points (when compared with a more export-oriented firm) when the domestic currency is floating, again suggesting that floats induce firms to internalize exchange rate risk correctly.

4.3 FINAL REMARKS

The literature on financial integration and the role of exchange rate regimes has continued to increase. To date, there is still lack of agreement on the pros and cons of globalization and the role of the exchange rate regime. Still, the conflictive empirical evidence on financial liberalization has shed some light onto this controversy by pointing to the time-varying effects of integration and to the causal links between integration and the quality of institutions. According to this evidence, financial deregulation strengthens the impetus for institutional reform, which in turn promotes less volatile financial markets and higher growth, but only in the long run. Importantly, these findings also suggest that dollarization may not play such an important role in the future as financial liberalization fuels better institutions, a reduction in distortions and more liquid capital markets.

NOTES

1. Professor, Economics Department, George Washington University, and National Bureau of Economic Research (NBER).
2. See, for example, Allen et al. (2002).
3. See, for example, Dooley (2000).
4. See, for example, Prasad et al. (2003) and Prasad, Rumbaugh and Wang (2005).
5. For an excellent discussion on the effects of asymmetric information in assets markets, see Eichengreen and Mussa (1998).
6. See Prasad et al. (2003) for a review of the literature on the effects of financial globalization on growth.
7. The 14 emerging economies are Argentina, Brazil, Chile, Colombia, Hong Kong, Indonesia, South Korea, Malaysia, Mexico, Peru, the Philippines, Taiwan, Thailand and Venezuela.
8. Rajan and Zingales (2003a, 2003b) argue that well-established firms (and therefore public officials) may in general oppose reforms that promote financial development because it breeds competition. These firms can even be hurt by financial development and liberalization as they imply better disclosure rules and enforcement (reducing the importance of these firms' collateral and reputation) and permit newcomers to enter and compete away profits. Rajan and Zingales (ibid.) conclude that opposition to reforms may be weaker in more open economies with abundant trade and cross-border flows. In this case, free access to international capital markets allows the largest and best-known domestic firms to tap foreign markets for funds, with their support for the policies that favour financial development and liberalization becoming stronger. Alessandria and Qian (2005) develop a general equilibrium model that endogenizes the efficiency of financial intermediaries after financial liberalization and show that removing restrictions on international capital flows may change the efficiency of intermediaries.
9. See Calvo and Reinhart (2002).
10. While Iannariello (2005) finds that fixed exchange rate regimes trigger dollarization, Berkmen and Cavallo (2007) do not find any significant effect. Since moral hazard problems triggered by exchange rate guarantees implicit in 'soft' pegs tend to be stronger in emerging markets, including both emerging and industrial countries in the sample – as done in Berkmen and Cavallo (ibid.) – may reduce the significance of this effect. In contrast, Iannariello (op. cit.) only includes emerging countries in her study.

REFERENCES

Alessandria, G. and J. Qian (2005), 'Endogenous financial intermediation and real effects of capital account liberalization', *Journal of International Economics*, **67** (1), 97–128.

Allen, F. and D. Gale (1999), 'Bubbles, crises, and policy', *Oxford Review of Economic Policy*, **15** (3), 9–18.

Allen, F. and D. Gale (2000), 'Bubbles and crises', *Economic Journal*, **110** (460), 236–55.

Allen, M., C. Rosenberg, C. Keller, B. Setser and N. Roubini (2002), 'A balance sheet approach to financial crisis', *IMF Working Paper* No. WP/02/210.

Bekaert, G., C. Harvey and C. Lundblad (2005), 'Does financial liberalization spur growth?', *Journal of Financial Economics*, **77** (1), 3–55.

Berkmen, Pelin and Eduardo A. Cavallo (2007), 'Exchange rate policy and liability dollarization: an empirical study', *IMF Working Paper* WP/07/33.

Burnside, C., M. Eichenbaum and S. Rebelo (2001), 'Hedging and financial fragility in fixed exchange rate regimes', *European Economic Review*, **45**, 1151–93.

Calvo, G. and C. Reinhart (2002), 'Fear of floating', *Quarterly Journal of Economics*, **117** (2), May, 379–408.

Chamon, M. and R. Hausmann (2002), 'Why do countries borrow the way they borrow?', *Working Paper*, Harvard University.

Chang, R. and A. Velasco (2004), 'Monetary policy and the currency denomination of debt: a tale of two equilibria', *NBER Working Paper* No. 10827.

Cowan, K., L. Herrera and E. Hansen (2005), 'Currency mismatches, balance sheet effects and hedging in Chilean non-financial corporations', *Inter-American Development Bank Working Paper* No. 521, January.

Dooley, M. (2000), 'A model of crises in emerging markets', *Economic Journal*, **110**, (460), 256–72.

Edison, H. and F. Warnock (2003), 'A simple measure of the intensity of capital controls', *Journal of Empirical Finance*, **10** (1–2), 81–103.

Eichengreen, B. (1999), 'Capital controls: capital idea or capital folly?', *Milken Review*.

Eichengreen, B. (2005), 'Capital account liberalization and the fund', paper prepared for the High Level Seminar on Capital Account Liberalization and the IMF, held at the Swiss Ministry of Finance and convened jointly by the Finance Ministries of Belgium, the Netherlands, Sweden and Switzerland, Bern, 12 December 2005, http://www.econ.berkeley.edu/~eichengr/policy/berne.pdf.

Eichengreen, B. and M. Mussa, with G. Dell'Ariccia, E. Detragiache, G.M. Milesi-Ferretti and A. Tweedie (1998), 'Capital account liberalization: theoretical and practical aspects', *International Monetary Fund Occasional Paper* No. 172, Washington, DC.

Galindo, A., A. Micco and G. Ordóñez (2002), 'Financial liberalization and growth: empirical evidence', paper presented at World Bank/George Washington University Conference, Financial Globalization: A Blessing or a Curse? 30–31 May, Washington, DC.

Gourinchas, P. and O. Jeanne (2003), 'The elusive gains from international financial integration', *NBER Working Papers* No. 9684.

Hellman, T., K. Murdock and J. Stiglitz (2000), 'Liberalization, moral hazard in banking, and prudential regulation: are capital requirements enough?', *American Economic Review*, **90** (1), 147–65.

Henry, P. (2000a), 'Stock market liberalization, economic reform, and emerging market equity prices', *Journal of Finance*, **55** (2), 529–63.

Henry, P. (2000b), 'Do stock market liberalizations cause investment booms?', *Journal of Financial Economics*, **58** (1–2), 301–34.

Iannariello, M. (2005), 'Financial dollarization levels and their response to shocks: an in-depth look at the relationship between financial dollarization and regime flexibility', PhD dissertation, George Washington University.

Ize, A. and E. Levy Yeyati (2003), 'Financial dollarization', *Journal of International Economics*, **29** (2), 323–47.

Kamil, H. (2006), 'Does moving to a flexible exchange rate regime reduce currency mismatches in firms' balance sheets?', paper presented at the 7th Jacques Polak Annual Research Conference, 9–10 November, International Monetary Fund.

Kaminsky, G. and C. Reinhart (1999), 'The twin crises: the causes of banking and balance-of-payments problems', *American Economic Review*, **89** (3), 473–500.

Kaminsky, G. and S. Schmukler (2003), 'Short-run pain, long-run gain: the effects of financial liberalization', *NBER Working Paper* No. 9787, June.

Kraay, Aart (1998), 'In search of the macroeconomic effects of capital account liberalization', World Bank, mimeo.

Krugman, P. (1998), 'Saving Asia: it's time to get radical', *Fortune*, 7 September, 74–80.

Loayza, N. and R. Ranciere (2004), 'Financial development, financial fragility, and growth', *Journal of Money, Credit and Banking*, **38** (4), 1051–76.

Martínez L. and A. Werner (2002), 'The exchange rate regime and the currency composition of corporate debt: the Mexican experience', *Journal of Development Economics*, **69** (2), 315–34.

Mishkin, F. (2003), 'Financial policies and the prevention of financial crises in emerging market countries', in M. Feldstein (ed.), *Economic and Financial Crises in Emerging Market Countries*, Chicago: University of Chicago Press, 93–130.

Prasad, E., T. Rumbaugh and Q. Wang (2005), 'Putting the cart before the horse? Capital account liberalization and exchange rate flexibility in China', *IMF Working Paper* No. 05/1 January.

Prasad, E., K. Rogoff, S. Wei and A. Kose (2003), 'The effects of financial globalization on developing countries: some empirical evidence', *Occasional Paper* No. 220, International Monetary Fund.

Rajan, R. and L. Zingales (2003a), 'The great reversals: the politics of financial development in the twentieth century', *Journal of Financial Economics*, **69** (1), 5–50.

Rajan, R. and L. Zingales (2003b), *Saving Capitalism from the Capitalists*, New York: Random House.

Rigobon, R. (2003), 'Identification through heteroskedasticity', *Review of Economics and Statistics*, **85** (4), 777–92.

Rodrik, D. (1998), 'Who needs capital-account convertibility?', *Essays in International Finance* No. 207, Department of Economics, Princeton University.

Schneider, M. and A. Tornell (2004), 'Balance sheet effects, bailout guarantees, and financial crises', *Review of Economic Studies*, **71** (3), 883–913.

Stiglitz, J. (2000), 'Capital market liberalization, economic growth, and instability', *World Development*, **28** (6), 1075–86.

Stulz, R. (1999), 'Globalization of capital markets and the cost of capital', *Journal of Applied Corporate Finance*, **12** (3), 8–25.

Tornell, A. and F. Westermann (2005), *Boom-Bust Cycles and Financial Liberalization*, Cambridge, Massachusetts: MIT Press.

5. Exchange rates from a multilateral and South-East Asian perspective

Hans Genberg[1]

This chapter discusses two issues related to international economic cooperation and policy strategies of small open economies. First, for multilateral consultations on and assessment of economic policies to be effective, they must have a basis in an appropriate pairing of instruments and objectives. In particular, the surveillance work of the IMF should de-emphasize the assessment of exchange rate levels, and instead focus on fundamental fiscal and monetary policy choices. The reason is that focusing on exchange rate levels to address current account imbalances is based on weak analytical foundations and is likely to be ineffective at best, and may in fact divert attention away from more fundamental policy adjustments required for lasting solutions to global imbalances.

Second, this chapter will discuss some aspects of monetary and exchange rate policy in small open economies with particular reference to economies in South-East Asia. The major point I would like to convey here is that there has been a substantial shift in the monetary policy strategies in the region in recent years, towards the adoption of price stability as the primary objective of policy and away from focusing on the exchange rate as a nominal anchor. This switch has important implications for monetary and financial cooperation in the region, as well as for how one should interpret their growth strategies.

5.1 INTERNATIONAL SURVEILLANCE OF ECONOMIC POLICIES: THE IMPORTANCE OF A PROPER PAIRING OF OBJECTIVES AND INSTRUMENTS

One of the recurring themes in recent discussions of international economic policy is the need for adjustments of exchange rates between the US dollar, the euro, the Chinese renminbi and the Japanese yen. The basic premise is that observed current account imbalances are unsustainable, and that coordinated exchange rate adjustments are needed to unwind them.

My contention is that the usual practice of translating goals for current account adjustment into specific recommendations for exchange rate adjustments is inappropriate. The main reasons for this are as follows:

1. Exchange rate changes have weak and uncertain effects on current account imbalances.
2. Even if an exchange rate adjustment would influence the current account, the exchange rate is either not a policy instrument or, when it is, the pairing of instruments to policy objectives according to the principle of comparative effectiveness suggests that exchange rate policy should be used for purposes other than current account adjustment.
3. It is often argued that a country with a freely floating exchange rate should not be bound by an assessment of the appropriateness of its exchange rate level. If this argument is carried to its logical conclusion, it would mean that there would be no need for international policy coordination if all countries adopted floating exchange rates.

Let me elaborate on each of these points.

5.1.1 Exchange Rate Changes Have Weak and Uncertain Effects on Current Account Imbalances

From an analytical perspective, it is almost certain that exchange rate policy does not have a particularly strong effect on current account imbalances. The current account by its very nature is the result of intertemporal decisions regarding savings and investment by the private sector and the government. As such it is influenced by variables that have an explicit time dimension: for example, the real rate of interest, expected income in the future relative to income today, the preference for consumption today relative to consumption in the future, or government taxes in the present versus government taxes in the future. The exchange rate on the other hand measures *current* relative prices, of monies in the case of the nominal exchange rate and of goods in the case of the real rate. For example, it would measure the price of a barrel of oil measured in euros versus the same barrel of oil measured in US dollars or the price of a bottle of California wine relative to a pair of shoes made in China. The link between these a-temporal relative prices and aggregate savings and investment decisions is indirect at best.

To appreciate this we must leave the confines of the partial equilibrium elasticity model and conduct the analysis in a general equilibrium setting, because then the tenuous link between exchange rate policy and the current account becomes evident. Let me just list some of the issues that must be taken into account:

- The real exchange rate is not a policy instrument once we consider a horizon beyond the short to medium term. Therefore the degree and duration of nominal price and wage rigidity must be explicitly considered.
- Pricing to market is prevalent in many countries and industries. This will reduce the impact of nominal exchange rate changes on relative prices in the importing country.
- Net international asset positions can be affected by exchange rate changes. The resulting changes in wealth can in turn influence savings behaviour. For example, an appreciation of the Chinese renminbi relative to the US dollar will almost surely reduce the net foreign asset position of Mainland China as a whole. Will this loss of wealth lead to an increase or decrease in the savings rate in China? How does the answer to this question depend on the fact that China's foreign assets are mainly held by the official sector, whereas the liabilities are more concentrated in the private sector?
- In some economies, production of exportables uses imported inputs. In this case a nominal appreciation of the domestic currency will raise production costs and thereby partly offset whatever benefits to profitability the appreciation brings when the good is exported.

This list of complications can be continued but the message should already be clear, namely that in a general equilibrium setting the link between exchange rate policy and the current account balance is precarious.

To avoid misunderstanding, note that asserting that autonomous exchange rate changes have limited effects on the current account does not imply that changes in the current account will have no exchange rate consequences. Several celebrated papers by Obstfeld and Rogoff, for example, demonstrate this very forcefully.[2] The framework developed by Obstfeld and Rogoff is designed to show what would happen to relative prices if changes in aggregate expenditures relative to output brought about a reduction in the current account deficit of the United States from its current level of some 5.5 per cent of GDP to some lower number that is judged to be more sustainable? As such it can be thought of as a modern sophisticated version of the classical transfer problem.

Thinking about the Obstfeld-Rogoff model in terms of the classical transfer problem is useful because it reminds us that the correlation between the current account balance and the real exchange rate will depend crucially on exactly how the current account is altered, that is, how the transfer is brought about. To make the point by means of an example: it is surely uncontroversial to suggest, for example, that the real exchange rate consequences of increases in expenditures in China on Boeing aircraft,

Humvees and French wine would be different from those that would result from increases in expenditures on non-traded goods in China even if their effect on the current account balance were the same.

So, to return to my main theme, current account imbalances and exchange rate changes may be correlated, but this does not mean that autonomous exchange rate movements will bring about current account adjustment. If such adjustments are judged to be necessary, other policies will have to be employed. There is no reason to translate current account targets into exchange rate assessments or targets for exchange rate adjustment.

5.1.2 Pairing Policy Instruments with Policy Objectives

What should then guide national and international efforts to design policies to deal with global current account imbalances? As the current account inherently reflects intertemporal decisions, it would seem natural to use policy instruments that have direct effects on savings and investment decisions. In previous research I have carried out with Alexander Swoboda and Michael Devereux, we have elaborated on this point in some detail, and shown that the basic intuition is robust to variations in modelling approaches. Policies that directly influence incentives to save and invest, for example tax incentives to saving, have reliable impacts on current account imbalances.[3] Similarly expenditure-reducing or expenditure-increasing policies such as government expenditures also have reliable effects on current accounts. On the other hand, expenditure-switching policies such as commercial policies or policies designed to alter the nominal exchange rate, have more limited effects on current account balances but can have stronger effects on relative prices.

5.1.3 Multilateral Surveillance in a World of Freely Floating Exchange Rates

The third reason why I believe it is unhelpful to translate current account objectives into exchange rate objectives stems from the practice of governments to argue that freely floating exchange rates can not be judged over- or undervalued as they are set by market forces. Although the validity of this notion may be disputed, simply take current practice as given and think about the fate of international policy coordination in a world where all (relevant) currencies are floating without interventions by the authorities. Imagine also that fiscal or other policies are generating current account imbalances that are judged unsustainable. In this situation, multilateral surveillance based on translating current account imbalances into an assessment of the appropriate level of the exchange rate would fail. Countries would simply refer to their floating exchange rates to argue that they would not need to make any policy adjustments.

The main conclusion from the above considerations is as follows: to the extent that multilateral assessment and cooperation on economic policies aims to resolve major current account imbalances, it should not be translated into exchange rate objectives and assessments. Instead it should focus on economic policies that are under the control of policy makers and that influence current accounts directly and robustly. The mission and advice of the IMF must reflect this fundamental reality.

5.2 MONETARY AND EXCHANGE RATE POLICY IN SMALL OPEN ECONOMIES WITH PARTICULAR REFERENCE TO SOUTH-EAST ASIA

In what follows I would like to report on some important developments regarding monetary and exchange rate policies in South-East Asia, restricting my comments to just one issue. This is that, contrary to what was the case before the financial crisis in the late 1990s, monetary policies in the region are now clearly focused on domestic objectives best described as domestic price stability. From this it follows that the enthusiasm for and the likelihood of exchange rate cooperation in the region is quite limited, and rightly so in my view. Let me elaborate.

When we look at official pronouncements as well as investigate actual behaviour, it is clear that there has been a shift in monetary policy strategies in the region in the ten years since the late 1990s. Central banks have now adopted policy strategies in which domestic price stability is the principal objective of monetary policies. This contrasts with the period before the 1997–98 financial crisis when exchange rate stability vis-à-vis the US dollar was quite prevalent, and to some extent a contributing reason for the crisis. At present six central banks in the region characterize their monetary policy as one of inflation targeting. These are the central banks of Australia and New Zealand, but also those of Indonesia, South Korea, the Philippines and Thailand. The Monetary Authority of Singapore can also be characterized as targeting inflation, albeit by using the effective exchange rate rather than a short-term interest rate as the policy instrument. Although it has been struggling to avoid deflation rather than inflation, the Bank of Japan has domestic price stability as the principal policy objective. This leaves three economies in the region where currency stability is mentioned as the policy objective. In two of them – Mainland China and Malaysia – currency stability is mentioned alongside price stability, whereas in the third, Hong Kong, the only objective is exchange rate stability.

There are important implications that follow from the predominant focus on domestic price stability. First, there is little official enthusiasm for any form of coordinated exchange rate policy, and rightly so. Such coordination would run the risk of creating conflicts with domestic objectives that would lead to a loss of central bank credibility and possibly speculative attacks on participating currencies.

In a recent paper with a colleague at the Hong Kong Monetary Authority, we discuss these issues in more detail, and suggest an alternative vision for regional cooperation.[4] Rather than focusing on exchange rates, we suggest an approach that centres on developing more liquid financial markets in the region in the foreseeable future. In the longer term, with a high level of both trade and financial integration, business cycles in the region will be more synchronized; in such a scenario, consultation and coordination in defining policy goals and institution-building can be beneficial.

If exchange rate coordination or complete monetary unification is desired by some subset of central banks, they can formally agree to centralize monetary policy decisions in a common central bank or they can decide to delegate it to an existing central bank. Adopting a common exchange rate policy or a single currency by all economies in the region is not required. The benefits from financial integration and monetary stability will be forthcoming anyway, even without a common exchange rate policy or a single currency.

The advantages of this approach to monetary integration are that it is compatible with increasing integration of financial markets, it naturally evolves from a system where central banks pursue similar objectives in their own self-interest, which makes it incentive-compatible, and it allows for a 'variable geometry' of the final area that adopts a common currency. Speculating on whether such a common currency area will eventually emerge in the region is, however, something that I will have to leave for another occasion.

NOTES

1. Executive Director, Research, Hong Kong Monetary Authority. The views expressed are those of the author and do not necessarily represent the views of the Hong Kong Monetary Authority.
2. See, for example, Obstfeld and Rogoff (2005).
3. See Genberg and Swoboda (1989) and Devereux and Genberg (2007).
4. Genberg and He (2007).

REFERENCES

Devereux, M. and H. Genberg (2007), 'Currency appreciation and current account adjustment', *Journal of International Money and Finance*, **26** (4), June, 570–86.

Genberg, H. and A. Swoboda (1989), 'Policy and current-account determination under floating rates', *International Monetary Fund Staff Papers*, **36** (1), March, 1–30.

Genberg, H. and D. He (2007), 'Monetary and financial cooperation among central banks in East Asia and the Pacific', *Hong Kong Monetary Authority Working Paper* No. 15/2007.

Obstfeld, M. and K. Rogoff (2005), 'The unsustainable US current account', mimeo, UC Berkeley.

PART II

Understanding exchange rates

6. Fundamentally lost? On the role of fundamentals in exchange rate economics in history and theory

Peter Mooslechner[1]

> Foreign exchange markets behave more like the unstable and irrational asset markets described by Keynes than the efficient markets described by modern finance theory. (Krugman, 1989)

> One of the key features of exchange rates when they are flexible is that they tend to be highly volatile. (MacDonald, 2007)

6.1 INTRODUCTION

The exchange rate is a strange and rather complicated animal. The difficulties already start with the method of quotation: most people – even those trained (to some extent) in economics – tend to be confused by the fact that a rise in the EUR/USD rate means a depreciation of the euro, and vice versa. A second complicated issue with exchange rates is the fact that they are (almost) the only directly observable relative prices, whereas people are used to dealing with prices of goods and services in absolute money terms in all other areas of economic behaviour. Other puzzles include questions like the random-walk characteristics of exchange rate movements as well as their speculative nature, which, on many occasions, drives exchange rates away from what is called 'fundamental value' – even if the precise nature of the relevant fundamental factors remains fundamentally unclear.

Obviously, the exchange rate is one of the most important links – if not *the* key link – between a country's domestic economy and the surrounding world. In particular in the small open economy case (SMOPEC) and given the less than fully flexible nature of domestic prices, the nominal exchange rate is key to determining the real exchange rate over the short and medium horizon. The real exchange rate, in turn, is crucial to a country's international competitiveness and macroeconomic performance. It is no surprise that under these premises exchange rate developments have received and continue to receive widespread attention in economic policy making – starting from the choice of the most suitable exchange rate regime to the central question of which factors are the main drivers of exchange rate movements in reality – which 'fundamentals' are 'fundamental'? In addition, the growing role of exchange rates in (international) financial crises in recent history, as well as the ongoing dynamic process of worldwide economic integration, have substantially increased the role of exchange rate fluctuations as a policy concern.

Over decades now, much attention has been given by economists to 'explain' exchange rate behaviour. In spite of these efforts, our understanding of what (really) determines exchange rate movements still seems to be rather limited. *The* main issue in this respect concerns the identification of the relevant 'fundamentals' that are key to the questions of if a country's exchange rate is overvalued or undervalued, if it is more or less in line with its determining factors or if speculative forces of whatever nature have driven it away from its fundamentally justified level. This chapter makes an attempt to relate the difficult question of fundamentals to the logic of exchange rate regimes on the one hand and to the determinants of exchange rates in a selection of economic theories on the other. The objective to confront historical exchange rate regimes and exchange rate theories is simply to shed some light on the main question, whether the basic concept of 'fundamentals' makes sense and to what extent history – of exchange rate regimes as well as theories of exchange rate determination – is able to tell us something in this respect.

6.2 THE FUNDAMENTALS OF EXCHANGE RATE REGIMES IN A HISTORICAL PERSPECTIVE

Much of the changes and the progress of international monetary systems reflects concerns with particular recurring historical episodes and puzzles. Exchange rate regimes chosen at a particular point in history inter alia reflect a certain degree of policy understanding of how exchange rates are determined on the one hand. On the other hand, the mechanics of exchange rate regimes contributed to the factors relevant for exchange rate behaviour. Therefore, knowledge about the broad strokes of monetary history are a useful contribution in understanding better which type of fundamentals were held important over different historical episodes and where the field of exchange rate economics has come from and where it is heading (Eichengreen, 1998).

6.2.1 The Classical Gold Standard as a Starting Point

During the late 19th century and the early days of the 20th century, exchange rate regimes were dominated by fixed exchange rate regimes until the breakout of World War I. In those days, the classical gold standard constituted the building block of the international monetary system. The classical gold standard may not be the beginning of exchange rate history, but it is a convenient starting point for considering the evolution of conventional wisdom on the subject (Crockett, 2003). Under the classical gold standard, the rate of exchange of the different currencies was given by the mint parity, that is, the rate of exchange of the domestic currency vis-à-vis the price of gold related to the rate of exchange of the foreign currency against the price of gold. Because governments credibly committed themselves to the fixed gold price and because of the free flow of gold across countries, private sector agents started gold arbitrage as soon as market prices departed from the official price. Consequently, fluctuations around the mint parity were actually delimited by the cost related to transporting gold from one country to another, like freight, insurance, handling (package and cartage), interest on money committed to the transaction and risk premium (Officer, 2001).

According to the gold standard, a gold outflow typically decreases the international assets of the central bank and hence the monetary base and money supply. The central bank's proper response was to raise interest rates to decrease domestic assets and the monetary base. A country experiencing a balance-of-payments deficit loses gold and its money supply decreases, both automatically and by policy in accordance with the gold standard rules, thereby increasing exports and decreasing imports. Similarly, a surplus country gains gold, the money supply increases, money income expands and the price level rises and balance-of-payments equilibrium is restored via the current account. This is called the 'price specie-flow mechanism'. The capital account also acts to restore balance, via interest rate increases in the deficit country inducing a net inflow of capital. What remains important is that under fixed exchange rates, gold flows simply adjust money supply to money demand; the money supply is not determined by policy and, also, prices, interest rates and incomes are determined worldwide.

6.2.2 The Unstable Interwar Gold Standard

The eruption of World War I in August 1914 led to the dissolution of the classical gold standard chiefly due to a run on the sterling. By that time, the reserve ratio in Britain, which is the ratio between gold reserves and liabilities to foreign governments (foreign sterling reserves), was extremely low. In this situation, the Bank of England decided to impose exchange rate controls, which led to the breakdown of the system. With the end of the war, most countries sought to re-establish exchange rate stability and returned, one after another, to a (sort of new) gold standard rule by the mid-1920s – only to give up gold again after the onset of the Great Depression in the early 1930s (Eichengreen, 1989 and 1992). The gold standard that apparently worked so well in the pre-World War I periods did not prevent chaos and depression in the 1920s and 1930s. What triggered this change? The short-lived interwar gold standard differed from the classical coin gold standard as it was a bullion gold standard or a gold exchange standard, in which a country's currency was backed by a reserve currency exchangeable to gold. This mechanism became more and more complicated as the US dollar developed to challenge the sterling as the dominant international reserve currency.

The features that fostered stability of the classical gold standard did not apply to the interwar standard; instead, many forces triggered instability – for example, the only partial process of establishing fixed exchange rates, resulting in disequilibrium exchange rates. The gold exchange standard concept became inherently unstable, because of the expansion of sterling and dollar liabilities to foreign central banks, expanding world liquidity. This instability was particularly severe in the interwar period for several reasons, such as the fact that many more countries were on the gold exchange standard than pre-war. But the prime problem with gold was not overall scarcity but rather maldistribution, as well as the even more precarious financial position of the UK. Together with internal balance as an important goal of policy this made balance-of-payments adjustment much more complicated than before – in many cases impossible. Finally, the end of the interwar gold standard occurred with the Great Depression, leading to balance-of-payments difficulties and the need for easy-money policy and destabilizing speculation, emanating from lack of confidence in authorities' commitment to currency convertibility.

6.2.3 Bretton Woods: A New Beginning

Another era of fixity in the global exchange rate system, which eventually lasted until 1973, came to be decided at the Bretton Woods conference in 1944. The Bretton Woods conference represented the first successful attempt to consciously design an international economic system. It reflected lessons drawn from both the fixed and floating period. The gold standard experience seemed to show that fixed exchange rates were more stable but required a credible domestic adjustment mechanism, a

Table 6.1 Chronology of exchange rate regimes

Period	Regime
1880–1914	Specie gold standard (bimetallism, silver), currency unions, currency boards, float
1919–45	Gold exchange standard, floats, managed floats, currency unions (arrangements), pure floats
1946–71	Bretton Woods adjustable peg, floats (Canada), dual/multiple exchange rates
1973–98	Free float, managed float, adjustable pegs, crawling pegs, basket pegs, target zones or bands, fixed exchange rates, currency boards; ('snake' and exchange rate mechanism [ERM] in Europe)
1999–present	European monetary union (plus ERM II), free float, managed float, adjustable pegs, crawling pegs, basket pegs, target zones or bands, fixed exchange rates, currency boards

Source: Adapted from Bordo (2004).

cooperative international environment and an absence of destabilizing capital flows. The floating rate period seemed to teach that exchange rates should be viewed as matters of mutual concern, since individually determined exchange rate policies could be inconsistent and unstable (McKinnon, 2005). The Bretton Woods system worked rather well as long as capital flows were modest, international inflationary and deflationary pressures were limited and countries accepted an obligation to direct domestic macroeconomic policies towards achieving external balance (Crockett, 2003).

The system was designed to provide fixed exchange rates, fluctuating not more than +/−1 per cent around the central parity of the participating countries against the US dollar, which served as the reserve currency and was tied to gold at a rate of USD 35 an ounce. This – very special type of – gold exchange standard worked smoothly until the US started having large current account deficits financed by US dollar supply, in particular related to the financing of the Vietnam War. This meant that the other central banks accumulated large US dollar reserves. At a certain point, rumours about the Fed's ability to convert those reserves into gold became more and more important and, finally, resulted in the disconnection of the dollar from gold in 1971 and the float of the German mark against the dollar in 1973.

In terms of exchange rate determination, the end of the Bretton Woods system marks the beginning of a new era of floating, in which demand and supply on the market determined the relative price of two currencies and in which gold lost its former central monetary stature and became a 'simple commodity', at least from an exchange rate regime perspective.

6.2.4 From the End of Bretton Woods . . .

Exchange rates between currencies have been highly unstable since the collapse of the Bretton Woods system of fixed exchange rates (James, 1996). Under floating exchange regimes, exchange rates are determined by agents buying and selling currencies in the foreign exchange markets. In fact, the instability of exchange rates came as a surprise to many (economists) and it was not expected that floating exchange rates would create so much macroeconomic uncertainty. In turn, this instability of exchange rates since the 1970s would not have surprised the founders of the Bretton Woods system, as the previous experience with floating exchange rates had been marked by massive instability (Bordo and Eichengreen, 1993). But given the tensions of the Bretton Woods system, economists and policy makers started to qualify exchange rate flexibility in a more favourable way. Unstable exchange rates were seen to be mainly caused by unstable policies and profit-maximizing speculators would always tend to stabilize, not destabilize, the exchange rate. Concern over the instability of floating exchange rates was replaced by the expectation of the greater flexibility that floating exchange rates would allow for macroeconomic policy, in particular independent domestic monetary policy, the adjustment to correct current account imbalances and to compensate for losses in international competitiveness (Friedman, 1953; Calvo and Reinhart, 2000).

In Europe, fears about the damaging effects of excessive exchange rate volatility were widely held to be important and prompted the creation of the so-called 'snake' in which the European Economic Community (EEC) countries' currencies were tied one to another, fluctuating in a tunnel against the dollar. The snake was superseded by the European Monetary System (EMS) in 1979, which paved the way for closer monetary ties in Europe. Monetary union, which had already been proposed earlier (Werner Plan in 1970), came back onto the agenda and was enshrined in the Maastricht Treaty in 1991. After turbulences in the EMS in 1992/93 – which led to substantial devaluations of some currencies and related enormous swings in countries' competitiveness – the momentum to monetary integration was regained and led, eventually, to the launch of the euro in 1999.[2] Eichengreen (1993), for example, indeed argues that the sequence of fixed to float and back again to fixed exchange rate regimes can be explained by (1) the presence or absence of a dominant power that takes the lead in securing fixed exchange rates, (2) the degree of international cooperation,

(3) the intellectual consensus regarding the desirability of either system, (4) macroeconomic volatility and (5) the coordination of fiscal and monetary policies.

6.2.5 . . . To European Monetary Union

Overall, the instability of rates since 1973 has been a severe disappointment. Only some of the changes in exchange rates could be attributed to differences in national inflation rates, but exchange rate volatility has been much larger than can be explained by differences in inflation rates or in other macroeconomic variables such as different growth rates in various countries' money supplies. Why did exchange rates turn out to behave in such an unstable way? Although no definite answer from theory was available (Obstfeld, 1985), practical experience – and policy concerns – paved the way for a renascence of fixed exchange rates in the 1990s in Europe. The increasing influence and the ongoing success of the hard currency block resulted in the decision to create the euro area, as a result of which the members' exchange rates were irrevocably fixed. EU acceding countries also tied their hands. Initially they used several hard currencies as an anchor for their exchange rate. Since the introduction of the euro they have either pegged their currency to the euro directly, run a currency board, or increased the euro's share in the baskets. In June 2004, shortly after EU enlargement, three countries (Estonia, Lithuania and Slovenia) joined ERM II, and in April 2005 three others (Latvia, Cyprus and Malta) followed, with Slovenia, Cyprus and Malta having since joined the euro area as well. This has further increased the number of countries that have given up the exchange rate as a policy instrument, as a preferred solution for smaller countries.

Finally, it has to be stressed that a considerable change in how the role of exchange rate developments is qualified has taken place, which broadly influences the hierarchy and sequence of economic policy strategies to be followed. After the breakdown of the Bretton Woods system and under the impression of the difficulties the system faced during its final decade, exchange rate movements and exchange rate flexibility were mainly seen as important economic policy tools to address important macroeconomic imbalances successfully. This perspective is also a dominant ingredient of the famous Mundell-Fleming (optimum currency area – OCA) approach of open economy macroeconomics (see Mundell, 1961 and Fleming, 1962) which attributes a rather strong position to the exchange rate as a policy instrument (Frankel and Rose, 1998). Compared with this – optimistic – view of the exchange rate as a macroeconomic policy tool, the experience of the 1980s and 1990s led to a completely different assessment of exchange rate developments. In the wake of the European exchange rate crises of the early 1990s, exchange rate developments were seen more and more as becoming a permanent source of international financial instability. This change in perspective led to the establishment of the euro area as an institutional framework that makes exchange rate volatility obsolete as a potential source of macroeconomic instability. In this new world, our overall understanding of the role of exchange rates in economic policy was not the only thing to change; the hierarchy of economic objectives and policies has also changed substantially. In particular, for countries intending to join the European Union and – eventually – monetary union, stabilizing the exchange rate, via participation in ERM II first, has become an overriding goal in the integration and convergence process (Backé and Mooslechner, 2004). This gives the exchange rate obviously a much higher weight in policy making even if countries are still at the beginning of the integration process.

6.3 EXCHANGE RATE THEORIES: THE DIFFICULT ROLE OF FUNDAMENTALS

The exchange rate determination literature has been in trouble since it was shown many times that a simple random-walk outperforms many, if not all, standard models in forecasting exchange rates in many, if not all, framework conditions (Sarno and Taylor, 2002; MacDonald, 2007; Dornbusch, 1980; Isard, 1995).

6.3.1 Purchasing Power Parity (PPP) and the PPP Puzzle: The Price Level Perspective

Purchasing power parity (PPP) is the most widely used and most traditional concept in exchange rate theory. The original simple concept has been around several centuries (Officer, 1982), many years before economics became a science in its own right. If price arbitrage equalizes the price of goods traded internationally, these goods would be sold in different countries at the same price and the 'law of one price' (LOOP) would hold. Unfortunately, even economists and economic policy nowadays often refers to the PPP and the LOOP concepts as the first – if not the only – ones when dealing with exchange rate issues. PPP provides a particularly simple theory of exchange rate determination, telling us that the relative price of two currencies will adjust to equal the ratio of the price levels of the two respective countries (Taylor and Taylor, 2004). But even if this adjustment doesn't take place for whatever reason, PPP is held to be a suitable reference point against which the value of a currency can be qualified as 'overvalued' or 'undervalued'.

Of course, nobody would claim that prices and differences in two countries' price levels play no role in the movement of two currencies relative to each other. Insofar as the exchange rate is an important determinant of a country's competitiveness, the interaction of prices and the exchange rate is an important factor. But even 25 years ago Frenkel (1982) wrote about the 'collapse' of the PPP hypothesis and Rogoff (1996) started a new strand of the literature dealing with the so-called 'PPP puzzle'. As empirical evidence shows, exchange rates and, especially, real exchange rates are characterized by a high degree of short-term volatility and instability, but they show (almost) no particular tendency to return to PPP values. There is now a rich variety of explanations for these permanent deviations of the exchange rate from its purchasing power parity and the explanations range from transactions costs to markets behaviour. Balassa (1964) and Samuelson (1964) have pointed out a particular important issue stemming from (relative) productivity developments, the so-called 'Dutch Disease' effect is another well-known factor driving exchange rates away from their PPP value. All in all, MacDonald (2007) concludes that, especially for the post-Bretton Woods era, PPP is not a useful construct in explaining exchange rate behaviour.

6.3.2 Interest Rate Parity: A First Financial Markets View

The second most widespread view regarding the determination of exchange rates relates to interest rates. It has long since been accepted that exchange rate movements can be influenced by changes in interest rates. Raising domestic interest rates could strengthen the value of the domestic currency and vice versa. No doubt, this different understanding of the determinants of exchange rates puts a completely different view on the understanding of what drives exchange rate developments. The two main forms of the interest rate parity hypothesis are covered interest rate parity and uncovered interest rate parity. The uncovered interest rate parity hypothesis is formulated in terms of expected future exchange rates and is, therefore, jointly related to the hypothesis of rational and unbiased exchange rate expectations. In this simplest form this 'efficient market hypothesis' can be seen as a model in which foreign exchange market participants behave rationally and risk-neutral. Under these conditions the gain from holding one currency instead of the other is offset by the opportunity cost, the interest rate differential. However, and regardless of the sophistication utilized, the efficient market hypothesis is rejected by the empirics of foreign exchange markets. Although interest rates cannot be rejected as having a particular impact on exchange rate developments, they are not seen to have a dominant influence in the medium run. Nevertheless, the appproach based on interest rates adds a completely different perspective to the analysis of foreign exchange markets compared with the PPP view.

6.3.3 The Balance-of-Payments Approach: The Mundell-Fleming (1961/62) Revolution

The classic Mundell-Fleming (MF) model introduced a completely different new approach into exchange rate determination compared with PPP or interest rate parity, although current account considerations were, of course, always present in economic policy discussions. The basic focus of the MF model is a macroeconomic one based on the assumptions of a small open economy. Related to this the model incorporates a given world interest rate as well as a limited selection of domestic and foreign assets. Therefore, residents of home and foreign countries are able to hold domestic and foreign currencies, and currency substitution as well as arbitrage are expected to happen. However, the main point of the MF or balance-of-payments view is its entirely macroeconomic background, introducing all kinds of macroeconomic factors and macroeconomic policies into the analysis of exchange rate movements. Under these conditions, the exchange rate becomes an endogenous part of macro considerations, in particular of relative macroeconomic developments in different countries.

6.3.4 Extensions and Refinements: The Monetary Model Beyond Mundell-Fleming

The Mundell-Fleming model was developed further in two distinct classes of monetary models of the exchange rate, the sticky-price monetary model and the flexible-price monetary model. These two types of models today still constitute the basis of exchange rate economics in many different variants. The sticky-price monetary model is primarily related to Dornbusch (1976). For the first time, it introduced the famous concept of 'overshooting' of the nominal and real exchange rates in the short and medium run above their long-run levels. These effects mainly stem from the specific characteristic of exchange rates and interest rates as 'jump variables', which have to correct for the stickiness of other variables, in particular, prices. Compared with this, the flexible-price monetary model can be interpreted as a market-clearing general equilibrium model in which purchasing power parity between countries' price levels is assumed. This points to one of the fundamental problems related to theories of exchange rate determination in general, which is the limited nature of their coverage of relevant factors. Open economy macroeconomics deal, at least, with six aggregate markets of an economy: the goods market, the labour market, the money market, the market for foreign exchange and the domestic bond market, as well as the foreign bond market. Needless to say that this number of relevant markets multiplies with the number of countries included and the number of more specific markets to be seen necessary to be included in the analysis, for example, foreign direct investment. Taking the flexible-price monetary model as an example, it can be shown that this model concentrates on the equilibrium condition of one of these markets only, the money market, whereas it is by no means clear that equilibrium in one particular of these markets implies equilibrium also in the other markets.

6.3.5 The Portfolio Approach: Towards Taking into Account the Reality of Financial Markets

One of the major limitations of many exchange rate models is seen in the fact that they concentrate on a very narrow range of assets only, in extreme cases only taking into account domestic and foreign money supply. The portfolio balance model broadens the range of assets available to investors in the home country as well as in foreign countries and it uses the well-known stock-flow adjustment framework to analyse the effects of changes in different kinds of asset markets on exchange rate movements and dynamics. In contrast to many other theoretical approaches the domestic and foreign asset markets are not considered to be perfect substitutes in portfolio models, thereby making the analysis much more realistic in terms of agents' behaviour. In the same vein, wealth effects are also explicitly taken into account. Investors hold a portfolio of currencies and instruments depending on their specific degree of risk aversion and the particular risk/return balance of all available assets. Nevertheless, the exchange rate is determined by supply of and demand for financial assets and the exchange rate remains the main determinant of the current account balance. In sum, the portfolio balance model is a dynamic model of exchange rate determination based on the interaction of asset markets and portfolios, current account balance and prices. An additional main feature of the model is that it allows the distinction between short-run flow equilibrium and long-run stock equilibrium adjustment. Taking these elements together, the portfolio balance model provides us with a much richer mechanism of analysing all kinds of effects in an exchange-rate-determining framework.

6.3.6 The New Open Economy Macroeconomics: Obstfeld-Rogoff (1995)

Once again, an entirely macroeconomic view of the issue was introduced by Obstfeld and Rogoff (1995) with a class of exchange rate models based on the so-called new open economy macroeconomics. Compared with the old Mundell-Fleming approach this approach is based on the optimizing behaviour of agents and specific assumptions concerning market structure and pricing behaviour of producers. Under these conditions, output therefore is essentially output determined with optimizing individuals and prices preset in an imperfectly competitive market. Issues like 'overshooting' and the interaction of current account balances and the real exchange rate are at the heart of the analysis. Country differences in net foreign assets, consumption dynamics and productivity developments become central factors in driving a country's exchange rate.

6.3.7 Lessons Learned: Models of Crisis and Speculative Attack

The currency crisis and speculative attack models were originally developed as an attempt to understand the specific economic developments in many Latin American countries in the 1970s and 1980s, in particular to understand the obvious failures of stabilization plans introduced. Initially, the relationship between a fixed exchange rate and inconsistent economic fundamentals, including fiscal and monetary policies, was the main focus of the analysis. For example, how excessive money supply under conditions of a fixed exchange rate could make an economy vulnerable to a currency attack and push an economy into crisis was one of the obvious questions to be addressed. An inappropriate macroeconomic policy mix was seen as the central issue to explain the sequence of currency attack and exchange rate crisis. But many of the exchange rate crises observed later on, in particular the crises that took place in the ERM in the 1990s, did not fit well into the modelling framework of these early models. A new generation of models was developed using a much richer modelling approach, including a broader set of variables that policy makers might be influenced by when deciding on how and how long to defend a fixed or pegged exchange rate. This set of variables also introduced a number of market-specific factors, like beliefs of market participants, self-fulfilling speculation or the existance of multiple equilibria. In the end, this type of model developed to show how a speculative attack on an exchange rate and a currency crisis may be unrelated to (macroeconomic) fundamentals and instead be based on moral hazard or herding behaviour like bank runs. All in all, these different strands of modelling speculative attack and exchange rate crisis are based on rather different views on how these situations can develop and lead to quite different policy conclusions as well, starting from finding the right policy mix in the early models and ranging to the risk management behaviour of foreign investors and the information available to them.

6.3.8 Market Microstructure: A Deeper Look at the Mechanics of Foreign Exchange Markets

The market microstructure approach is one of the most recent innovations in exchange rate theory, motivated mainly by the massive amount of trading on worldwide foreign exchange markets and the difficulties explaining this from a macroeconomic point of view (Vitale, 2007). In a nutshell, much more trading is observed on foreign exchange markets than can be explained by standard macroeconomic exchange rate theory. Therefore, a micro-based approach was developed concentrating on micro aspects of the foreign exchange market such as price formation or trade dynamics. Trading volumes much larger than those strictly needed to fulfil the direct needs of those who initiated the basic transactions are seen to fulfil other important functions, for example, risk management purposes. The market microstructure approach concentrates on the mechanics of trading and on the price formation process. It deals with the amount and quality of information available to market participants and, in particular, it analyses the heterogeneity of agents as well as the heterogeneity of their expectations based on differences in beliefs or preferences. In practice, order flows and bid-ask spreads are at the centre of microstructure models of exchange rates.

6.3.9 Behavioural Finance: Dealing with Currencies

Strongly based on the knowledge gained in putting more focus on analysing the microstructure of foreign exchange markets recently, DeGrauwe and Grimaldi (2006) present a behavioural finance model of exchange rate determination. As Williamson (2008) strongly concluded in this respect, up to now 'the profession has never taken the next step of replacing models in which everyone is assumed to believe they have a perfect understanding of how the system works . . . by one that recognizes diversity in agents' beliefs and thought processes'. He also concludes, by the way, that 'the conventional exchange rate model is an empirical failure'. DeGrauwe and Grimaldi base their model on heterogeneous traders, fundamentalists and chartists. The first group acts on the belief that exchange rates tend to return to their long-run equilibrium level, however determined (a negative, stabilizing feedback rule), whereas the second group of actors extrapolate recent changes into the future, thereby reinforcing already realized current moves in the exchange rate (a positive, destabilizing feedback rule). In their model setting, 'disconnection' of exchange rate movements from fundamentals becomes 'a natural outcome of the complex dynamics', low-probability events happen much more frequently than according to a normal distribution and (from time to time) involve bubble-and-crash dynamics.

6.4 CONCLUSIONS

Which exchange rate regime is suitable for which country and what is the role of (which?) fundamentals in determining the exchange rate regime and with regard to qualifying the right level of the exchange rate? Judging from the history of, and experience with, exchange rate regimes and judging from the history of exchange rate theories, no clear-cut answer seems available. The history and experience of exchange rate regimes tells us that exchange rate regimes have become much more complicated to work and that the high expectations put in floating exchange rates to make life easier never materialized. To the contrary, exchange rate fluctuations have more and more complicated international financial conditions while Europe, as a consequence, introduced a stabilizing element into the international financial system by establishing a monetary union. The history of exchange rate theories shows that there is no easy explanation available. At the same time, it has become evident that the forces that drive exchange rates have become increasingly complicated and volatile.

It is still a stylized fact that out-of-sample forecasts of exchange rates produced by structural models based on economic fundamentals are no better than those obtained using a naive random-walk or no-change model of the nominal exchange rate (Sarno and Valente, 2008). This evidence may be taken as suggesting that there are speculative forces at work in the foreign exchange market that are not reflected in the usual menu of economic fundamentals. These constitute, for example, key elements of the 'exchange rate disconnect puzzle' (Obstfeld and Rogoff, 2000). What seems to be necessary under these circumstances is to develop a framework for modelling and understanding exchange rates that explicitly takes into account that there are changing parameters in economic fundamentals and that no fundamentals model appears to perform well for long periods of time and allows for shifts in the weights attached to the fundamentals over time.

Because volatile expectations and departures from rationality are likely to be one important element for the failure of exchange rate models, Bacchetta and van Wincoop (2004), for example, provide a theory of exchange rate determination that incorporates the fact that practitioners in the foreign exchange market regularly change the weight they attach to different economic variables. Over time the weights attributed to economic variables change. Surprisingly little attention has been directed towards assessing the potential of these considerations for establishing an economically meaningful relationship between exchange rates and fundamentals. Other authors have argued that the poor forecasting performance recorded in this literature may be due to the fact that the parameters in the estimated equations are unstable. This instability may be rationalized on a number of grounds, including policy regime changes, instabilities in the money demand or puchasing power parity equations, or also agents' heterogeneity leading to different responses to macroeconomic developments over time. Other researchers have claimed that volatile expectations or departures from rationality are likely to account for the failure of exchange rate models. Any promising new approach has to take into account the fact that there are changing weights in the economic fundamentals driving exchange rates and that no model of fundamentals appears to perform well for long periods of time: the same set of economic fundamentals that explains reasonably well the exchange rate developments in the past may not be useful in forecasting exchange rate developments for the future. Exchange rate forecasting remains just as hard today as in the seminal work of Meese and Rogoff (1983), and the exchange rate is often well approximated by a driftless random-walk for prediction purposes. If combined, different models somehow average out the errors made by various misspecified models.

NOTES

1. Director of the Economic Analysis Department, Oesterreichische Nationalbank, Austria.
2. Triffin (1991) qualified the entire situation of turbulences and instability as a 'scandal'.

REFERENCES

Bacchetta, P. and E. van Wincoop (2004), 'A scapegoat model of exchange rate fluctuations', *NBER Working Paper* No. 10245.

Backé, P. and P. Mooslechner (2004), 'From transition to monetary integration: Central and Eastern Europe on its way to the euro', *Comparative Economic Studies*, **46** (1), 177–90.

Balassa, Bela (1964), 'The purchasing-power parity doctrine: a reappraisal', *Journal of Political Economy*, **72** (6), 584–96.

Bordo, M. (2004), 'Exchange rate regimes for the 21st century: a historical perspective', in: *60 Years of Bretton Woods*, OeNB Workshops, No. 3, Oesterreichische Nationalbank.

Bordo, M.D. and B. Eichengreen (eds) (1993), *A Retrospective on the Bretton Woods System: Lessons for International Monetary Reform*, Chicago: University of Chicago Press.

Calvo, G.A. and C.M. Reinhart (2000), 'Fear of floating', *NBER Working Paper* No. 7993.
Crockett, A. (2003), 'Exchange rate regimes in theory and practice', in P. Mizon (ed.), *Monetary History, Exchange Rates and Financial Markets*, Cheltenham, UK and Northampton, MA, USA: Edward Elgar.
De Grauwe, P. and M. Grimaldi (2006), *The Exchange Rate in a Behavioral Finance Framework*, Princeton, NJ: Princeton University Press.
Dornbusch, R. (1976), 'Expectations and exchange rate dynamics', *Journal of Political Economy*, **84** (6), 1161–76.
Dornbusch, R. (1980), 'Exchange rate economics: where do we stand?', *Brookings Papers on Economic Activity*, No. 1, 143–85.
Eichengreen, B. (1989), 'The comparative performance of fixed and flexible exchange regimes: interwar evidence', *NBER Working Paper* No. 3097.
Eichengreen, B. (1992), *Golden Fetters*, New York and Oxford: Oxford University Press.
Eichengreen, B. (1993), 'The endogeneity of exchange rate regimes', *NBER Working Paper* No. 4361.
Eichengreen, B. (1998), *Globalizing Capital: A History of the International Monetary System*, Princeton, NJ: Princeton University Press.
Fleming, J. (1962), 'Domestic financial policies under fixed and floating exchange rates', *IMF Staff Papers*, 369–79.
Frankel, J. and A. Rose (1998), 'The endogeneity of the optimum currency area', *The Economic Journal*, **108** (449), July, 1009–25.
Frenkel, Jacob A. (1981), 'The collapse of purchasing power parities during the 1970s', *European Economic Review*, **16** (1), 145–65.
Friedman, M. (1953), 'The case for flexible exchange rates', *Essays in Positive Economics*, Chicago: University of Chicago Press.
Isard, P. (1995), *Exchange Rate Economics*, New York: Cambridge University Press.
James, H. (1996), *International Monetary Cooperation since Bretton Woods*, New York and Oxford: Oxford University Press, July, pp. 52–63.
Krugman, P. (1989), *Exchange Rate Instability*, Cambridge, Massachusetts: MIT Press.
MacDonald, R. (2007), *Exchange Rate Economics*, London and New York: Routledge.
McKinnon, R. (2005), *Exchange Rates under the East Asian Dollar Standard*, Cambridge, Massachusetts: MIT Press.
Meese, R. and K. Rogoff (1983) 'Empirical exchange rate models of the seventies: do they fit out of sample?', *Journal of International Economies*, **14** (1), 3–24.
Mundell, R. (1961), 'A theory of optimum currency areas', *American Economic Review*, **51** (4), 657–65.
Obstfeld, M. (1985), 'Floating exchange rates: experience and prospects', *Brookings Papers on Economic Activity*, No. 2, 369–450.
Obstfeld, M. and K. Rogoff (1995), 'Exchange rate dynamics redux', *Journal of Political Economy*, **103** (3), 624–60.
Obstfeld, M. and K. Rogoff (2000), 'The six major puzzles in international macroeconomics: is there a common cause?', *NBER Working Paper* No. 7777.
Officer, L. (1982), *Purchasing Power Parity and Exchange Rates: Theory, Evidence and Relevance*, Greenwich, Connecticut: JAI Press.
Officer, L. (2001), 'Gold standard', *EH.Net Encyclopedia*, edited by Robert Whaples, http://eh.net/encyclopedia/article/officer.gold.standard.

Rogoff, Kenneth (1996), 'The purchasing power parity puzzle', *Journal of Economic Literature*, **34** (2), 647–68.
Samuelson, P. (1964), 'Theoretical problems on trade problems', *Review of Economics and Statistics*, **46** (2), 145–54.
Sarno, L. and M. Taylor (2002), *The Economics of Exchange Rates*, Cambridge, UK: Cambridge University Press.
Sarno, L. and G. Valente (2008), 'Exchange rates and fundamentals: footloose or evolving relationship?', *CEPR Discussion Paper* No. 6638, January.
Taylor, Alan M. and Mark P. Taylor (2004), 'The purchasing power parity debate', *Journal of Economic Perspectives*, **18** (4), 135–58.
Triffin, R. (1991), 'The IMS (International Monetary System . . . or Scandal?) and the EMS (European Monetary System . . . or Success?)', *Banca Nazionale del Lavoro, Quarterly Review* No. 179.
Vitale, P. (2007) 'A guided tour of the market microstructure approach to exchange rate determination', *Journal of Economic Surveys*, **21** (5), 903–34.
Williamson, J. (2008), 'Exchange rate economics', *Peterson Institute Working Paper Series* No. WP08-3, February.

7. Macroeconomic fundamentals and the exchange rate

Ronald MacDonald[1]

7.1 INTRODUCTION

There is a widespread perception in the economics profession that exchange rates are disconnected from macroeconomic fundamentals and this can be illustrated using two puzzles in international finance, namely the levels puzzle and the volatility puzzle. In this chapter we consider these puzzles and argue that they really aren't so puzzling after all. Our main conclusion is that macro fundamentals are important determinants of exchange rates, that they can explain exchange rate volatility, and that they can also be used to provide exchange rate forecasts that dominate a random-walk at even short horizons.

The levels puzzle was generated initially by Meese and Rogoff (1983), who demonstrated that macroeconomic-based models of the exchange rate were unable to outperform a random-walk in an out-of-sample forecasting context. For many years, this result has seemed almost impossible to overturn and it has become something of a stylized fact that the predictability of exchange rates, in terms of macro fundamentals, only kicks in at 'long' horizons (horizons of three years or greater); forecasting exchange rates at shorter horizons is therefore something of a futile exercise (Frankel and Rose, 1995 and Rogoff, 1999). In this chapter we argue that this stylized result reflects the use of inappropriate estimation methods rather than the inappropriateness of macro fundamentals.

The volatility puzzle has inter- and intra-regime dimensions. In terms of inter-regime volatility, the perception is that in moving from fixed to floating exchange rates the volatility of macro fundamentals stays unchanged, but the volatility of the exchange rate increases dramatically. Intra-regime volatility refers to the behaviour of exchange rates with respect to macro fundamentals in flexible rate regimes: here the perception is that the volatility of the macro fundamentals cannot explain the volatility of the exchange rate and the latter is in some sense 'excessive'. However, as we shall see in this chapter, there are a number of theoretical explanations for the excessive volatility of exchange rates with respect to macro fundamentals, and, in any case, the empirical evidence is not entirely clear-cut that the excessive volatility is indeed in the data. The inter-regime volatility result is also explicable if an appropriate set of macroeconomic fundamentals is analysed.

The outline of the remainder of this chapter is as follows. In the next section we look at the volatility puzzle in some detail and, specifically, focus on explanations of the puzzle, both theoretical and empirical. In the third section we go on to show how macroeconomics-based exchange rate models can be used to outperform a random-walk in an out-of-sample forecasting context, thereby overturning the well-known Meese and Rogoff paradigm. The final section concludes.

7.2 THE VOLATILITY PUZZLE

The volatility puzzle has two aspects: inter- and intra-regime volatility. A standard asset pricing framework would imply:

$$Var(s_t) \leq Var(\hat{s}_t) \tag{7.1}$$

where $\hat{s}_t$ is some measure of the fundamental-based exchange rate, but in actuality what we observe in flexible rate regimes is:

$$Var(s_t) > Var(\hat{s}_t). \tag{7.2}$$

This is the intra-regime puzzle (see, for example, Frankel and Meese, 1987 and MacDonald, 1999) – the stylized fact that exchange rates in floating regimes seem to be excessively volatile relative to macroeconomic fundamentals. However, and as we shall see below, a number of macroeconomic models predict that the direction of the variance inequality in (7.2) is correct. The concept of inter-regime volatility (Baxter and Stockman, 1989 and Flood and Rose, 1999) is that in moving from fixed to floating rates the volatility of macroeconomic fundamentals remains unchanged but the volatility of exchange rates – both real and nominal – increases dramatically. For example, Baxter and Stockman (1989) examine the variability of output, trade variables and private and government consumption and the real exchange rate between Bretton Woods and post-Bretton Woods and they are: 'unable to find evidence that the cyclic behaviour of real macroeconomic aggregates depends systematically on the exchange rate regime. The only exception is the well known case of the real exchange rate'. In the next sub-section we look at a range of theoretical models that can be used to explain the intra- and inter-regime puzzles and we then go on to consider some of the empirical evidence on both aspects of the volatility puzzle.

7.2.1 Fundamentals-based Models and Exchange Rate Volatility

The well-known monetary exchange rate model can be used in a straightforward way to say something about exchange rate volatility. Consider the following standard representation of the monetary model:

$$s_t = m_t - m_t^* - \beta_0(y_t - y_t^*) + \beta_1 E_t(s_{t+1} - s_t), \tag{7.3}$$

which may be rearranged for the current exchange rate as:

$$s_t = z_t + \theta E_t(s_{t+1}), \tag{7.3'}$$

where

$$z_t = (1 + \beta)^{-1}[m_t - m_t^* - \beta_0(y_t - y_t^*)],$$

and

$$\theta = \beta_1(1 + \beta_1)^{-1}.$$

With rational expectations the expected exchange rate in period $t+1$ may be obtained by leading (7.3′) one period and taking conditional expectations:

$$E_t s_t = E_t z_{t+1} + \theta E_t s_{t+2}.$$

By recursively substituting out the expected exchange rate for all future periods the forward extension of the monetary model may be obtained as:

$$s_t = \sum_{i=0}^{\infty} \theta^i E_t[z_{t+i}] \tag{7.4}$$

where the transversality or terminal condition – $\lim_{i\to\infty} \theta^i E_t s_{t+i+1} = 0$ – is assumed to hold. A key implication of (7.4) is that changes in current fundamentals can have a more than proportionate, or magnified, effect on s to the extent they influence the future profile of expectations. This may be seen more clearly by posing the following example: what does a current change in the money supply signal to agents? To answer this question we assume the time series properties of the composite fundamental term have an AR1 representation:

$$z_t = \phi z_{t-1} + u_t \quad |\phi|<1. \tag{7.5}$$

Using this expression in (7.4) a closed-form solution for the exchange rate may be derived as:

$$s_t = (1 - \phi\theta)^{-1} z_t, \tag{7.6}$$

since the term $(1 - \phi\theta)^{-1}$ is greater than unity, a current change in m will have a magnified effect on s. So in answer to the above question a current change in the money supply, by signalling to agents through (7.6) further changes in the future, produces a more than proportionate movement in the current exchange rate relative to current fundamentals. On the basis of this model, one potential explanation for the apparent excess volatility of the exchange rate with respect to current fundamentals is that such a comparison misses the dramatic effect that expectations can have on exchange rate volatility and so on this view the intra-regime puzzle is not such a puzzle after all.

Obstfeld and Rogoff (2000) have used a stochastic version of their new open economy macroeconomic (NOEM) model to generate a variant of the forward-looking monetary model. The basic difference with the model above is that the introduction of uncertainty means that the forward-looking reduced form features a risk premium term:

$$s_t = \frac{\bar{i}\varepsilon}{1 + \bar{i}\varepsilon} \sum_{s=t}^{\infty} \left(\frac{1}{1 + \bar{i}\varepsilon} \right)^{s-t} E_t \left[m_s - m_s^* + \frac{v_s - v_s^*}{\bar{i}\varepsilon} \right], \tag{7.7}$$

where the risk premium, $v_t - v_t^*$, is given by:

$$v_t - v_t^* = \frac{1}{2}(\sigma^2_{p^*,t} - \sigma^2_{p,t}) + \rho(\sigma_{cp^*,t} - \sigma_{cp,t}) \tag{7.8}$$

and the subscript p denotes the log of the price level and the overbar above the interest rate term reflects a non-stochastic steady state value (which arises because the non-linearity of money equilibrium condition makes it necessary to approximate it in the neighbourhood of a non-stochastic steady state), and ε is the consumption elasticity of the demand for money. The term involving $[v_s - v_s^*]_{s=t}^{\infty}$ is referred to as the 'level' risk premium, and is not exactly equal to the standard forward market risk premium because of the existence of $1/\bar{i}\varepsilon$. There are two key insights here. First, the risk premium can affect the level of the exchange rate, and not just the predictable excess return, which has been studied extensively in the literature. This is important because it means that higher moments of economic variables can affect the volatility of the exchange rate and not just the first moments – if the forward risk premium is quite volatile, this could have important implications for exchange rate volatility. Second, the effect of the risk premium on the exchange rate may potentially be very large because of the scaling factor, $1/\bar{i}\varepsilon$. A rise in the covariance of c and p would lead to a fall in v, which, in turn, would produce a fall in the interest rate and from (7.7) an exchange rate appreciation. Obstfeld and Rogoff view this as capturing the idea of a portfolio shift toward the home currency or, equivalently, of a 'safe haven' effect on the home currency.

Other applications of the NOEM model to the issue of exchange rate volatility, include Duarte (2003), who uses a variant of the two-country NOEM model in which asset markets are incomplete and prices are set one period in advance in the buyer's currency (that is, local currency pricing), to address the intra-regime volatility issue. In this set-up, changes in expectations about future variables can translate into changes in the exchange rate without directly affecting other macroeconomic variables, thereby offering an explanation for the excess volatility result.

Duarte and Stockman (2003) exploit the same two-country model used in Duarte (2003) to highlight the role of the risk premium in explaining the intra-regime volatility result. Their key prediction is that new information that results in agents revising their perceptions of the risk premium can produce exchange rate volatility without there being any changes in the current macroeconomic variables. Exogenous shocks to money growth and productivity growth, with time-varying second moments, cause endogenous changes in the risk premium. Such shocks result from regime shifts that affect the covariances of shocks, and these generate 'rational speculation', in the sense of altering equilibrium risk premia. The model of Duarte and Stockman generates a strong correlation between changes in exchange rates and changes in risk premia. Other applications of the NOEM to explain the excess volatility issue are: Betts and Devereux (1996), Devereux and Engel (2001), Bacchetta and van Wincoop (2003) and Monacelli (2004).

A number of theoretical models are therefore able to explain both the inter- and intra-regime volatility effects. What of the empirical evidence?

7.2.2 Empirical Evidence on Intra- and Inter-regime Volatility

Flood and Rose (1995, 1999) demonstrate the existence of inter-regime volatility by constructing so-called virtual fundamentals (VF) and total fundamentals (TF). Consider again the monetary reduced form:

$$s_t = m_t - m_t^* - \beta_0(y_t - y_t^*) + \beta_1(i_t - i_t^*), \tag{7.9}$$

which can be rearranged as:

$$s_t - \beta_1(i_t - i_t^*) = m_t - m_t^* - \beta_0(y_t - y_t^*),$$

where the left-hand side becomes the 'virtual fundamental' $VF_t = s_t - \beta_1(i_t - i_t^*)$ and the right-hand side is the 'traditional fundamental', $TF_t = m_t - m_t^* - \beta_0(y_t - y_t^*)$. Flood and Rose estimate the conditional volatility of VF and TF (and also for variants in which they allow money demand disturbances) for a sample period spanning both the Bretton Woods and post-Bretton Woods periods. The countries studied are: the UK, Canada, France, Germany, Holland, Italy, Japan and Sweden; and the numeraire country/currency is the US. In sum, their results indicate that the volatility of VF increases dramatically as countries move from fixed to floating, but the volatility of TF does not. Frankel and Rose demonstrate that this finding is robust to different values of the coefficient specifications. Flood and Rose's key conclusion is that exchange rate models cannot explain the volatility of the exchange rate in the recent floating period. They draw the implication that what changes in the move from fixed to flexible exchange rates is the market microstructure and so this should be the focus in trying to understand high-frequency exchange rate movements.

Arnold, MacDonald and de Vries (2005) (AVM) revisit the Flood and Rose finding and argue that it is important to turn the question from why do exchange rates appear excessively volatile in flexible rate regimes to why are fundamentals not more volatile in fixed rate regimes? In this regard they argue it is important to recognize the role played by distortions in fixed rate regimes and modify the monetary exchange rate equation to:

$$s = E[m_j - m_j^*] - E[x_j - x_j^*] + \ln\frac{R}{I} - \ln\tau\frac{\tau^*\omega^*}{\omega} + E[\ln\tau_j + \ln\omega_j^* - \ln\omega_j] + \Omega, \tag{7.10}$$

where τ capital control distortion and ω trade distortion and is the risk premium comprising the sum of variances and covariances of the individual variables:

$$\Omega = \frac{1}{2}\{[\sigma^2_{m_j^*} - \sigma^2_{m_j}] + [\sigma^2_{x_j} + \sigma^2_{\ln\tau_j/\omega_j} + 2\sigma_{p_j^*,x_j} - 2\sigma_{p_j^*,\ln\tau_j/\omega_j} - 2\sigma_{x_j,\ln\tau_j/\omega_j}]$$
$$- [\sigma^2_{x_j^*} + \sigma^2_{\ln\omega_j^*} + 2\sigma_{p_j^*,x_j^*} + 2\sigma_{p_j^*,\ln\omega_j^*} + 2\sigma_{x_j^*,\ln\omega_j^*}]\}. \tag{7.11}$$

Arnold et al. (2005) tackle the results of Flood and Rose (1995) in terms of two key distortions: IMF support and capital controls. In a monetary framework, volatility should show up in reserves under fixed exchange rates, but Flood and Rose have argued there is no volatility of reserves trade-off. However, AVM show with a specific case study for the UK through Bretton Woods and post-Bretton Woods that IMF credit facilities *can* dramatically distort the reserve trade-off and that IMF support is quantitatively important enough to include in an analysis of the volatility trade-off and when it is, there is indeed a volatility trade-off.

Additionally, using the offshore/onshore interest rate differential as a measure of capital controls, AVM show for the UK during Bretton Woods and post-Bretton Woods that it is striking how marked the volatility of the onshore/offshore differential is for the former period. Indeed it is demonstrated that the volatility of the offshore/onshore differential is almost the reverse of the stylized exchange rate volatility – that is, highly volatile in Bretton Woods and hardly any volatility in the floating rate period. AVM also demonstrate this is also an important source of volatility for France and Italy during the sub-period when capital controls were in force in the ERM period (that is, 79.01–83.03).

AVM also assess the post-Bretton Woods intra-regime volatility issue by constructing standard deviations of Δs and Δf, that is, $\Delta((m - m^*) - (y - y^*))$, with both the US and Germany as alternate numeraire. They report the striking result: the order of magnitude of volatility in total fundamentals is not very different from Δs. A further finding of AVM is that for the ERM period the magnitude of exchange rate volatility is clearly dependent on whether realignments are excluded or not. With realignments included, s rate volatility turns out to be much greater compared with the non-realignment position. Flood and Rose (1995) and others do not include s realignments in their work. AVM conclude that the intra- and inter-regime volatility disconnection is overplayed – there is a clear connection between macro fundamentals in both intra- and inter-regime comparisons, especially if the appropriate fundamentals are utilized.

7.3 THE LEVELS PUZZLE AND OUT-OF-SAMPLE FORECASTING

The levels puzzle was kicked off by Meese and Rogoff (1983), who demonstrated that a standard set of macroeconomic fundamentals generated from a monetary model were unable to beat a random-walk in an out-of-sample forecasting context, and this despite giving the fundamentals-based model an unfair advantage by using the actual data outcomes of the fundamentals rather than forecasting the fundamentals themselves (which would have to be done in a real-time forecasting exercise – that is, producing forecasts that could potentially have been used at the time). Ever since the publication of the Meese and Rogoff paper the ability of an exchange rate model to beat a random-walk has become something of an acid test, indeed, *the* acid test of how successful an exchange rate model is. Indeed, it has become the equivalent of the R squared metric by which an exchange rate model is judged.

More specifically, Meese and Rogoff (ibid.) take various versions of the monetary model and estimate these models for the dollar-mark, dollar-pound, dollar-yen and the trade-weighted dollar. The sample period studied was March 1973 to November 1980, with the out-of-sample forecasts conducted over the sub-period December 1976 to November 1980. In particular, the models were estimated from March 1973 to November 1976 and one- to 12-step-ahead forecasts were conducted. The observation for December 1976 was then added in and the process repeated up to November 1980. Rather than forecasting all of the right-hand side variables from a particular exchange rate relationship simultaneously with the exchange rate, to produce real-time forecasts, Meese and Rogoff gave the monetary class of models an unfair advantage by including actual data outcomes of the right-hand side variables. Data on the latter variables were available to them due to the historical nature of their study, but of course they would not have been available at the time of forecasting to a forecaster producing 'real-time' forecasts. To produce the latter all of the right-hand side variables would have had to be forecast simultaneously with the exchange rate. Out-of-sample forecasting accuracy was determined using the mean bias, mean absolute bias and the root mean square error criteria. The benchmark comparison is, as we have noted, a simple random-walk with drift:

$$s_t = s_{t-1} + \kappa + \varepsilon_t, \tag{7.12}$$

where κ is a constant (drift) term and ε_t is a random disturbance. Since the RMSE (root mean square error) criterion has become the measure that most subsequent researchers have focused on we note it here as:

$$RMSE = \sqrt{\frac{\sum (F_t - A_t)^2}{n}}$$

where F is the forecast and A is an actual outcome. By taking the ratio of the RMSE obtained from the model under scrutiny, to the RMSE of the random-walk process, a summary measure of the forecasting performance can be obtained as:

$$RMSE^r = \frac{RMSE^m}{RMSE^{rw}} \tag{7.13}$$

where $RMSE^r$ is the root mean square error ratio (this is equivalent to the Theil statistic).

In sum, Meese and Rogoff were unable to outperform a random-walk at horizons of between one and 12 months ahead, although in four instances (out of a possible 224) the VAR (vector auto-regressive) model produced a $RMSE^r$ ranking that was less than one at longer horizons (one outperformance of the model at six months and three outperformances at 12 months), although this is still a number that is less than that expected by chance. The reason why the Meese and Rogoff finding has been interpreted as a particularly telling indictment against fundamentals-based models is because they deliberately gave their models an unfair advantage by using actual data outcomes of the fundamentals, rather than forecasting them simultaneously with the exchange rate. The Meese and Rogoff result has been confirmed more recently by Mark (1995) and Chinn and Meese (1995), although these researchers do find that predictability kicks in at 'longer horizons', that is, horizons of 36 months and above.

The Meese and Rogoff (1983) finding has had an enduring impression on the economics profession. For example, surveying the post-Meese and Rogoff literature, Frankel and Rose (1995) argue (emphasis added): 'the Meese and Rogoff analysis of *short horizons* [less than 36 months] has never been convincingly overturned or explained. It continues to exert a pessimistic effect on the field of empirical exchange rate modelling in particular and international finance in general'.

One potential reason why Meese and Rogoff may have been unable to beat a random-walk is because all but one of their empirical relationships were either static or had very limited dynamics. However, we know from the PPP (purchasing power parity) literature that exchange rate dynamics tend to be quite complex and adjustment to PPP takes a considerable number of periods. A similar story is true for the money market relationships, which are so central to the monetary model – all of the available evidence from money demand studies indicates that adjustment to equilibrium is often quite complex. Clearly for an empirical exchange rate model to be successful it should incorporate these kinds of dynamics. As we shall now demonstrate, when these dynamics are accounted for in the estimation process, the random-walk model is convincingly beaten.

One way of addressing the dynamic adjustments underlying is to use a modelling method such as the so-called general-to-specific dynamic modelling approach proposed by Hendry (1995) and others. Although in one of their estimated models, Meese and Rogoff did allow for rich dynamic interactions using a VAR, it is likely that such a system is overparameterized in terms of its use of information and such systems generally do not forecast well. Interestingly, Meese and Rogoff in a footnote cite this as a potential reason for the poor performance of the VAR-based implementation of the model. The general-to-specific approach can be used to produce parsimonious VARs or parsimonious VECM (vector error correction mechanism) models.

The general-to-specific approach to exchange rate modelling, and its implications for exchange rate forecastability, can be illustrated using the approach of MacDonald and Taylor (1991). In particular, they use cointegrating methods and a general-to-specific approach to produce a dynamic error correction equation of the following form:

$$\Delta s_t = \underset{(0.073)}{0.244}\,\Delta s_{t-2} - \underset{(0.235)}{0.417}\,\Delta_2 \Delta m_t - \underset{(0.343)}{0.796}\,\Delta y_t - \underset{(0.003)}{0.008}\,\Delta^2 i^*_t - \underset{(0.013)}{0.025}\,z_{t-1} + \underset{(0.003)}{0.005} \tag{7.14}$$

This equation was shown to pass a standard set of in-sample diagnostic tests (not reported here). Of perhaps more significance, however, is the ability of this model to outperform a random-walk in an out-of-sample forecasting exercise. In order to produce truly dynamic out-of-sample forecasts, MacDonald and Taylor implemented a dynamic forecasting exercise over the last 24 observations using the procedure of Meese and Rogoff (1983); that is, they sequentially re-estimated the model for every data point from January 1989 onwards, computing dynamic forecasts for a number of forecast horizons. The RMSE ratio from this model is less than unity at all horizons from one month to 12. Clearly this result is in marked contrast to those of Meese and Rogoff.

However, despite the apparent success in beating a random-walk, MacDonald and Taylor continue to use the actual right-hand side variables in their forecasting exercise and therefore although this is consistent with the original Meese and Rogoff article, these forecasts could not have been used by practitioners to make 'real-time' exchange rate forecasts. Furthermore, although the RMSE ratios are less than unity, it is not clear that they are significantly less than one. In order to address these kinds of issues MacDonald and Marsh (1997) propose a modelling technique that produces fully simultaneous forecasts of all of the model variables and they also provide significance levels for the RMSE ratios. MacDonald and Marsh take the so-called UIP-PPP approach, which involves combining relative interest rates (UIP = uncovered interest parity) with the nominal exchange rate and relative prices to produce a stationary (cointegrating) relationship. That is, they focus on the following vector:

$$x' = [s, p, p^*, i^l, i^{l*}].$$

The modelling approach involves generating the structural econometric modelling (SEM) of Hendry and Mizon (1993) and Johansen and Juselius

(1994). A key advantage of this SEM modelling strategy is that it results in a full system of equations, rather than a single reduced form, and it can therefore be used to provide forecasts for all of the variables in the model. The essential point made by MacDonald and Marsh is that an exchange rate model that incorporates a sensible long-run equilibrium and dynamic properties, which are rich enough to capture the underlying data-generating process, should do better than a static model or one with very simple dynamics (which is essentially the kind of model used by other researchers).

MacDonald and Marsh focus on the yen, mark and pound against the US dollar, over the period January 1974 to December 1992, with the last 24 observations held back for forecasting purposes. The forecasts constructed are fully simultaneous and dynamic and could therefore have been used by a potential forecaster. The success of the forecasts is gauged in three ways. First, using the $RMSE^r$ criterion, discussed above. Second in terms of the directional ability calculated as:

$$D = \frac{(1 \text{ if forecast direction} = \text{actual, else } 0)}{n}.$$

On the basis of chance D is expected to be 0.5, and therefore any number above 0.5 means that the model does better in terms of its predictive ability than simply tossing a coin. Finally, RMSE ratios were constructed for the model projections relative to a panel of 150 professional forecasts, located in the G-7 financial centres, and as collected by Consensus Economics of London (gauged using the $RMSE^r$ criterion). In sum, MacDonald and Marsh demonstrate that fundamentals-based SEM models have forecasting properties that easily dominate a random-walk at horizons as short as two months ahead, have average directional forecast ability across the three currencies and horizons of 0.75, and dominate the forecasts of the professional forecasters.

In a follow-up book, MacDonald and Marsh (1999) extend their earlier analysis by using a tripolar model of the yen, dollar and German mark and demonstrate once again the ease with which the random-walk model can be beaten in an out-of-sample forecasting context once appropriate dynamics and long-run relationships have been incorporated into an exchange rate model. Other recent examples of the dominance of fundamentals-based models over the random-walk are: La Cour and MacDonald (2000) and Mark and Sul (2001).

Cheung, Chinn and Pascual (2005) estimate a monetary approach reduced forms, and variants thereof, which incorporate 'real' factors such as a Balassa-Samuelson effect. Their sample period is 1973 Q2 to 2000 Q4 and they consider five currencies against the US dollar and Japanese yen. They report that 'no model consistently outperforms a random walk, by a mean squared error criterion; however, along a direction-of-change dimension, certain structural models do outperform a random walk with statistical significance'. In the light of our discussion above, this result seems surprising especially since Cheung et al. use an error correction specification, in addition to a first difference specification. However, crucially the error correction models estimated are not rendered parsimonious by the deletion of insignificant dynamics and MacDonald and Marsh have shown that this aspect of exchange rate modelling is crucial in the process of obtaining accurate exchange rate forecasts.

We believe that the research presented in this chapter demonstrates clearly that the random-walk paradigm no longer rules the roost in terms of exchange rate forecasting. There is now a sufficient body of evidence to suggest that the random-walk can be beaten in a large variety of samples and for a number of different currencies. This, of course, is not to say that the random-walk model can always be beaten, but it does, at least, indicate that the pessimism that many have levelled against fundamentals-based exchange rate models is unwarranted.

7.4 CONCLUDING COMMENTS

In this short chapter we have re-examined the perceived wisdom that a standard set of macro fundamentals are unable to explain exchange rates in an out-of-sample forecasting context and that the same kinds of fundamentals are unable to explain the volatility of exchange rates both across and within regimes. The main objective of this chapter has been to show that when appropriate account is taken of long-run equilibrium relationships and short-run dynamics it is relatively straightforward to beat a random-walk at horizons as short as two months ahead, and to beat the random-walk significantly in a statistical sense. We have also shown that there are a number of theoretical models that offer explanations for the apparently excessive volatility of exchange rates with respect to fundamentals and these models are compatible with rational, forward-looking behaviour. Again, when appropriate macro fundamentals are used, neither the intra-regime nor the inter-regime puzzles seem that puzzling from an empirical perspective.

NOTE

1. Adam Smith Professor of Political Economy, University of Glasgow, and Fellow of CESifo research network, Munich. This chapter draws on chapters 3, 5 and 10 of *Exchange Rate Economics: Theories and Evidence* by Ronald MacDonald (2007), London: Routledge.

REFERENCES

Arnold, I., R. MacDonald and C. de Vries (2005), 'Fundamental volatility is regime specific', mimeo, University of Glasgow.

Bacchetta, P. and E. van Wincoop (2003), 'Can information heterogeneity explain the exchange rate determination puzzle?', *NBER Working Paper* No. 9498.

Baxter, M. and A. Stockman (1989), 'Business cycles and the exchange-rate system', *Journal of Monetary Economics*, **23** (3), 377–400.

Betts, C. and M. Devereux (1996), 'The exchange rate in a model of pricing to market', *European Economic Review*, **40** (3), 1007–21.

Cheung, Y.-W., M. Chinn and A.G. Pascual (2005), 'Empirical models of the 90s: are any fit to survive?', *Journal of International Money and Finance*, **24** (7), 1150–75.

Chinn, M. and R. Meese (1995), 'Banking on currency forecasts: how predictable is the change in money?', *Journal of International Economics*, **38** (1–2), 161–78.

Devereux, M. and C. Engel (2001), 'Endogenous currency price setting in a dynamic open economy model', *NBER Working Paper* 8559.

Duarte, M. (2003), 'Why don't macroeconomic quantities respond to exchange rate variability?', *Journal of Monetary Economics*, **50** (4), 889–913.

Duarte, M. and A.C. Stockman (2003), 'Rational speculation and exchange rates', *Journal of Monetary Economics*, **52** (1), 3–29.

Flood, R.P. and A.K. Rose (1995), 'Fixing exchange rates: a virtual quest for fundamentals', *Journal of Monetary Economics*, **36** (1), 3–37.

Flood, R.P. and A.K. Rose (1999), 'Understanding exchange rate volatility without the contrivance of macroeconomics', *Economic Journal*, **109** (459), F660–72.

Frankel, J.A. and R. Meese (1987), 'Are exchange rates excessively variable?', in S. Fischer (ed.), *NBER Macroeconomics Annual*, Cambridge, Massachusetts: MIT Press, pp. 117–53.

Frankel, J.A. and A. Rose (1995), 'A survey of empirical research on nominal exchange rates', in S. Grossman and K. Rogoff (eds), *The Handbook of International Economics*, vol. 3, Amsterdam: North Holland.

Hendry (1995) *Pc-Give*, Oxford: Oxford University Press.

Hendry, D.F and G. Mizon (1993), 'Evaluating dynamic econometric models by encompassing the VAR', in P.C.B Phillips (ed.), *Models, Methods and Applications of Econometrics*, pp. 272–300, Oxford: Blackwell.

Johansen, S. and K. Juselius (1994), 'Identification of the long-run and the short-run structure. An application to the ISLM model', *Journal of Econometrics*, **63** (1), 7–36.

La Cour, L. and R. MacDonald (2000), 'Modelling the ECU against the US dollar: a structural monetary interpretation', *Journal of Business Economics and Statistics*, **18** (4), 436–50.

MacDonald, R. (1999), 'Exchange rates: do fundamentals matter?', *Economic Journal*, **109** (459), 673–91.

MacDonald, R. and I.W. Marsh (1997), 'On Casselian PPP, cointegration and exchange rate forecasting', *Review of Economics and Statistics*, **79** (4) November.

MacDonald, R. and I.W. Marsh (1999), *Exchange Rate Modelling*, Boston: Kluwer.

MacDonald, R. and M.P. Taylor (1991), 'The monetary model of the exchange rate: long-run relationships and coefficient restrictions', *Economics Letters*, **37** (2), 179–85.

Mark, N.C. (1995), 'Exchange rates and fundamentals: evidence on long-horizon predictability', *American Economic Review*, **85** (1), 201–18.

Mark, Nelson C. and Donggyu Sul (2001), 'Nominal exchange rates and monetary fundamentals: evidence from a small post-Bretton Woods panel', *Journal of International Economics*, **53** (1), 29–52.

Meese, R. and K. Rogoff (1983), 'Empirical exchange rate models of the seventies: do they fit out of sample?', *Journal of International Economics*, **14** (1), 3–24.

Monacelli, T. (2004), 'Into the Mussa puzzle: monetary policy regimes and the real exchange rate in a small open economy', *Journal of International Economics*, **62** (1), 191–217.

Obstfeld, M. and K. Rogoff (2000), 'Risk and exchange rates', *NBER Working Paper* No. 6694.

Rogoff, K. (1999), 'Monetary models of dollar/yen/euro nominal exchange rate: dead or undead?', *Economic Journal*, **109** (459), F655–9.

8. Understanding exchange rates: a micro-based perspective on the importance of fundamentals

Martin D.D. Evans[1]

8.1 INTRODUCTION

The apparent disconnect between the dynamics of spot exchange rates and macroeconomic variables over short- and medium-term horizons has been a long-standing puzzle. Surveys of the empirical literature by Frankel and Rose (1995) and Cheung, Chinn and Pascual (2005) conclude that changes in macroeconomic variables, so-called exchange rate fundamentals, can account for very little of the observed variation in spot rates over months, quarters or a year. At the same time, there is a new but rapidly growing body of evidence showing that order flows – a measure of trading patterns in the foreign exchange (FX) market – can account for a very large proportion of the variation in spot rates over days, weeks and months (for a recent survey, see Evans, 2008, Ch. 7). Many students of the FX market have interpreted these new micro-based findings as a confirmation that exchange rates are disconnected from fundamentals. Indeed, the prevalent view is that the trading patterns summarized in order flow are largely independent of macroeconomic activity, so the empirical success of micro-based models leaves little role for traditional fundamentals as a source of exchange rate dynamics.

This chapter puts forward a different view. I shall argue that the micro-based evidence on the importance of order flows leaves plenty of room for macroeconomic fundamentals as a driver of exchange rates. In fact, micro-based models represent a new perspective, based on the microeconomics of FX trading, which allows us to investigate the link between exchange rates and the macroeconomy with much greater resolution. As a result, recent micro-based research points to the existence of a more nuanced link between macroeconomic fundamentals and spot exchange rates.

8.2 TRADITIONAL AND MICRO-BASED EXCHANGE RATE MODELS

To understand why the micro-based approach provides a new perspective on the role of fundamentals as a driver of exchange rate dynamics, it is useful to delineate how traditional exchange rate models differ from their micro-based counterparts. In particular, I want to focus on the key difference between the two modelling approaches that opens up new conceptual space for studying the connections between exchange rates and macroeconomic variables.

Traditional exchange rate models pay little attention to how trading in the FX market actually takes place. The implicit assumption is that the details of trading (that is, who quotes currency prices and how trade takes place) are unimportant for the behaviour of exchange rates over months, quarters or longer. This simplifying assumption carries little weight when all information relevant to the determination of the spot rate is common knowledge. In such a world, all market participants have the same information about the structure and state of the economy, and so have no difficulty in agreeing on the 'appropriate price' at which trade in foreign currency could take place. The fact that trade takes place or follows a particular pattern in terms of who buys and sells foreign currency is irrelevant for the determination of spot rates.

Trading patterns may also be largely irrelevant for the determination of spot rates in the absence of common information. If market participants have different information but are able to reach a consensus quickly concerning the 'appropriate price' for FX, most of the variations in spot rates we observe at macroeconomic frequencies will be unrelated to trading activity. Bacchetta and van Wincoop (2006) develop an exchange rate model in this genre. They study the dynamics of the spot rate in a standard monetary model where investors have different exchange rate exposures and private information concerning future macroeconomic fundamentals. As is standard in the literature, the rational expectations equilibrium (REE) spot exchange rate is identified as the rate that sets aggregate excess demand for foreign currency equal to zero. This rate is not the one at which market participants would first agree to trade because it embodies information that is not yet known by any one investor. However, it is possible to identify conditions under which the REE rate is established after only one round of trading in a limit order market (see, for example, Evans, 2008, Ch. 8). If these conditions hold true, the high pace of FX trading suggests that deviations of actual spot rates from the REE values should be very short-lived. As a result, these so-called microstructure effects should be dominated by the impact of new information concerning fundamentals when we consider the behaviour of spot rates over months, quarters or years. In short, the presence of heterogeneous information may give rise to short-lived microstructure effects, but they may be safely ignored if we are interested in understanding the behaviour of spot rates over macro-relevant horizons.

Micro-based exchange rate models differ from their traditional counterparts in that they examine the determination and behaviour of spot exchange rates in an environment that replicates the key features of trading in the FX market. In particular, they focus on how information relevant to the pricing of foreign currency becomes reflected in the spot exchange rate via the trading process. According to this approach, trading is not an ancillary market activity that can be ignored when considering exchange rate behaviour. Rather, it is an integral part of the process through which spot rates are determined and evolve.

The focus on trading necessitates the specification of a rich informational environment. Micro-based exchange rate models start from the premise that much of the information about the current and future state of the economy is dispersed across agents (that is, individuals, firms and financial institutions). Agents use this information in making their everyday decisions, including decisions to trade in the FX market at the prices quoted by dealers. Dealers quote prices (for example, dollars per unit of foreign currency) at which they stand ready to buy or sell foreign currency; they will purchase foreign currency at their bid quote, and sell foreign currency at their ask quote. Agents that choose to trade with an individual dealer are termed the dealer's customers. The difference between the value of purchase and sale orders *initiated* by customers during any trading period is termed customer order flow. Importantly, order flow is different from trading volume because it conveys information. Positive (negative) order flow indicates to a dealer that, on balance, their customers value foreign currency more (less) than his or her asking (bid) price. Interdealer order flow is similarly defined for transactions between dealers.[2] By tracking who initiates each trade, order flow provides a measure of the information exchanged between counterparties in a series of financial transactions.

At their heart, micro-based models describe the process by which the dispersed macroeconomic information on fundamentals contained in the customer order flows becomes known across the market, and hence embedded into FX quotes. As part of this process, dealers extract information from their trades with customers and other dealers by solving a series of inference problems. Under some circumstances, these problems are sufficiently simple for every dealer to learn all there is to know about fundamentals in a few rounds of interdealer trading. In this case, the pace of information aggregation is very fast, so that new information concerning fundamentals is quickly reflected in dealer quotes whether the news is initially dispersed or common knowledge. The resulting dynamics for exchange rates over weeks, months or quarters will be indistinguishable from the predictions of traditional models. Here micro-based models provide the theoretical justification for the prevalent assumption that micro-structure effects may be safely ignored when our concern is the behaviour of spot rates over macro-relevant horizons.

The real potential of the micro-based approach comes to the fore when the inference problem facing individual dealers is sufficiently complex to slow down the pace of information aggregation. Under these circumstances, it takes many rounds of interdealer trading before the dispersed information concerning fundamentals becomes known across the market. This scenario is much more likely from a theoretical perspective because the conditions needed for fast information are quite stringent (Evans and Lyons, 2004). When these conditions are not met, variations in spot rates over macro-relevant horizons primarily reflect the process through which existing (dispersed) information concerning fundamentals becomes embedded into FX quotes rather than changes in actual fundamentals. It is this process of information aggregation that constitutes the new conceptual space for studying the connections between exchange rates and macroeconomic variables.

8.3 THE ROLE OF FUNDAMENTALS

How do micro-based models provide a new perspective on the role played by fundamentals in the determination and evolution of spot exchange rates? To address this question, let us consider the determination of the equilibrium exchange rate in a micro-based model.

Evans and Lyons (2007) develop a model of foreign exchange trading embedded within an otherwise standard two-country dynamic general equilibrium model. The model contains two key features: first, the equilibrium spot exchange rate is identified from the optimally determined price of foreign currency quoted by dealers at a point in time. This means that information about the current and future state of the economy (that is, fundamentals) will only impact on exchange rates when, and if, it affects dealers' quotes. The second feature concerns dealers' information. Each dealer receives information from two sources: (1) macro data releases and (2) the foreign currency orders from customers (that is, households and firms) and other dealers. Taken together, these sources provide incomplete information about current and future fundamentals.

The structure of trading in the foreign exchange market is far too complex to be modelled in great detail. Instead, micro-based models describe a trading environment that captures key facets of actual trading in an analytically tractable setting. In practice this means that trading is assumed to follow a simple sequence of events. In Evans and Lyons (2007), dealers quote FX prices to customers at the start of each period. Each dealer then receives orders from a subset of firms and households that comprise his or her customers. Dealers next quote prices in the interdealer market. These prices, too, are good for any quantity and are publicly observed. Dealers then have the opportunity to trade among themselves. Interdealer trading is simultaneous and trading with multiple partners is feasible.

In this trading environment, optimal quote decisions take a simple form; all dealers quote the same FX price to both customers and other dealers. We can represent the period-t quote as:

$$s_t = (1 - b)\sum_{i=0}^{\infty} b^i E[f_{t+i}|\Omega_t^D], \tag{8.1}$$

where $0 < b < 1$, s_t is the log price of foreign currency quoted by all dealers, and f_t denotes exchange rate fundamentals. The form for fundamentals differs according to the macroeconomic structure of the model. In Evans and Lyons (2007), f_t includes home and foreign money supplies and household consumption. In models where central banks conduct monetary policy via the control of short-term interest rates, f_t will include variables used to set policy. More generally, f_t will also include a term that compensates dealers for providing liquidity to customers wanting to trade foreign currency. This is the source of the micro-based foreign exchange risk premium.

While equation (8.1) takes the present value form familiar from standard international macro models, it is crucial to recognize that it represents how dealers quote the price for foreign currency in equilibrium. All dealers choose to quote the same price in this trading environment because doing otherwise opens them up to arbitrage, a costly proposition. Consequently, the period-t quote must be a function of information known to all dealers. Equation (8.1) incorporates this requirement with the use of the expectations operator, $E[.|\Omega_t^D]$, which denotes expectations conditioned on information common to all dealers at the start of period t, Ω_t^D. This is not to say that all dealers have the same information. On the contrary, the customer order flows received by individual dealers represent an important source of private information, so there may be a good deal of information heterogeneity across dealers at any one time. Dealers use their private information in initiating trade with other dealers, and, in so doing, contribute to the process through which all dealers acquire information.

We can now use equation (8.1) to examine the role of fundamentals as a driver of exchange rate dynamics. Iterating (8.1) forward one period and rearranging gives:

$$\Delta s_{t+1} = \tfrac{1-b}{b}(s_t - E[f_t \mid \Omega_t^D]) + \varepsilon_{t+1}, \qquad (8.2)$$

where $\Delta s_{t+1} = s_{t+1} - s_t$ and

$$\varepsilon_{t+1} = \tfrac{1-b}{b}\sum_{i=1}^{\infty} b^i (E[f_{t+i} \mid \Omega_{t+1}^D] - E[f_{t+i} \mid \Omega_t^D]). \qquad (8.3)$$

Equation (8.2) provides us with a very useful decomposition for thinking about the channels through which fundamentals contribute to the dynamics of the spot rate. It says that the change in the log spot rate (that is, the depreciation rate for the home currency) comprises two components: the expected depreciation rate, $E[\Delta s_{t+1}|\Omega_t^D]$, identified by the first term; and the unexpected change, $\varepsilon_{t+1} = s_{t+1} - E[s_{t+1}|\Omega_t^D]$, shown in equation (8.3). The expected depreciation rate is proportional to the difference between the current spot rate and dealers' expectations concerning the current level of fundamentals. Equation (8.1) implies that this difference equals the present value of future changes in fundamentals:

$$s_t - E[f_t \mid \Omega_t^D] = \sum_{i=1}^{\infty} b^i E[\Delta f_{t+i} \mid \Omega_t^D]. \qquad (8.4)$$

where $\Delta f_{t+1} = f_{t+1} - f_t$. Thus, if dealers expect fundamentals to grow in the future, they also anticipate quoting a higher future price for foreign currency, which in turn contributes to the realized depreciation rate, Δs_{t+1}. The second term in (8.2), $\varepsilon_{t+1} = s_{t+1} - E[s_{t+1} \mid \Omega_t^D]$, identifies the impact of new information received by all dealers between the start of periods t and t+1. Equation (8.3) shows that new information impacts on the FX price quoted in period t+1 to the extent that it revises forecasts of the present value of fundamentals based on dealers' common information.

While fundamentals can contribute to the dynamics of spot rates in a micro-based model via two channels, they need not be equally important. Indeed, the relative importance of each channel depends on the behaviour of fundamentals and the quality of dealers' information. Let us consider these factors in turn. If there is little serial correlation in the change in fundamentals, dealers' forecasts of future changes in fundamentals will be small even if they have complete information about current fundamentals. Under these circumstances, dealers will not anticipate any significant change in the prices they will quote for foreign currency in the future. And, as a result, fundamentals exert little influence on Δs_{t+1} via the expected depreciation rate. Similarly, if dealers have very incomplete information about the current state of the fundamentals, their forecasts for future changes in fundamentals may be small even though the changes appear to be serially correlated. In this case, fundamentals exert little influence on spot rate dynamics via the expected depreciation rate because the information available to dealers was insufficient to exploit the time series properties of fundamentals that become apparent ex post.

These observations provide a simple explanation for the well-known fact that depreciation rates are very hard to forecast. As Engel and West (2005) and others have noted, the variables that comprise fundamentals in many traditional exchange rate models appear to follow non-stationary I(1) processes with little serial correlation in their first difference. It would therefore be rather surprising to find that dealers' forecasts of future changes in fundamentals were significant even if they had complete information about the current state of the economy. Add to this a more realistic view about how incomplete dealers' information actually is, and it is little wonder that under most circumstances dealers quote FX prices that imply an expected depreciation rate that is close to zero.[3]

The fact that depreciation rates are very hard to forecast does not imply that exchange rates are disconnected from fundamentals. It simply means that the dynamics of spot rates must be largely attributable to the effects of news. Here micro-based models have a big advantage over their traditional counterparts because their trade-based foundations provide detail on how news affects spot rates. In particular, as equation (8.3) indicates, micro-based models focus on how new information about fundamentals reaches dealers and induces them to revise their FX quotes. It is here that micro-based models provide the new conceptual space for studying the connections between exchange rates and macroeconomic variables.

News concerning fundamentals can reach dealers either directly or indirectly. Common knowledge (CK) news operates via the direct channel. CK news contains unambiguous information about current and/or future fundamentals that is simultaneously observed by all dealers and immediately incorporated into the FX price they quote. In principle, macroeconomic data releases on say GDP, industrial production or unemployment could be a source for CK news, but in practice they rarely contain much unambiguous new information. In fact, CK news events appear rather rare.

The indirect channel operates via order flow and conveys dispersed information about fundamentals to dealers. Dispersed information comprises micro-level information on economic activity that is correlated with fundamentals. Examples include the sales and orders for the products of individual firms, market research on consumer spending, and private research on the economy conducted by financial institutions. Dispersed information first reaches the FX market via the customer order flows received by individual dealers. These order flows have no immediate impact on dealer quotes because they represent private information to the recipient dealer. The information in each customer flow will only impact on quotes once it is known to all dealers. Interdealer order flow is central to this process. Individual dealers use their private information to trade in the interdealer market. In so doing, information on their customer orders is aggregated and spread across the market. Dispersed information is incorporated into dealer quotes once this information aggregation process is complete.

To summarize, the micro-based approach to exchange rate modelling opens up new conceptual space for understanding the link between fundamentals and spot rates because it provides the analytical framework for studying how new information about fundamentals becomes embedded in dealers' quotes via trading. This is an important theoretical step forward for two reasons. First, the near-legendary difficulty of forecasting future changes in the spot rate (that is, beating the 'random-walk') provides compelling empirical evidence that the assimilation of new information accounts for most of the variations in spot rates. Second, micro-based models make novel empirical predictions about how the assimilation process takes place and so offer the foundation for new empirical research on the link between spot rates and fundamentals.

8.4 EMPIRICAL EVIDENCE

Two strands of recent research provide empirical support for the idea that information concerning fundamentals is assimilated by dealers as a result of trading activity. The first strand considers the impact of macroeconomic data releases; the second provides direct evidence that order flows carry information about the macroeconomic variables that comprise exchange rate fundamentals. Let me review these strands in turn.

8.4.1 Information Assimilation from Macroeconomic Announcements

There is a large literature studying the impact of macroeconomic data releases (so-called macroeconomic announcements) on exchange rates and other asset prices. A common finding in this literature is that macroeconomic announcements account for a small fraction of the total variation in spot rates. For example, Klein, Mizrach and Murphy (1991) find that announcements concerning the US trade balance can account for approximately 40 per cent of the variance of the USD/DEM and YEN/USD spot rates measured at a daily frequency. This is an impressive result, but it only applies to the days when the announcements were made. If we include all other days, the announcements account for less than 3 per cent of the daily changes in spot rates. This finding extends beyond the trade balance. Andersen et al. (2003) find that spot rates respond immediately to a number of different macroeconomic announcements, but taken together they account for a small fraction of the total variation in spot exchange rates at macro-relevant frequencies.

One interpretation of these findings is that spot rates are primarily driven by factors that are unrelated to the new information contained in macroeconomic announcements. Quite what these factors are remains a mystery, but they do not appear to be related to the fundamentals identified in traditional exchange rate models. From this perspective, the announcements' literature appears to confirm that spot rates are largely disconnected from fundamentals. Micro-based models provide an alternative interpretation: macroeconomic announcements do contain new information about fundamentals, but most of this information is transmitted indirectly to spot rates via order flow – a mechanism that is overlooked by existing research on announcement effects. The reason for this is most easily understood with the aid of an example.

Suppose a scheduled announcement on US GDP growth is greater than the expectations of FX market participants. Furthermore, let us assume that everyone agrees that unexpectedly high US GDP growth represents good news for the international value of the dollar. If everyone agrees that GDP growth is x per cent higher than expected, and as a result, the dollar is y per cent more valuable in terms of Japanese yen, dealers will immediately quote a YEN/USD rate that is y per cent higher. This is the standard mechanism through which news directly impacts on currency prices – a mechanism that does not appear to be very empirically important.

Now suppose that everyone agrees that the GDP announcement represents good news for the dollar, but that there are diverse opinions as to how large the appreciation should be. Under these circumstances, the initial rise in the YEN/USD spot rate may be viewed as too large by some market participants and too small by others. Those who view the rise as too small will place orders to purchase the dollar, while those who view the rise as too large will place orders to sell. In aggregate, the balance of these trades represents the order flow that dealers use to further revise their spot rate quotes. In particular, positive (negative) order flow signals that the initial YEN/USD spot rate was below (above) the balance of opinion among market participants concerning the implications of the GDP announcement for the value of the dollar. Importantly, there is no theoretical limit to the duration of this price adjustment process. It may take a matter of minutes when market participants can easily infer each others' views from their trading actions, or much longer when incomplete information concerning order flow across the market make inferences less precise. In the latter case, it will be impossible to estimate the full impact of announcements on currency prices without data on order flows – data that was not utilized in the existing announcements literature. Consequently, the results from the existing literature do not rule out the possibility that macroeconomic announcements contain significant new information about fundamentals that is transmitted indirectly to spot rates via order flow.

Recent results in Evans and Lyons (2008) provide strong empirical support for this view. This study examined how the joint behaviour of spot rates and order flow is affected by the arrival of macroeconomic news at intraday and daily frequencies. In particular, the paper estimates models where diverse views about the implications of a news item creates volatility in order flow, which in turn feeds through to changes in currency prices. Estimates based on intraday data show that order flow contributes more to changing FX prices in the period immediately following the arrival of news than at other times. This evidence points to the importance of the indirect channel. Estimates based on daily data imply that approximately two-thirds of the effect of macroeconomic news on spot rates is transmitted via order flow, the remainder being the direct effect. With both the direct and indirect channels operating, the estimates imply that macroeconomic news accounts for 36 per cent of the total daily variation in spot rates. This is a far higher figure than suggested by the earlier announcements literature and provides some direct evidence connecting the behaviour of spot rates to the macroeconomy.

8.4.2 Information Assimilation from Order Flows

The second strand of recent research focuses on the source of the strong contemporaneous relationship between depreciation rates and order flows documented by Evans and Lyons (2002a and 2002b), Payne (2003), Froot and Ramadorai (2005) and others. These papers show that order flows can account for as much as 80 per cent of the variation in daily depreciation rates, but they do not provide evidence on why order flows have this high level of explanatory power.

Recent research by Evans and Lyons (2007) sheds light on this issue. They develop a model in which order flows drive depreciation rates because they convey information about fundamentals. Although order flows are determined endogenously, their impact on spot rates can be easily understood using equations (8.2) and (8.3) (repeated here for convenience):

$$\Delta s_{t+1} = \tfrac{1-b}{b}(s_t - E[f_t \mid \Omega_t^D]) + \varepsilon_{t+1}, \tag{8.2}$$

$$\varepsilon_{t+1} = \tfrac{1-b}{b}\sum_{i=1}^{\infty} b^i (E[f_{t+i} \mid \Omega_{t+1}^D] - E[f_{t+i} \mid \Omega_t^D]). \tag{8.3}$$

In the Evans and Lyons model, the FX orders placed by households and firms at the start of day t are correlated with information concerning the fundamentals that is not currently known to FX dealers. (This correlation arises because the microeconomic conditions driving the trading decisions of individual agents represent a change in aggregate economic activity that is not CK.) As a result, the customer order flows received by individual dealers contain new information about fundamentals, information that is spread across the whole market via interdealer trade. Hence, the aggregate interdealer order flow observed on day t provides a measure of the market-wide information flow that dealers use to revise their quotes between the start of days t and $t+1$. In other words, interdealer order flows carry much of the new information identified by ε_{t+1} in equation (8.3).

This mechanism not only provides a theoretical rationale for the strong empirical link between spot rate changes and order flows, it also delivers two new testable implications: first, transaction flows should have superior forecasting power for future fundamentals than current spot rates. Second, insofar as the transactions flows received by individual dealers predict what 'the market' will learn about fundamentals in the future, those flows should have forecasting power for future exchange rate returns. Let us consider each of these predictions in more detail.

In the Evans and Lyons model, dealers are forward-looking when quoting FX prices, so spot rates embody their forecasts for fundamentals based on common information, Ω_t^D, as in equation (8.1). One empirical implication of this observation is that spot exchange rates should have forecasting power for fundamentals. While there is some evidence that this is true for variables that comprise fundamentals in many models (Engel and West, 2005), the forecasting power is rather limited. The forecasting implication of the Evans and Lyons model is more exacting. If order flows convey information about fundamentals that is not yet CK to all dealers (that is, not in Ω_t^D), then they should have *incremental* forecasting power for fundamentals, beyond the forecasting ability of any variable in Ω_t^D. This is a strong prediction: it says that order flow should add to the forecasting power of all other variables in Ω_t^D, including the history of spot rates and the fundamental variable itself. Nevertheless, Evans and Lyons (2007) find ample support for this prediction using customer order flows and candidate fundamental variables such as output, inflation and money supplies. These findings provide direct evidence on the information content of customer order flows, and provide a new perspective on the link between exchange rates and fundamentals.

Evans and Lyons (2005) showed that customer order flows had significant forecasting power for *future* depreciation rates, both in- and out-of-sample. For example, at the four-week horizon the out-of-sample forecasts accounted for a highly significant 15.7 per cent of the variation in excess returns. This forecasting result is surprising in its own right. However, it is even more interesting if we consider its implications for the flow of information concerning fundamentals. More specifically, if it takes some time for all the dealers in the market to assimilate the information about fundamentals that was originally carried by a subset of customer orders, those orders should have forecasting power for spot rates because they predict what 'the market' will learn about fundamentals in the future. Again, Evans and Lyons (2007) find ample empirical support for this prediction.

Taken together, these results represent the first findings that link macro fundamentals, transaction flows and exchange rate dynamics. They provide strong support for the idea that exchange rates vary as 'the market' assimilates dispersed information regarding macro fundamentals from transaction flows.

8.5 CONCLUSION

Micro-based models provide a new perspective on the links between macroeconomic fundamentals and spot exchange rates by focusing on the process through which participants in the FX market assimilate information. The power of this approach lies in its ability to relate the transmission of macroeconomic information to trading activity, thereby generating testable empirical implications that are absent in traditional exchange rate models. Although research in this area is still in its early stages, the results to date look promising. At this point it seems safe to say that spot rates are not completely disconnected from fundamentals. Instead, they appear to evolve, in part, as information concerning fundamentals is assimilated by 'the market' via trading. Understanding this process is an important goal of micro-based research, and will have far-reaching implications for a variety of issues in international finance.

NOTES

1. Professor of Economics, and Professor of Finance, Georgetown University and NBER. Department of Economics and MSB, Georgetown University, Washington, DC 20057, USA; tel: (202) 687-1570; e-mail: evansm1@georgetown.edu.
2. Interdealer trading can take place directly (that is, when one dealer asks another for a bid-and-ask quote, and then decides whether he or she wishes to trade) or indirectly via a limit order book run by a broker. In the latter case, order flow is defined as the difference between the value of market orders to purchase and sell foreign currency. In recent years electronic brokerages have come to dominate interdealer trading.
3. One likely exception to this observation occurs during financial crises. If dealers view the

current state of the economy as unsustainable, they will forecast future changes in fundamentals even though they lack complete information about the current state of the economy. Under these circumstances, anticipated future changes in their FX quotes will become an important driver of the spot rate.

REFERENCES

Andersen, T., T. Bollerslev, F. Diebold and C. Vega (2003), 'Micro effects of macro announcements: real-time price discovery in foreign exchange', *American Economic Review*, **93** (1), 38–62.

Bacchetta, P. and E. van Wincoop (2006), 'Can information heterogeneity explain the exchange rate determination puzzle?', *American Economic Review*, **96** (3), 552–76.

Cheung, Yin-Wong, M. Chinn and A. Pascual (2005), 'Empirical exchange rate models of the nineties: are any fit to survive?', *Journal of International Money and Finance*, **24** (7), 1150–75.

Engel, C. and K. West (2005), 'Exchange rates and fundamentals', *Journal of Political Economy*, **113** (3), 485–517.

Evans, M. (2008), *The Foundations of Foreign Exchange*, manuscript in preparation for the Princeton Series in International Finance, Princeton University Press. Chapters available at: http://www9.georgetown.edu/faculty/evansm1/book/outline.htm.

Evans, M. and R. Lyons (2002a), 'Order flow and exchange rate dynamics', *Journal of Political Economy*, **110** (1), 170–80.

Evans, M. and R. Lyons (2002b), 'Informational integration and FX trading', *Journal of International Money and Finance*, **21** (6), 807–31.

Evans, M. and R. Lyons (2004), 'A new micro model of exchange rates', *NBER Working Paper* No. 10379, March.

Evans, M. and R. Lyons (2005), 'Meese-Rogoff redux: micro-based exchange rate forecasting', *American Economic Review*, **95** (2), 405–414, May.

Evans, M. and R. Lyons (2007), 'Exchange rate fundamentals and order flow', *NBER Working Paper* No. 13151, June.

Evans, M. and R. Lyons (2008), 'How is macro news transmitted to exchange rates?', *Journal of Financial Economics*, **88** (1), 26–50.

Frankel, J. and A. Rose (1995), 'Empirical research on nominal exchange rates', in G. Grossman and K. Rogoff (eds), *Handbook of International Economics*, Elsevier Science, vol. III, pp. 1689–1729.

Froot, K. and T. Ramadorai (2005), 'Currency returns, intrinsic value, and institutional-investor flows', *Journal of Finance*, **LX** (3), 1535–65.

Klein, M., B. Mizrach and R.G. Murphy (1991), 'Managing the dollar: has the plaza agreement mattered?', *Journal of Money, Credit and Banking*, **23** (4), 742–51.

Payne, R. (2003), 'Informed trade in spot foreign exchange markets: an empirical investigation', *Journal of International Economics*, **61** (2), 307–29.

9. Real exchange rate dynamics in transition economies: the role of investment in quality

Jan Brůha[1] and Jiří Podpiera[2]

9.1 INTRODUCTION

The real exchange rate is an important policy variable, for instance determining – to some extent – monetary policy conditions in open economies and conditioning the optimal timing for monetary integration. In addition, to the extent the real exchange rate trend is an equilibrium convergence phenomenon it does not adversely impact converging country competitiveness. Therefore, an explanation of the trend real exchange rate dynamics that is consistent with the rest of the economic variables is an important step for appropriate policy implementation and, in a European context, also for monetary union integration.

Economic developments in transition countries in Central and Eastern Europe, specifically the so-called Visegrad-4 countries – the Czech Republic, Hungary, Poland and Slovakia – during the transition decade 1995–2005 (that is, with the basic institutional foundations of a market economy already in place) can be summarized with five facts:[3]

- Fact 1: GDP per capita convergence of the Visegrad-4 country average to the EU-15 average attained 1 per cent a year on average over the decade.
- Fact 2: Significant trade integration pushed up the average export-to-GDP ratio of the Visegrad-4 countries by 2 per cent a year over the decade. Thus, the trade balance, initially in deficit by around 5 per cent, reached a balanced position at the end of the decade.
- Fact 3: The privatization and economic attractiveness of the region resulted in a significant inflow of foreign direct investment (FDI); on average FDI inflows to Visegrad-4 countries reached 5 billion USD a year over the decade. The foreign-owned firms gradually increased their share in total exports, in some countries even up to 90 per cent.

- Fact 4: The real exchange rates – also in the sub-index of tradable goods – of Visegrad-4 currencies vis-à-vis the euro appreciated by an average slightly exceeding 2 per cent a year.
- Fact 5: The share of medium-high and high-tech products in total exports rose by 1.5 to 2 per cent a year; see Fabrizio, Igan and Mody (2007).

Even though most stylized facts (Fact 1 through 3 and 4 in parts) materialized as predicted by mainstream economic theory, represented by Obstfeld and Rogoff (1995), the mechanism used to explain the real exchange rate dynamics apparently did not work in practice. This constitutes a puzzle that we address in this chapter.

9.2 THE PUZZLE

Although economic developments and especially real exchange rate developments traditionally receive special attention in the literature, the recent trend real exchange rate appreciation in the majority of the Central and Eastern European countries constitutes a puzzle for mainstream international macroeconomics (Obstfeld and Rogoff, 1995).

Since the bulk of real exchange rate appreciation stems from the real exchange rate for tradable goods – see Cincibuch and Podpiera (2006) and Égert, Lommatzsch and Lahrèche-Révil (2006) – the scope for the mainstream theoretical explanation of real exchange rate appreciation, that is, the Harrod-Balassa-Samuelson type of convergence, is very limited.

In addition, in absence of the Harrod-Balassa-Samuelson effect on the real exchange rate, as documented, for instance, by Flek, Podpiera and Markova (2003) and Mihaljek and Klau (2006), mainstream theory would predict the real exchange rate of converging economies to depreciate rather than to appreciate.

We take the deficit of the mainstream models in explaining the experience of converging countries as a starting point for an implicit assumption that, along the transition path, products have comparable qualities across all countries. Consequently, an increasing supply of products in a converging economy causes domestic product prices to go down given the downward sloping demand curve, and apparently causes the real exchange rate to depreciate.

Against this backdrop, real exchange rate appreciation may reflect changes in the quality of production, especially with regard to tradables. This is evident from the difference between Slovenia and the Visegrad-4 countries during 1995–2005. While the proportion of medium and high-tech products was high and constant, and no real exchange rate was observed in Slovenia, the Visegrad-4 countries started from low proportions and experienced a significant but gradual shift towards high-tech products, and recorded trend real exchange rate appreciation; see Fabrizio et al. (2007).

9.3 MODELS WITH PRODUCT QUALITY

Recent models by Melitz (2003) and Ghironi and Melitz (2005) introduce a limited role for the quality of product baskets in explaining real exchange rate appreciation. In their model, the number of basket varieties can be taken as a metaphor for the quality of the basket of products through the love-for-variety. The love-for-variety attribute of consumers' utility makes consumers pay more for a basket with a wider variety, and an increase in varieties overestimates observed price indices. If the number of varieties expands in the converging economy relatively more to its advanced counterpart, the real exchange rate based on the observed consumer price indices (as opposed to the rate computed using welfare-theoretic indices) will appreciate for the converging economy.

The strength of this effect is, however, conditional on two aspects. First, the effect will be stronger for a converging economy with a relatively smaller initial variety (that is, the greater the gap in development, the stronger the effect from varieties). Second, the strength of the effect will depend on the degree of initial openness and the dynamics of integration of the converging economy, since a significant part of the increases in varieties is facilitated by varieties imported into the converging economy. Nevertheless, the real exchange rate appreciation seems neither strictly linked to the state of development nor to the degree of openness or speed of opening up. Slovenia for instance, started its convergence to the euro area countries at a much higher level of GDP per capita than the Visegrad-4 countries, had a similar degree of openness and experienced roughly the same speed of integration via foreign trade, yet unlike the Visegrad-4, whose currencies appreciated by 30 to 50 per cent from 1995 to 2005, did not experience real exchange rate appreciation.

Besides, as has been shown by Brůha and Podpiera (2007c) using simulations for a reasonable range of parameters, the effect of quality (variety) is insufficient for explaining the typical pace of real exchange rate appreciation of transition economies, especially in Central and Eastern Europe. Therefore, we propose to use an extension of the model by Ghironi and Melitz (2005) by introducing a direct vertical quality investment margin, which proves to be an important determinant of the dynamics of the real exchange rate. This is similar to the model by Dury and Oomen (2007), who studied the impact of exogenous quality shocks on the real exchange rate. They show that if shocks that increase the quality content also increase unit production costs, then they cause the quality-unadjusted real exchange rate to appreciate. Note that although 'quality' shocks and their relation to unit costs are exogenous in the model by Dury and Oomen (ibid.), Brůha and Podpiera's (2007b, 2007c) model treats investment decisions endogenously, and the relation between unit costs and quality investment is derived from a rigorous microeconomic production function. The extended model is briefly sketched in the Appendix to this chapter.

In essence, apart from the effect of varieties, the quality of the product basket in the model developed by Brůha and Podpiera (2007b) is given by optimal corporate decisions to invest in quality. As in Ghironi and Melitz (2005), quality is taken to be the source of the observed real exchange rate appreciation. Using simulations with the extended model for a reasonable range of parameters, Brůha and Podpiera (2007c) show that the endogenous mechanism of quality decisions in a converging transition economy readily generates the observed pace of real exchange rate appreciation.

9.4 MODEL SIMULATIONS

Using the model developed in Brůha and Podpiera (2007b, 2007c) and the calibration of the model for the Visegrad-4 countries presented in Brůha and Podpiera (2007a), we simulate convergence paths of the real exchange rate for the convergence period. In particular, we assume that the convergence in total factor productivity (TFP) will follow a logistic curve and, using a fit of the convergence from 1995–2005, we derive the future path of productivity convergence for 2006–2020.

Using the calibrated parameters for each Visegrad country and its TFP convergence, we simulate the transition dynamics of the endogenous variables. The key macroeconomic endogenous variables include the ratio of GDP per capita of a Visegrad country to GDP per capita of the EU-15, the empirical real exchange rate, the trade balance, the financial account balance, consumption and investment.

Table 9.1 shows the results for the transition dynamics of the real exchange rate (yearly change in real exchange rate) and the path of the GDP per capita ratio of a converging country to the EU-15 GDP average, starting in 1995 until 2020.

As we can see from the table, the convergence of the Visegrad-4 countries is projected to continue until 2020, when the GDP per capita reaches the average of the EU-15. The convergence is consistent with the empirical real

Table 9.1 Convergence dynamics projections

	1995–2005		2005–10	2010–15	2015–20
	Data	Model	Model	Model	Model
Czech Republic					
GDP ratio[a]	0.6	2.4	0.9	0.8	0.4
Real exchange rate[b] %	1.6	1.1	0.7	0.5	0.4
Hungary					
GDP ratio	1.2	1.7	1.5	1.5	0.6
Real exchange rate %	1.5	1.2	1.5	0.7	0.8
Poland					
GDP ratio	1.0	1.2	1.9	2.3	0.8
Real exchange rate %	0.8	1.2	1.5	0.7	0.8
Slovakia					
GDP ratio	1.0	1.3	1.5	1.5	0.4
Real exchange rate %	1.4	0.8	1.5	1.1	0.6

Notes:
a. GDP ratio refers to the average change (in percentage points) in the ratio of GDP per capita of the converging economy to the GDP per capita of the EU-15 (in purchasing power parity).
b. Real exchange rate refers to the percentage change in the real exchange rate over the period with the convention that the positive values mean appreciation.

Source: Brůha and Podpiera (2007a).

exchange rate appreciation, which is still quite significant over the short horizon but moderates in the medium term and significantly slows around 2015. For this reason, the year 2015 seems to be the most appropriate date for the majority of Visegrad-4 countries to contemplate adopting the euro since there is a sufficiently high probability of having an acceptable inflation differential after joining the monetary union at this stage of convergence.

9.5 CONCLUSION

In this chapter we propose a new explanation (investment in quality) for the exchange rate dynamics in transition economies, especially in the Visegrad-4 countries, which reconciles some of the stylized facts that mainstream literature has not adequately explained: in particular, the increasing share of high-tech products in exported goods by Visegrad-4 countries, the observed real exchange rate appreciation in the tradable good sector and the very small empirical evidence for the Balassa-Samuelson effect.

Using a two-country model with trade and investment costs enriched with the vertical investment margin proved to be a powerful tool for explaining the very significant real exchange rate appreciation that was observed in European transition economies. Solving the model for transition dynamics for Visegrad-4 countries, under the assumption of a total factor productivity convergence along the logistic curve to the level of EU-15 and chosen values of calibrated parameters, we derive the projected convergence trajectories.

As follows from the projected real exchange rate, the Visegrad-4 countries would be expected to enter a phase of real exchange rate moderation and stabilization around 2015. Based on this finding, the appropriate timing for the monetary integration of the Visegrad-4 countries would be beyond this horizon.

APPENDIX: THE CORE OF THE BRŮHA-PODPIERA MODEL

There are two countries that are modelled in an infinite-horizon discrete-time setting. Both countries are populated by a representative competitive household, which has recursive preferences over discounted streams of period utilities, derived from consumption. Production takes place in heterogeneous production entities called firms.

9A.1 Firms

There is a continuum of firms in both countries. In each period there is an unbounded mass of new, ex ante identical, possible entrants. Firms differ ex post by the total factor productivity: upon entry, a firm draws a shock z from a distribution $G(z)$. At the end of each period, there is an exogenous probability δ that a firm is hit by an exit shock, independent on aggregate and individual states. Hit firms shut down.

The production function maps two inputs into two outputs. One type of input is fixed and labelled as 'capital', the other one is variable and labelled as 'labour', which is available in inelastic supply in each country and is immobile between countries. One type of output is quality h and if the firm j uses k_j units of capital, then the quality of its product is given simply as $h_j = k_j$. Capital investment can be considered an improvement in quality. The second output production function is the physical quantity of produced goods x. The production function is given as follows: $x_{jt} = z_j A_t \ell(l_{jt}, k_j)$. The production function ℓ is strictly increasing in the first argument (labour), but strictly decreasing in the second argument. The quality investment is costly for two reasons: first, it requires fixed input k_j and, second, more labour is required to produce better goods. The total factor productivity A_t pertains to the ownerships: at time t firms owned by the domestic household enjoy the productivity A_t^H, while firms owned by the foreign household enjoy the productivity A_t^F.

We assume that the final output of the firm is given by the product of quality and quantity: $q_{jt} = h_j x_{jt}$ and that this final quality-quantity bundle is what is sold at the market. The quality-quantity decomposition of the final good is assumed to be able to derive the movements of the real exchange rate. The production of the final-good bundle can be thus described using the production function f: $q_{jt} = z_j A_t f(k_j, l_{jt})$, where f is given as $f(k_j, l_{jt}) \equiv k_j \ell(l_{jt}, k_j)$. The quality investment is a fixed factor, set at the time of entry, while labour can be freely adjusted.

The optimal decision of the firm will be demonstrated on a domestic firm (that is, a firm owned by the domestic agent and located in the domestic country). In this respect, p^d_{jt} denotes the price of a good produced by a firm j located in the domestic country at time t sold to the domestic market, p^m_{jt} is the price of a good j imported to the domestic market from the foreign country, and p^{m*}_{jt} is the price of a good from the domestic country sold to the foreign household. We further assume that prices are denominated in the currency of the market of sale.

The t-period profit of the domestic firm of vintage τ and owned by the domestic household $\Pi^d_{j\tau t}$ satisfies:

$$\Pi^d_{j\tau t} = \left[\kappa_{jt} p^d_{jt} + (1 - \kappa_{jt}) \frac{s_t}{1 + \mathbf{t}} p^{m*}_{jt} \right] A^H_t z_j f(k_j, l_{jt}) - \omega_t l_{jt},$$

where $0 \leq \kappa_{jt} \leq 1$ is a share of product q_{jt} sold in the domestic market, s_t being a nominal *foreign exchange rate*, and $\mathbf{t} \geq 0$ represents unit iceberg exporting costs. Firms of different vintages and different ownership have different levels of investment in quality; that is why $\Pi^d_{j\tau t}$ will be naturally different along these dimensions.

Firms may export only if special fixed costs are sunk. If a firm at the time of entry decides to sink the fixed export costs, then it becomes eligible to export in all subsequent periods, otherwise it remains ineligible to export in all periods. Nominal investment costs are assumed to take the following form: $P_t(k + c^\xi)$, $\xi \in \{e,n\}$, where P_t represents the 'ideal' price index, which is the price of both consumption and investment goods. We assume that:

$$c^e > c^n > 0$$

where the superscript refers to eligibility, that is e – *eligible* or n – *non-eligible*: eligible firms pay larger fixed costs. This implies, as in Melitz (2003), that in equilibrium there is an endogenous cut-off productivity value $\bar{z}$, such that firms with lower idiosyncratic productivity $z_j < \bar{z}$ will not invest to become eligible, while firms with a sufficiently high productivity level $z_j \geq \bar{z}$ will do.

We assume that a firm's manager maximizes the expected stream of discounted profits. Thus, the value of the profit stream of the domestic firm of vintage τ, enjoying the idiosyncratic productivity level z_j and owned by the domestic household in real terms is:

$$V^d_\tau(z_j) = \max_{\xi, k, \{l_t\}} \sum_{t=\tau}^{\infty} (1 - \delta)^{t-\tau} \mu^t_\tau \frac{\Pi^d_{j\tau t}}{P_t} - (c^\xi + k),$$

where $\Pi^d_{j\tau t}/P_t$ is the t-time real profit of a firm of vintage τ, enjoying the productivity level j under the optimal production plan, and the effective discount factor is given as $(1-\delta)^{\tau-t}\mu_\tau^t$, where μ_τ^t is the marginal rate of intertemporal substitution between dates τ and t of the domestic household.

The final good Q is composed of a continuum of intermediate goods, some of them are produced in the home country and some are imported. The intermediate goods are aggregated using the constant elasticity of substitution (CES) production function with the parameter θ.

The optimal production and investment plans can be derived using backward induction. We present the derivation for a domestic firm. Standard results of monopolistically competitive pricing under the CES market structure suggest that prices are set as a mark-up over marginal costs. Simultaneously with setting prices, firms also decide κ_j. In what follows, the *real* quantities are denoted by the Monotype Corsiva scripts: $\mathcal{P}^d_{j\tau t} \equiv \Pi^d_{j\tau t}/P_t$ is the real profit of a domestic firm and $\mathcal{W}_t \equiv w_t/P_t$ is the real domestic wage.

Now, let us take the perspective of a non-eligible firm of vintage τ and productivity level A_t^H. Its real profit $P^d_{j\tau t}$ in a period t is given – conditional on non-eligibility status, aggregate productivity and idiosyncratic productivity z_j, – as a solution to the following problem:

$$\mathcal{P}^d_{j\tau t} = \max_{l_{jt}} \{\frac{p_{jt}}{P_t} A_t^H z_j f(k_j, l_{jt}) - \mathcal{W}_t l_{jt}\}.$$

Similarly, the real profit of an eligible firm $\mathcal{P}^d_{j\tau t}$ of vintage τ in a period t is given by:

$$\mathcal{P}^d_{j\tau t} = \max_{l_{jt}} \{ [\kappa_{jt} \frac{p_{jt}}{P_t} + (1-\kappa_{jt}) \frac{\eta_t}{1+t} \frac{p^*_{jt}}{P^*_t}] A_t^H z_j f(k_j, l_{jt}) - \mathcal{W}_t l_{jt}\}.$$

The expected present value of profit streams is as follows:

$$\mathcal{P}^{d\xi}_{j\tau} = \sum_{t=\tau}^{\infty} \mu_\tau^t (1-\delta)^{t-\tau} \mathcal{P}^d_{j\tau t},$$

where $\xi \in \{n, e\}$. The expected present value depends on idiosyncratic productivity z_j, invested capital k_j as well as the future path of productivities, real wages and demands.

The optimal investment decision of a domestic eligible firm, which enjoys a productivity level z_j, maximizes the value of the firm given as:

$$V_\tau^{de}(k_j \mid z_j) = \mathcal{P}^{de}_{j\tau}(z_j, k_j, \{\mathcal{W}_{t+\tau}, \mathcal{Q}_{\tau+t}, \mathcal{Q}^*_{\tau+t}, A^H_{\tau+t}, \eta_{\tau+t}\}_{t=0}^{\infty}) - (c^e + k_j)$$

and similarly for a non-eligible firm:

$$V_\tau^{dn}(k_j \mid z_j) = \mathcal{P}^{dn}_{j\tau}(z_j, k_j, \{\mathcal{W}_{t+\tau}, \mathcal{Q}_{\tau+t}, A^H_{\tau+t}\}_{t=0}^{\infty}) - (c^n + k_j).$$

Maximization of $V_{\tau}^{de}(k_j|z_j)$ (resp. $V_{\tau}^{dn}(k_j|z_j)$) yields the optimal demand for quality investment (capital) for eligible (respectively non-eligible) firms, and the value of a firm is:

$$V_{\tau}^{d\xi}(z_j) = \max_{k_j \geq 0} V_{\tau}^{d\xi}(k_j \mid z_j),$$

where $\xi \in \{n,e\}$. The value functions $\Omega_{\tau}^{dn}(z_j)$, $V_{\tau}^{de}(z_j)$ implicitly define the cut-off value $\bar{z}$, which is the least idiosyncratic shock, which makes the export-eligibility investment profitable. Thus, it is defined as:

$$\bar{z}_{\tau}^{d} = \min_{z_j} (\Omega_{\tau}^{de}(z_j) \geq V_{\tau}^{dn}(z_j)).$$

The value of a firm is given by:

$$\Omega_{\tau}^{d}(z_j) = \max_{\xi \in \{n,e\}} \Omega_{\tau}^{d\xi}(z_j) = \begin{cases} V_{\tau}^{de}(z_j) \; if \; z_j \geq \bar{z}_{\tau}^{d} \\ V_{\tau}^{dn}(z_j) if \;\; z_j < \bar{z}_{\tau}^{d} \end{cases},$$

and the expected value of a new entrant, owned by the domestic household, of vintage τ, $\mathbf{V}_{\tau}^{d}$ is: $\mathbf{V}_{\tau}^{d} = \int_{z_L}^{z_U} \Omega_{\tau}^{d}(z) G(dz)$. This completes the backward induction.

9A.2 Households

The home country is populated by a representative competitive household, which has recursive preferences over discounted streams of period utilities, derived from consumption of the aggregate good. Households can trade international bonds.

The domestic household maximizes:

$$\max U = \sum_{t=0}^{\infty} \beta^t u(C_t),$$

subject to

$$B_t = (1 + r_{t-1}^*) B_{t-1} + \frac{1}{\eta_t}\left(- C_t + \frac{W_t}{P_t} L \right) + \frac{1}{\eta_t}\left(\sum_{\sigma \leq t} (1-\delta)^{t-\sigma} n_{\sigma}^{d} \frac{\tilde{\Pi}_{\sigma,t}^{d}}{P_t} - \tilde{\chi}(n_t^d) \right) +$$
$$\left(\sum_{\sigma \leq t} (1-\delta)^{t-\sigma} n_{\sigma}^{f} \frac{\tilde{\Pi}_{\sigma,t}^{f}}{P_t^*} - \tilde{\chi}(n_t^f) \right) - \frac{\Psi_B}{2} B_t^2 + \mathcal{T}_t$$

where B_t is the real bond holding of the domestic household. Bonds are denominated in the foreign currency by our convention; however, since the model is deterministic, this assumption is completely innocent. C_t denotes consumption and r^*_{t-1} is the real interest rate of the internationally traded bond. The parameter Ψ_B represents adjustment portfolio costs to stabilize the model and $\mathcal{T}_t$ is the rebate of these costs in a lump-sum fashion to the household.

The number of new domestically located entrants owned by the domestic household in time t is n^d_t, while $\tilde{\chi}(n^d_t)$ presents the investment cost associated with entry of n^d_t entrants. Similarly, n^f_t denotes the number of new entrants in the foreign country owned by the domestic household. The associated costs are given as $\hat{\chi}(n^f_t)$. The two functions $\tilde{\chi}, \hat{\chi}$ differ by the parameters Ψ_d, Ψ_f only.

From the first-order conditions, the asset demand can be derived (see Brůha and Podpiera, 2007b):

$$(1 + \Psi_B B_t) = \frac{\eta_{t+1}}{\eta_t}(1 + r^*_t)\mu^{t+1}_t,$$

$$\tilde{c}^d_t + \Psi_d n^d_t = \sum_{v \geq 0}(1 - \delta)^v \mu^{t+v}_t \frac{\tilde{\Pi}^d_{t,t+v}}{P_{t+v}},$$

$$\eta_t(\tilde{c}^f_t + \Psi_f n^f_t) = \sum_{v \geq 0}(1 - \delta)^v \eta_{t+v} \mu^{t+v}_t \frac{\tilde{\Pi}^f_{t,t+v}}{P^*_{t+v}},$$

where the marginal rate of substitution between times t_1 and t_2 is defined as:

$$\mu^{t_2}_{t_1} \equiv \beta^{t_2 - t_1} \frac{u'(C_{t_2})}{u'(C_{t_1})}.$$

The part of the model related to the foreign household is derived analogously. Note that although there is idiosyncratic variance at the firm level, the uncertainty is cancelled at the aggregate level due to the law of large numbers. Thus, the household optimization is deterministic.

9A.3 General Equilibrium

The general equilibrium is defined as a time profile of prices and quantities such that all households optimize and all markets clear. The simulation of the dynamic path proved to be convenient for applications of efficient numerical methods if we rewrite the model in the recursive (first-order) form. See Brůha and Podpiera (2007b) for a discussion of a possible approach.

9A.4 A Note on the Real Exchange Rates

The prices p_{jt} and the corresponding price indexes P_t and P_t^* are quality-adjusted prices. Therefore, the real exchange rate η_t is measured in the terms of qualities. Due to imprecise quality adjustment in real-world price indexes, in order to obtain comparable indexes, we have to define aggregate indexes over prices pertaining to physical quantities. Let us denote such indexes as $\wp_t$ and $\wp_t^*$. One can use a simple approximation and set $\wp_t = \mathcal{K}_t P_t$, where $\mathcal{K}_t$ is the total amount of quality investment by firms selling their products in the domestic country:

$$\mathcal{K}_t = \sum_{\xi \in \{d,d^*\}} \int_{\Omega^\xi} k_{j\tau} d\Gamma_t^\xi(j,\tau) + \sum_{\xi \in \{f,f^*\}} \int_{\Omega_e^\xi} k_{j\tau} d\Gamma_t^\xi(j,\tau).$$

Nevertheless, $\wp_t$ might differ from the CPI-based real-world indexes by one more term. The market structure based on the CES aggregation implies the *love-for-variety* effect. Hence, the quality-unadjusted CPI-based real exchange rate (empirical real exchange rate) is the correct model counterpart of the *measured real exchange rate in reality* and is defined as:

$$\eta_t^e = \left(\frac{n_t^*}{n_t}\right)^{\frac{1}{\theta-1}} \frac{\mathcal{K}_t^*}{\mathcal{K}_t} \eta_t.$$

NOTES

1. Economist, External Economic Relations Division, Czech National Bank.
2. Director of External Economic Relations Division, Czech National Bank.
3. The index of price liberalization compiled by the European Bank for Reconstruction and Development (EBRD) shows that all these countries have liberalized prices to the level 3 that is comparable to advanced industrialized countries by 1993. Similarly, all these countries liberalized trade and foreign exchange until 1995 to the extent (level 4, EBRD index) considered as standard for advanced industrialized countries. And finally, both small- and large-scale privatization was completed (level 4, EBRD index) by 1995 and 1997, respectively. For a more extensive discussion of institutional foundation and reform implementation, see Roland (2004).

REFERENCES

Ahnert, H. and G. Kenny (2004), 'Quality adjustment of European price statistics and the role for hedonics', *Occasional ECB Working Paper* No. 15.

Brůha, J. and J. Podpiera (2007a), 'Transition economy convergence in a two-country model: implications for monetary integration', *ECB Working Paper* No. 740.

Brůha, J. and J. Podpiera (2007b), 'Inquiries on dynamics of transition economy convergence in a two-country model', *ECB Working Paper* No. 791.
Brůha, J. and J. Podpiera (2007c), 'Real exchange rate in emerging economies: the role of different investment margins', Czech National Bank, mimeo.
Cincibuch, M. and J. Podpiera (2006), 'Beyond Balassa-Samuelson: real appreciation in tradables in transition countries', *Economics of Transition*, **14** (3), 547–73.
Dury, K. and O. Oomen (2007), 'The real exchange rate and quality improvements', *Bank of England Working Paper* No. 320.
Égert, B., K. Lommatzsch and A. Lahrèche-Révil (2006), 'Real exchange rates in small open OECD and transition economies: comparing apples with oranges?', *Journal of Banking and Finance*, **30** (12), 3393–406.
Fabrizio, S., D. Igan and A. Mody (2007), 'The dynamics of product quality and international competitiveness', *IMF Working Paper* No. WP/07/97.
Flek, V., J. Podpiera and L. Markova (2003), 'Sectoral productivity and real exchange rate appreciation: much ado about nothing?', *Czech Journal of Economics and Finance*, **53** (3–4), 130–53.
Ghironi, F. and M. Melitz (2005), 'International trade and macroeconomic dynamics with heterogeneous firms', *Quarterly Journal of Economics*, **CXX** (August), 865–915.
Melitz, M. (2003), 'The impact of trade on intra-industry reallocation and aggregate industry productivity', *Econometrica*, **71** (6), 1695–725.
Mihaljek, D. and M. Klau (2006), 'The Balassa-Samuelson effect and the Maastricht criteria: revising the debate', in N. Batini (ed.), *Monetary Policy in Emerging Markets and Other Developing Countries*, IMF.
Obstfeld, M. and K. Rogoff (1995), 'Exchange rate dynamics redux', *Journal of Political Economy*, **103** (3), 624–60.
Roland, G. (2004), 'After enlargement: institutional achievements and prospects in the new member states', in C. Detken, V. Gaspar and G. Noblet (eds), *The New EU Member States Convergence and Stability*, proceedings of the Third ECB Central Banking Conference, 21–22 October 2004, pp. 35–58.

10. The impact of exchange rate interventions and communication over the medium term

Marcel Fratzscher[1]

10.1 INTRODUCTION

Since the mid-1980s, some monetary authorities, such as those in Japan, have periodically conducted substantial purchases or sales in FX markets, often supported by 'oral interventions'. Others, such as the US and euro area authorities, basically abandoned direct market interventions in the mid-1990s and have since relied on communication as their primary policy tool to affect exchange rates.

Assessing the success of those different routes, the literature on FX market interventions has found mixed and partly supportive evidence that FX purchases and sales may help move currencies in the desired direction (for example, Edison, 1993; Sarno and Taylor, 2001). More recently, policy makers (Rubin and Weisberg, 2003) have argued and academic research (for example, Fratzscher, 2004; Jansen and de Haan, 2005) has found that communication may have a significant impact on exchange rates. The literature on the role of communication, while still in its infancy, constitutes a first step towards understanding appropriate monetary policy design.

Two important questions arise from the literature that have not been answered conclusively yet. First, through which channels do oral and actual interventions affect exchange rate developments? Second, how effective are such interventions in the longer term?

From a conceptual perspective, interventions may affect exchange rates through three channels. First, through the portfolio balance channel: FX purchases or sales by a monetary authority alter the relative supply and demand of domestic versus foreign assets, thus altering the exchange rate even given sterilized interventions due to imperfect substitutability of the underlying assets (for example, Dominguez and Frankel, 1993). Second, through the signalling channel: actual or oral interventions may be perceived by markets as indicating future policy (measures) (Mussa, 1981;

Lewis, 1995; Kaminsky and Lewis, 1996; Bonser-Neal, Roley and Sellon, 1998). Exchange rate communication may also induce market participants to anticipate actual future interventions. Both these channels would imply that interventions have only a one-off and immediate effect on exchange rates if markets are efficient and incorporate all relevant information immediately.

From a market microstructure perspective, based on the work by Peiers (1997) and Evans and Lyons (2002), interventions may influence exchange rates also through a third channel, the coordination channel (Sarno and Taylor, 2001). Functioning as a coordination device for investors, actual and oral interventions may alter the dynamics of FX markets, implying dynamic and long-term effects on exchange rates. Evans and Lyons (2005) provide compelling evidence for a gradual incorporation of macroeconomic news into prices that takes several days. They relate this gradual absorption to the trading that takes place between end-users, such as hedge funds and mutual funds, as trading itself provides relevant information to market participants. This result is also consistent with Andersen et al. (2003), who find that volatility effects of news often rise over time and are quite persistent.

The question of key policy relevance is precisely how permanent and long-lasting intervention effects are. This chapter addresses this question empirically, by analysing the communication strategy of G-3 monetary authorities (the United States, Japan and the euro area), and by assessing its long-run effectiveness and actual interventions since 1990. The chapter starts by outlining how exchange rate communication is measured and classified. While any measurement and classification of communication is prone to be incomplete and to reflect imprecisely the intentions of policy makers, the aim is to take a financial market perspective and to understand how market participants react to (exchange rate) news that become available to them.

Whereas oral, and to some extent also actual, interventions are found to have a significant contemporaneous impact on G-3 exchange rates on the days authorities intervene, the effects cannot be shown to be statistically significant beyond two or three days (based on cumulated impulse responses obtained from an EGARCH[2] model specification). The chapter argues that this finding cannot be interpreted as evidence against long-term effectiveness of interventions; the effect of individual interventions is simply not sufficiently large to dominate all other factors that influence exchange rates. Even the impact of important macroeconomic news, such as announcements of US non-farm payroll employment and of the German Ifo business confidence index, cannot be shown to be statistically significant beyond a few days.

To gauge longer-term effectiveness, the final part of the chapter turns to forward-looking indicators of exchange rates. Two key results emerge. First, whereas exchange rate communication has a statistically significant effect on forward rates for a horizon up to six months, actual interventions do so only over a shorter horizon. Second, communication mostly reduces historical volatility of spot rates, based on the EGARCH specification, as well as the implied volatility of over-the-counter option contracts, whereas actual interventions mostly increase both types of volatility. These key differences may reflect the different ways in which interventions are conducted: actual interventions, often carried out in secret, induce a significant degree of uncertainty among market participants about whether interventions took place, how large they were and whether they are part of a longer series of interventions. By contrast, communication provides a public signal to all participants, thus possibly reducing the heterogeneity of information and beliefs and helping reduce volatility.

The chapter is structured as follows. The next section introduces the data, also discussing some caveats underlying communications data measurement. The third section presents the empirical results on the long-term effectiveness of interventions based on an EGARCH model for spot rates and option contracts. The fourth section concludes.

10.2 THE DATA: COMMUNICATION AND ACTUAL INTERVENTIONS

With regard to exchange rate communication, the first issue is how to measure it. Ideally, one would compile all statements in which policy makers express a view about the domestic exchange rate. Since the objective of this chapter is to measure whether such communication is successful in moving FX markets in the intended way, one should look in particular at all those statements that become available to market participants. Representing the most likely source of information, the newswire service Reuters News, was chosen as the source from which to extract all headline statements made by relevant G-3 policy makers since 1990. Since any one statement may be followed by several newswire reports, we made sure to include only the first reports published. In most cases, such reports are posted within minutes of a policy maker's statement. This allows conducting the empirical analysis using a daily frequency, with all exchange rate quotes used throughout the paper at 18:00 US Eastern Standard Time (EST).

A second issue was which policy makers to include in the analysis. In the United States and in Japan, exchange rate policy is in the realm of the Treasury and the Ministry of Finance, respectively. As officials at the Federal

Reserve and the Bank of Japan also occasionally make statements about the exchange rate, the list further includes the US Treasury Secretary, his deputy and the members of the FOMC (Federal Open Market Committee); and Japan's Minister of Finance and his deputy plus the Governor and two Vice Governors of the Bank of Japan.[3] For the United States, the great majority of statements extracted indeed comes from the Treasury officials, while relatively few come from the Federal Reserve. For instance, only seven statements were extracted for Chairman Greenspan for the entire 1990–2003 period.

By contrast, exchange rate policy in Europe has traditionally been the responsibility of the respective central banks, with finance ministry officials usually providing relatively few statements on the exchange rate overall. For the period starting with the establishment of the euro area in 1999, the 18 members of the Governing Council are included in the analysis; for the period 1990–98 the members of the Bundesbank Zentralbankrat.

Specifically, we extracted all statements fulfilling two sets of search criteria, namely the words 'exchange rate' or the given currency name; and the title or name of the relevant policy maker. In the third and most difficult step, content analysis (for example, Holsti, 1969; Kassarjian, 1977), it was necessary to classify the statements systematically depending on whether they support a stronger or a weaker domestic currency, or whether the policy maker is neutral, so that the classification is:

$$IO_t = \begin{cases} +1 & \textit{if `strengthening' oral statement} \\ 0 & \textit{if `ambiguous' oral statement} \\ +1 & \textit{if `weakening' oral statement} \end{cases}$$

Content analysis presupposes clear classification rules. We applied the four-eye principle and discarded all statements that had been classified differently. The more difficult statements to classify were often those by US policy makers attempting to weaken the US dollar, and those by euro area policy makers intended to weaken the euro or Deutschmark. As explained by Robert Rubin (Rubin and Weisberg, 2003), policy makers often tend to use very subtle and slight changes in their language to indicate a shift in policy. However, the advantage of using newswire reports is that they convey interpretations by professionals who are aware of these nuances and most experienced in interpreting such changes.

With regard to caveats for using such an analysis to extract a communication database, newswire reports may not reflect the true intention of the policy maker. Moreover, a further potential drawback is that not all statements may be reported, causing the extracted list to be incomplete. Yet given the objective of this chapter to analyse market reaction to communication, it seems sensible to focus only on those statements that actually

Table 10.1 Exchange rate communication, 1990–2003

	US		Japan		Euro Area	
	Strengthen	Weaken	Strengthen	Weaken	Strengthen	Weaken
Number of interventions						
1990–2003	125	30	66	71	77	37
1990–94	18	15	34	16	13	4
1995–98	31	5	16	4	3	15
1999–2003	76	10	16	51	61	18

Source: Reuters News, author's categorization.

become available to market participants, and Reuters News is among those providers who receive the greatest attention among traders and investors.

Table 10.1 and Figure 10.1 show the oral interventions by the three authorities since 1990. Most importantly, one can identify very distinct communication regimes over time. Whereas US authorities were more ambiguous about the USD exchange rate in the early 1990s, they have been pursuing a policy of supporting a strong US dollar since 1994, with a few exceptions. Similarly, the German and euro area authorities mostly supported a stronger domestic currency, though in particular in 1995/96 they attempted to push for a weaker Deutschmark. By contrast, the Japanese authorities mostly aimed at weakening the yen with a few notable exceptions, such as in 1997/98 and in the early 1990s.

Table 10.2 and Figure 10.2 show that US and euro area authorities basically stopped conducting interventions in August 1995, with the mentioned exception of September and November 2000, while Japanese authorities intensified interventions in 2003 and early 2004. Moreover, the magnitude of the interventions by the Bank of Japan has increased substantially in recent years. The average daily intervention in the period 1999–2003 was around USD 3.2 billion – or about eight times larger than the roughly USD 400 million average interventions in the period 1990–94. In 2003 alone, Japanese authorities bought around USD 180 billion to weaken the yen, and around USD 140 billion in the first quarter of 2004.

10.3 LONG-TERM EFFECTIVENESS OF INTERVENTIONS

Do communication and actual interventions move exchange rates? And if so, does this imply that such interventions have a long-term effect? This

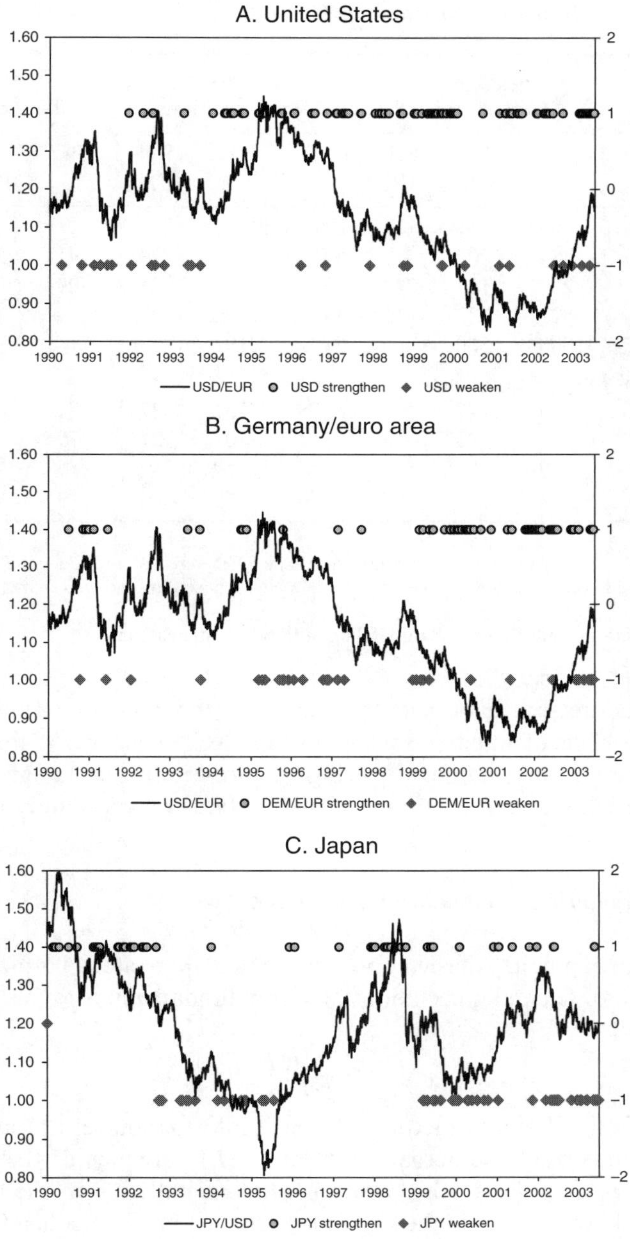

Source: Author's estimations.

Figure 10.1 Exchange rate communication

Table 10.2 Actual interventions, 1990–2003

	USA All interventions			Japan All interventions			Euro Area All interventions		
	All	Buy FX	Sell FX	All	Buy FX	Sell FX	All	Buy FX	Sell FX
Magnitude of interventions (average, USD million)									
1990–2003	284	202	323	1554	1697	223	1591	2589	617
1990–94	203	125	242	385	427	223	1709	2811	634
1995–98	821	833	819	1706	1706	–	419	419	–
1999–2003	1500	1500	–	3192	3192	–	n/a	–	n/a
Number of intervention days									
1990–2003	84	27	57	278	251	27	87	43	44
1990–94	74	25	49	131	104	27	79	39	40
1995–98	9	1	8	59	59	0	4	4	0
1999–2003	1	1	0	88	88	0	4	0	4

Note: Amounts for the actual interventions of the ECB were not announced. The numbers used here are those reported by Reuters News, based on financial market reports.

Sources: US Federal Reserve, Bank of Japan, Bundesbank, Reuters.

section addresses this issue by analysing the contemporaneous and dynamic effects of interventions in an EGARCH framework, first for the spot exchange rate, and then by using forward-looking exchange rate indicators based on over-the-counter (OTC) option contracts and other asset prices.

10.3.1 Empirical Methodology and Hypotheses

As the starting point, the evolution of the exchange rate (s_t) is modelled as a function of agents' expectations of future fundamentals f_{t+i}:

$$s_t = (1 - \theta) \sum_{i=0}^{\infty} \theta^i E_t(f_{t+i} | \Omega_t) \tag{10.1}$$

where θ is the discount factor and Ω_t the information set at time t. Oral interventions (IO_t) and actual intervention (IA_t) are part of the information set Ω_t, as well as other relevant fundamentals X_t. In the empirical framework, the change in the log spot exchange rate (Δs_t) is therefore modelled as a function of the difference in interest rates between the two countries (i^*–i), both types of interventions, fundamentals and day-of-the-week effects (W_t):

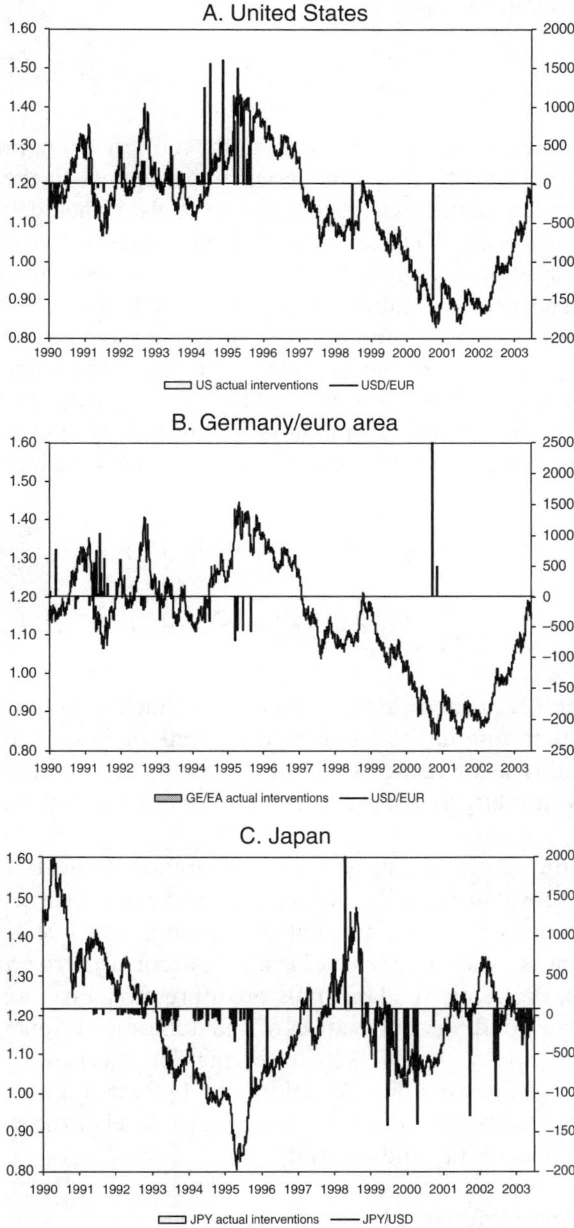

Source: Author's estimations.

Figure 10.2 Actual FX interventions

$$\Delta s_t^{USD/EUR} = \alpha + \delta\,(i_t^{US} - i_t^{EA}) + \sum_d \eta^d W_t^d + \sum_l \chi^l X_t^l$$
$$+ \sum_j (\beta^j IA_t^j + \gamma^j IO_t^j) + \varepsilon_t \quad j = US,EA, \qquad (10.2)$$

which constitutes the estimation equation for the conditional mean of the USD–EUR exchange rate; an analogous model applies to the JPY–USD exchange rate. The set of macroeconomic controls X_t includes a broad set of 12 US, ten euro area/German and ten Japanese news items.

For daily data, the change in the log exchange rate exhibits strong non-normality, in particular significant heteroskedasticity with $\varepsilon_t \sim (0,h_t)$, excess kurtosis and skewness. A commonly employed way to correct for this is to model the conditional second moment explicitly using some form of a GARCH(1,1) model. Here I use an EGARCH(1,1) specification of Nelson (1991), which has the advantage that no non-negativity constraints on the coefficients of the conditional second moments need to be imposed:

$$\log(h_t) = \tau + \omega\left(\left|\frac{\varepsilon_{t-1}}{\sqrt{h_{t-1}}}\right| - \sqrt{2/\pi}\right) + \phi\log(h_{t-1}) + \kappa\left(\frac{\varepsilon_{t-1}}{\sqrt{h_{t-1}}}\right)$$
$$+ \sum_j \left(\mu^j \left|IA_t^j\right| + \lambda^j \left|IO_t^j\right|\right) + \sum_d \xi^d W_t^d \quad j = US,EA \qquad (10.3)$$

The model is estimated using a standard log likelihood function. While part of the literature has focused on the effects of interventions on FX market volatility using related GARCH or other frameworks,[4] the results shown below are largely robust to using alternative specifications of the model.

The hypotheses concerning the contemporaneous effects of interventions (I_t) are shown in Table 10.3. First, in an efficient market setting, selling foreign exchange or credible communication in support of the domestic currency (that is, when markets believe that it conveys true and relevant signals about economic fundamentals or future monetary policy) should lead to a corresponding appreciation of the domestic currency. Second, a credible intervention should help lower market uncertainty and hence reduce exchange rate volatility. And third, an intervention that is not credible is expected to have no significant effect on the level of the exchange rate while raising uncertainty and volatility.

10.3.2 Evidence from Spot Exchange Rates

I first turn to the empirical results of the model based on spot exchange rates for daily data over the period 1990–2003. As outlined in Table 10.3,

Table 10.3 Hypotheses of contemporaneous effects of actual and oral interventions

	US dollar–Euro		Yen–US dollar	
	Conditional mean	Conditional variance	Conditional mean	Conditional variance
Credible	$\beta_1^{EA}, \gamma_1^{EA} > 0$	$\mu_1^{EA}, \lambda_1^{EA} \leq 0$	$\beta_2^{JA}, \gamma_2^{JA} < 0$	$\mu_2^{JA}, \lambda_2^{JA} \leq 0$
Intervention I_t	$\beta_1^{US}, \gamma_1^{US} < 0$	$\mu_1^{US}, \lambda_1^{US} \leq 0$	$\beta_2^{US}, \gamma_2^{US} > 0$	$\mu_2^{US}, \lambda_2^{US} \leq 0$
Not credible or ambiguous	$\beta_1^{EA}, \gamma_1^{EA} = 0$	$\mu_1^{EA}, \lambda_1^{EA} > 0$	$\beta_2^{JA}, \gamma_2^{JA} = 0$	$\mu_2^{JA}, \lambda_2^{JA} > 0$
Intervention I_t	$\beta_1^{US}, \gamma_1^{US} = 0$	$\mu_1^{US}, \lambda_1^{US} > 0$	$\beta_2^{US}, \gamma_2^{US} = 0$	$\mu_2^{US}, \lambda_2^{US} > 0$

Source: Author's estimations.

parameters β and γ in the conditional mean equation (10.2) measure the contemporaneous effect of oral and actual interventions by the respective authorities. The results, shown in Table 10.4, are controlled for the macroeconomic news X_t, day-of-the-week effects W_t and the interest rate differential.

The key result is that both oral and actual interventions by the G-3 authorities have a highly significant contemporaneous effect on the exchange rate on the day they occur. On average, communication moves the daily exchange rate by between 0.14 per cent and 0.22 per cent. By contrast, the impact of FX interventions varies substantially: an intervention by German authorities of USD 1 billion moved the exchange rate by about 1.1 per cent, whereas US interventions only had a significant effect on the JPY–USD exchange rate. The smallest effect of FX interventions are those by the Bank of Japan where a USD 1 billion purchase or sale moved the exchange rate by a mere 0.087 per cent. This is very similar to the contemporaneous effect found by Ito (2002).

However, as mentioned above, US and euro area authorities basically stopped intervening in August 1995, whereas Japanese authorities continued and even intensified their interventions in 2003 and early 2004, purchasing around USD 180 billion in 2003 and about USD 140 billion in the first quarter of 2004. Hence, the smaller effect of Japanese interventions may merely reflect the fact that the rapid rise in financial integration and in trading volumes in FX markets require larger interventions to move the exchange rate by the desired magnitude. To provide a yardstick, the purchase of USD 180 billion by Japanese authorities in 2003, and given a point estimate of 0.087, implies that Japanese interventions helped to weaken the yen by more than 15 per cent on a cumulative basis.

Table 10.4 Impact effect of interventions on spot exchange rate

	Cond. Mean Eq.[a]		Cond. Variance Eq.[a]	
	Coef.	*Std. error*	Coef.	*Std. error*
A. USD–EUR exchange rate				
US oral intervention IO^{US}	−0.144**	*0.072*	−0.026*	*0.014*
GE/EA oral intervention $IO^{GE/EA}$	0.216**	*0.101*	−0.031**	*0.014*
US actual intervention IA^{US}	−0.505	*0.309*	0.044	*0.052*
GE/EA actual intervention $IA^{GE/EA}$	1.125***[d]	*0.286*	0.556***	*0.134*
Interest rate differential[b]	–0.002	*0.006*		
LR test[c]	8.356***			
B. JPY–USD exchange rate				
US oral intervention IO^{US}	0.143***	*0.067*	−0.016*	*0.008*
JA oral intervention IO^{JA}	−0.142***	*0.051*	−0.007	*0.016*
US actual intervention IA^{US}	1.150***	*0.390*	0.398	*0.298*
JA actual intervention IA^{JA}	−0.087***	*0.012*	0.822***	*0.119*
Interest rate differential[b]	0.014	*0.072*		
LR test[c]	8.200***			

Notes:
a. Results are based on an EGARCH model and controlled for macroeconomic news.
b. The interest rate differential for the USD–EUR (JPY–USD) exchange rate is the difference between US and euro area (Japanese) three-month money market rates.
c. Tests whether a model with intervention variables has a higher explanatory power than a model without intervention variables.
d. ***, **, * indicate significance at the 99%, 95%, 90% levels, respectively.

Source: Author's estimations.

The results for the macroeconomic news X_t and day-of-the-week effects W_t are statistically significant in several cases and confirm the results commonly found in the literature (for example, Andersen et al., 2003; Ehrmann and Fratzscher, 2005). They are not shown for reasons of brevity since they are included as controls and our focus is on the impact of oral and actual interventions. The interest rate differential is never significant, and this holds also when including first differences of interest rates rather than the differential in equation (10.2).

A number of robustness checks were conducted. The first set of columns in Table 10.5 shows the contemporaneous effects when using indicator functions for both oral and actual interventions, coding them as +1 if they attempt to strengthen the domestic currency and –1 if they aim at weakening it. This specification thus makes the effects of communication and actual interventions more directly comparable. As expected, the point estimates for actual interventions are somewhat less statistically significant,

Table 10.5 *Robustness tests of impact effect of interventions on spot exchange rate*

	Other IA Definition[a]		Sub-sample: Pre-1996	
	Coef.	*Std. error*	Coef.	*Std. error*
A. USD–EUR exchange rate				
US oral intervention IO^{US}	−0.144**	*0.071*	−0.155***	*0.055*
GE/EA oral intervention $IO^{GE/EA}$	0.216**	*0.101*	0.186**	*0.091*
US actual intervention IA^{US}	−0.109	*0.204*	−0.548	*0.358*
GE/EA actual intervention $IA^{GE/EA}$	0.149*	*0.076*	1.088***	*0.306*
Interest rate differential[b]	−0.003	*0.006*	−0.002	*0.007*
LR test[c]	8.026***[d]		8.859***	
B. JPY–USD exchange rate				
US oral intervention IO^{US}	0.143***	*0.067*	0.139**	*0.070*
JA oral intervention IO^{JA}	−0.142***	*0.051*	−0.130***	*0.058*
US actual intervention IA^{US}	0.129**	*0.063*	1.194***	*0.436*
JA actual intervention IA^{JA}	−0.044*	*0.025*	−0.435***	*0.330*
Interest rate differential[b]	0.010	*0.042*	0.020	*0.079*
LR test[c]	7.923**		8.296***	

Notes:
a. Results are based on an EGARCH model where *IA* is an indicator function being + 1 for purchases and –1 for sales of the domestic currency.
b. The interest rate differential for USD–EUR (JPY–USD) exchange rate is the difference between US and euro area (Japanese) three-month money market rates.
c. Tests whether a model with intervention variables has a higher explanatory power than a model without intervention variables.
d. ***, **, * indicate significance at the 99%, 95%, 90% levels, respectively.

Source: Author's estimations.

given that the magnitudes of interventions are ignored. The key result is that the point estimates of actual interventions are somewhat smaller than those of oral interventions, which implies that, overall, the contemporaneous effects of both types of interventions are roughly comparable.

Furthermore, the data were tested for significant changes over the sample period. The second set of columns of Table 10.5 shows the results when estimating the model only over the period 1990–95. Estimating the model for the period 1996–2003 is problematic as the United States and Germany/the euro area never intervened during that period (see Section 10.2). The results for the period 1990–95 show that there were little or no changes in the impact of communication over time as the point estimates for oral interventions are very similar for the first sub-period as compared with the whole period. Moreover, the coefficient of Japanese FX interventions is substantially higher in the earlier period. What this implies is that actual interventions nowadays need to be much larger to have the same desired effect on the exchange rate. This is not surprising as FX markets today are indeed substantially deeper than 10–15 years ago.

A potentially important caveat to all estimations is that interventions may inherently be endogenous, that is, they may not only alter current and future exchange rate movements, but they react to past exchange rate movements or trends. Kearns and Rigobon (2004) suggest a methodology for correcting for such an endogeneity bias by modelling directly the potential behaviour and reaction of central banks on the days they intervene. However, it is not clear to what extent and over what horizons policy makers react to past exchange rate developments. Moreover, the literature (for example, Sarno and Taylor, 2001) has shown that, in particular, actual interventions tend to be of the leaning-against-the-wind type, going against the previous exchange rate trend. This implies that if endogeneity really constituted a bias, it would be a downward bias, and the true effect of communication and actual interventions may even be somewhat larger.

10.3.3 Dynamic Effects of Interventions

Given the contemporaneous effects shown in Tables 10.4 and 10.5, the central question is how permanent and long-lasting these effects are. One way of analysing the permanence of the effects is to formulate the mean equation in a dynamic context to test whether oral and actual interventions have a lagged effect on future exchange rate movements:

$$\Delta s_t^{USD/EUR} = \alpha + \delta\,(i_t^{US} - i_t^{EA}) + \sum_d \eta^d W_t^d + \sum_l \chi^l X_t^l$$
$$+ \sum_{k=0}^{T} \sum_j (\beta_k^j IA_{t-k}^j + \gamma_k^j IO_{t-k}^j) + \varepsilon_t \quad j = US, EA, \qquad (10.4)$$

which is identical to the model of equation (10.2), only that now it is tested whether interventions have a significant effect on the exchange rate up to an order of $t = 40$ days. I then estimate the cumulated impulse responses:

$$H_0\colon \sum_k \beta_k = 0, \ \sum_k \gamma_k = 0$$

Figures 10.3 and 10.4 show the responses of the USD–EUR and the JPY–USD exchange rates to different types of intervention events (contemporaneous response with up to 40 lags) and their 90 per cent confidence bands. Two key results stand out from the cumulated impulse responses.

First, for several interventions the point estimate of the effect remains relatively stable and changes little over time. In other words, the largest effect of interventions on exchange rates is the contemporaneous one, while exchange rates seem to be unaffected by interventions thereafter. This suggests that markets are indeed efficient in incorporating the information from interventions into prices on the day interventions occur. Moreover, the effects of interventions on exchange rates appear *economically* meaningful, as discussed above for Table 10.4.

The second key result is that *statistically* the effect of interventions becomes insignificant after a few days, usually after two to three days, in those cases where the contemporaneous effect is significant. This does not seem surprising as many different pieces of news affect exchange rates every day, so that interventions clearly cannot be said to be dominant but are only one source of important factors driving exchange rates.

An alternative way of testing the duration of intervention effects on exchange rates is to use different time windows for the model (10.2)–(10.3), such as two-day returns, three-day returns and so on, for the change in the log spot exchange rate (Δs_t). The results, however, are qualitatively very similar to those using cumulated impulse responses, and are not shown here for reasons of brevity.

To allow for a comparison with other factors driving exchange rates, Figure 10.5 shows the cumulated impulse responses for two of the most important macroeconomic news, US non-farm payroll employment releases and the Ifo business confidence indicator for the euro area.[5] Again, the macroeconomic news have a highly statistically significant contemporaneous effect on exchange rates, which disappears beyond a few days after the release of these news.

In summary, the evidence based on time-series analysis suggests the presence of a significant contemporaneous effect of both oral and actual interventions on exchange rates. However, statistically this effect becomes insignificant after a few days. This does not necessarily imply that interventions do not have a permanent, long-run effect, but merely that news reported in the days after interventions do not allow empirically measuring the permanent effect precisely.

10.3.4 Evidence from Forward Rates and OTC Option Contracts

Clearly, the problem of obtaining the true permanent or long-run effect of oral and actual interventions of equation (10.2) is that other news reported in the days after an intervention introduce 'noise' that render the point estimates statistically insignificant after a few days. An alternative way of assessing the long-run effectiveness of interventions is to look at purely

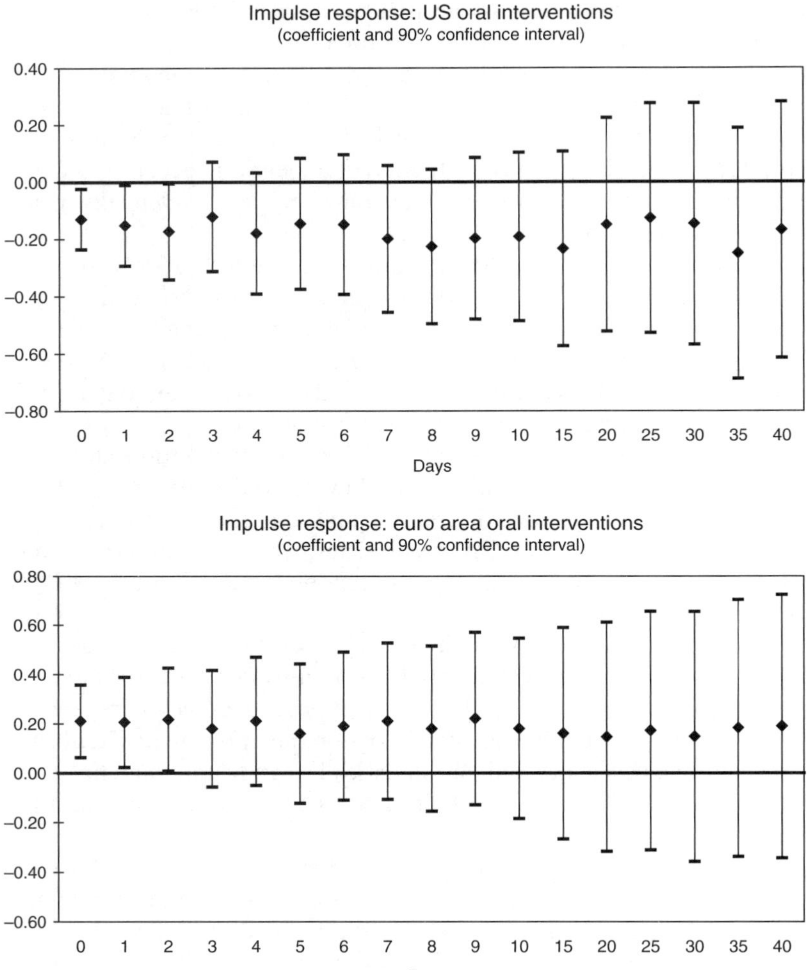

Source: Author's estimations.

Figure 10.3 Cumulated impulse responses of US and euro area interventions, USD–EUR exchange rate

forward-looking asset prices. This sub-section analyses intervention effects on OTC option contracts ranging from one day to one year in their horizon. The effect of communication and of actual interventions on such contracts over various horizons provides an indirect measure of their long-term effectiveness. All estimates presented in the sub-section are based on

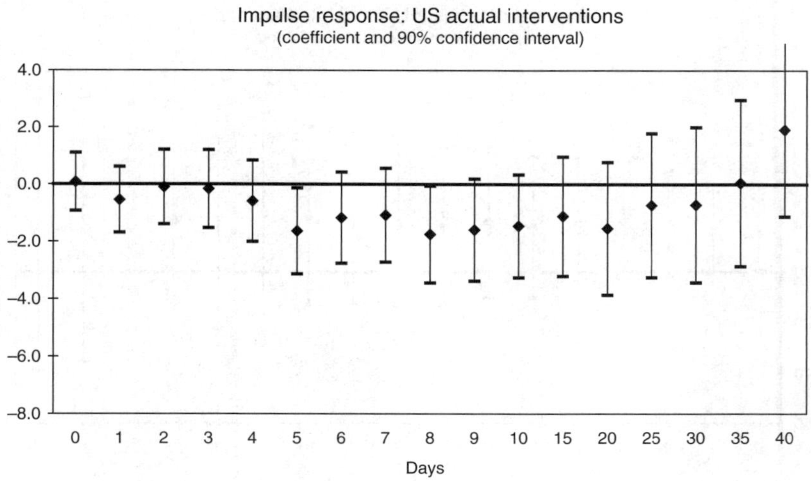

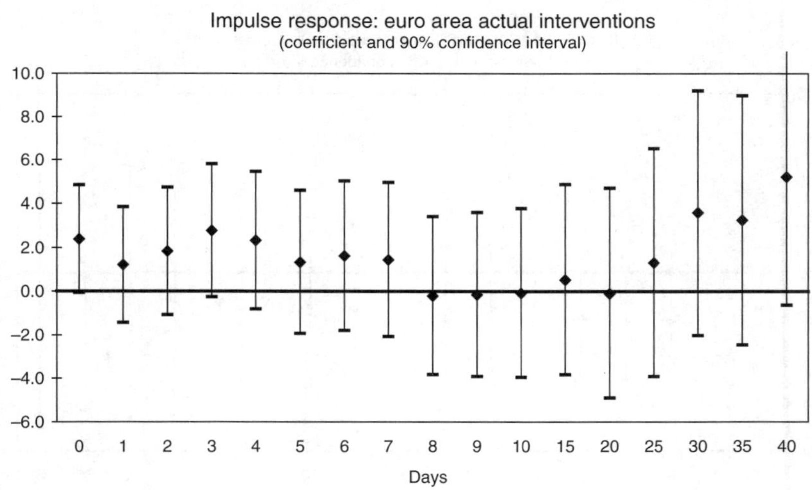

Figure 10.3 (continued)

the same specification as equation (10.2), only that the independent variable uses the first difference of the respective forward or option contract.

In more detail, we use the option contracts for the USD–EUR and the JPY–USD options of Citigroup, one of the largest players in these OTC markets. Moreover, OTC currency markets are substantially larger, with a substantially higher trading volume than that of FX-traded option

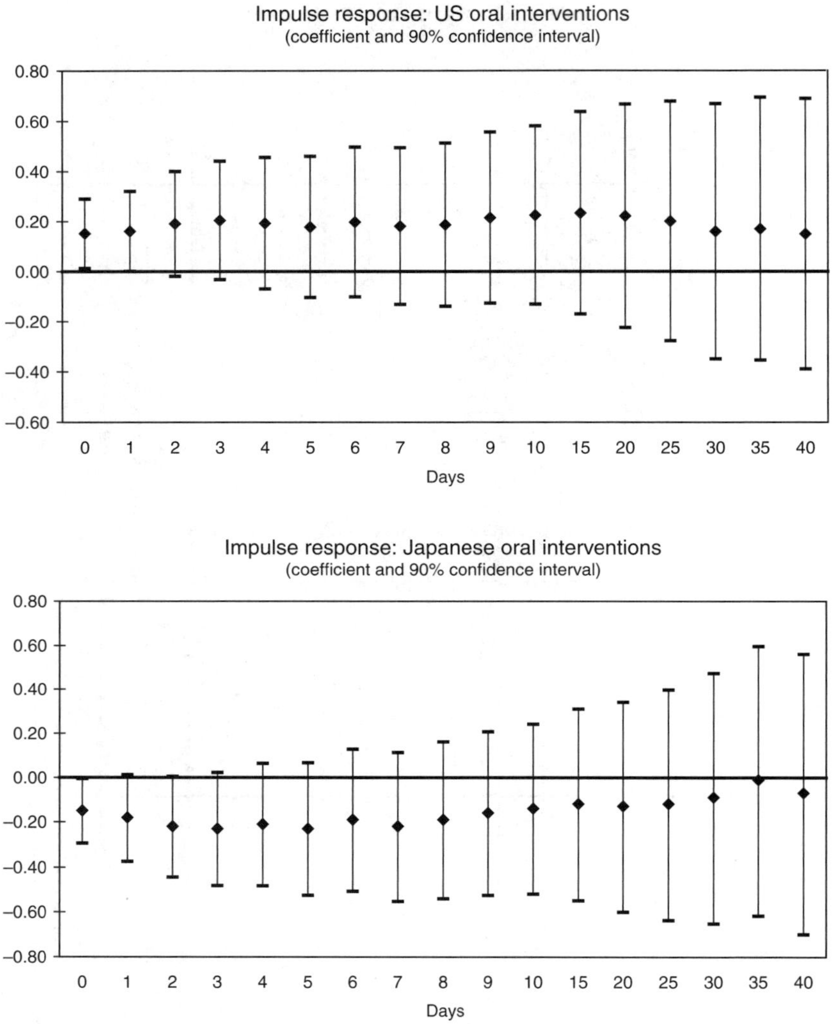

Source: Author's estimations.

Figure 10.4 Cumulated impulse responses of US and Japanese interventions, JPY–USD exchange rate

contracts. An additional advantage of the OTC contracts is that their daily quotes are based on fixed moneyness, that is, the distance between the strike price of the option with the corresponding forward rate. By contrast, quotes from FX-traded options are usually based on the distance between

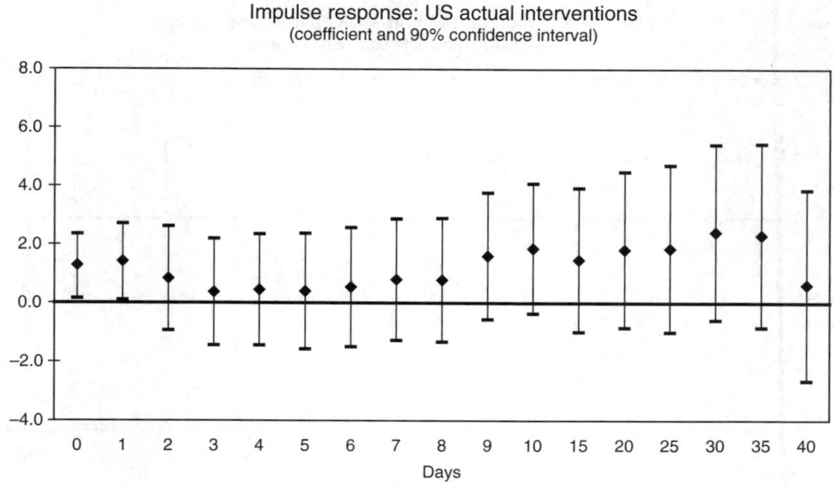

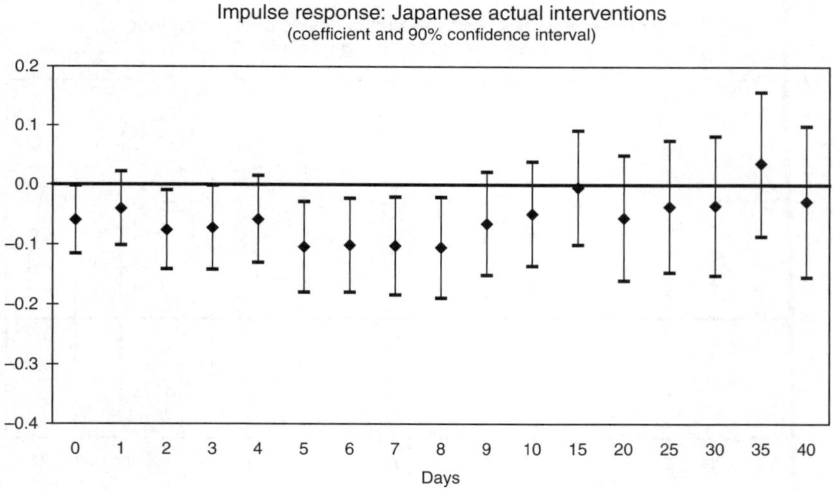

Figure 10.4 (continued)

fixed strike prices and time-varying forward contracts so that the horizon of the quotes varies over time.

Finally, this sub-section looks at different types of OTC contracts. In addition to forward rates, the OTC contracts analysed are implied volatilities, risk reversals and strangles. In contrast to the backward-looking volatility measure obtained from conditional variance equation (10.3) of the

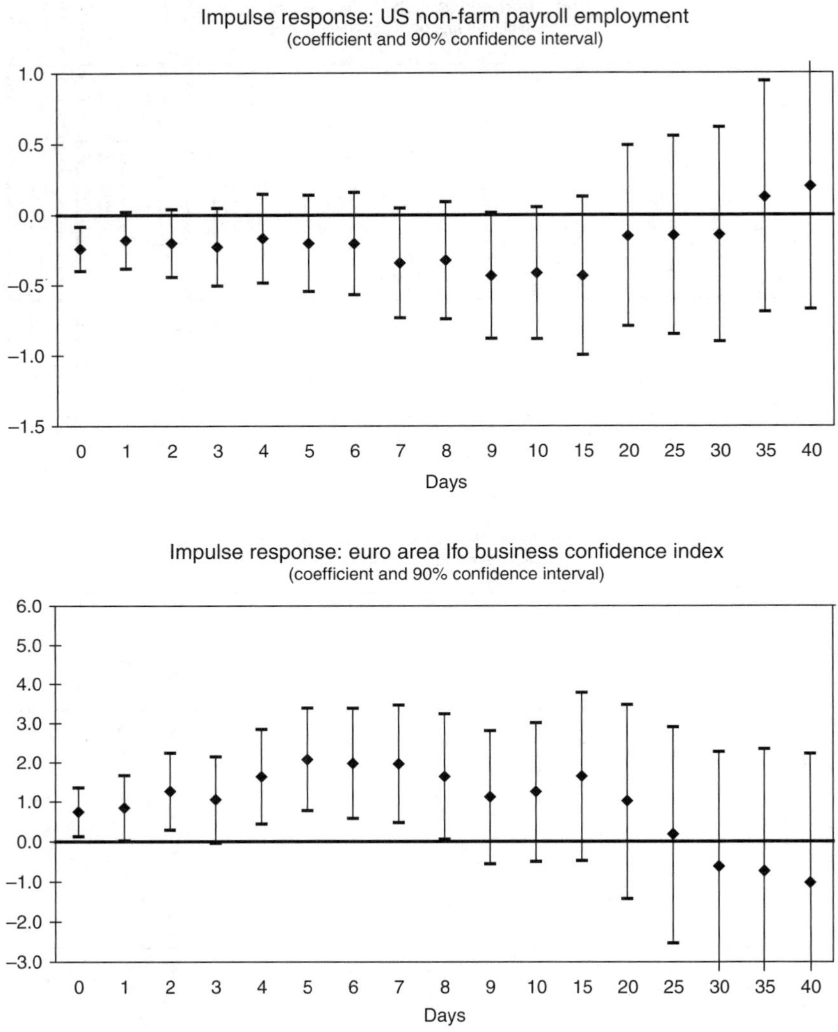

Source: Author's estimations.

Figure 10.5 Cumulated impulse responses of selected macroeconomic news, USD–EUR exchange rate

EGARCH model, the implied volatility is a purely forward-looking measure that reflects the degree of uncertainty among market participants about the exchange rate outlook. Risk reversals and strangles combine different types of options. A risk reversal is a simultaneous sale of an out-of-the-money put option and purchase of an out-of-the-money call option. It provides a positioning indicator about market expectations about the future direction of the exchange rate. As an example, a positive price of a USD–EUR risk reversal contract indicates that markets are long in euro and thus put a larger probability on a euro appreciation. By contrast, a strangle combines the simultaneous purchase of an out-of-the-money call option and an out-of-the-money put option. It provides a proxy for expectations about large future exchange rate movements.[6]

In short, these option contracts provide different and mutually complementary information about how communication and actual interventions may affect expectations of exchange rate movements and underlying risks over the medium to long run. As a starting point, Figures 10.6 and 10.7 show the response of forward contracts with horizons ranging from one day to one year to oral and actual interventions in the USD–EUR market (Figure 10.6) and the JPY–USD market (Figure 10.7). In all cases the forward rates of contracts with shorter maturities react more strongly to oral and actual interventions than those with longer maturities. A key finding of the analysis is that forward rates of up to and including six months react statistically significantly to communication from US and euro area authorities. By contrast, actual interventions affect forward rates only of at most one month for the JPY–USD exchange rate, and even only one week for the USD–EUR exchange rate.

Overall, a first key finding therefore is that communication affects forward rates over a longer horizon than actual interventions. This may be interpreted as evidence in favour of the long-term, or at least medium-term, effectiveness of exchange rate communication. However, as a caveat it should be recalled that actual interventions tend to lean against the exchange rate trend relatively more often than exchange rate communication. Hence, at least part of this difference may be explained by the different conditions under which oral and actual interventions take place.

The next step of the analysis focuses on the different option contracts – implied volatility, risk reversal and strangle – as outlined above. Table 10.6 shows the results for both types of interventions and for both USD–EUR and JPY–USD exchange rates. The central finding is that communication tends to *reduce* implied volatility in most cases whereas actual interventions *raise* implied volatility. This implies that communication tends to lower market uncertainty, whereas actual interventions increase it. This is consistent with the finding of Table 10.4 on historical volatility from the EGARCH model. It underlines a fundamental difference between communication versus actual interventions.

One possible explanation for this finding may arise from the very different ways official statements about the exchange rate and actual interventions are

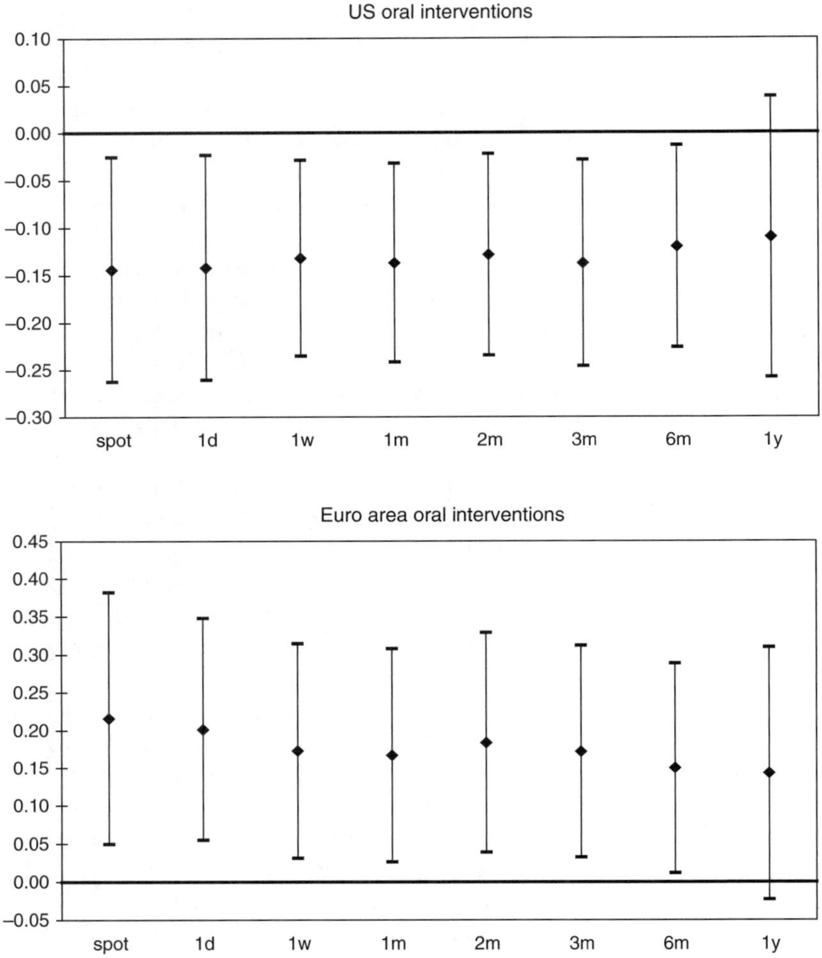

Source: Author's estimations.

Figure 10.6 Effect of interventions on forward exchange rates, USD–EUR

made. On the one hand, communication is available to all market participants in the same way and the great majority of market participants may interpret a statement in the same way. Hence, exchange rate communication that is considered to offer relevant information tends to reduce the heterogeneity of beliefs among market participants and thus lowers market volatility. On the other hand, actual interventions are mostly conducted in secret, without policy makers announcing that such interventions have

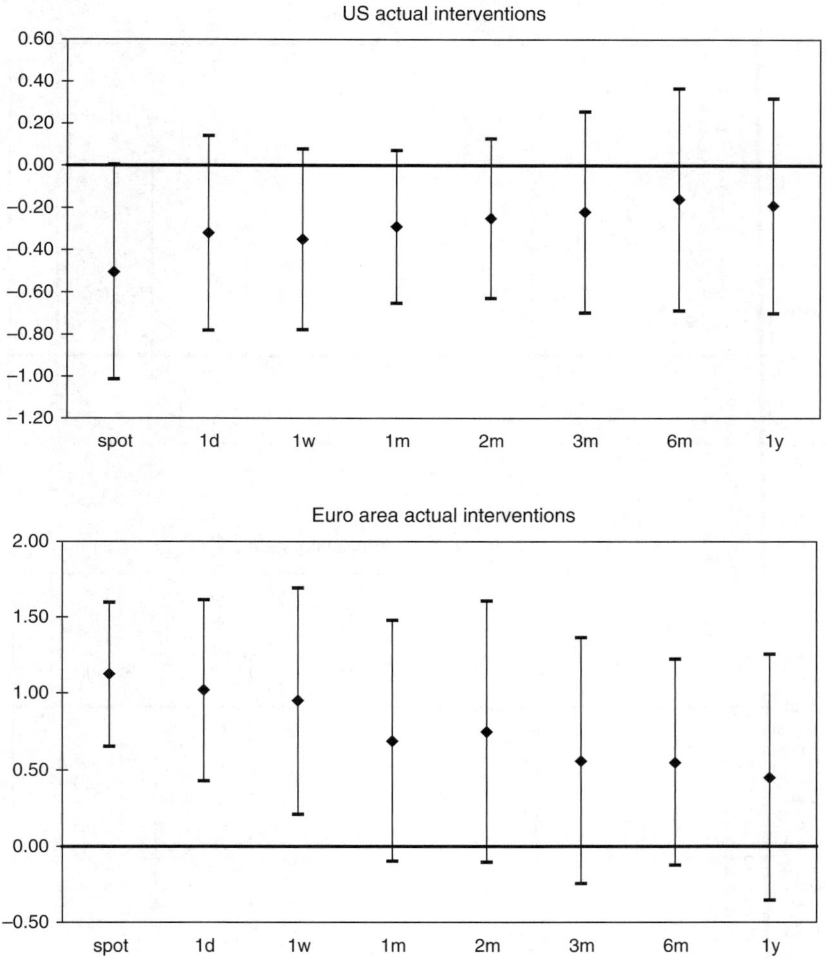

Figure 10.6 (continued)

taken place. Although many market participants may have an indication that an actual intervention by a central bank has occurred, views about the scale, frequency and likelihood of future interventions may differ widely across market participants. Hence, one may indeed expect such actual interventions to raise the degree of market uncertainty.

Finally, Table 10.7 shows the response of other asset prices – equity returns, short-term and long-term interest rates – to communication and actual interventions. While there is some modest reaction of equity markets

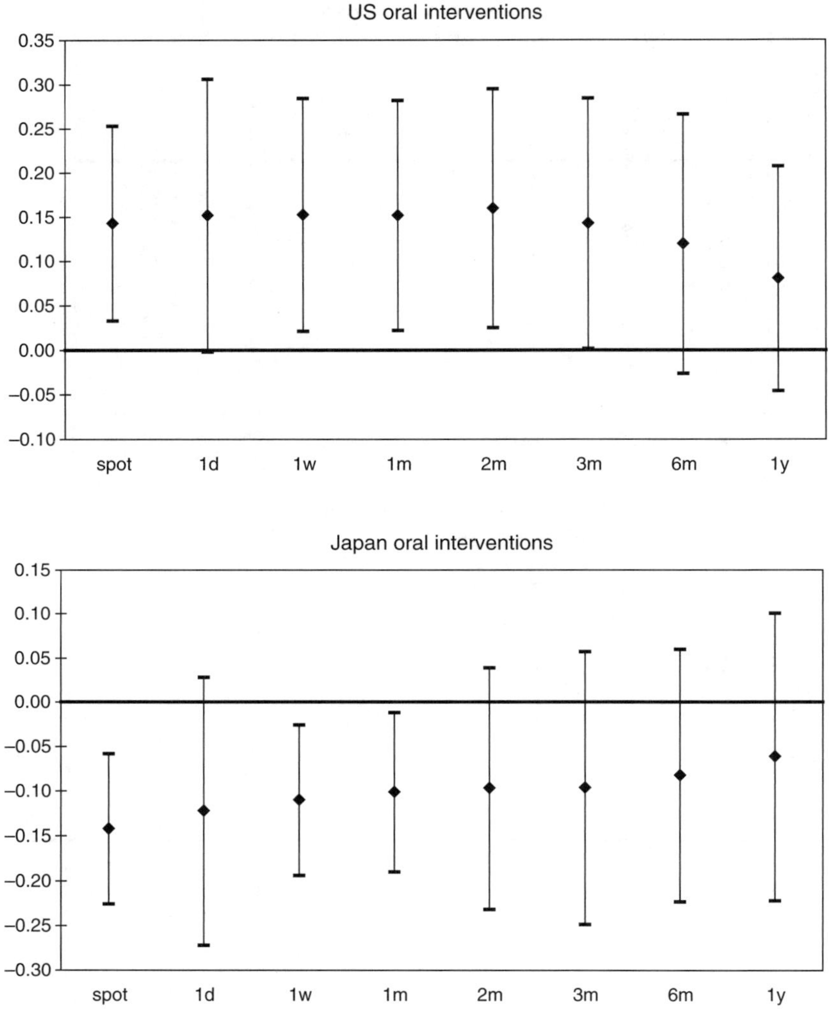

Source: Author's estimations.

Figure 10.7 Effect of interventions on forward exchange rates, JPY–USD

to US oral and actual interventions, neither short-term nor long-term interest rates respond significantly to either communication or actual interventions. One interpretation of this finding is that market participants do not see either type of intervention as providing a signal for future monetary policy decisions so that interest rates remain broadly unchanged.

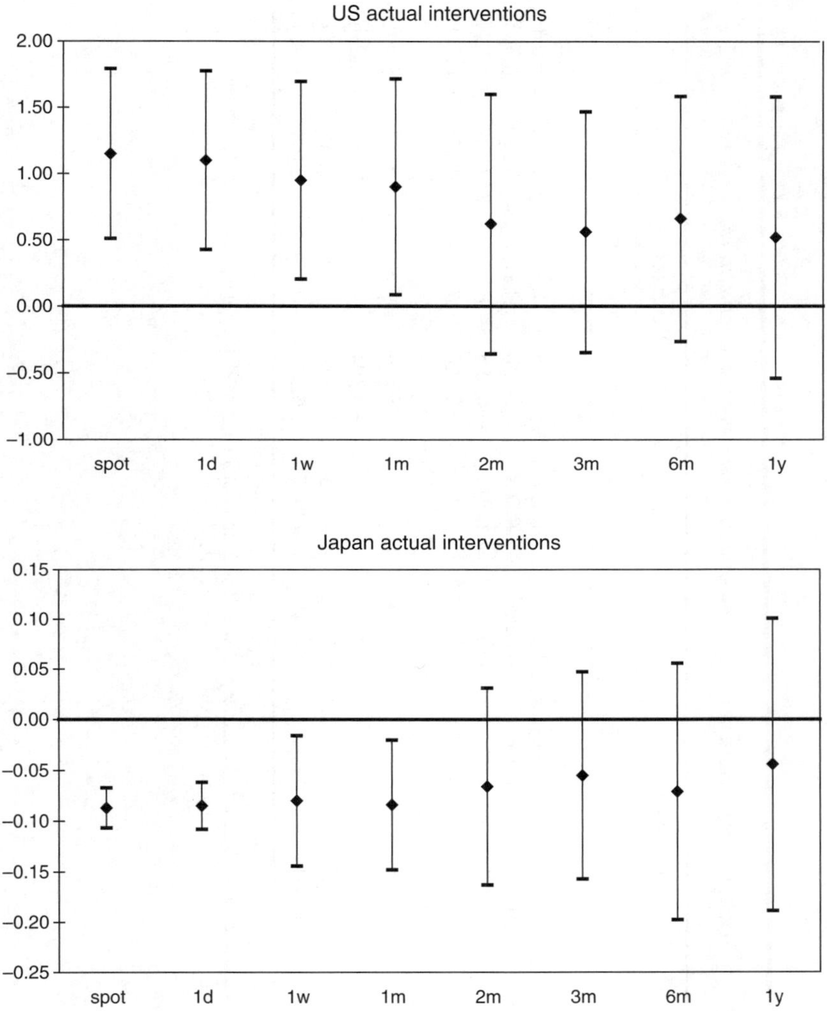

Figure 10.7 (continued)

10.4 CONCLUSIONS

Communication and actual interventions are two direct policy tools monetary authorities have to influence exchange rate developments. Over the past two decades, several monetary authorities, in particular those in the United States and in the euro area, basically abandoned the use of actual

Table 10.6 Impact effect of interventions on forward-looking (one-month) exchange rate indicators

	Forward Rate		Implied Volatility		Risk Reversal		Strangle	
	Coef.	*Std. error*	Coef.	*Std. error*	Coef.	*Std. error*	Coef.	*Std. error*
A. USD–EUR exchange rate								
US oral intervention IO^{US}	−0.137**	*0.064*	−0.235***	*0.098*	−1.569	*5.465*	−0.184	*0.690*
GE/EA oral intervention $IO^{GE/EA}$	0.167*	*0.086*	−0.606***	*0.198*	−2.380	*3.213*	0.529	*0.648*
US actual intervention IA^{US}	−0.291	*0.224*	0.057***	*0.017*	−0.985	*0.926*	0.188	*0.236*
GE/EA actual intervention $IA^{GE/EA}$	0.691	*0.483*	0.237***	*0.035*	−0.466	*0.696*	0.228	*0.199*
B. JPY–USD exchange rate								
US oral intervention IO^{US}	0.152*	*0.079*	−0.391*	*0.197*	−1.110	*1.810*	0.391	*0.329*
JA oral intervention IO^{JA}	−0.101*	*0.054*	−0.279	*0.239*	−0.394	*0.623*	0.088	*0.236*
US actual intervention IA^{US}	0.906**	*0.495*	0.132	*0.095*	−0.912	*0.691*	0.201	*0.611*
JA actual intervention IA^{JA}	−0.081**	*0.039*	0.194**	*0.092*	−0.323*	*0.161*	0.096	*0.364*

Note: ***, **, * indicate significance at the 99%, 95%, 90% levels, respectively. The estimation of the model is done analogously to models (10.4)–(10.5) for spot rates. As implied volatility takes only positive values, the absolute values of the communication and actual intervention variables are used.

Source: Author's estimations.

Table 10.7 Impact effect of interventions on other asset prices

	Equity Market		Short Interest Rates		Long Interest Rates	
	Coef.	*Std. error*	Coef.	*Std error*	Coef.	*Std. error*
US oral intervention IO^{US}	0.219**	*0.109*	0.008	*0.041*	0.005	*0.005*
GE/EA oral intervention $IO^{GE/EA}$	0.119*	*0.056*	0.013	*0.023*	−0.001	*0.006*
JA oral intervention IO^{JA}	−0.050	*0.168*	−0.004	*0.004*	−0.002	*0.007*
US actual intervention IA^{US}	0.198*	*0.091*	0.003	*0.002*	0.004	*0.004*
GE/EA actual intervention $IA^{GE/EA}$	−0.094	*0.154*	0.004	*0.005*	−0.015	*0.065*
JA actual intervention IA^{JA}	0.154	*0.091*	0.001	*0.001*	0.001	*0.001*

Note: ***, **, * indicate significance at the 99%, 95%, 90% levels, respectively.

Source: Author's estimations.

purchases and sales in FX markets in the mid-1990s and have since relied almost exclusively on communication to alter exchange rate developments. Others, such as the Japanese authorities, have gone through periods in which they intensified both actual interventions and exchange rate communication.

Focusing on the G-3 economies, the chapter analysed whether exchange rate policies have been effective in altering the path of exchange rates over the medium to long run. For the contemporaneous effect, the chapter found that communication of all three monetary authorities has a significant impact on exchange rates in the order of between 0.14–0.21 per cent. With regard to effects beyond the immediate, contemporaneous reach, cumulated impulse responses based on an EGARCH model of daily exchange rate changes indicate that no statistically significant effect of either communication or actual interventions can be found beyond two or three days after an intervention takes place. However, the chapter argues that this does not necessarily imply that interventions do not have a long-run or permanent effect, but merely that other news that influence exchange rates in the days following an intervention do not allow us to identify such an effect statistically.

With regard to forward-looking indicators, the results indicate that communication affects forward rates over a longer horizon than actual interventions. The finding thus may be interpreted as evidence in favour of the long-term, or at least medium-term effectiveness of exchange rate communication. However, as a caveat it should be recalled that actual interventions tend to lean against the exchange rate trend relatively more often than exchange rate communication. Hence, at least part of this difference may be explained by the different conditions under which oral and actual interventions take place.

A further central finding of the chapter is that communication tends to *reduce* historical as well as implied volatility in most cases whereas actual interventions *raise* volatility. This implies that communication tends to lower market uncertainty, whereas actual interventions increase it. This finding may result from the very different ways official statements about the exchange rate and actual interventions are made. Communication is available to all market participants in the same way and may be understood in a similar way by the majority of market participants. Hence, exchange rate communication that is considered to offer relevant information tends to reduce the heterogeneity of beliefs among market participants and thus market volatility. By contrast, actual interventions are mostly conducted in secret. Although many market participants may have an indication that an actual intervention has taken place, views about the scale, frequency and likelihood of future interventions may differ widely across market participants, thus inducing higher market uncertainty.

The literature on analysing and understanding the importance of communication for asset prices, and in particular for exchange rates, is still in its infancy. However, from a policy perspective it is important to understand the role communication may play as a policy tool and what its limitations are. The objective of the chapter has been to contribute towards a better understanding of this role of communication, though many open issues, in particular concerning the channels through which communication works, remain for future work.

NOTES

1. Marcel.Fratzscher@ecb.int, Senior Adviser at the European Central Bank. An earlier version of this chapter was published in the *Journal of International Money and Finance*, **25** (1), 146–67, February 2006. I would like to thank Terhi Jokipii for excellent research assistance. Comments and suggestions from seminar participants at the ECB and at the JIMF-CRIF-TAFI conference on Foreign Exchange Markets are gratefully acknowledged. The views expressed in this chapter are those of the author and do not necessarily reflect those of the ECB.
2. Exponential generalized autoregressive conditional heteroskedasticity.
3. There have been numerous discussions in the past about the importance attached by markets to 'Mr Yen', Eisuke Sakakibara, Japan's Director General of the International Finance Bureau and Vice Finance Minister in the second half of the 1990s. His statements about exchange rate developments almost always received close scrutiny from financial markets. For instance, on 21 June 1999, Mr Sakakibara stated in a press conference: 'we do not want a premature strengthening of the yen'. The yen fell by 1.7 per cent against the

US dollar on that day. On 21 April 1998 Reuters quotes Mr Sakakibara's reply to a question of reporters as: 'excessive yen weakness has caused a rise in trade surplus in goods and services. In that sense, it is not desirable'. The yen appreciated by 0.6 per cent against the US dollar on that day.

4. See, for instance, Bonser-Neal and Tanner (1996), Baillie and Osterberg (1997) and Dominguez (2003). Also EGARCH models with higher-order lags were tested and showed that the EGARCH(1,1) model is sufficient to address the non-normality of the data. Moreover, using a standard FIGARCH specification did not yield qualitatively different results from the EGARCH(1,1) model employed here. Moreover, it has been argued by Beine, Bénassy-Quéré and Lecourt (2002) that a fractionally integrated GARCH (FIGARCH) model may be a more appropriate way than a standard GARCH(1,1) model to formulate the conditional variance. However, using a standard FIGARCH specification did not yield qualitatively different results from the EGARCH(1,1) model employed here.
5. Andersen et al. (2003) and Ehrmann and Fratzscher (2005) test for the impact of a broad set of US and European macroeconomic news on exchange rates, also showing that these two are particularly important news, among others.
6. Galati and Melick (2002) provide a detailed discussion of the OTC market and also offer an empirical analysis of the effect of actual interventions on exchange rates.

REFERENCES

Andersen, Torben G., Tim Bollerslev, Francis X. Diebold and Clara Vega (2003), 'Micro effects of macro announcements: real-time price discovery in foreign exchange', *American Economic Review*, **39** (1), 38–62.

Baillie, Richard T. and William P. Osterberg (1997), 'Central bank intervention and risk in the forward market', *Journal of International Economics*, **43** (3–4), 483–97.

Beine, Michel, Agnès Bénassy-Quéré and Christelle Lecourt (2002), 'Central bank intervention and foreign exchange rates: new evidence from FIGARCH estimations', *Journal of International Money and Finance*, **21** (21), 115–44.

Bonser-Neal, Catherine and Glenn Tanner (1996), 'Central bank intervention and the volatility of foreign exchange rates: evidence from the options market', *Journal of International Money and Finance*, **15** (6), 853–78.

Bonser-Neal, Catherine, V. Vance Roley and Gordon H. Sellon (1998), 'Monetary policy actions, intervention, and exchange rates: a reexamination of the empirical relationships using federal funds rate target data', *Journal of Business*, **71** (2), 147–77.

Dominguez, Kathryn M. (2003), 'The market microstructure of central bank intervention', *Journal of International Economics*, **59** (1), 25–45.

Dominguez, Kathryn M. and Jeffrey A. Frankel (1993), 'Does foreign exchange intervention matter? The portfolio effect', *American Economic Review*, **83** (5), 1356–69.

Edison, Hali J. (1993), 'The effectiveness of central-bank intervention: a survey of the literature after 1982', *Special Papers in International Economics*, No. 18, Princeton University.

Ehrmann, Michael and Marcel Fratzscher (2005), 'Exchange rates and fundamentals: new evidence from real-time data', *Journal of International Money and Finance*, **24** (2), 317–41.

Evans, Martin D. and Richard K. Lyons (2002), 'Order flow and exchange rate dynamics', *Journal of Political Economy*, **10** (1), 170–80.

Evans, Martin D. and Richard K. Lyons (2005), 'Do currency markets absorb news quickly?', *Journal of International Money and Finance*, **24** (2), 197–219.
Fratzscher, Marcel (2004), 'Communication and exchange rate policy', *ECB Working Paper* No. 363, May.
Galati, G. and W. Melick (2002), 'FX interventions and market expectations', *BIS Economic Paper* No. 10.
Holsti, O. (1969), *Content Analysis for Social Sciences and Humanities*, Reading: Addison-Wesley.
Ito, Takatoshi (2002), 'Is foreign exchange intervention effective? The Japanese experience in the 1990s', *NBER Working Paper* No. 8914, April.
Jansen, D.-J. and J. de Haan (2005), 'Talking heads: the effects of ECB statements on the euro-dollar exchange rate', *Journal of International Money and Finance*, **24** (2), 343–61.
Kaminsky, Graciela L. and Karen K. Lewis (1996), 'Does foreign exchange intervention signal future monetary policy?', *Journal of Monetary Economics*, **37** (2), 285–312.
Kassarjian, Harold H. (1977), 'Content analysis in consumer research', *Journal of Consumer Research*, **4** (1), 8–18.
Kearns, Jonathan and Roberto Rigobon (2004), 'Identifying the efficacy of central bank interventions: evidence from Australia and Japan', *Journal of International Economics*, **66** (1), 31–48.
Lewis, Karen K. (1995), 'Are foreign exchange intervention and monetary policy related and does it really matter?', *Journal of Business*, **68** (2), 185–214.
Mussa, Michael (1981), *The Role of Official Intervention*, New York: Group of Thirty.
Nelson, Daniel B. (1991), 'Conditional heteroskedasticity in asset returns: a new approach', *Econometrica*, **59** (2), 347–70.
Peiers, Bettina (1997), 'Informed traders, intervention, and price leadership: a deeper view of the microstructure of the foreign exchange market', *Journal of Finance*, **52** (4), 1589–614.
Rubin, Robert and Jacob Weisberg (2003), *In an Uncertain World: Tough Choices from Wall Street to Washington*, New York: Random House Publishers, November.
Sarno, Lucio and Mark Taylor (2001), 'Official intervention in the foreign exchange market: is it effective and, if so, how does it work?', *Journal of Economic Literature*, **39** (3), 839–68.

11. Using the microstructure approach to foreign exchange markets in a central bank

Áron Gereben[1]

11.1 INTRODUCTION

In recent years the analysis of currency markets and exchange rates using the tools of market microstructure theory has gained popularity in the academic literature. Although these methods are not yet considered to be a part of the standard toolkit of central bank analysts, some of the results they yield could be potentially used for providing regular decision-making support and policy advice in central banks. The aim of this chapter is to give an overview of the research on the foreign exchange (FX) microstructure conducted at the Magyar Nemzeti Bank (the central bank of Hungary, MNB), and to highlight some of the policy-relevant applications.

The structure of the chapter is the following. The next section highlights the importance of the exchange rate in the conduct of monetary policy in Central and Eastern European (CEE) economies in general, and in Hungary in particular. The third section presents our main motivating factors to study the microstructure of the FX market. The fourth gives insights into our data sources. The fifth summarizes the key research results we obtained. To conclude, the final section elaborates on the potential for policy-related, practical applications of the microstructure approach for a central bank.

11.2 WHY DO WE CARE ABOUT THE EXCHANGE RATE?

There are several reasons why the MNB considers the exchange rate as a factor of key importance when conducting monetary policy. Hungary is an emerging market and, as such, its financial markets are relatively vulnerable to global, regional and internal shocks. The risk premia associated with

Hungarian asset prices, and the exchange rate of the local currency – the forint – in particular, have been reacting significantly to shifts in these external and internal factors in the past.

The central bank operates an inflation targeting regime. However, rather unusually, due to a joint agreement between the government and the central bank, an exchange rate target zone relative to the euro is also in place. This exchange rate band is rather wide, +/–15 per cent, thus leaving room for relatively large exchange rate fluctuations. However, the existence of two simultaneous targets – the inflation target and the exchange rate band – carries the potential of a conflict between the two. Such a conflict emerged in mid-January 2003, when, against a rising inflationary outlook, a speculative attack had been launched against the strong edge of the exchange rate band. The attack was successfully defended by the central bank through large-scale intervention on the FX markets on one hand, and interest rate cuts to increase the relative costs of speculation on the other (see Barabás, 2003).[2]

As Hungary is a small, open, export-oriented economy, the wealth and income of a large number of economic agents – producers, consumers, borrowers and so on – are exposed directly or indirectly to exchange rate fluctuations. Furthermore, as the level of domestic credit relative to the size of the economy is relatively small compared with more developed countries with deeper financial intermediation, the part of the economy exposed to interest rate changes is comparatively low. As a consequence, the role of the exchange rate channel is of key importance within the transmission mechanism of monetary policy.

An additional need for better understanding the determinants and the dynamics of the exchange rate stems from the fact that in order to join the euro area, Hungary will be part of the exchange rate mechanism (ERM) II at some point in the future. To perform successfully within ERM II, and to meet the exchange rate stability criterion of the Maastricht Treaty, the central bank will need to have an in-depth knowledge of the key factors that generate the dynamics of the forint/euro exchange rate.

11.3 MOTIVATIONS FOR STUDYING THE MICROSTRUCTURE OF THE FX MARKETS

The main motivation for starting an empirical research programme on the microstructure of the FX markets originated from previous observations of links between some financial flows and the exchange rate. The MNB has been collecting FX flow data from commercial banks for a long time. Casual observations indicated that some of these flow indicators showed relatively strong co-movement with daily exchange rate fluctuations. However, in order to use these seemingly ad hoc linkages in our day-to-day support for monetary policy decision-making, we felt that we needed some theoretical support.

Canonical models of exchange rate determination cannot explain such co-movements. These models assume frictionless financial markets and homogeneous information structure. As a consequence, new information is incorporated into prices immediately, without any adjustments in quantities.

Microstructure-based models, on the other hand, release some of these assumptions. They emphasize the importance of the mechanism of trading, and allow participants to trade on the basis of differing information sets. The trading mechanism itself plays a crucial role in the process through which scattered pieces of information on the 'fair' value of the exchange rate are distributed among traders and customers. As a consequence, the quantities and the direction of trading has an impact on the dynamics of the exchange rate. Thus, it was a natural decision for us to turn towards this approach, as it promised to provide a theoretical explanation for our empirical observations.

Having studied the recent empirical literature on the micro approach to the FX market, we realized that some of the bank's data on the Hungarian FX market were quite unique and particularly suitable for testing the implications of the microstructure approach. This provided additional motivation for us to go further down the FX microstructure route.

11.4 DATA SOURCES FOR MICROSTRUCTURE ANALYSIS

Good data sets for analysing the microstructure of FX markets are relatively scarce. First, in many instances, it is useful to have data at relatively high, preferably intra-day frequencies, or at transaction level. Second, besides price data, the analysis often requires data on transacted quantities, too. Third, to calculate *order flow*, a key variable in the microstructure approach representing the net balance of transactions initiated by buyers and sellers, one needs to identify who played the active role in a given transaction – the buyer or the seller. Although there are techniques to estimate this information from bid-ask spreads, these methods are rather uncertain, therefore it is better to have first-hand data on the initiating party for each trade.

As such, data sets are usually not readily available, researchers typically obtain their data for empirical studies from three main sources. One source is the major electronic FX trading platforms, such as Reuters or EBS, who occasionally provide transaction-level data on interbank trading for such purposes. Such data were used by Evans and Lyons (2002), or Berger et al. (2006), among others. Another option is to obtain trading-level data from an individual bank with a substantial market share, and assume that its trading activity is representative for the market as a whole. For major currency pairs, data from Citibank and the Royal Bank of Scotland have been used by several studies – see Evans and Lyons (2005a, 2005b) or Osler (2003). The third route is to use data based on banks' FX transaction reports to central banks or other authorities. Such data are available only for some currency pairs, where monetary authorities or other agencies collect such reports. Examples of the use of such data are D'Souza (2002) or Bjønnes, Rime and Solheim (2005).

The MNB has two data sets describing the spot forint/euro trading. The first one is based on domestic banks' daily FX transactions report. This data set allows us to create series of *customer order flow*, the net balance of buyer- and seller-initiated trades between the market-making banks and their customers. The second data set comes from Reuters's D3000 Spot Matching system, the most important electronic interdealer trading platform of the forint/euro market, and can be used to create series of *interdealer order flow*, the net balance of buyer- and seller-initiated trades between market-making banks.

Domestic banks in Hungary are required to report their FX transactions above a certain size to the central bank once a day. These reports contain the price (exchange rate) and the quantity for each transaction, and also some auxiliary information on the residence (domestic/non-resident) and the background (bank/non-bank financial institution/non-financial company) of the given counterparty. This information can be used to calculate order flow measures for the different customer segments. For example, order flow from foreign non-financial companies measures whether this particular customer group was a net initiator of Hungarian forint sales, or forint purchases. Data are available with a two-day lag, and are thus suitable for continuous monitoring and regular policy use. The data are available from November 2001, and include periods of large market turbulences.

The source of the other data set, the Reuters D3000 trading platform, is an electronic limit order book, where the participating banks can submit limit and market orders, and the system automatically pairs the matching ones. Our database contains all orders submitted to the system in a given period, and all trades that were actually concluded, with time stamps at the precision of a tenth of a second. By combining the trade and the order data, we can infer for each trade whether it was initiated by the buyer or the seller, and thus calculate the aggregate interdealer order flow at various frequencies. These data are not available real time; Reuters provided historical series to us on a one-off basis on request. Currently we possess the data for two full years: 2003 and 2004.[3]

11.5 RESEARCH RESULTS

One of the main issues that we have been focusing on in our research programme on the FX microstructure was the relationship between customer order flows and the exchange rate. A key result of the FX microstructure literature is that the dynamics of the order flow can explain a large part of exchange rate fluctuations. This result was first established by Evans and Lyons (2002) using interdealer order flow, and was subsequently extended to customer order flows (see, for example, Fan and Lyons, 2002).

Specifically, we have been seeking to answer the following questions. Can order flow explain the dynamics of emerging market exchange rates, such as the forint/euro? Does it matter what kind of clients originate the order flow? Are we able to identify customers whose order flow typically conveys price-relevant information ('push' customers) and ones who act as liquidity providers ('pull' customers)?

The methodology we used was based on other studies done for more developed currency markets, such as Carpenter and Wang (2003), Mende and Menkhoff (2003), Bjønnes, Rime and Solheim (2005) and Marsh and O'Rourke (2005). Data from the banks' daily FX report were particularly suitable for this type of analysis.

To illustrate, let us take a look at Table 11.1. It shows two regression runs, where we attempted to explain daily changes in the exchange rate by daily order flow from different customer groups. In the first regression shown in column 1, the explanatory variables are the order flows from foreign banks, foreign non-financials and the central bank, the so-called 'push' customers. The negative sign of the coefficients indicate that forint purchases by these client types usually coincide with a forint appreciation, and their sales with depreciation. Their order flow explains about 30 per cent of the dynamics of the exchange rate. In the second regression (column 2), the order flows from domestic agents are on the right-hand side. The sign of the coefficient indicates that forint purchases by these customers usually coincide with depreciations, and sales with appreciations. This suggests that these customers are more likely to be liquidity providers on the market.

Our key finding, namely that customer order flow is able to explain a significant part of the fluctuations of the forint/euro exchange rate, was in line with studies for other currency pairs. Also, the data is consistent with the model of 'push' and 'pull' customers. Our analysis suggests that foreign

Table 11.1 Spot market order flow and the exchange rate

Variables	(1) Model with Push Customers	(2) Model with Pull Customers
Constant	−0.114	0.054
	(−1.55)	(0.57)
Foreign banks' order flow	**−0.127**	–
	(−21.42)	
Foreign non-banks' order flow	**−0.201**	–
	(−14.22)	
Domestic (non-market-making) banks' order flow	–	**0.278**
		(13.86)
Domestic non-banks' order flow	–	**0.115**
		(7.23)
Central banks' order flow	**−0.169**	–
	(−28.64)	
Domestic (non-market-making) banks' order flow speculative attack dummy*	–	***−0.441***
		(−19.32)
Diagnostics		
Adjusted R^2	0.305	0.141
P-value, serial correlation Q-test (lags: 1, 5)	0.17, 0.23	0.45, 0.66
P-value, ARCH LM test for heteroskedasticity (lags: 1, 5)	0.84, 0.75	0.80, 0.94

Notes:

a. Dependent variable: daily logarithmic change of the forint/euro exchange rate.
b. Parameter z-statistics are in parentheses.
c. Sample period: 8 Nov 2001–3 Oct 2005.
d. Number of observations: 979.
e. Estimation method: maximum likelihood, with a GARCH (2,1) structure. The ARCH and GARCH components are not reported here.
f. To test for serial correlation, null probabilities derived from a Ljung-Box Q-test using 1 and 5 lags are shown. To test for heteroskedasticity, p-values derived from the ARCH LM test (using F-statistics) are shown.
g. Parameter estimates significant at a 1% level are shown with bold typeface.

Source: Gereben et al. (2006).

clients and the central bank seem to play the role of push customers: information embedded in their trades seems to drive the dynamics of the exchange rate. Their order flow is positively correlated with the exchange rate. Domestic clients, on the other hand, play the role of 'pull' customers, providing the liquidity to the market. Their order flow is negatively correlated with the exchange rate (see Gereben et al., 2006).

Another research objective was to obtain a better understanding of the functioning of the spot forint/euro market using high-frequency data from the Reuters database. Besides looking at how different measures of market liquidity – such as the bid-ask spreads, the number of quotes and trades, the depth and the width of the order book – evolve intra-day, we also wanted to test whether interdealer order flow has an explanatory power for the dynamics of the exchange rate.

One interesting feature of the data is that it enables us to study the cross-section of the Reuters D2000 order book. Figure 11.1a shows such a cross-sectional snapshot for a given moment of a regular trading day. The stepwise graph shows the cumulated amount of bid and ask quotes for each level of the exchange rate. It can be seen that the market is fairly balanced, as both the quantities, and the slopes of the demand and supply schedules are relatively symmetric.

It is worthwhile taking a look at how the order book changes during times of market turbulence. Figure 11.1b shows a similar snapshot taken during the speculative attack of January 2003, when the strong edge of the forint/euro exchange rate band was tested by the market. Obviously, the market was much more skewed this time. The bid-ask spread became narrower, and both the quantities quoted, and the slopes of the demand and supply schedules became highly asymmetric. The quantities offered also increased significantly.

All in all, we found that, although the Hungarian FX market is much smaller in terms of size and liquidity than its more developed peers, the intra-day patterns of various liquidity indicators are quite similar. Also, interdealer order flow can explain a large part of the exchange rate dynamics, as shown by Evans and Lyons (2002) for the major currency pairs and by Scalia (2004) for some emerging FX markets. Gereben and Kiss M. (2006) discuss these results in more detail.

An interesting area of research is to explore what kind of role does the trading itself play in the transmission of information about fundamentals into prices. Traditional models of the exchange rate assume homogeneous information, and do not leave room for different interpretations of the same news item. Microstructure models allow different agents to interpret the same information differently. In the case of this more realistic assumption, trading itself may be a channel through which the market reaches a consensus about what is the new 'fair' value of the currency in the light of the particular news.

Building on previous works in this field, such as Love and Payne (2006), Evans and Lyons (2003, 2005a) and Berger et al. (2006), we looked at whether macroeconomic news are incorporated directly and immediately into the forint/euro exchange rate, or the order flow between dealers plays a role in transmitting information and reaching a new equilibrium price.

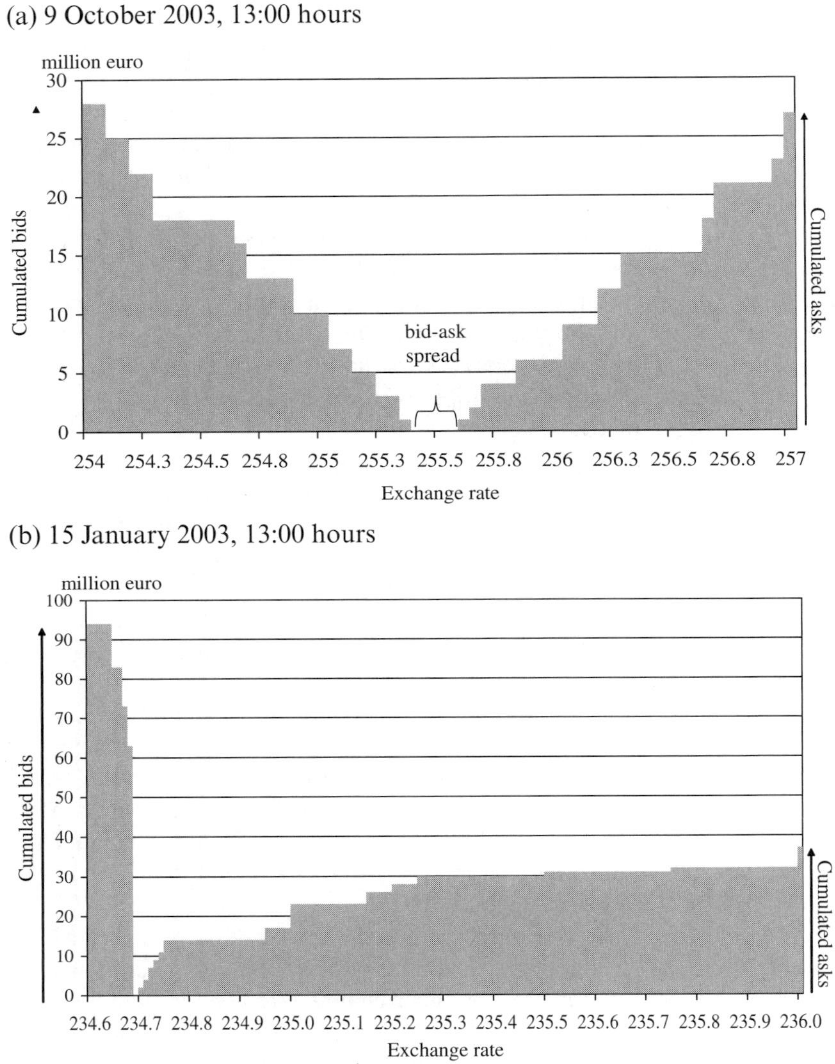

Source: Gereben and Kiss M. (2006).

Figure 11.1a and b The width and depth of the order book

First of all, we found that besides the exchange rate, order flow also heavily reacts to news. Second, according to our data, only a small part of the effects of news releases are impounded into prices directly and immediately. About 60 per cent of the news impact is channelled into the

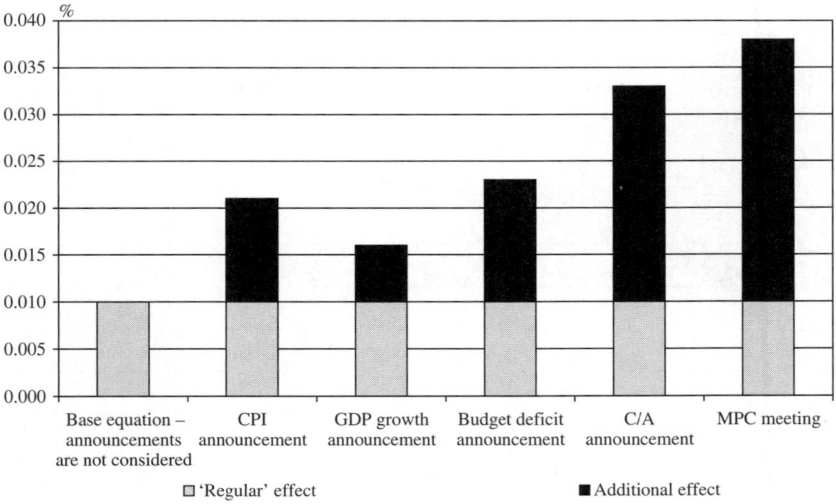

Source: Frömmel, Kiss M. and Pintér (2008).

Figure 11.2 The impact of order flow on the exchange rate during news releases

exchange rate through the trading process, via the order flow. Third, we also observed that the impact of order flow on the exchange rate is larger around news releases than during 'normal' times. These findings confirm some earlier results for other markets.

Figure 11.2 illustrates this latter point. It shows the size of the order flow's impact coefficients on the exchange rate during normal market conditions, and around news announcements. The size of the coefficient increases around the announcements. It seems that in the case of the forint/euro exchange rate, the order flow has the largest impact on the exchange rate around the releases of the current account statistics, and when the Monetary Council announces its interest rate decisions. A more detailed description of the methodology and the results can be found in Frömmel, Kiss M. and Pintér (2008).

The period covered by our data sets includes times of relatively severe market turbulences. An example of this is the January 2003 speculative attack, but there are other events characterized by exceptional exchange rate volatility in the database. It is interesting to examine whether the relationship between the order flow and the exchange rate remains the same during these times of market stress. Some studies, such as Luo (2001), suggest so, and emerging market currencies, such as the forint seem to be good testing grounds for this issue.

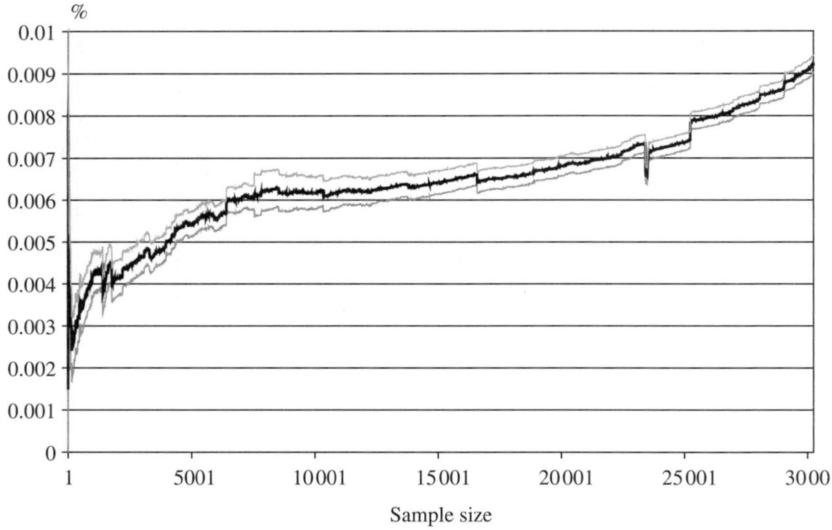

Source: Author's calculations.

Figure 11.3 Recursive estimation of the order flow's impact parameter with the sample sorted by daily volatility

Although our work in this area is in its initial phase, some preliminary results are worth mentioning. One experiment we conducted was that we took our intra-day exchange rate return and order flow observations, and sorted these observations by the daily volatility of the exchange rate. Then we ran a recursive regression between the order flow and the currency returns on this sorted sample. Figure 11.3 shows the evolution of the order flow's impact parameter on the exchange rate. It seems that the impact of a given amount of order flow on the exchange rate increases with volatility. This may suggest that the impact of the order flow is larger when the market is turbulent. Such a result would be in line with some of the theoretical models of trading, such as Kyle (1985).

11.6 POLICY USE

Besides the research interest, the most interesting issue for a central bank is, of course, whether the results of a particular area of study could be used and implemented in the day-to-day policy-oriented work. There are indeed many aspects of the microstructure-based analysis of the FX market that have practical applications for a monetary authority.

One aspect that has proven to be quite useful at the MNB was the knowledge about the key customer types of the Hungarian FX market. Knowing the 'typical' behaviour, market role and price impact of the key groups of domestic and foreign market participants can be valuable. In the past, this type of information proved a good complement to price data and market intelligence for analysing particular shifts in the exchange rate. It allowed us to draw a more detailed and richer picture of market events, and helped us to better understand the strategies and processes underlying market dynamics. As the customer order flow data is available on a daily basis with a two-day lag, we are able to include this information regularly and promptly into the briefing materials to the bank's decision-making bodies.

Another useful application derives from high-frequency information. Previously, the key information source on the intra-day patterns of liquidity, turnover and other market conditions was our market intelligence. It can give great insight into the market processes, but it cannot provide, obviously, a fully representative and unbiased view. High-frequency microstructure analysis provided us with objective benchmarks on how the intra-day patterns of liquidity indicators and turnover evolve under various conditions, against which day-to-day market intelligence can be evaluated.

A key potential benefit for central banks to study the microstructure of the FX market is that it could help to better prepare for potential interventions on the FX market. This kind of knowledge might be particularly useful for EU candidate countries, who may be likely to resort to market intervention to meet the exchange rate stability criterion during their planned ERM II membership.

First, microstructure-based analyses quantifying the impact of the order flow on the exchange rate can provide the monetary authorities with clues on the potential effect of an official intervention. Second, the microstructure approach shows that the same intervention could produce a very different impact on the exchange rate depending on the circumstances. Our own results so far suggest that interventions may be more effected when aligned with macroeconomic news. Similarly, intervention in turbulent times may have a larger impact than intervention under regular market conditions.

NOTES

1. Deputy Head of Financial Analysis, Magyar Nemzeti Bank. The views presented here are the result of a substantial body of work with various experts, in particular Michael Frömmel, György Gyomai, Norbert Kiss M. and Klára Pintér. All remaining errors are those of the author. The views expressed here do not necessarily represent the official view of the Magyar Nemzeti Bank.

2. The exchange rate band was abolished on 25 February 2008. Since then the Hungarian forint has been freely floating.
3. A more detailed description of these data sources can be found in Gereben, Gyomai and Kiss M. (2006) and Gereben and Kiss M. (2006).

REFERENCES

Barabás, Gyula (ed.) (2003), 'Coping with the speculative attack against the forint's band', *MNB Background Studies* No. 2003/3, Magyar Nemzeti Bank (The Central Bank of Hungary).

Berger, David W., Alain Chaboud, Sergey Chernenko, Edward Howorka, Raj S.K. Iyer, David Liu and Jonathan H. Wright (2006), 'Order flow and exchange rate dynamics in electronic brokerage system data', *Federal Reserve Board International Finance Discussion Paper* No. 830, September.

Bjønnes, Geir H., Dagfinn Rime and Haakon O. Aa. Solheim (2005), 'Liquidity provision in the overnight foreign exchange market', *Journal of International Money and Finance*, **24** (2), 177–98.

Carpenter, Andrew and Jianxin Wang (2003), 'Sources of private information in FX trading', University of New South Wales, typescript, January.

D'Souza, Chris (2002), 'A market microstructure analysis of foreign exchange intervention in Canada', *Bank of Canada Working Paper* No. 2002-16, June.

Evans, Martin D.D. and Richard K. Lyons (2002), 'Order flow and exchange rate dynamics', *Journal of Political Economy*, **110** (1), 170–80.

Evans, M.D. and R.K. Lyons (2003), 'How is macro news transmitted to exchange rates?', *NBER Working Paper* No. 9433, 22 January.

Evans, M.D. and R.K. Lyons (2005a), 'Do currency markets absorb news quickly?', *Journal of International Money and Finance*, **24** (2), 197–217.

Evans, Martin D.D. and Richard K. Lyons (2005b), 'Meese-Rogoff redux: micro-based exchange-rate forecasting', *American Economic Review Papers and Proceedings*, **95** (2), 405–14.

Fan, Mintao and Richard K. Lyons (2002), 'Customer trades and extreme events in foreign exchange', in Paul Mizen (ed.), *Essays in Honor of Charles Goodhart*, Edward Elgar, Cheltenham, UK and Northampton, MA, USA, pp. 160–79.

Frömmel, Michael, Norbert Kiss M. and Klára Pintér (2008), 'Macroeconomic announcements, communication and order flow on the Hungarian foreign exchange market', *MNB Working Papers*, forthcoming.

Gereben, Áron and Norbert Kiss M. (2006), 'A brief overview of the characteristics of interbank forint/euro trading', *MNB Bulletin*, Magyar Nemzeti Bank (The Central Bank of Hungary), **1** (2), December, 21–6.

Gereben, Áron, György Gyomai and Norbert Kiss M. (2006), 'Customer order flow, information and liquidity on the Hungarian foreign exchange market', *MNB Working Papers* No. 2006/8, Magyar Nemzeti Bank (The Central Bank of Hungary).

Kyle, Albert S. (1985), 'Continuous auctions and insider trading', *Econometrica*, Econometric Society, **53** (6), 1315–35, November.

Love, R. and R. Payne (2006), 'Macroeconomic news, order flows, and exchange rates', manuscript, London School of Economics.

Luo, Jinhui (2001), 'Market conditions, order flow and exchange rates determination', manuscript, London School of Economics, December.
Marsh, Ian W. and Ceire O'Rourke (2005), 'Customer order flow and exchange rate movements: is there really information content?', City University, *EMG Working Paper Series*, EMG-01-2005.
Mende, Alexander and Lukas Menkhoff (2003), 'Different counterparties, different foreign exchange trading? The perspective of a median bank', typescript, University of Hannover.
Osler, Carol L. (2003), 'Currency orders and exchange-rate dynamics: explaining the success of technical analysis', *Journal of Finance*, **58** (5), 1791–821.
Scalia, Antonio (2004), 'Liquidity and volatility of Central European currencies', manuscript, Bank of Italy.

12. How do central banks and FX traders interact?

Antonio Scalia[1]

12.1 INTRODUCTION

The purpose of this contribution is to comment[2] on Chapter 10 ('The impact of exchange rate interventions and communication over the medium term' by Marcel Fratzscher) and Chapter 11 ('Using the microstructure approach to foreign exchange markets in a central bank' by Áron Gereben) and to complement their findings with my own research conducted for the Czech Republic.

Although Chapters 10 and 11 adopt different approaches, they share a common interest in the market interaction between central banks and foreign exchange (FX) traders, a theme that has clear implications for the monetary authorities. My key point is as follows: the results on the effectiveness of intervention for the major central banks should not be extrapolated as a guide for future actions in the market of currencies with limited liquidity. Communication may not be as successful, particularly if the economy is in transition and the monetary authorities face the associated special challenges. On the other hand, the small scale of the market is such that the impact of order flow on price is bigger, and this has important implications for the monitoring activity of the central bank as well as for possible, direct market intervention.

The next section presents my discussion of the chapters by Fratzscher and Gereben. The third section shows some results on intervention effectiveness in the case of a currency with limited liquidity, namely the Czech koruna (CZK). The fourth describes the stylized facts about the microstructure of the foreign exchange market in the case of the Polish zloty, the Czech koruna and the Hungarian forint. The final section contains concluding remarks.

12.2 DISCUSSION OF THE CHAPTERS

In the first place, I will point out what in my opinion is the main contribution made by each chapter and the issues that are still open. The scope of both presentations is extremely wide, and they are complementary to each other. The analysis by Fratzscher sheds light on the evolution of intervention techniques and their effectiveness in the case of the major currencies. They are traded in a market environment where central banks used to be big and respected players in the past, but have become less powerful in recent times, owing partly to the growth of market turnover. In light of these developments, let me point out that I see the increasing use of communication and 'oral intervention' by the monetary authorities as a necessity rather than a virtue. In many cases, traditional intervention in the market has featured large transaction volumes and short-lived effects. Against this background, communication has lent itself as a less expensive alternative.

On the other hand, intervention in the market has retained much of its flavour in the case of small currencies, like the Hungarian forint. I will argue that, although the issue of intervention effectiveness is not the main focus of Gereben's chapter, its analysis of market microstructure raises some issues that are relevant for the monetary authorities. I will also show some estimates taken from a recent paper of mine, to illustrate this point.

I would like to praise Marcel Fratzscher for the width of the database on oral intervention that he has put together for the FX markets of the United States, Japan and the euro area (G-3). I also liked the array of robustness checks that he has performed. The data show that, although with a little decline in the volatile period 1995–98, the practice of communication has been very popular among monetary authorities.

The main result of the chapter is that oral intervention has indeed been an effective tool for foreign exchange policy of the G-3 currencies. It is interesting to observe that monetary policy moves increase the effectiveness of subsequent communication. This is consistent with the notion that monetary policy directly affects the fundamentals of the economy, to which the exchange rate ultimately responds.

From a technical viewpoint, let me also note that some regressions seem to make an unconventional use of explanatory variables. This applies in particular to the equations that include a dummy for future monetary policy decisions. They seem to imply that market players in the model have perfect foresight. This issue might deserve some clarification.

Should we expect the general conclusion of the chapter, that communication does influence foreign exchange rates, to hold now and for the future? This is not obvious in my view. First, the FX market has experienced a large growth in turnover. In the last four years, just following the end of the sample period used in the study, turnover has increased by 70 per cent (see BIS, 2007). Second, international portfolio diversification in asset management has surged as well. The large players and those that are most active in the FX market, like the hedge funds, have grown in their number compared with four years ago.

My next question is: can we extend the conclusion of the study to small currencies? The link here is even weaker. The weight of international asset managers in the case of small currencies is stronger. Besides, in many cases the monetary authorities of small economies face a transition period, like the convergence process towards the adoption of the euro. This implies that they are in the process of establishing credibility, which is a prerequisite for the effectiveness of oral intervention.

Turning to Gereben's chapter, his empirical research is also based on a fine data set. This enables the author to distinguish the information content of foreign and domestic investors.

What is special about foreign investors? They are often big players; in addition, they may possess private information on international customers' order flow. They may see portfolio shifts occurring in the major currencies and thus infer the direction of possible shifts in smaller currencies. It is also remarkable that domestic banks act as liquidity providers in the market, as revealed by the estimates. The finding that the spot market is the primary channel for information aggregation is also interesting, and it is in line with other studies. That's all valuable information for the central bank, for monitoring purposes as well as for possible actions in the market.

Let's turn to an open issue. The estimates produced by Gereben provide encouraging results on the ability of customer order flow to forecast exchange rate moves using daily time series. This applies to the Meese-Rogoff-type equations and, to a lesser extent, to the order flow model, which excludes contemporaneous order flow values. However, the author seems to be only partially satisfied, because the forecasting performance in the latter model is not statistically significant.

My point is that order flow and, more generally, the micro working of the market may reveal useful information for the central bank also at higher frequency. One possible direction for future research is the use of intra-day data. In particular, in the case of a small currency with limited liquidity it may be important to estimate the impact of buy and sell orders in the very short run, and to see whether dealers react differently in various states of the market. In this respect, the probability of intervention by the central bank is clearly an important state variable.

Table 12.1 Intervention effectiveness (intra-day estimates for the CZK/EUR, July–December 2002)

	Same-hour Exchange Rate Impact per EUR 10 Million Order Flow	Persistent Effect
1. The central bank intervenes secretly (either side), the likelihood of intervention is low	6.60 basis points (20 pips)	89%
2. The central bank intervenes secretly; the likelihood of intervention is high	9.31 basis points (28 pips)	74%
3. The central bank intervenes discreetly, the likelihood of intervention is high ex ante and the market learns that intervention is occurring	(9.31 + 2.93 =) 12.24 basis points (37 pips)	74%

Source: Scalia (2008).

12.3 A CASE STUDY ON INTERVENTION EFFECTIVENESS

Let me briefly show you some results from a recent paper (Scalia, 2008). I studied the Czech koruna market in the second half of 2002, using hourly data on signed order flow. That period featured several rounds of direct market intervention performed by the Czech National Bank (CNB) to stem the appreciation of the koruna. These interventions were discreet and took place between July and September. In those months the market perceived a high likelihood of intervention ex ante, owing to the strength of the koruna. From October onwards, owing partly to a political crisis, the koruna weakened. The market thus perceived a low intervention probability. As a matter of fact, the CNB did not intervene in the last quarter. Using data from the Reuters Dealing market, I estimate the impact of order flow (see Section 12.4). Taking 10 million euros as a reference measure of signed order flow on the CZK/EUR contract, the same-hour impact was equal to 6.60 basis points when intervention probability was low, and to 9.31 basis points when it was high (see Table 12.1).

In the days when the central bank was known to be in the market, although with some delay, the hourly impact increased to 12 basis points. Of these, the persistent component lasting throughout the day was roughly 75 per cent.

These results look quite interesting to me. The estimates are much bigger than similar estimates obtained for large currencies. In their study of the DEM/USD market with intra-day data, Evans and Lyons (2002) find that the exchange rate impact of order flow is equivalent to 0.6 basis points per USD 10 million. My estimate is over 12 times as large as that. Froot and Ramadorai (2005) provide projections of order flow on exchange rate returns for the G-10 currencies against the US dollar at various frequencies. At the daily frequency, the highest available, these projections lie in a range between 0.5 basis points per USD 10 million order flow for the Canadian dollar and 2.4 basis points for the Australian dollar, with the euro area at 0.9 basis points. Based on the estimates of Domaç and Mendoza (2004), the price impact corresponding to a USD 10 million intervention would be 0.8 basis points for the Mexican peso and 2.0 basis points for the Turkish lira, respectively. The difference between my estimates and those from previous studies seems related to the different degree of liquidity of the CZK/EUR contract compared with the major currency pairs.

Let me also make a second remark. The above results reveal to the central bank what the impact might have been had it performed watertight secret intervention, or other non-policy-related operations in the FX market, for example, as an agent for the government or for portfolio investment purposes.

12.4 THE MARKET MICROSTRUCTURE OF CENTRAL EUROPEAN CURRENCIES

Has the evidence on the Czech koruna anything to say for the companion currencies of Central Europe, in particular the Polish zloty (PLN) and the Hungarian forint (HUF)? I will argue affirmatively. To understand why, let me present a simple comparison of some key microstructure figures for the three currencies, in the same sample period as in the analysis of the koruna intervention episodes, namely the second half of 2002 (Scalia, 2004).

It should be noted that, unlike the koruna, neither the Polish zloty nor the Hungarian forint were subject to market intervention by the respective monetary authorities in that period. However, as we will see, the three currencies share some important properties.

From the middle of 2001 to the end of 2002 the Polish currency was extremely volatile, also as a reflection of the swings in the sentiment of international portfolio investors. In the second half of 2002 the average PLN/EUR exchange rate was equal to 4.04, with a variation range of +4.7/–2.9 per cent.

After a sharp appreciation in the spring of 2002, the HUF/EUR experienced a period of high volatility, which went on through the rest of the year. In the sample period, the daily average HUF/EUR exchange rate was equal to 242.5 and it fluctuated in the range +4.7/–3.0 per cent. The unilateral central parity against the euro remained stable at 276.1.

The koruna strengthened from end-2001 to mid-2002, following large capital inflows related to the privatization process. At the beginning of the summer of 2002 the CZK/EUR was trading slightly above 29. In the sample period the average exchange rate was 30.54, with a variation range equal to +3.6/–5.2 per cent.

In terms of liquidity, the closest survey of foreign exchange activity (BIS, 2002) shows that total daily turnover in the spot market against all other currencies as of April 2001 was equivalent to USD 736 million for the CZK, USD 160 million for the HUF, USD 2340 million for the PLN. For the sake of comparison, daily spot transactions in the Danish krone (DKK), the only other participant in the exchange rate mechanism (ERM) II with the euro during the sample period, were equivalent to USD 2988 million.

My microstructure evidence is based on a detailed data set from the Reuters Dealing 3000 Spot Matching system. This is a multilateral trading platform operated as an electronic limit order book, that is a system where dealers can place either orders with a price limit (limit orders) or orders to be executed at the best outstanding quotes (market orders), for a wide range of currency pairs. All orders are firm and they are automatically matched against the best available quotes (that is, limit orders), up to the threshold set by the bilateral credit lines. The system updates the order book and shows the best quotes to all dealers together with the flow of quotes and trades.

The data set includes all incoming orders and trades executed during 8:00–17:00, Monday through Friday, between 1 July and 31 December 2002. Each record (quote or trade) includes the date, time and currency pair. In addition each quote record shows the side of the quote plus the firm price and quantity, the latter in millions of euros or US dollars. Each transaction record gives the price and quantity with a bought/sold indicator.

In the case of the zloty, the most liquid currency pair is the PLN/USD, not the PLN/EUR. Therefore I consider the former. Summary statistics on a daily basis for the CZK/EUR, HUF/EUR and PLN/USD are shown in Table 12.2, Panels A to C. The sample includes 128 working days. The trade flow statistics refer to 'signed' transactions, whereby any filled buy (sell) market order is attributed a + (–) sign. Daily turnover on CZK/EUR is EUR 169.6 million. Average trade flow is EUR +5.9 million, indicating net euro purchases against the koruna over the sample period. The HUF/EUR pair has an average turnover of EUR 120.5 million and trade flow of EUR +8 million. The PLN/USD pair has a daily turnover of USD 273.7 million and trade flow of USD +1.3 million. The average daily return for the koruna is positive, indicating a tendency to depreciate against the euro over the sample period. The forint and the zloty show the opposite phenomenon, with negative average returns. Volatility, measured as the squared daily

Table 12.2 Transactions on Reuters Dealing 3000, summary statistics and sample correlation – daily data[c] (July–December 2002)

Panel A – CZK/EUR						
Summary statistics	Obs.	Mean	Std. dev.	Sum	Min.	Max.
Turnover[a]	128	169.6	79.0	21713	33	429
Trade flow[a]	128	5.9	31.4	752	−82	89
Log rate change[b]	127	6.2	47.4	792.8	−99.0	142.4
Volatility[d]	127	0.23	0.37		0	2.03
Spread[e]	128	7.5	2.9		3.0	22.6
Cross-correlation	Trade flow		Log rate change		Volatility	Spread
Log rate change	0.49***[f]					
Volatility	0.30***		0.49***			
Spread	0.03		0.01		0.18**	
Turnover	0.24***		0.29***		0.49***	−0.10
Panel B – HUF/EUR						
Summary statistics	Obs.	Mean	Std. dev.	Sum	Min.	Max.
Turnover	128	120.5	72.9	15419	8	364
Trade flow	128	8	23.7	1024	−50	72
Log rate change	127	−2.7	31.3	−343.6	−133.5	95.2
Volatility	127	0.10	0.22		0	1.78
Spread	128	7.2	4.0		1.7	37.7
Cross-correlation	Trade flow		Log rate change		Volatility	Spread
Log rate change	0.57***					
Volatility	0		−0.23***			
Spread	−0.02		−0.01		0.10	
Turnover	0.21 **		−0.03		0.54***	−0.27***
Panel C – PLN/USD						
Summary statistics	Obs.	Mean	Std. dev.	Sum	Min.	Max.
Turnover	128	273.7	119.7	35034	54	698
Trade flow	128	1.3	34.1	163	−118	86
Log rate change	127	−3.7	52.5	−475.7	−152.9	135.4
Volatility	127	0.27	0.40		0	2.34
Spread	128	5.8	3.5		3.3	30.5
Cross-correlation	Trade flow		Log rate change		Volatility	Spread
Log rate change	0.51***					
Volatility	0.02		0.04			
Spread	0.06		0.12		0.01	
Turnover	−0.05		0.09		0.45***	0.03

Notes:

a. Turnover and trade flow are in millions of euros or US dollars.
b. The log rate change is multiplied by 10 000.
c. The daily rate is given by the last traded rate before 17:00 Central European Time daily.
d. Volatility is the squared log rate change multiplied by 10 000.
e. The spread is given by the average intra-day inside spread divided by the rate level and multiplied by 10 000, that is, in basis points.
f. *** denotes significance of correlation at the 1% level, ** denotes significance at the 5% level.

Source: Scalia (2004).

return, is large for the zloty and the koruna, at 0.27 and 0.23 basis points respectively, and relatively smaller for the forint, at 0.10 basis points.

The data set does not record when a given quote has been matched or cancelled by the proponent. Hence, the bid-ask spread at any point in time cannot be directly observed but must instead be estimated on the basis of some assumptions about the life of each quote. Taking a simple stance, in view of the relatively low liquidity of the three currency pairs and of casual inspection, I assumed that each quote expires after five minutes, if it has not been previously matched. At each point in time I thus obtain an estimate of the prevailing inside spread, given by the difference between the best outstanding ask and the best outstanding bid.

The daily spread is a weighted average of the intra-day spreads. For comparison across the three currencies, the spread is normalized and expressed as a percentage of the exchange rate times 100, that is, in basis points. The PLN/USD pair displays the lowest average spread, equal to 5.8 basis points; the CZK/EUR and HUF/EUR show an average spread of 7.5 and 7.2 basis points respectively.

The lower section of each panel in Table 12.2 gives the cross-correlation between the above market variables for each currency pair. An important fact stands out: signed order flow and returns display a large positive correlation, in the range 0.49–0.57.

Table 12.3, Panels A–C provides similar statistics as in Table 12.2, at hourly intervals within each day. The intra-day data confirm that the cross-correlation between order flow and return is high, with the same order of magnitude through all currency pairs, in the range 0.45–0.49. This is consistent with the notion that order flow has a direct impact on exchange rate changes also contemporaneously, a key hypothesis in the micro portfolio balance model of Evans and Lyons (2002). The spread displays positive correlation with volatility, with the highest value, equal to 0.23, for the PLN/USD.

Scalia (2004) performs econometric regressions of intra-day order flow for the zloty and the forint, in the same spirit as the analysis of intervention effectiveness in the case of the Czech koruna. It turns out that the same-hour exchange rate impact of order flow is extremely significant. In the case of PLN/USD it is equal to 6.0 basis points per USD 10 million; in the HUF/EUR it is equal to 7.0 basis points per EUR 10 million.

12.5 CONCLUDING REMARKS

I derive some stylized facts from the above evidence. In the first place, liquidity in Central European currency markets is relatively low, as revealed

Table 12.3 Transactions on Reuters Dealing 3000, summary statistics and sample correlation – hourly[c] data (8:00–17:00 CET)

Panel A – CZK/EUR

Summary statistics	Obs.	Mean	Std. dev.	Min.	Max.
Turnover[a]	1130	18.1	17.9	1	166
Trade flow[a]	1130	0.5	10.1	−42	73
Log rate change[b]	1058	0.17	18.82	−73.5	136.3
Volatility[d]	1056	0.04	0.10	0	1.9
Spread[e]	1147	8.1	8.3	0.01	150.8

Cross-correlation	Trade flow	Log rate change	Volatility	Spread
Log rate change	0.47***[f]			
Volatility	0.12***	0.30***		
Spread	−0.01	0.03	0.10***	
Turnover	0.14***	0.17***	0.37***	−0.13***

Panel B – HUF/EUR

Summary statistics	Obs.	Mean	Std. dev.	Min.	Max.
Turnover	1080	13.3	14.4	1	132
Trade flow	1080	0.8	8.0	−46	64
Log rate change	1063	−0.49	12.56	−81.7	60.1
Volatility	1063	0.02	0.05	0	0.7
Spread	1135	7.8	10.0	0	140.7

Cross-correlation	Trade flow	Log rate change	Volatility	Spread
Log rate change	0.49 ***			
Volatility	0.01	−0.15***		
Spread	0	−0.04	0.09***	
Turnover	0.15***	−0.01	0.38***	−0.15***

Panel C – PLN/USD

Summary statistics	Obs.	Mean	Std. dev.	Min.	Max.
Turnover	1133	28.8	22.9	1	206
Trade flow	1133	0.1	11.8	−52	60
Log rate change	1077	−0.17	17.8	−128.4	128.5
Volatility	1077	0.03	0.11	0	1.7
Spread	1149	5.8	9.2	0.9	189.5

Cross-correlation	Trade flow	Log rate change	Volatility	Spread
Log rate change	0.45***			
Volatility	0.01	−0.05		
Spread	0.02	0.10***	0.23***	
Turnover	−0.01	−0.01	0.20***	−0.04

Notes:

a. Turnover and trade flow are in millions of euros or US dollars.

b. The log rate change is multiplied by 10 000.

c. The hourly rate is given by the last mid-quote available at the end of each hour.

d. Volatility is the hourly squared log rate change multiplied by 10 000.

e. The spread is given by the average hourly inside spread divided by the rate level and multiplied by 10 000, that is, in basis points.

f. *** denotes significance of correlation at the 1% level.

Source: Scalia (2004).

by market volume and the spread levels. Looking at the most recent BIS central bank survey (BIS, 2007), between 2001 and 2007 the share of FX market turnover has increased above the average for the Polish zloty: from 0.5 to 0.8 per cent of global transactions. In the case of the forint and the koruna, the share has remained unchanged and equal in both cases to 0.2 per cent. It should also be recalled that in the last seven years, global turnover has more than doubled.

The second fact that stands out is the relatively large value of volatility. Third, the order flow evidence shows that the FX markets respond quite fast and considerably to new information, as impounded into incoming transactions. The koruna case reveals that such response is largely affected by the state of the market, and the presence of the central bank is an important conditioning variable.

I fully subscribe to the indication given by Martin Evans in Chapter 8: the knowledge of market microstructure brings in much greater resolution for understanding exchange rate determination. The study of order flow data is an additional source of information on what is happening in the economy. This is particularly true in the case of small currencies, where the central bank might consider market intervention also in view of the limited liquidity of the market.

In light of the important differences in the market structure of the major currencies, as opposed to currencies with limited liquidity, one should pay attention to extrapolate Fratzscher's general conclusion, that communication is to a large extent an effective policy tool.

My bottom line for future research in the study of small currencies is an encouragement to pursue the analysis of intra-day market behaviour, combined with the use of order flow data.

NOTES

1. Head of Risk Management Division, Monetary and Foreign Exchange Policy Department, Banca d'Italia.
2. This contribution reflects the author's personal views, and not necessarily the views of the Banca d'Italia.

REFERENCES

BIS (Bank for International Settlements) (2002), *Triennial Central Bank Survey – Foreign Exchange and Derivatives Market Activity in 2001*, Basel: BIS.

BIS (Bank for International Settlements) (2007), *Triennial Central Bank Survey – Foreign Exchange and Derivatives Market Activity in 2007*, Basel: BIS.

Domaç, I. and A. Mendoza (2004), 'Is there room for foreign exchange intervention under an inflation targeting framework? Evidence from Mexico and Turkey', *World Bank Policy Research Working Paper* No. 3288.

Evans, M. and R. Lyons (2002), 'Time varying liquidity in foreign exchange', *Journal of Monetary Economics* **49** (5), 1025–51.

Froot, K. and T. Ramadorai (2005), 'Currency returns, intrinsic value, and institutional investor flows', *Journal of Finance*, **60** (3), 1535–66.

Scalia, A. (2004), 'Liquidity and volatility of Central European currencies', *Banca d'Italia Working Paper*.

Scalia, A. (2008), 'Is foreign exchange intervention effective? Some micro-analytical evidence from the Czech Republic', *Journal of International Money and Finance*, **27** (4), 529–46.

PART III

Understanding economic competitiveness

13. Competitiveness in a monetary union

Josef Christl[1]

International competitiveness ranks among the most widely discussed topics, both within economics and within politics. And the issue truly deserves this prominent standing. Competitiveness is one of the most important and far-reaching features of an economy and is referred to in such diverse contexts as in wage negotiations, industrial and structural policy, exchange rate developments or international trade. Quite a few of the 'growth miracles' of the last decades may be traced to impressive gains in international competitiveness and export-led growth. Prominent examples include emerging Asia and China.

Competitiveness is a very broad concept and touches many areas, as is reflected by the broad range of indicators that have been devised to measure it. These include unit labour costs, sectoral and regional trade structures, quality and technology upgrading of produce and location factors like tax systems. The most prominent and most widely used concepts, however, are different exchange rate indicators.

Against this backdrop, this chapter discusses whether the exchange rate is in fact as important a measure of national competitiveness as it used to be – approaching the exchange rate subject from the special perspective of the countries of the euro area.

In my opinion, exchange rates are significant for competitiveness, but they are certainly not the only important factor. For example, one defining feature of the catching-up process of the Central and Eastern European countries (CEECs) was and still is real appreciation, partly due to productivity differentials between the tradable and non-tradable sector (also known as the Balassa-Samuelson effect). Nevertheless, the countries in Central and Eastern Europe have managed to increase their economic wealth substantially within a comparatively short period of time. Such gains in welfare were often associated with very robust developments of external trade. Exports as well as imports have been increasing strongly for an extended time span, and countries have become more and more integrated into international production networks.

This dynamic development seemingly conflicts with real appreciation as this should increase imports and decrease exports, provided all other factors were to remain constant. But other factors are rarely constant. The CEECs managed to transform their economies from centrally planned systems to market economies. Substantial progress has been achieved in the areas of property rights and privatization, as well as capital and trade liberalization. The 12 countries that joined the EU in 2004 and 2007 have anchored their institutional structures to the EU, and now they are being viewed as increasingly secure places for investing and doing business in general.

This in connection with an initial productivity boost after the overcoming of certain weaknesses inherited from the Communist era – like labour hoarding, overemphasis of heavy industry or inefficient management practices – contributed to an ever-improving standing of the region vis-à-vis the rest of the world. This is underlined, for example, by increasing world market shares or strong foreign direct investment inflows. During the past few years some of the countries also managed to upgrade successfully the technological and quality structure of their export production, which helped to secure existing market shares and to gain further importance in international trade. Against the backdrop of those improvements, appreciation did not pose a serious obstacle to competitiveness and economic development. This seems to underline that the external value of a currency is not the only decisive feature when it comes to the competitive position of a country.

A specific setting where exchange rates do not matter at all for competitiveness is within a monetary union. The countries constituting the union have given up the tool of national exchange rate policy for the benefits of introducing a common currency. But of course the absence of national currencies and therefore the absence of exchange relationships among them does not mean that questions of competitiveness lose their importance. In a certain sense they are even more important in such a context, as the exchange rate can no longer act as an adjustment mechanism to adverse developments. All the burden of adjustment then lies on wages and prices, and this may – as experience tells us – be a painful and tedious experience.

But what does matter for quantitative competitiveness in a monetary union is the development of unit labour costs. If increases in unit labour costs in a particular country are substantially larger than average for an extended time span, the country in question loses competitiveness vis-à-vis the other members. Production becomes relatively more expensive, and exporters are increasingly facing difficulties to compete in the internal market. This will ultimately impact the current account, economic activity and employment. As devaluing the currency is no longer an option in national economic policy making, such a development could result in prolonged stagnation. Some observers have even noted that such effects may threaten the stability of the whole monetary union.

In the euro area, the growth pattern of unit labour costs is indeed divergent. In some countries, unit labour costs have been increasing substantially stronger than average for an extended period of time (for example, in Ireland, Greece, Spain, Italy, Luxembourg, Portugal). In most of the cases this can be traced to comparatively weak productivity developments and strong wage increases (Spain, Italy, Luxembourg, Portugal). However, there is also one example – Ireland – where rising wages have accompanied very solid productivity developments.

Excessive unit labour cost growth is a concern per se. However, it can be more of a problem for some countries than for others, depending on the underlying drivers of wages and productivity. Differences in unit labour cost may be the outcome of a catching-up process, they may reflect different positions of countries within the economic cycle or country-specific shocks. But adverse developments may also be the consequence of structural shortcomings or inappropriate policies. In a catching-up setting or in a scenario of cyclical fluctuations, pronounced unit labour cost differentials should not constitute a long-term phenomenon. However, inflexible labour markets, a lack of competition in product markets or inefficient taxation systems, for example, may well permanently constrain productivity and increase wage pressure. Such causes tend to lead to more serious problems as they are potentially long-lasting.

Against this backdrop, increasing importance should be attached to policies that will meaningfully combat such deficiencies. Structural reforms as, for example, laid down in the Lisbon Agenda, constitute an especially useful policy option. Not only do they help increase competitiveness by improving cost-efficiency and by lifting innovative capacity as well as educational attainment, they also boost growth and employment.

With a view to competitiveness, paramount measures include structural reforms to stimulate productivity growth, especially in the services sector, to foster competition and to improve the functioning of market mechanisms, especially in the labour markets. An important advantage of such a set of policy actions is that they create conditions that allow wages to increase without putting pressure on prices and reduce the required adjustment of nominal wages in situations when competitiveness losses must be restored.

Needless to say, the single monetary policy of the Eurosystem cannot and will not address competitiveness problems in individual countries. But a credible monetary policy aimed at maintaining price stability in the medium term and solidly anchoring medium- and long-term inflation expectations can decisively contribute to a stable economic environment. In a stable macroeconomic context, it is not only easier to single out where reforms are needed, but the benefits of reforms are also made more visible and convincing, thus supporting their acceptance.

Ambitious structural reforms are not only important from a domestic perspective. Globalization and far-reaching international integration of financial markets have led to the build up of sizeable current account mismatches in the world. Against the backdrop of a current account close to balance, the euro area can best contribute to an orderly unwinding by making its economy more flexible and adoptive, and this is exactly what the Lisbon Agenda aims to achieve. Financial market reform and further deregulation of product and labour markets would positively impact saving and investment decisions in Europe and increase economic momentum. This would not only reduce the risk emanating from global imbalances but would also help to buffer the negative economic impact of an abrupt unwinding, should it finally occur. The manifold positive effects of structural reforms make their implementation a priority.

With regard to developments in the foreign exchange market, we saw quite some appreciation of the euro vis-à-vis the dollar in the course of 2007. In some countries this triggered fears that their economy may be unduly affected by the strong euro. Subsequently, discussions ensued of whether the monetary policy strategy of the European Central Bank (ECB) should be expanded to explicitly incorporate exchange rate considerations. Such requests, in my opinion, are ill-conceived.

Although a strong euro reduces sales abroad, it boosts spending at home. Cheaper imports raise the real income of households and thereby fuel consumption. In the euro area, where household spending has been sluggish, a shift in demand away from exports would be welcome. Cheaper imports also keep a lid on inflation. This seems especially important in times of high and rising oil prices. Finally, a deliberate management of the exchange rate can only act as a short-term cure for competitiveness problems and may well have adverse effects in the long run. The euro's strength is a powerful market signal that induces productivity advances in the export-oriented sector and may speed up a necessary shift in resources to more profitable lines of work. In that sense, the exchange rate can act as an agent for structural change and contribute to an elevated level of productivity. This will ultimately impact growth and competitiveness and easily outweigh the short-lived gains of active exchange rate management.

NOTE

1. Executive Director, Oesterreichische Nationalbank.

14. Real and nominal convergence: policy challenges in a monetary union

Lorenzo Bini Smaghi[1]

14.1 INTRODUCTION

The Maastricht Treaty – and, for that matter, the Reform Treaty – says very little on the real economy, aside from the fact that growth and employment are an objective of the European Union. The articles contained in the monetary chapters of the Treaty all refer to *nominal* variables, be they monetary policy or inflation, and so does the section that describes the criteria and procedure for the adoption of the euro. This does not mean, though, that the underlying developments in the *real* economy are unimportant. In fact, there is a burgeoning literature on the impact that the euro has had on the convergence of the member economies. Among such a wide range of academic contributions, let me refer in particular to papers presented at a conference organized by the ECB in June 2005, which provide evidence of the changes brought about by the euro with respect to trade integration, structural reforms, financial integration, business cycle synchronization and inflation differentials.[2]

Against this backdrop, one may wonder: is it a problem that the criteria for adopting the euro refer to nominal variables – the inflation rate, the long-term interest rate and the exchange rate – and to the budget deficit and debt ratios? Should the Treaty have been drafted differently? I will argue to the contrary. However, while it is wrong to suggest that the adoption of the euro solves all problems, it is equally wrong to suggest that real convergence does not pose considerable challenges in the path towards the adoption of the euro. The key policy message is that these challenges can be addressed as long as one is aware of them and explicitly takes them into consideration. Hiding the issues does not help. It might actually backfire if and when difficulties arise as people might be inclined to think that the root of all problems lies with the euro and its early adoption, rather than inappropriate policy actions in other fields. This is not just a hypothesis. It's what we observe every day, even within the euro area, with politicians claiming that Europe and the euro are to blame for their lack of success.

I would like to consider the case of countries that are converging in real and nominal terms towards the euro area.[3] Can both processes take place in parallel? What are the challenges? How can monetary, fiscal and structural policies best tackle them?

Let me also emphasize that the issue is relevant not only for the countries concerned but also for the whole of the European Union, in light of the existing strong economic ties. For example, the trade share of the 'new' EU member states, excluding Slovenia, is 18 per cent for Germany, 9 per cent for France and 12 per cent for Italy. These shares are comparable to that of the United States and exceed China's share. Links through financial and foreign direct investment (FDI) are also equally, if not more, important. Of course, the euro area is also very important for the new EU member states, representing 62 per cent of their external trade. It is not far-fetched to say that to some extent we are 'all in the same boat'.

In this chapter, I will first propose an analytical framework to examine the issue in a systematic way. I will then discuss some examples within the euro area. Finally, I will try to draw some policy lessons from both theory and experience.

14.2 ANALYTICAL FRAMEWORK

Let me start by laying out a framework to interpret real and nominal economic convergence.

14.2.1 Structural Forces Driving Convergence, Real Appreciation and External Deficits

Let us take two hypothetical countries, an advanced one, which I'll call for simplicity 'West', and one that is emerging and catching up, named 'East'. Real economic convergence should imply a higher marginal return on capital in East compared with West, due to the fact that capital is scarcer and due to decreasing returns on capital accumulation. In a closed economy, this translates into a higher real equilibrium interest rate in East compared with West. In a world with full financial integration, we would observe large capital flows from West to East. Since people in East expect to be richer tomorrow and want to smooth consumption over time, they will borrow, the more so the higher the expected economic growth rate.

This phenomenon will not happen if there are financial frictions and borrowing constraints in East that prevent the real interest rate from rising or the borrowing demand from being satisfied. In that case we might even observe that the flow of capital is reversed, from East to West. This is the so-called Lucas paradox; it's what we are currently observing, for example, in some East Asian economies, notably in China, and what we saw in Western Europe in the 1950s and 1960s. In Central and Western European countries, there does not seem to be such a paradox. There are, by and large, no borrowing constraints as countries are bound by what is called the *acquis communautaire*, in other words, all the laws and agreements, including the treaties that apply in the EU. Perhaps what is more important, they have implemented banking sector reforms that have led to an increase in banking competition.[4] So in the case of the European Union the theory works.

Another element of the theory that seems to be working to some extent is the Balassa-Samuelson effect, which contributes to a real exchange rate appreciation in East.[5] The real exchange rate appreciation associated with real convergence can obviously happen in two ways (or a combination of them): first, with a stable nominal exchange rate and high inflation, as in Japan in the post-war period up to the early 1970s; second, with an appreciating nominal exchange rate and stable low inflation, as in Japan in the subsequent period up to the early 1990s. I will not dwell on the choice of the exchange rate regime, apart from noting that the second channel of real appreciation is obviously precluded after a country joins the monetary union.

14.2.2 'Disequilibrium' Real Appreciation

While the theory suggests that real appreciation and balance of payments deficits are the natural consequences of real convergence, it does not follow that any such appreciation or deficit is justified in size. Real appreciation and external deficits may become excessive as a result of inappropriate policies and/or excessively optimistic expectations by economic agents.[6] Conceptually, this is no different from bubbles and busts in asset prices, which may be initially triggered by a real, fundamental reason (such as higher productivity growth or monetary policy shocks) but may then be inflated disproportionately by excessive self-fulfilling expectations.

In our example of East converging to West, the above risk may materialize when investor exuberance in East, supported by expectations of rapid economic and monetary integration, generates excess demand and inflationary pressures. Risk premia in East may be excessively squeezed,[7] leading to asset price misalignments (for example, in housing) and over-indebtedness in a context of still abundant global liquidity and strong risk appetite. Irrational optimism on the side of wage earners can add to the risk. Such a scenario represents an 'out-of-equilibrium' real appreciation, leading to an overshooting that is typically observed in boom-and-bust cycles. There is abundant literature on this phenomenon. The key question is what to do to avoid such a scenario.

14.2.3 Adjustment in a Monetary Union

Let us consider first the case of both East and West participating in a monetary union, which puts a constraint on real exchange rate movements or, more precisely, a constraint on competitiveness within the union. Let us go back to the idea that the expected real marginal product of capital is higher in East. If the nominal exchange rate is fixed and there is sufficient capital mobility within the union, capital inflows in East must be accompanied by a combination of (1) balance-of-payments deficits, and (2) higher inflation. This should gradually be reversed as the real convergence process runs its course and the excess return on investment opportunities is absorbed.

What is the adjustment mechanism? If inflation rises above the average in a given country, it loses competitiveness and this has, over time, a dampening impact on inflation. The point can be illustrated clearly using an open economy Phillips curve where the real exchange rate appears as a determinant of inflation.[8] What effect prevails, and at what speed, depends on the relative importance of the two channels in the Phillips curve. Ceteris paribus, the more integrated and flexible a country, the likelier it will be that the forces of convergence prevail over those of divergence. Research shows that in the euro area the competitiveness channel works satisfactorily and that, abstracting from trends related to Balassa-Samuelson effects, deviations from purchasing power parity (PPP) are mean-reverting. According to this research, the adjustment in the euro area is actually found to be quicker in the Economic and Monetary Union (EMU) than in regions of the United States.[9] However, more research is needed on this important issue; moreover, the situation is clearly different across countries, depending on the degree of integration and flexibility.

Due consideration should be given to the fact that the adjustment channels might be impaired in some cases. If nominal and real rigidities as well as financial frictions are limiting the scope for relative price changes, or weakening the expenditure-switching role of relative inflation differentials, the convergence process in a monetary union could be rather bumpy. This may occur, for example, if the massive inflow of capital and exceptionally low risk premia are rapidly reversed and followed by an equally large outflow as the adjustment takes place and as risks are re-appreciated.

It is important to recognize that membership of a monetary union increases the likelihood of excessively low risk premia and a pro-cyclical behaviour of real interest rates, which might temporarily slow down or even destabilize the structural adjustment process. Indeed, within a monetary union, forces exerting upward pressures on inflation tend to become self-sustained and more likely to give rise to an abrupt adjustment. Since the nominal interest rate is fixed at the union level, any shock bringing inflation above the union average will reduce the real interest rate and fuel further inflationary pressures, in a self-reinforcing mechanism.[10]

In a boom-and-bust scenario, such as the one I have described, which is a real risk in a monetary union or with a fixed exchange rate regime, policy makers undoubtedly face the very difficult challenge of having to avoid an overheating of the economy in the face of surging capital inflows and rapid credit growth. An independent monetary policy could be a suitable instrument to tackle such a problem but it is simply not available to East as long as it has not joined the monetary union. With a fixed exchange rate regime, however, monetary policy makes things even worse for East, because it is set by West with a view to ensuring price stability in West itself. Given the convergence process and the required higher rate of growth of productivity and income in East, as compared with West, the monetary policy set by West is too expansionary for East. As an illustration, a 4 per cent interest rate might be appropriate for an economy growing at a steady state rate of 2 per cent and with 2 per cent inflation – I'm giving these numbers for purely illustrative reasons – but is certainly not appropriate for an economy growing in real terms at 6 per cent or more, as required by the catching-up process. As the inflationary pressures arise in East, the monetary policy becomes pro-cyclical, further destabilizing the economy and making the adjustment more abrupt later on.

The recent financial turbulence in the United States and Europe has shown the dangers of keeping interest rates too low, compared with the economy's underlying rate of productivity and income growth, for a prolonged period of time. When I raised the issue myself, in 2005, I noted that there was still very little literature on this issue.[11] Some progress has been made, but the issue is still not sufficiently recognized in academic and policy fora. Indeed, when one looks at the current situation in many emerging market economies, one cannot but be struck by the huge gap between these two variables, which, in my view, is the sign of a major distortion in the allocation of resources that might lead to future abrupt adjustment.[12]

Fiscal policy can be activated to attenuate the inflationary pressures arising from the monetary stimulus, but the size of the fiscal restraint might have to be quite ample. Banking supervision and related prudential measures could also be implemented to limit credit expansion. Their quantitative impact is of course uncertain, especially in an environment of full capital mobility. Capital controls might be applied to contain inflows, but they are not allowed in the EU.

14.2.4 Summing Up

What can we learn from all this? Let me recap the reasoning in three main developments that can be expected from real convergence in a monetary union:

- First, real convergence may entail a higher return on capital for some time in the catching-up country and a substantial appreciation of the real exchange rate, which is to be considered, to some extent, as an equilibrium phenomenon and a natural consequence of real catching-up dynamics.
- Second, within a monetary union or with a fixed exchange rate system, the appreciation of the real exchange rate may take place through a higher inflation rate.
- Third, as a consequence of the above, the inflationary process associated with the real exchange rate appreciation may fuel an inflationary spiral that entails an overshooting of inflation and a boom-and-bust cycle. In this context, nominal convergence is not consistent with the continuation of real convergence and might imply large adjustment costs.

How can these last developments be avoided? The key word is flexibility. Let me elaborate on this. First, there must be flexibility in the wage and price adjustment setting. Since the process of real convergence requires significant movements in the real exchange rate and since in a monetary union the nominal exchange rate cannot be used as an adjustment tool, it is of paramount importance that prices can move quickly in the required direction. A key aspect is thus wage formation. Movements in the real exchange rates must be rapidly reflected in movements of real wages – in the opposite direction (!) – in order to preserve the competitiveness of the economy. We do have some evidence that some new EU member states score quite well in terms of labour market flexibility.[13] However, the situation is not the same across countries.

Movements in the real exchange rate should, and will, bring about demand shifts between tradable and non-tradable goods and more generally between different sectors of the economy. In the era of globalization, this cannot only be described as a problem for EU countries. In fact, membership of the EU and of the monetary union can be characterized as a 'regional globalization' due to the trade-enhancing effects of the euro.[14] It is of great importance that the economy is flexible and able to reallocate physical and human capital across different production locations. The ability to shift production seamlessly from the less competitive to the more competitive sectors is a hallmark of countries dealing successfully with globalization. It is also true for success in the monetary union.

A study of the administrative burdens in the new EU member states on the basis of indicators published by the Fraser Institute shows that the business environment has significantly improved in those states over the past few years.[15] However, on average in 2004 it had still not reached the average level of the euro area countries and there remained significant differences between the new EU member states. Another indicator, the OECD's country score index on barriers to trade and investments, shows an overall decline from 1998 to 2003 both in the euro area and in the four largest new EU member states, but on average, they remain higher in the latter. This would suggest that more needs to be done to make the economies of the new member states more flexible so that they can respond to the challenges they face in the process of real and nominal convergence.

14.3 SOME INTERESTING EXAMPLES

Let us now see how the conceptual framework that I have just described works out in practice.

14.3.1 Some Stylized Facts

Let me consider the experiences of countries that are already in the euro area. This might teach us something useful about the challenges that the new member states may face in converging towards the euro adoption. In 1995, that is, a few years before the launch of the euro, there were a handful of countries with a real GDP per capita significantly below the euro area average: Greece, at 65 per cent, Spain, at 79 per cent, Portugal, at 65 per cent and Ireland, at 89 per cent. If we look at the new EU member states (data for 2006), we see a range of between 34 per cent (Romania and Bulgaria) and 72 per cent (Czech Republic) of euro area GDP per capita. For some of these countries, we are already in a situation similar to that of the countries catching up with the euro area in 1995; currently, the Czech Republic already has a higher income per capita than Portugal and is very close to Greece and Slovenia.[16] For some other countries, however, and notably for Bulgaria and Romania, the degree of the required catching up is nowhere near to the income gap for the original euro area members. We are therefore in a new situation here.

A stylized fact in the adoption of the euro in 1999 was that the convergence of nominal interest rates was accompanied by the convergence of the real interest rate.[17] The real interest rate of previously high-inflation countries such as Greece, Spain, Italy and Ireland fell substantially as these countries were able to slash inflation and exchange rate risk premia. In Italy, for example, the real short-term interest rate fell from over 5 per cent in the nine years before the euro to 1 per cent in the nine years thereafter. Nevertheless, convergence has not been completed. This is related to persistent inflation differentials among the euro area countries, which has been the subject of quite some attention in the literature.[18] Higher-inflation countries, such as Spain and Ireland, have experienced systematically lower (and in the Irish case often negative) real interest rates than lower-inflation countries such as Germany, despite their higher (potential) growth.

In theory, as I mentioned earlier, the self-sustaining nature of real interest rates in the different countries of a monetary union can fuel divergences within the union. But these forces are partly countered by the loss of competitiveness, which has a dampening effect on inflation. If you want to see the glass half empty, you could argue that this second force has not yet been strong enough to prevent persistent inflation differentials across countries. I prefer to see the glass half full by noting that inflation differentials within the euro area have remained at a relatively low level, fully comparable with divergence among US regions and well below the cross-country variation seen before the mid-1990s. This observation is also true when we look at business cycle fluctuations, which appear to be quite synchronized within the euro area. This is not to say – of course – that the differences between real interest rates across countries are of no concern.

14.3.2 Ireland Versus Portugal

Let me now focus on two extremely different performances within the euro area: Ireland and Portugal. Real GDP per capita in Ireland was 89 per cent of the euro area average in 1995, but was already above the average in 1998. Between 1998 and 2006, real income per capita increased by almost 25 percentage points, to reach 131 per cent of the euro area average in 2006, which is the second highest after Luxembourg. (Based on these numbers, it is surprising how many people still speak of Ireland as a catching-up economy.) As for Portugal, its income per capita was 65 per cent of the euro area average in 1995, a figure that has changed little in over a decade (it was 67 per cent in 1998 and 68 per cent in 2006). The bottom line is that real per capita income in the two countries was not very different in the early 1990s but became twice as large in Ireland by 2006. How could that happen?

The answer to this question may well matter since Ireland and Portugal in 1995 were in a situation not unlike that of some new EU member states now (though, as we have seen, for some of them the starting point is significantly lower).[19] One approach to understanding the difference can be found in growth accounting exercises. The stellar growth performance of Ireland was not just due to higher labour and capital input but also, and mainly, due to labour productivity growth, which has been close to 3 per cent per year since the introduction of the euro and, according to available estimates, almost entirely due to growth in total factor productivity (TFP). In Portugal, growth in labour productivity has been less than 1 per cent per year on average, reflecting subdued TFP growth.

In the decade before joining the euro area both Portugal and Ireland went through a boom, with annual average GDP growth rates at 2.8 per cent and 6.7 per cent, respectively (1990–98). This strong growth masked substantive differences. While fiscal policy was pro-cyclical in Portugal, reinforcing domestic demand pressures, it was much more disciplined in Ireland. While growth in unit labour costs and HICP (Harmonized Index of Consumer Prices) inflation was high in Portugal (7.6 per cent and 6.2 per cent on average between 1990 and 1998, respectively), cost and price pressures remained contained in Ireland (1.4 per cent and 2.3 per cent, respectively). Competitiveness was hurt in Portugal, resulting in a rising current account deficit (to 8.9 per cent of GDP in 1999), while competitiveness was relatively well preserved in Ireland and the current account position broadly neutral (0.3 per cent of GDP in 1999). Thus, the longer-term track record before joining monetary union regarding low inflationary pressures and a balanced current account was impressive in Ireland. This shows that even very rapid catching up does not need to be associated with high inflation or large imbalances.

After the euro changeover – between 2000 and 2003 – a sharp downward adjustment occurred in Portugal as consumption and investment slowed considerably. Competitiveness problems and the need to improve the fiscal position added to the downturn. Annual real GDP growth in Portugal in the period 1999–2006 averaged 1.7 per cent. In Ireland, real output growth continued instead at a strong pace (at 6.5 per cent on average) in this period and the fiscal balance was in slight surplus. Following the slowdown in activity, unit labour cost growth and inflation pressures diminished in Portugal (to 3.1 per cent and 3.0 per cent on average, respectively), while they gradually picked up in Ireland (3.2 per cent and 3.5 per cent, respectively, on average) in the period 1999–2006. Since 1999, the Portuguese economy has not succeeded in improving its competitiveness and its sizeable current account deficit remains.

In principle, one could imagine that stronger productivity growth should contribute to containing unit labour costs, making Ireland more competitive than Portugal. This is true, but not in the most obvious sense. If one computes unit labour costs in Ireland and Portugal, numbers are approximately the same. However, export performance has been much stronger in Ireland than in Portugal, which has resulted in a trade surplus in the balance of payments (against a large deficit in Portugal). The large profit outflows in the factor income account in Ireland negatively affect the current account position. In 2006, the current account stood at –4.2 per cent of GDP in Ireland, against –9.9 per cent of GDP in Portugal. What has happened? Quite simply, cost competitiveness is not the only determinant of competitiveness. Shifting production to higher value-added sectors is as important as keeping unit labour costs under control, if not more. There is evidence that Ireland and Portugal have been competing in quite different products and markets in the past decade, with the latter country being subject to stronger competitive pressures from new EU member states and emerging market economies.

To a large extent, the divergence can be traced back to the key structural features of the two economies. The first is a different degree of flexibility. Indicators of product and market regulation, compiled by the OECD, signal significantly more rigidity in Portugal than in Ireland; the same is true for other measures of market friendliness such as the World Bank's Doing Business index.[20] Another crucial difference is in the availability of physical and human capital, as evidenced by the discrepancy in educational attainment of the labour force, research and development expenditure, penetration of information technology, and so on. Ireland has also benefited, in part, from the removal of the exchange rate risk after the adoption of the euro, which has favoured large FDI inflows (though countries like Portugal should have benefited from this as well). Labour market and wage and price flexibility have contributed to preventing inflation from rising excessively and becoming entrenched and ultimately unsustainable for the country's competitiveness.

Another interesting and telling difference between Ireland and Portugal has been in the field of fiscal policy. Public debt, public expenditure and budget deficits have all been significantly lower in Ireland than in the rest of the euro area, noticeably so when compared with Portugal. This shows that the discretionary use of fiscal policy is hardly a recipe for stimulating growth, especially when the 'fiscal house' is not in order.

At the same time, one should not be complacent about developments in Ireland. Several years of very low and even negative real interest rates, coupled with buoyant growth, may have led some sectors of the economy, and the housing market in particular, to levels that are unsustainable over the medium term. We still do not know of policies that have been reliably deployed to prevent the risk of misallocation of capital in an environment of very low real interest rates. Only time will tell. Moreover, the success of Ireland, a small country with little more than 4 million inhabitants, may not be easily replicated elsewhere, especially in larger countries. Nonetheless, it shows that equally flexible and dynamic economies in Eastern Europe could do just as well if they were to join the euro area.

To sum up, the differences between Ireland and Portugal are not so much in the behaviour of the real exchange rate and in standard measures of cost competitiveness. The Irish example shows that it is possible to prosper in the monetary union while having a higher potential growth rate than the rest of the union. This does not need to be 'paid' in terms of divergent or explosive inflationary outcomes and/or in unsustainable competitiveness for the country. The Portuguese example, in contrast, provides a stark warning that entering the monetary union per se does not guarantee a satisfactory growth performance. In order to obtain the full benefits of monetary union, the appropriate economic structures and national policies have to be in place.

14.4 CONCLUSION

Economic and monetary union should never be considered as a final destination, but only as a departure point. Joining the euro area is not, in itself, a recipe for economic success. Countries need to be well equipped in order to thrive in it. The recipes for success are known: flexibility in the wage and price formation process, flexibility in the production structure, human and physical capital, dynamism. These features are not very different from those that are needed anyway in an era of globalization, but participation in EMU makes them even more compelling. Real convergence is therefore not, per se, an impediment to joining the monetary union. Nonetheless, there is no doubt that real convergence creates some challenges of its own that need to be properly addressed by policy makers before joining a monetary union. Not doing so will lead to both economic and political problems.

The recent experience of Slovenia, which adopted the euro on 1 January 2007, is a confirmation of what I just said. The economy is growing fast and inflationary pressures are mounting, with the latest numbers exceeding 5 per cent. Monetary policy evidently cannot cure this problem. On the other hand, fiscal policy in Slovenia is too lax, out of line with what would be required for macroeconomic stabilization. Deregulation of the product and labour markets has not yet been completed. Wages are growing faster than productivity, in particular in the public sector. The risks of a boom-and-bust cycle are looming.

In the face of this worrying scenario, what is the reaction of the policy authorities? Very predictable: they blame the euro for the price increases.[21] 'Déjà vu all over again': whenever things go wrong in a country, the policy makers blame Europe.

It's obviously not the right response, and it won't help the Slovenian people understand where the problems lie. Whether Slovenia will turn out to be more like Ireland than Portugal in the next few years depends entirely on Slovenia. And this will be true for any new member of the euro area.

NOTES

1. Member of the Executive Board, European Central Bank. The views expressed in this chapter reflect only those of the author. I thank L. Stracca, M. Darracq-Paries, M. Andersson, G. Fagan, O. Tristani, K. Masuch and F. Mongelli for input and comments.
2. See Mongelli and Vega (2006).
3. Note that I will not touch upon demographics, given that the Central and Eastern European countries are not very different in that respect from the countries currently in the euro area.
4. See Arratibel et al. (2007) for a survey of these developments.
5. Égert, Halpern and MacDonald (2006) calculate that the Balassa-Samuelson effect could contribute to real exchange rate appreciation in some new EU member states by around one to two percentage points annually, but not in all countries.
6. See Boz (2007) for a theoretical analysis related to emerging countries.
7. See, for instance, Luengnaruemitchai and Schadler (2007).
8. See Flamini (2007) for an analytical derivation, and Leith and Malley (2007) for empirical estimates for G7 countries.
9. See Berk and Swank (2007). Note, however, that this conclusion is dependent on the assumption that the PPP trends are entirely due to the Balassa-Samuelson effect and therefore reflect equilibrium phenomena.
10. See Allsopp and Vines (1998).
11. 'Inflation, expectations and current challenges to monetary policy', speech at the European Inflation-linked Conference, Rome, 10 October 2005.
12. In addition, low nominal interest rates may be also, if not more, important than low real interest rates in leading to asset price misalignments; see Shiller (2007).
13. Buettner (2007) finds that regional wage flexibility is significantly higher in new EU member states (NMS) than in the euro area; in particular, wage formation within regions is more sensitive to local unemployment in the NMS. See also Blanchflower (2001) on the response of wages to unemployment in the NMS.
14. See Rose (2000).
15. Arratibel et al. (2007), in particular pp. 27–9.
16. The figure for Poland, by far the largest new EU member state, is 48 per cent of the euro area average in 2006, up from 37 per cent in 1995.
17. See Arghyrou, Gregoriou and Kontonikas (2007). However, they reject full real interest rate convergence for Greece, Spain and Italy as well as the UK.
18. See Angeloni and Ehrmann (2002) and Ortega (2003) among the academic contributions; see also ECB (2003, 2005) especially on the policy implications.
19. In part, this might reflect the fact that the statistical data for real GDP are different from real GNP in the Irish case. Therefore, the increase in real domestic product has not necessarily entirely benefited the Irish people to the same extent. However, the quantitative importance of this discrepancy is low. We are therefore left with the task of understanding the causes of this divergence in economic performance.

20. Ireland is ranked 8th and Portugal 37th in the World Bank's ease of Doing Business index, which ranks economies from 1 to 178. The index is calculated as the ranking on the simple average of country percentile rankings on each of ten topics covered in the *Doing Business 2008* report. See http://www.doingbusiness.org/economyrankings/.
21. See the statement by Slovenia's Prime Minister Jansa on 16 November 2007: 'I was warned by other countries' leaders that we would see price increases after euro adoption'.

REFERENCES

Allsopp, C. and D. Vines (1998), 'The assessment: macroeconomic policy after EMU', *Oxford Review of Economic Policy*, **14** (3), 1–23.

Angeloni, I. and M. Ehrmann (2002), 'Euro area inflation differentials', *ECB Working Paper* No. 388.

Arghyrou, M.G., A. Gregoriou and A. Kontonikas (2007), 'Do real interest rates converge? Evidence from the European Union', *Cardiff Economics Working Paper* No. E2007/26.

Arratibel, O., F. Heinz, R. Martin, M. Przybyla, L. Rawdanowicz, R. Serafini and T. Zumer (2007), 'Determinants of growth in the Central and Eastern European EU member states – a production function approach', *ECB Occasional Paper* No. 61.

Berk, J.M. and J. Swank (2007), 'Regional real exchange rates and Phillips curves in monetary unions: evidence from the US and EMU', *DNB Working Paper* No. 147/2007.

Blanchflower, D. (2001), 'Unemployment, well-being and wage curves in Eastern and Central Europe', *Journal of the Japanese and International Economies*, **15** (4), 364–402.

Boz, E. (2007), 'Can miracles lead to crises? The role of optimism in emerging markets crises', *IMF Working Paper* No. 07/223.

Buettner, T. (2007), 'Unemployment disparities and regional wage flexibility: comparing EU members and EU accession countries', *Empirica*, **34** (4), 287–97.

ECB (European Central Bank) (2003), 'Inflation differentials in the euro area: potential causes and policy conclusions', *ECB Working Paper Series* No. 388.

ECB (European Central Bank) (2005), 'Monetary policy and inflation differentials in a heterogeneous currency area', *ECB Monthly Bulletin*, May, 61–77.

Egert, B., L. Halpern and R. MacDonald (2006), 'Equilibrium exchange rates in transition economies: taking stock of the issues', *Journal of Economic Surveys*, **20** (2), 257–324.

Flamini, A. (2007), 'Inflation targeting and exchange rate pass-through', *Journal of International Money and Finance*, **26** (7), 1113–50.

Leith, C. and J. Malley (2007), 'Estimated open economy Phillips curves for the G7', *Open Economies Review*, **18** (4), 427–51.

Luengnaruemitchai, P. and S. Schadler (2007), 'Do economists and financial markets perspectives on the new members of the EU differ?', *IMF Working Paper* No. WP/07/67.

Mongelli, P. and J.L. Vega (2006), 'What effects is EMU having on the euro area and its member countries? An overview', *ECB Working Paper Series* No. 599.

Ortega, E. (2003), 'Persistent inflation differentials in Europe', *Banco de España Working Paper* No. 03/05.

Rose, A.K. (2000), 'One money, one market: estimating the effect of common currencies on trade', *Economic Policy*, **30**.

Shiller, R. (2007), 'Low interest rates and high asset prices: an interpretation in terms of changing popular economic models', paper prepared for the Celebration of BPEA conference, 6–7 September.

15. Product quality and international competitiveness in the new member states of the EU[1]

Deniz Igan[2]

15.1 INTRODUCTION

Of the new members entering the European Union (EU) in May 2004, several had achieved a decade of impressive export growth, expanding significantly their shares of world markets. What factors lay behind this performance? This chapter places in international context the achievements of the eight Central and Eastern European countries (the CEE-8).[3] Though the timing and pace varied, the gains in market shares are evident for six of these eight countries (Figure 15.1); only Slovenian and Latvian market shares remained relatively flat. In benchmarking this performance, the goal of the chapter is to help identify more broadly the determinants of international competitiveness.

The puzzle is that the market share gains by the CEE-8 were achieved despite the appreciation of real exchange rates (Figure 15.1). Of course, the bivariate relationship between real exchange rates and evolution of market shares does not control for other developments during this period. Nevertheless, the question does arise: is the real exchange rate irrelevant? If not, what other factors compensated for the appreciation to explain the apparently strong competitiveness of these economies? And will these favorable factors continue to power export growth?

The key to the puzzle is that a structural transformation was also achieved during this period. This transition from planned economic systems was accompanied by extensive privatization and restructuring, alongside the dismantling of trade barriers and the inflow of foreign direct investment. Forced to compete with international producers, domestically and in foreign markets, firms in the CEE-8 survived by reducing their quality-adjusted prices. This, in turn, required both cost reduction and quality enhancement. Meanwhile, the composition of production shifted toward higher-technology products. This chapter documents that transformation. Building

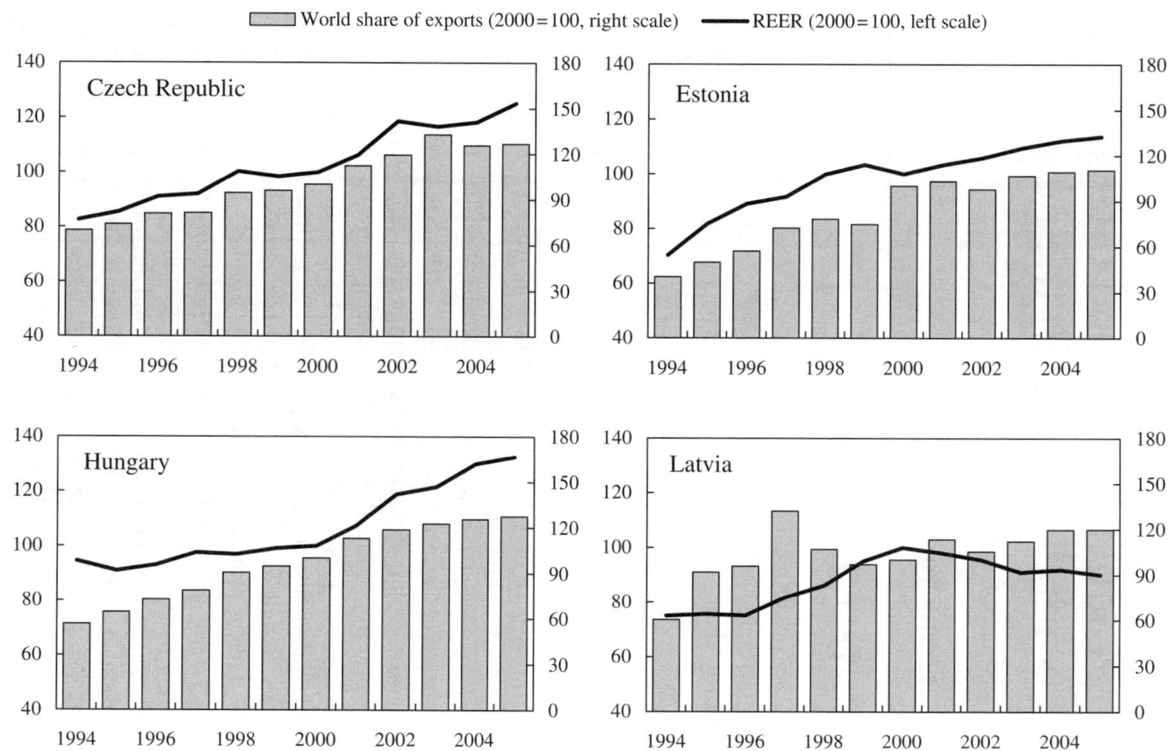
World share of exports (2000=100, right scale)
REER (2000=100, left scale)
Czech Republic
Estonia
Hungary
Latvia
140
120
100
80
60
40
180
150
120
90
60
30
0
1994
1996
1998
2000
2002
2004

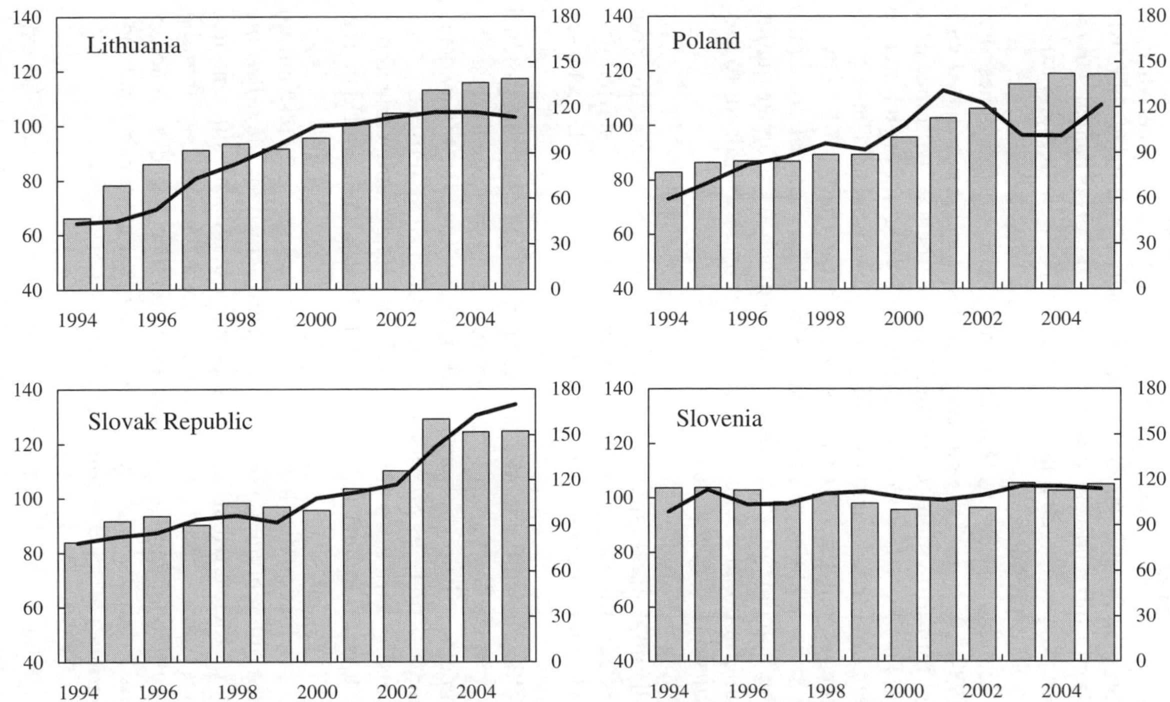

Note: * Market share is the share in per cent of a country's manufacturing exports in the global manufacturing trade.

Sources: UN Comtrade database; IMF, International Financial Statistics; author's calculations.

*Figure 15.1 CEE-8: market share and real effective exchange rate (REER), 1994–2005** from data at the six-digit level of disaggregation, the evidence shows an impressive shift in product quality – measured by the unit value of a country's exports relative to the unit value of world exports – and in the technological intensity of exports (Figure 15.2). At the same time, while the pace and timing of the shift once again varied across countries, there was also a movement from relatively low-technology products principally to the medium-technology range, and more slowly, to the production and export of high-technology products.

The empirical analysis shows that, in a cross-section of countries, over the period 1994–2004, quality and technology upgrading associated with the structural transformation were, indeed, also associated with increased market share. The analysis strongly suggests that, when trading in international markets, countries benefit from higher product quality. The implication, therefore, is that the observed association for the CEE-8 between improved product quality and increased market share was not accidental but rather the outcome of the apparent value attached to higher-quality products in international markets. The cross-country analysis leads to four specific conclusions of relevance to the CEE-8:

- A small initial market share allows for a catch-up process: coming out of their transition from planned economies, the CEE-8 started with relatively small market shares and took advantage of the catch-up potential.
- Controlling for initial market share, both a higher starting product quality, proxied by the unit value ratio, and an increase in this ratio over time have helped expand market share; however, the evidence also suggests that this process may have diminishing returns.
- Once quality variations are accounted for, real exchange rate appreciation appears to hurt a country's ability to expand its world market share.
- Higher product quality has, as expected, been especially relevant for so-called differentiated products, which are valued for the range and quality of their attributes. Higher product quality of differentiated products from a country appears 'twice blessed' in the sense that this quality also helps gain market share in 'reference-priced' and 'homogeneous' products, possibly by enhancing that country's reputation or economies of scale in sourcing and transportation costs.

The message for the CEE-8, therefore, is complimentary but also cautionary. These countries have gone through a catch-up phase during which they have also put to good use their human capital in moving up the technology and quality ladder. These factors have allowed them to maintain the dynamism of their exports despite exchange rate appreciations. However, looking ahead, the task will become harder, for several reasons. First, the market share gains made possible by the particularly small world market shares at the time of transition have been largely achieved. Second, the task of technology and quality upgrading was facilitated by the opportunities for relatively easy gains through privatization and restructuring. A new generation of restructuring and technical progress will require more sophisticated efforts and measures. Finally, there is some evidence that technological upgrading may have diminishing returns. However, it will be necessary to keep pace with technical change in competitor economies to maintain market shares and limit the risk of falling behind. Hence, the pressures for continued productivity gains will only increase over time.

This chapter builds on an incipient empirical literature linking product quality and export performance. Dulleck et al. (2005) report the improvements in the product quality and technology content of exports from the CEE-8. In their empirical analysis, however, they focus on assessing whether improved product quality/technology of a particular product is associated with an increasing share of that product in the country's basket of exports. Instead, the question we ask is whether the country's share of world markets (either for all goods or for different baskets of goods) is a function of country product quality.

The rest of this chapter is organized as follows. In the next section, we present several bivariate relationships to motivate an empirical framework for analyzing the evolution of market shares. The third section reports the basic regressions results, explaining the changes in market shares for 58 countries (accounting for almost 94 per cent of the world trade) over the period 1994 to 2004. The fourth reports results that distinguish between differentiated, reference-priced, and homogeneous products. The final section concludes.

15.2 EXPLAINING MARKET SHARES: AN EMPIRICAL FRAMEWORK

We begin with the proposition that a large initial market share constrains the subsequent increase in market share. This intuition is based on the presumption that, whereas newer entrants have a significant catch-up possibility, a country's share saturates at some point. To test this intuition, an appropriate measure of market share is needed. To motivate such a measure, Figure 15.3 plots, for select economies, the share of their GDP in world GDP against the share of their exports in world trade. Figure 15.3a, for 1994, shows the countries clustered around the 45-degree line; the CEE-8

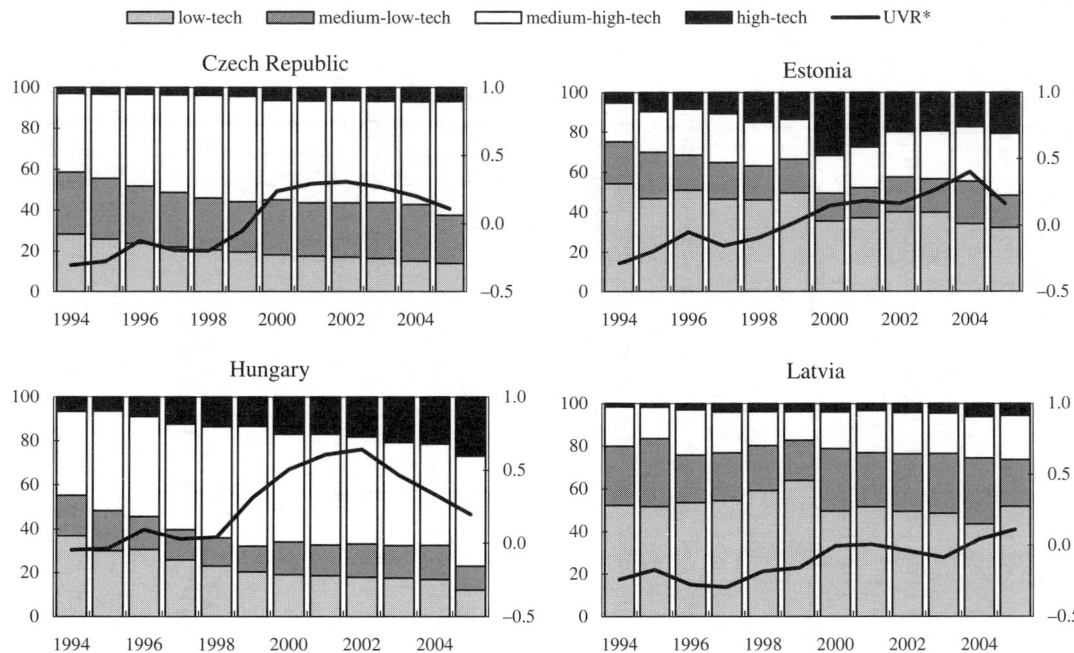
low-tech
medium-low-tech
medium-high-tech
high-tech
UVR*
Czech Republic
Estonia
Hungary
Latvia
100
80
60
40
20
0
1.0
0.5
0.0
–0.5
1994
1996
1998
2000
2002
2004

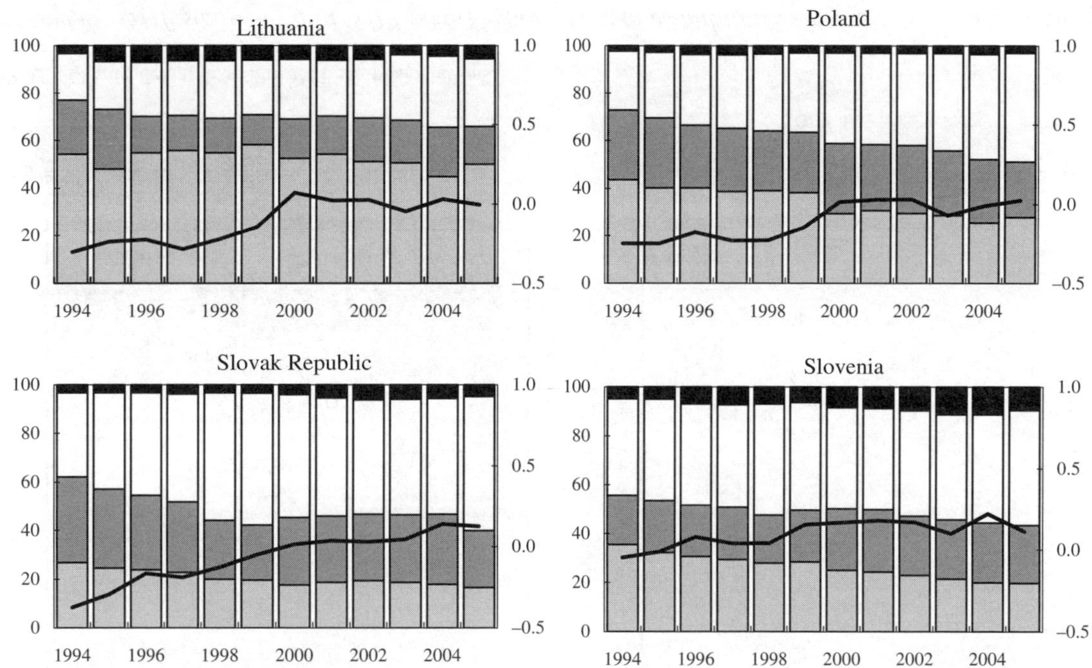

Note: * UVR is the unit value of a country's exports divided by the unit value of world exports. Expressed in logarithm so that a value of zero means country unit value equals world unit value.

Sources: UN Comtrade and author's calculations.

Figure 15.2 New member states: moving up the technology and quality ladder, 1994–2005 (share in per cent of country exports)

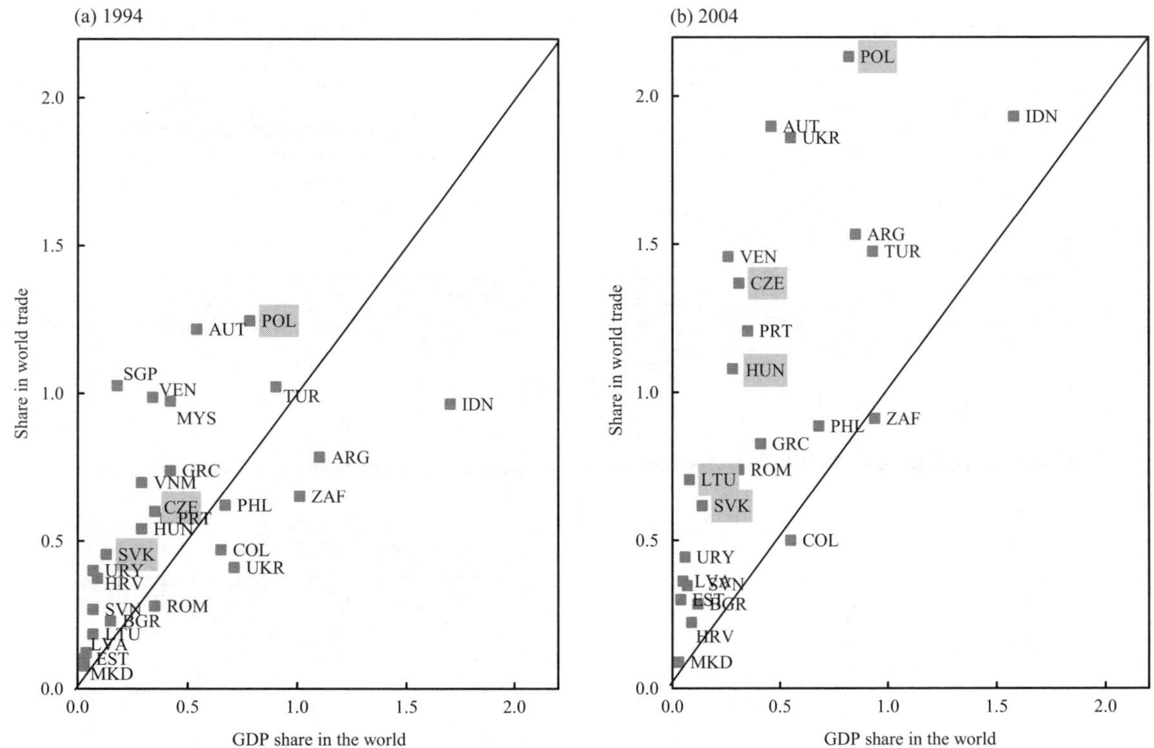

Sources: IFS, UN Comtrade database and IMF staff calculations.

Figure 15.3a and b GDP share in world GDP versus export share in global trade, 1994 and 2004 (in purchasing power parity, in per cent) were already slightly above that line, especially Slovakia and Slovenia. By 2005, these countries had acquired more of a presence in world GDP but especially in world trade. In conducting the analysis, therefore, two measures of market share are possible. First, the simple share of exports in world markets, as shown in Figure 15.3, can be used. The concern with such a measure is that it also reflects the size of the country and not just its competitive capability. Second, the export share can be normalized by the country's GDP share in world GDP. This latter measure is a metric of how far ahead a country's trading relationships are relative to its production capabilities. A large normalized market share would indicate reduced potential for further inroads into world markets, absent expansion of domestic production capacity. Because this analysis relies primarily on within-country variation over a decade, the change in country size during that period can be quantitatively important in some cases; however, in general, the findings remain similar irrespective of the measure used.

The data do support the expected inverse relationship between initial share and the subsequent increase in market shares. Figure 15.4a shows this relationship for the simple measure of market share, and Figure 15.4b for the normalized measure. Countries with smaller shares in 1994 had made, on average, larger gains by 2005, showing the possibility of catch up. The countries in Eastern Europe benefited from this process. Note also, for example, that the Czech Republic is above the line, implying that its market share gain was due to more than its low level of initial market penetration and despite its substantial exchange rate appreciation during this period. Other CEE-8 countries are in a similar position. This finding prompts us to examine what other factors were at work.[4]

To examine the role of technology and quality upgrading in the evolution of market shares, we constructed measures along two dimensions: quality and technology composition. As noted, based on trade data detailed at the six-digit level according to the Harmonized System (HS), unit value ratios (UVRs) are constructed. These are the ratios of a country's export unit values to the global average. For every country in the sample, we fix the basket of goods throughout the period under consideration.[5] By considering an unchanging basket of goods, we eliminate effects arising from greater product variety exported by a country (which may be of value to international buyers) and the shift to products with higher technology content, both of which may allow a country to raise the average prices at which it sells its exports. With these two effects eliminated, and because the analysis focuses on changes over time within a country, the UVR, in principle, proxies product quality, on the premise that a higher price reflects higher quality (see Hallak and Schott, 2005). The concern remains that the UVR is picking up other influences, especially if local

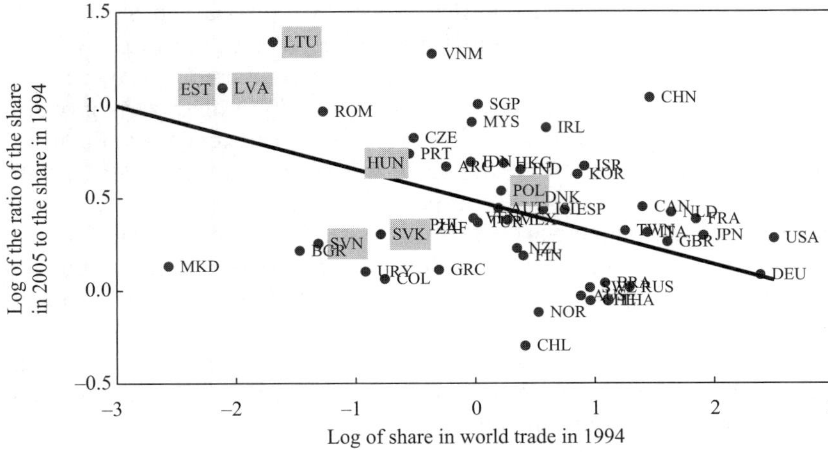

Figure 15.4a Increases in market shares relative to initial market shares, 1994–2005

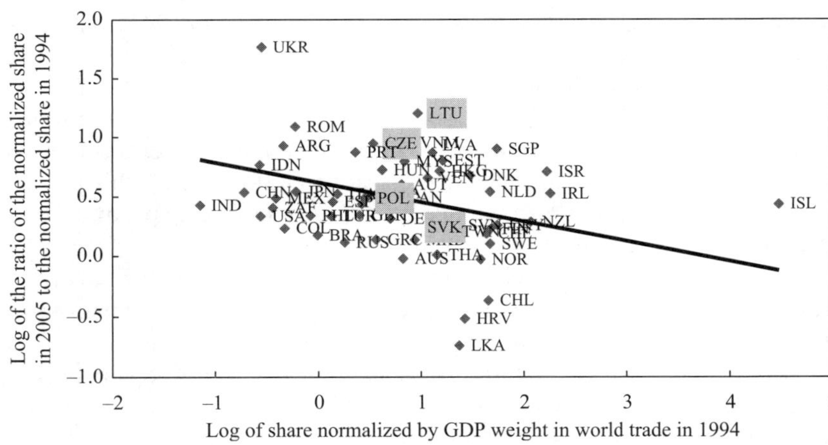

Figure 15.4b Increases in normalized market shares relative to initial normalized market shares, 1994–2005

monopolies exist and competition does not arbitrage away differences in quality-adjusted prices. To the extent that is the case and the UVR does not measure 'quality', the estimates will be biased downward. Hence, a finding that a higher UVR helps increase market share would provide a conservative estimate of the effects of quality. There remains the possibility that the UVR is picking up changes in the relative shares of products within the fixed basket of goods. To control for this, using higher R&D intensity as a

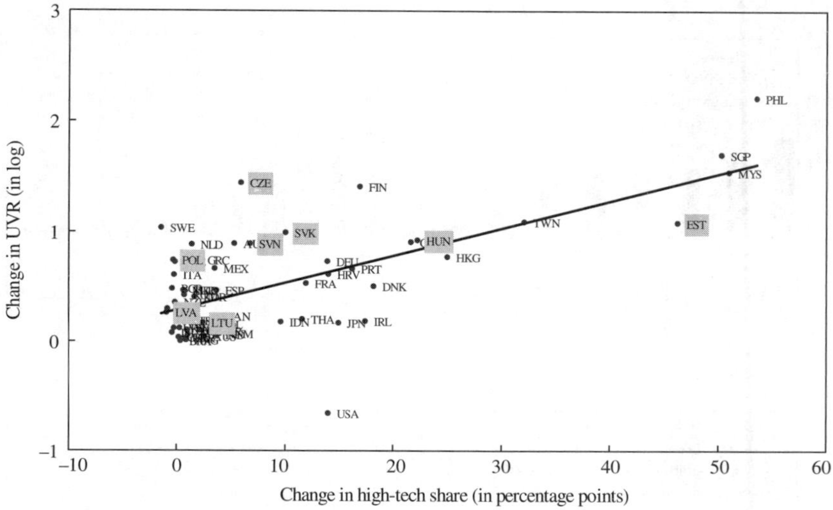

Source: UN Comtrade and author's calculations.

Figure 15.5 Change in unit value ratio vs change in high-tech share, 1994–2005

metric for higher technology, we obtain measures of a country's technology composition (for the fixed basket of goods, the technology composition changes to the extent that shares within that basket evolve).[6] Figure 15.5 shows that an increase in the high-tech share of a country's export composition is (imperfectly) correlated with its unit value ratios. Among developing countries/emerging markets, East Asia and the CEE-8 were the forerunners in technology and quality upgrading, whereas Latin America lagged (Figure 15.6).

These considerations lead to the following base empirical specification:

$$\log\,(\textit{normalized market share}_{i,t+1}/\textit{normalized market share}_{i,t}) \\ = \mathrm{f}\,(\textit{log normalized market share}_{i,t},\ \textit{log UVR}_{i,t},\ \Delta UVR_{i,t+1},\ \Delta REER_{i,t+1}).$$

Throughout, we use the change in the *normalized market share* as the variable to be explained. i refers to a country. ΔUVR_{t+1} is the log change in UVR from period t to period $t+1$, and $\Delta REER_{t+1}$ is the log change in the real effective exchange rate (REER) from period t to period $t+1$. Thus, we examine if the initial UVR influences the subsequent evolution of a country's market share and allow also for the possibility that the change in the UVR helps gain market share over the period considered. Because of

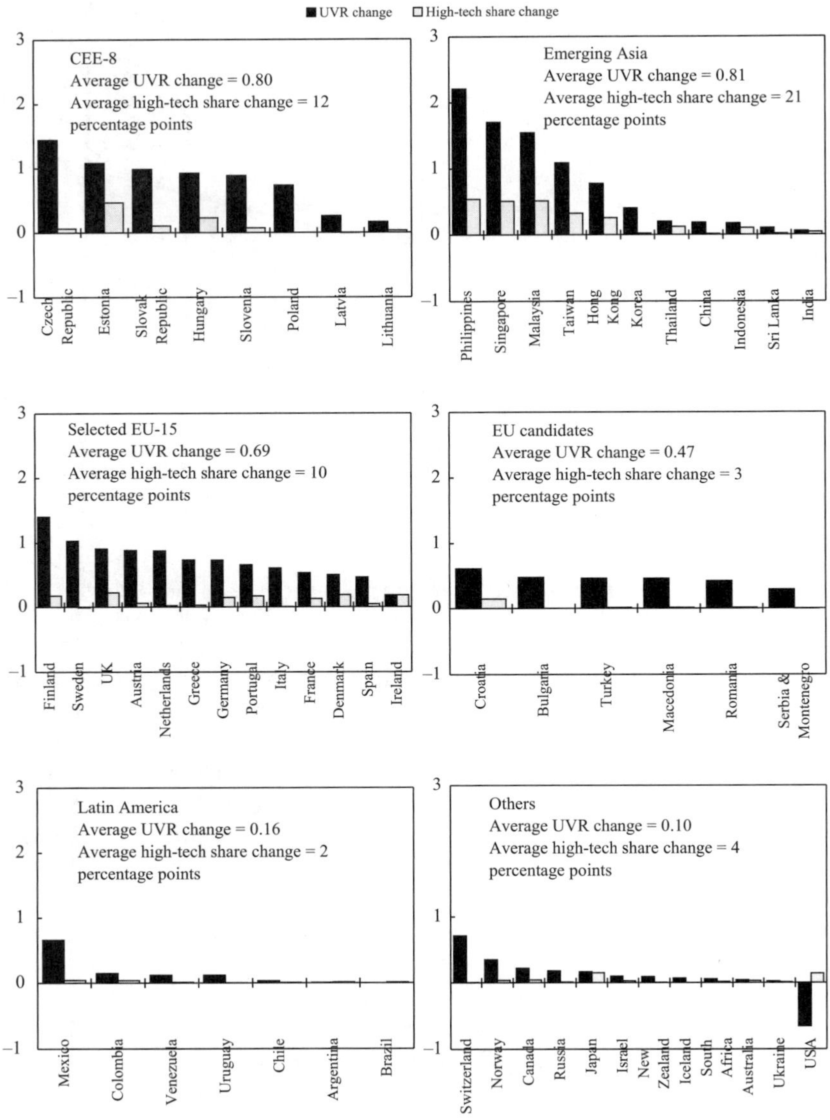

Note: * Average changes in UVR and high-tech shares are unweighted means across each country group. The changes are computed as the log difference for UVR and as the absolute change for high-tech share.

Sources: UN Comtrade, author's calculations.

*Figure 15.6 Change in unit value ratio and high-tech share, 1994–2005** the difficulties in measuring the equilibrium value of the exchange rate, especially for developing economies, we consider only the change in REER.

Panel regressions with country fixed effects allow analysis of within-country changes in market shares. The period from 1994 to 2005 is divided into three sub-periods, 1994–97, 1998–2001 and 2002–05, since annual changes are too noisy to give reliable results. We also ran the regressions for five-year periods with very similar findings. All regressions include country dummies, which are not reported. Since the dependent variable is the change in the market share, which, on average, does not change systematically for all countries in the same direction over time, we do not include time dummies. For 58 countries (covering almost 94 per cent of world trade) and the three time periods, we have, in principle, 174 observations. The Appendix lists the countries.

15.3 BASE RESULTS

Three factors are found to be significant in determining the evolution of market shares (Table 15.1). First, as Figure 15.4 above foreshadowed, the change in market share is inversely related to the starting share. Second, the initial UVR is positively associated with the subsequent increase in market share at a high level of statistical significance. Thus, of two countries starting each with a 1 per cent share of the world market, the one with a starting unit value at the world average (and, hence, a log UVR equal to zero) will see its market share unchanged over the next three-year period (assuming no change in UVR and REER). A similar country with a starting unit value that is 10 per cent above the world average will increase its market share to 1.05 per cent. Third, the change in UVR over the three-year period is also positively and significantly associated with an increased market share. Once we control for these factors, the direction of the effect of a real exchange rate change is such that an appreciation hurts; however, in this specification, the statistical significance is weak.

These relationships work differently for developed and developing countries.[7] Not surprisingly, the inertia set by initial market shares is significant in developed countries (Table 15.2, columns 1 and 2), implying that it is difficult for them to increase their international presence from their well-established world market positions. Because the initial market share is so potent, the effect of other variables is more modest, though the initial UVR has a strong bearing for exports from the EU-15. REER has the 'wrong' sign for developed economies. In contrast, the developing country group is less constrained by its market share history (Table 15.2, columns 3–5), allowing more space for market share increase through technology and

Table 15.1 Base specification – dependent variable: ratio of end-of-period share to beginning-of-period share

	(1)	(2)	(3)	(4)
Initial share	−0.936***	−1.021***	−1.009***	−1.031***
	(7.25)	(8.48)	(8.55)	(8.72)
Initial UVR		0.326***	0.492***	0.492***
		(4.61)	(5.09)	(5.12)
UVR change			0.189**	0.183**
			(2.46)	(2.40)
REER change				−0.229
				(1.50)
Constant	0.649***	0.629***	0.572***	0.588***
	(8.30)	(8.70)	(7.70)	(7.88)
Observations	174	174	174	174
Number of countries	58	58	58	58
R-squared	0.31	0.42	0.45	0.46

Note: Absolute value of t-statistics in brackets. * significant at 10%; ** significant at 5%; *** significant at 1%. All variables are in logarithms.

quality upgrading. Also, developing countries are apparently punished more for real exchange rate appreciations. Figure 15.7 plots how much quality upgrading is required to compensate for a given level of exchange rate appreciation in order to keep a country's market share constant. Using the coefficients in Table 15.2, column 3, we calculate the UVR change that would leave the market share unchanged if a 10 per cent REER appreciation occurred. Since this calculation takes the initial share and initial UVR in 1994 as given for each country, the required rise in UVR depends on the actual initial conditions a country starts with and, therefore, differs across countries. Reflecting the catch-up effect, countries with smaller initial market shares and higher initial quality levels can do less upgrading than those with less advantageous initial conditions and still achieve the same results.

The evidence is mixed on whether the gains from technology and quality upgrading are non-linear (Table 15.3). In the rest of the analysis, we focus only on developing countries. In exploring a number of extensions, we first briefly consider if quality variations have non-linear effects. The square of UVR does have a negative sign, indicating that continued UVR enhancement brings declining gains, though the coefficient is not significant at the 5 per cent level. However, the sum of the evidence, including the observation noted above that such quality enhancements play a limited role for developed economies, suggests that there are limits to gains from this upgrading process. This (and their already large market shares) may explain

Table 15.2 Differences between developed and developing countries – dependent variable: ratio of end-of-period share to beginning-of-period share

Sample	(1) EU-15	(2) Developed Countries	(3) Developing Countries	(4) EU-8, Emerging Asia, Latin America	(5) EU-8, EU Candidates, Emerging Asia, Latin America
Initial share	−1.944***	−1.765***	−0.899***	−1.039***	−0.909***
	(6.11)	(6.75)	(7.14)	(5.57)	(7.04)
Initial UVR	0.247*	0.135	0.504***	0.569***	0.489***
	(1.94)	(0.96)	(4.63)	(5.73)	(4.55)
UVR change	0.055	−0.096	0.285***	0.288***	0.283***
	(0.45)	(0.78)	(3.39)	(3.98)	(3.40)
REER change	1.669***	1.089***	−0.478***	−0.517***	−0.559***
	(4.25)	(3.38)	(2.93)	(3.11)	(2.96)
Constant	1.711***	1.415***	0.430***	0.465***	0.423***
	(5.68)	(6.34)	(6.52)	(4.98)	(6.16)
Observations	42	63	111	81	99
Number of countries	14	21	37	27	33
R-squared	0.84	0.75	0.51	0.57	0.55

Note: Absolute value of t-statistics in brackets. * significant at 10%; *** significant at 1%. All variables are in logarithms.

the smaller gains made recently by East Asian countries (compared with the CEE-8) despite their continued impressive technology and quality upgrading.

Finally, two other considerations deserve attention. First, does the quality improvement reflect technical change? In other words, within the fixed basket of goods we consider, does a higher UVR primarily reflect the fact that the composition of this fixed basket is moving to higher-tech products with higher unit values? Table 15.4 shows that taken by itself, a move toward higher technology is associated with an increase in market shares. However, in the 'horse race' between UVRs and technology shares, UVRs win. The implication is that there is some collinearity between improving product quality and technological upgrading, that is, countries experiencing one process also go through the other. However, within the fixed basket of goods, better quality of the individual products is more important than shifts to higher-technology products.[8]

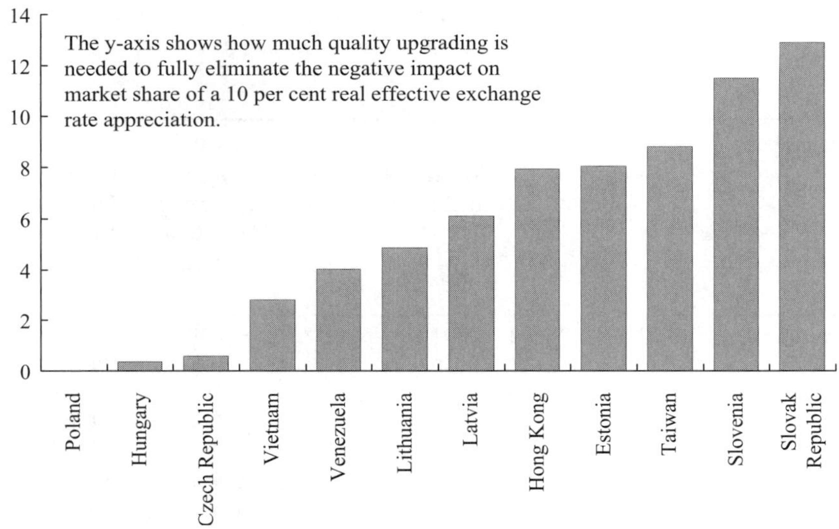

Sources: UN Comtrade and author's calculations.

Figure 15.7 UVR upgrade requirement to compensate for 10 per cent REER appreciation (in per cent)

Second, could the apparent influence of UVRs be a proxy for the possibility that countries are able to sell products at higher prices to importing countries growing rapidly and, hence, that the gain arises from astute selection of destination rather than from the effort to raise product quality? Table 15.4 shows that the growth of partner country GDP per capita is important: countries exporting to rapidly growing partners experience more rapid expansion of international market shares.[9] However, this finding does not negate the importance of quality improvements.

We pursue the relative roles of partner country growth and product quality in Table 15.5. As discussed in Section 15.2, there is a presumption that richer countries have a higher propensity to buy higher product qualities. The first column of Table 15.5 shows that more rapid partner country growth is mainly relevant when the partner country is a developing economy. In other words, the more rapid growth of developing country buyers helps expand international market shares in a way that growth of industrialized country partners does not. In contrast, quality matters more for selling to industrialized economies. We interact the change in UVRs separately with developing and industrialized partner country growth. The results imply that if the developing country partner is not growing, the elasticity of change in market share with respect to change in UVR is about

Table 15.3 Non-linearities in the effects of quality upgrading – dependent variable: ratio of end-of-period share to beginning-of-period share

Sample	(1) Developing Countries	(2) Developing Countries	(3) Developing Countries
Initial share	−0.856***	−0.879***	−0.868***
	(6.79)	(6.61)	(6.43)
Initial UVR	0.753***	0.552***	0.602***
	(4.33)	(3.73)	(3.52)
UVR change	0.251***	0.289***	0.325***
	(2.97)	(3.40)	(3.11)
REER change	−0.436***	−0.478***	−0.474***
	(2.69)	(2.92)	(2.88)
Initial UVR, squared	−0.166*		
	(1.82)		
Initial share*Initial UVR		−0.057	−0.123
		(0.48)	(0.76)
Initial share*UVR change			−0.07
			(0.60)
Constant	0.414***	0.422***	0.419***
	(6.31)	(6.16)	(6.06)
Observations	111	111	111
Number of countries	37	37	37
R-squared	0.53	0.51	0.51

Note: Absolute value of t-statistics in brackets. * significant at 10%; ** significant at 5%; *** significant at 1%. All variables are in logarithms.

0.65. This elasticity falls to zero if the developing country partner growth is 5 per cent a year. In contrast, the elasticity is almost double for zero industrialized country growth and remains high for the observed range of industrialized country growth rates.

15.4 IDENTIFYING QUALITY EFFECTS ACROSS PRODUCT CATEGORIES

Presumably, quality matters more for some products than for others. In his important contribution, Rauch (1999) has identified the degree to which product varieties are differentiated within a product group. He concludes, using supporting evidence, that the degree of differentiation influences the

Table 15.4 Does quality upgrading reflect technology upgrading? Dependent variable: ratio of end-of-period share to beginning-of-period share

Sample: Developing Countries	(1)	(2)	(3)	(4)	(5)	(6)	(7)
	High- and Medium-tech Upgrading			High-tech Upgrading		Impact of Trading Partners' Income	
Initial share	−0.900***	−0.842***	−0.864***	−0.902***	−0.862***	−0.886***	−1.160***
	(6.98)	(6.11)	(6.59)	(7.16)	(6.93)	(6.81)	(8.72)
Initial UVR	0.421***			0.365**			0.498***
	(3.63)			(2.15)			(5.27)
UVR change	0.289***			0.218**			0.394***
	(3.37)			(2.12)			(5.07)
REER change	−0.467***	−0.489***	−0.481***	−0.453***	−0.476***	−0.440**	−0.388***
	(2.89)	(2.78)	(2.76)	(2.77)	(2.86)	(2.52)	(2.74)
Initial high- and medium-tech share	0.15	0.262**	0.226***				
	(1.51)	(2.59)	(3.01)				
High- and medium-tech share change	−0.009	0.043					
	(0.12)	(0.54)					
Initial high-tech share				0.08	0.167***	0.087***	
				(1.46)	(4.58)	(3.58)	
High-tech share change				0.041	0.090***		
				(1.08)	(2.84)		
Trading partners' GDP per capita growth							0.118***
							(4.36)
Constant	0.696***	0.942***	0.899***	0.743***	1.120***	0.870***	−0.002
	(4.09)	(5.60)	(6.10)	(3.32)	(7.72)	(7.18)	(0.01)
Observations	111	111	111	109	109	109	108
Number of countries	37	37	37	37	37	37	36
R -squared	0.54	0.44	0.43	0.55	0.52	0.46	0.65

Note: Absolute value of t-statistics in brackets. * significant at 10%; ** significant at 5%; *** significant at 1%. All variables are in logarithms.

Table 15.5 *Differences between developing and industrial trading partners – dependent variable: ratio of end-of-period share to beginning-of-period share*

Initial share	−1.257***	−1.226***	−1.238***
	(11.90)	(11.96)	(12.16)
Initial UVR	0.464***	0.348***	0.354***
	(6.40)	(4.35)	(4.54)
UVR change	0.341***	1.091***	0.620***
	(5.39)	(4.22)	(5.74)
REER change	−0.196*	−0.215*	−0.218*
	(1.70)	(1.92)	(1.96)
Developing trading partners' income growth	0.091***	0.084***	0.093***
	(4.92)	(4.63)	(5.24)
Industrial trading partners' income growth	−0.065	−0.022	−0.049
	(1.15)	(0.40)	(0.89)
UVR change*Developing trading partners' income growth			−0.065***
			(3.13)
UVR change*Industrial trading partners' income growth		−0.208***	
		(2.99)	
Constant	0.457***	0.299*	0.360**
	(2.81)	(1.80)	(2.26)
Observations	171	171	171
Number of countries	57	57	57
R-squared	0.70	0.73	0.73

Note: Absolute value of t-statistics in brackets. * significant at 10%; ** significant at 5%; *** significant at 1%. All variables are in logarithms.

information necessary to trade these products. The more differentiated the product, Rauch finds, the greater the role of informal (ethnic) information networks in successfully conducting international trade in that product. In this section, we examine whether the degree of product differentiation is also consistent with quality variations that allow greater scope for pricing differentials.

Following Rauch (ibid.), we classify goods into three categories, reflecting the differences in their price-setting mechanisms:[10]

- Differentiated products do not have well-defined product standards and are not traded on specialized exchanges. They carry the largest potential for quality variation.
- Reference-priced products are goods that have referable standards with reference prices that are available in specialized publications;

*Table 15.6 Scope of quality variation across product groups**

Year	Differentiated Goods	Reference-priced Goods	Homogeneous Goods
1994	0.29	0.30	0.11
1998	0.75	0.42	0.21
2001	0.54	0.41	0.31
Total	0.65	0.39	0.23

Note: * The table summarizes the standard deviation of UVRs.

however, they are not traded on organized exchanges. Quality variation is possible but less so than for differentiated goods.

- Homogeneous products are goods that have clearly defined standards and/or are internationally traded on organized exchanges. Hence, they have well-defined prices and the smallest potential variation in quality.

Table 15.6 reports the standard deviations of the UVRs for the three categories. As expected, differentiated products have the highest standard deviations, followed by reference goods, and then by homogeneous goods (which are clustered quite tightly around a single international price). Notice, however, that there is some tendency for homogeneous products to become more differentiated over time, as the information intensity in trade increases and technological advances help expand the spectrum of product varieties. Figure 15.8 shows the UVRs for all three categories in the CEE-8. The changes in the aggregate country UVRs are driven by the changes in the UVRs of differentiated products, for which quality differentiation is intuitively expected to be the strongest.

The analysis in Section 15.3 is repeated for these three categories of products (Table 15.7). Some findings stand out. First, for the differentiated and reference-priced products, their initial UVR and the UVR change work strongly, but these variables have little influence on the market shares of commodities. This is as we would expect, though the fact that quality levels and changes work at least as strongly for reference-priced goods as for differentiated goods is something of a surprise (Hallak, 2006, obtained a similar result). Second, differentiated goods, however, appear to play a special role, through spillover benefits for reference-priced goods. One interpretation is that the quality of a country's differentiated goods serves as a signal of a country's general ability to develop quality products; as such, a high UVR for these goods benefits other exports. In contrast, if the UVR of reference-priced goods is higher, the exporting country makes less

Table 15.7 Product groups according to price-setting mechanism – dependent variable: ratio of end-of-period share to beginning-of-period share (calculated specifically for each product group)

Sample: Developing Countries	(1)	(2)	(3)	(4)	(5)	(6)
	Differentiated Goods		Reference-priced Goods		Homogeneous Goods	
Initial share	−1.176***	−1.130***	−1.160***	−1.201***	−0.825***	−0.782***
	(11.28)	(10.71)	(5.63)	(6.09)	(5.85)	(5.61)
Initial UVR of differentiated goods	0.515***	0.561***		0.235***		0.13
	(6.44)	(6.80)		(2.76)		(0.99)
Initial UVR of reference-priced goods		−0.206*	0.683***	0.498**		0.294
		(1.84)	(3.04)	(2.22)		(1.55)
Initial UVR of homogeneous goods					0.165	0.066
					(0.34)	(0.14)
UVR change	0.337***	0.343***	0.477**	0.404**	−0.172	−0.18
	(4.93)	(5.09)	(2.48)	(2.18)	(0.60)	(0.64)
REER change	−0.456***	−0.458***	−0.162	−0.146	−0.408	−0.37
	(2.93)	(2.99)	(0.89)	(0.84)	(1.50)	(1.38)
Trading partners' GDP per capita growth	0.038	0.032	0.210***	0.155***	0.191***	0.156***
	(1.15)	(0.99)	(6.85)	(4.41)	(4.37)	(3.11)
Constant	−0.019	0.007	−0.324**	−0.095	−0.109	−0.04
	(0.12)	(0.05)	(2.03)	(0.54)	(0.50)	(0.17)
Observations	108	108	108	108	108	108
Number of countries	36	36	36	36	36	36
R-squared	0.72	0.74	0.54	0.59	0.50	0.54

Note: Absolute value of t-statistics in brackets. * significant at 10%; ** significant at 5%; *** significant at 1%. All variables are in logarithms.

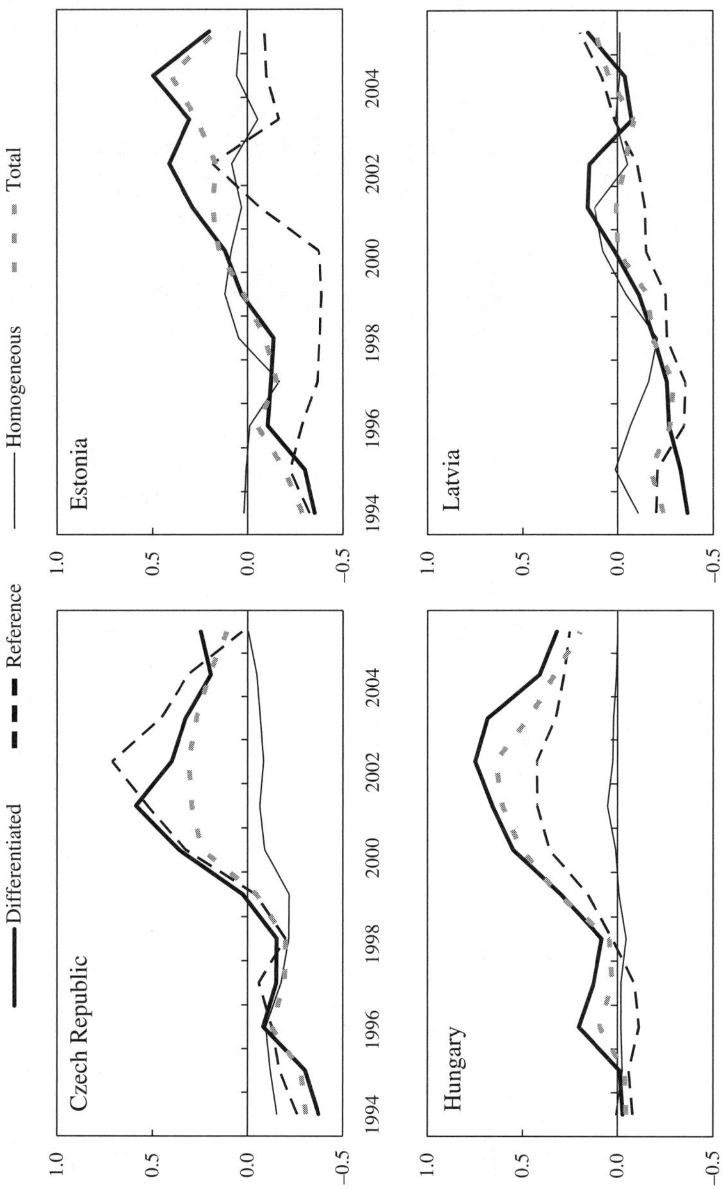

Differentiated
Reference
Homogeneous
Total
Czech Republic
Estonia
Hungary
Latvia
1.0
0.5
0.0
–0.5
1994
1996
1998
2000
2002
2004

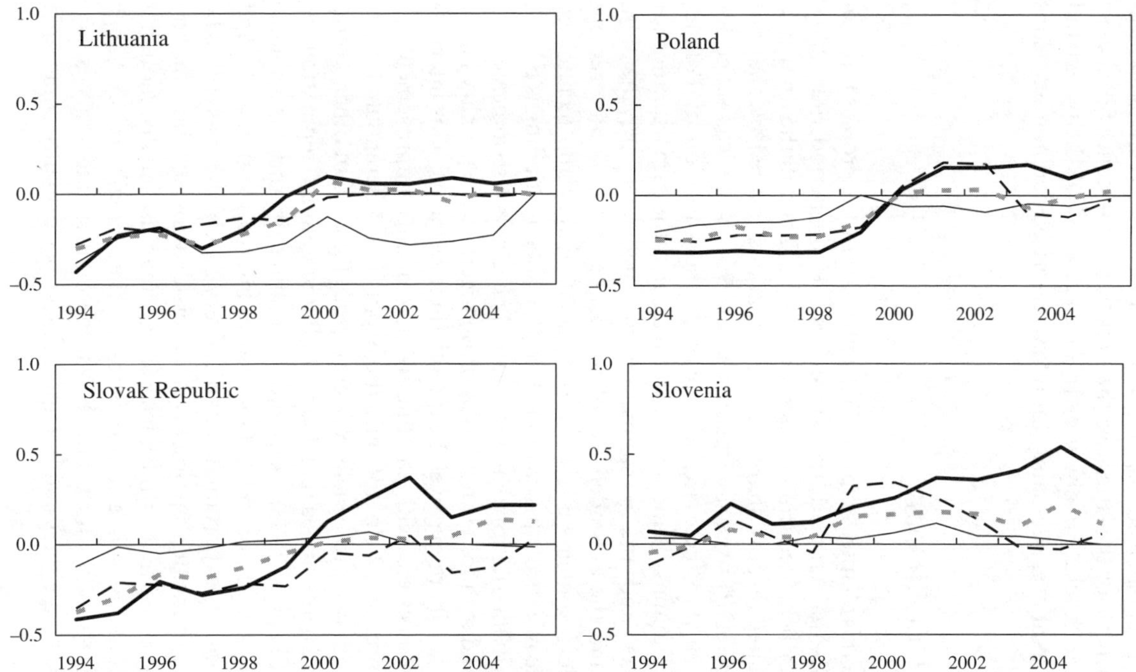

Note: UVR is the unit value of a country's exports divided by the unit value of world exports. Expressed in logarithm so that a value of zero means country unit value equals world unit value.

Source: UN Comtrade database and author's calculations.

*Figure 15.8 CEE-8: UVRs according to potential quality differentiation, 1994–2005** headway in differentiated goods – as if resources were diverted to the reference-priced goods. Third, the appreciation of the real exchange rate has the expected negative effect. This effect is, surprisingly, most pronounced for differentiated goods, followed by homogeneous and reference-priced goods, where for the latter two the statistical significance falls below the conventional levels. Finally, growth of partner GDP helps expand market shares, as above, but mainly for reference-priced and homogeneous goods.

15.5 CONCLUSIONS

The analysis in this chapter helps explain some part of the process through which the CEE-8 gained world market shares over the period 1994–2005. Essentially, they benefited from a catch-up process. Though their normalized export shares (export shares in world markets divided by share of GDP in world GDP) were not small even in 1994, there was scope for expansion, given that these are, with perhaps the exception of Poland, small, open economies. Trade liberalization created the opportunities for expanded trade, and the economic reforms instigated privatization, restructuring and the expanded use of foreign capital and management skills. These developments allowed a process of quality and technology upgrading. The results of this chapter show that such upgrading is consistent with gains in international market share. The results also indicate that, while quality and technology tend to improve together, the primary factor in gaining market share may well be quality improvements. This interpretation is also consistent with the finding that quality improvements in differentiated products help not only the exports of differentiated products but also 'spillover' to benefit reference-priced goods. In other words, quality improvements appear related to building country reputation (as suggested by Shapiro, 1983). Reputation-building, in turn, is valuable when a country is still not well established in international markets and information about its export quality and delivery capabilities has still to be established. That the catch-up process is associated with such information signaling is also consistent with Rauch's (1999) analysis. Finally, though it appears in a simple bivariate comparison that the real effective exchange rate appreciation did not hurt the CEE-8, the multivariate analysis suggests that, if exchange rates had not appreciated, performance could have been even better.

Looking ahead, the task becomes challenging for several reasons. First, the increased market share makes further gains more difficult. Second, there is some evidence of decreasing returns to improved quality. Thus, with reduced prospects of catching up, and continued (and possibly heightened) technological competition, the pressure to maintain market shares will increase. Continued policy efforts to raise productivity will therefore be needed.

To the evolving analysis of competitiveness, this chapter adds some new dimensions. There may be merit in examining not only export shares in the global economy but also the normalized shares to assess how export performance is responding to changes in domestic production capabilities. Second, the role of product quality and technology upgrading could be important in some circumstances, but its importance will need to be assessed in context. In any event, this study demonstrates that a careful harnessing of disaggregated data can provide useful insights into the structural change of a country's export composition. Finally, analyzing exports along the dimensions in which they are differentiated can also have an important bearing on competitiveness. The analysis of competitiveness, therefore, has not become easier!

APPENDIX

The Appendix reports on the country sample, data sources, industry taxonomies, construction of the UVR and selected products under the Rauch (1999) classification of traded goods.

15A.1 The Sample

We started with 119 countries, accounting for approximately 99 per cent of world manufacturing trade in the period 1994–2005. We ranked these countries according to their market shares and examined data coverage, both for trade-related variables and the control variables mentioned above. We retained those countries that had the data necessary for this analysis. The final data set covers the period between 1994 and 2005 for 58 countries. In Table 15A.1, we provide the list of these countries, with the names of those countries classified as 'developing countries' in bold. These countries account for 93.5 per cent of global trade in manufactured products. For the purpose of this chapter, we compute each country's export share as a fraction of the global trade in manufacturing products (Table 15A.2).

15A.2 Data Sources

The trade data come from the UN Comtrade database and consist of the trade values and quantities of export flows. The export data are at the six-digit product level, according to the Harmonized System (HS) classification, the most disaggregated level available from Comtrade.[11,12] For each product, an observation consists of the country of origin, time, trade value in dollars, quantity and units in which the quantity is expressed.

The real effective exchange rate, based on the consumer price index (CPI), is taken from the IMF's *International Financial Statistics* (IFS).

The income level of trading partners is calculated using the GDP per capita from *International Financial Statistics* and the trade weights from the *World Economic Outlook* database. To check robustness, both nominal and purchasing power parity (PPP) based measures are used. The results reported here use trading partners' income level in PPP terms, but the results using the alternative measure based on nominal GDP per capita are virtually the same.

15A.3 Construction of Variables

We construct measures of technology and quality change at the country level using the detailed trade data at the product level. As in similar studies,

*Table 15A.1 List of countries**

Argentina	Germany	**Malaysia**	Spain
Australia	Greece	**Mexico**	**Sri Lanka**
Austria	**Hong Kong SAR**	Netherlands	Sweden
Brazil	**Hungary**	New Zealand	Switzerland
Bulgaria	Iceland	Norway	**Taiwan POC**
Canada	**India**	**Philippines**	**Thailand**
Chile	**Indonesia**	**Poland**	**Turkey**
China	Ireland	Portugal	**Ukraine**
Colombia	**Israel**	**Romania**	United Kingdom
Croatia	Italy	**Russia**	United States
Czech Republic	Japan	**Serbia and Montenegro**	**Uruguay**
Denmark	**Korea, Rep. of**	**Singapore**	**Venezuela**
Estonia	**Latvia**	**Slovak Republic**	**Vietnam**
Finland	**Lithuania**	**Slovenia**	
France	**Macedonia**	**South Africa**	

Note: * Countries that are classified as 'developing countries' are in bold.

the sample of products is limited to those of the manufacturing sectors. We use the Classification of Economic Activities in the European Community (NACE). Manufactures of coke products, refined petroleum products and nuclear fuel are excluded from the analysis.

The technology content of products is based on the taxonomy provided by Hatzichronoglou (1997). Products are classified into four groups: high technology, medium-high technology, medium-low technology and low technology.[13] This classification is based on a cut-off procedure using R&D intensities in select OECD economies in two-digit International Standard Industrial Classification (ISIC) product categories.

The measure of product quality is the relative unit value of a country's exports with respect to the unit value of all exports to a given market. Referred to as the 'unit value ratio (UVR)' and commonly used in the trade literature, this concept of measuring quality by relative unit value has its basis in the idea that consumers would be willing to pay more for the same product if they perceive it to be of better quality.

We first calculate the unit value of each product that a specific country exports by dividing the trade value by the quantity. Then, we calculate the world unit value for the same basket of goods. We then divide the country's unit value for each product in the basket by the world unit value for the corresponding products. Finally, we aggregate these product unit value ratios into a single unit value ratio, using the weights of each product in the overall exports of the country. The reported UVR takes the logarithm of

*Table 15A.2 Country exports as a share of world exports**

	1994	1997	2002	2005
Argentina	0.42	0.48	0.46	0.49
Australia	0.91	0.85	0.79	0.70
Austria	3.10	2.62	2.71	3.20
Brazil	0.39	0.37	0.36	0.43
Bulgaria	0.68	1.08	1.09	1.23
Canada	1.29	1.56	1.43	1.10
Chile	1.36	1.22	1.14	1.34
China	0.42	0.39	0.45	0.55
Colombia	0.21	0.21	0.29	0.27
Croatia	1.49	0.88	0.88	1.16
Czech Republic	1.49	1.79	2.63	3.04
Denmark	3.51	2.98	2.92	3.17
Estonia	1.20	2.16	3.08	2.45
Finland	2.75	2.84	2.86	2.80
France	1.99	1.89	1.91	2.01
Germany	2.44	2.48	2.57	2.99
Greece	0.58	0.55	0.50	0.51
Hong Kong SAR	3.55	2.89	2.35	1.99
Hungary	1.22	1.83	2.44	2.81
Iceland	3.91	3.19	3.25	2.73
India	0.19	0.19	0.18	0.19
Indonesia	0.40	0.40	0.54	0.46
Ireland	4.75	4.16	5.00	6.30
Israel	1.69	1.69	2.04	1.92
Italy	1.75	1.68	1.61	1.77
Japan	0.86	0.90	0.92	0.99
Korea	1.23	1.29	1.34	1.52
Latvia	0.61	1.34	1.15	0.97
Lithuania	0.50	0.98	1.17	1.28
Macedonia	1.48	1.11	0.76	0.77
Malaysia	1.91	1.96	2.07	1.93
Mexico	0.32	0.51	0.61	0.47
Netherlands	3.49	3.75	3.51	3.98
New Zealand	1.85	1.74	1.73	1.39
Norway	1.81	1.58	1.48	1.52
Philippines	0.51	0.55	0.64	0.51
Poland	0.75	0.77	1.02	1.32
Portugal	1.76	1.67	1.54	1.69
Romania	0.53	0.66	1.05	1.26
Russia	0.36	0.45	0.51	0.43
Serbia and Montenegro	0.09	0.62	0.58	0.86

Table 15A.2 (continued)

	1994	1997	2002	2005
Singapore	4.66	4.96	4.24	4.56
Slovak Republic	1.66	1.76	2.22	2.95
Slovenia	3.78	3.47	3.51	3.72
South Africa	0.53	0.62	0.69	0.62
Spain	1.34	1.38	1.37	1.50
Sri Lanka	0.87	0.82	0.84	0.70
Sweden	3.84	4.17	3.52	3.72
Switzerland	5.30	4.85	4.37	5.21
Taiwan POC	2.30	1.90	1.91	1.80
Thailand	1.09	1.06	1.30	1.23
Turkey	0.62	0.58	0.84	1.02
Ukraine	0.23	0.57	0.64	0.68
United Kingdom	1.44	1.53	1.42	1.27
Uruguay	1.43	1.10	0.88	0.77
USA	0.55	0.64	0.63	0.48
Venezuela	0.49	0.49	0.40	0.43
Vietnam	0.41	0.61	0.76	0.87

Note: * Shares are computed using the common basket of products for the country and the benchmark (world). Trade values are summed up across products within a country and then divided by the sum of trade values of the same products exported by all countries.

Sources: UN Comtrade database and staff calculations.

this ratio. Hence, a negative UVR corresponds to a quality lower than world standard.

Four remarks on UVR follow. First, products that fail to appear consistently in a country's export basket are excluded from the UVR calculations. Thus, the UVR measures the changes in the relative quality of the products that the country has been exporting on a continuous basis. Second, the basket of goods on which UVR calculations are based is the intersection of the set of goods a country exports and the set of goods comprising the world exports. To calculate the UVR, the quantities should be expressed in the same units across the sample of countries. Third, the weights used in aggregating the country's product unit values change as the export composition changes. Hence, the aggregated unit value reflects not only the quality but also the composition of exports. Finally, market shares are calculated using the same basket of goods as for the UVR.

Table 15A.3 Partial list of products in Rauch (1999) classification

Differentiated	Reference-priced	Homogeneous
Soya sauce	Soya bean flour and meal	Coffee, not roasted or decaffeinated
Vitamins and their derivatives	Tar distilled from coal or lignite	Barley
Beauty, make-up, skin-care	Propane, liquefied	Rice in the husk (paddy or rough)
Artificial waxes	Mercury	Soya beans
Chemical preparations for photography	Sulphates of copper	Crude soya-bean oil
Activated carbon	Methanol (methyl alcohol)	Raw cane sugar, in solid form
Prepared rubber accelerators	Ionones and methylionones	Raw beet sugar, in solid form
Articles of apparel and clothing accessories	Vaccines for human medicine	Cocoa beans, whole or broken, raw
Vulcanized rubber thread and cord	Medicaments of alkaloids or derivatives	Tobacco, not stemmed/stripped
Hygienic or pharmaceutical articles	Fertilizers	Ores and concentrates
Articles of apparel of leather	Cellulose and its chemical derivatives	Lignite, not agglomerated
Wooden frames for paintings and photographs	Plates of polymers of ethylene	Petroleum oils and oils
Parquet panels of wood	Gummed or adhesive paper	Carbon
Textile wall coverings	Woven fabrics of cotton	Aluminium oxide, other than artificial
Articles of gold or silversmith	Woven fabrics of synthetic fibres	Natural rubber latex, in primary form
Flanges, stainless steel	Asphalt or similar material article	Latex of synthetic rubber
Chain, roller, iron or steel	Ferro-alloys	Cotton, not carded or combed
Table knives having fixed blades	Flat-rolled products of stainless steel	Wood in rough form
Carbon or graphite electrodes	Rails, iron or steel	Diamonds unsorted whether worked or not
Electrical insulators	Pipes and tubes, copper-zinc base	Silver in unwrought forms
Rail locomotives	Chain and parts thereof of copper	Gold in unwrought forms, nonmonetary
Automobiles	Plates, sheet, strip and foil, nickel	Platinum, unwrought or in powder form
Aircraft undercarriages and parts	Foil, aluminium	Iron, unrefined
Optical devices, appliances and instruments	Tin bars, rods, profiles and wire	Copper-zinc base alloys, unwrought
Clocks and watches	Molybdenum and articles thereof	Nickel, unwrought, not alloyed
Playing cards	Magnesium and articles thereof	Powders, molybdenum
Ballpoint pens	Nickel-iron electric accumulators	Magnesium

NOTES

1. This is a shorter and updated version of the *IMF Working Paper*, No. WP/07/97 by Stefania Fabrizio, Deniz Igan and Ashoka Mody (2007).
2. International Monetary Fund. The views expressed in this chapter are those of the author and do not necessarily represent those of the IMF or IMF policy. Deniz Igan is an Economist in the Research Department, Financial Studies Division, of the IMF.
3. The Czech Republic, Estonia, Hungary, Latvia, Lithuania, Poland, the Slovak Republic and Slovenia.
4. Noteworthy is China's impressive performance. Figure 15.4a shows that China's absolute gain in market share between 1994 and 2004 was large. However, Figure 15.4b suggests that China's export expansion was largely commensurate with its catch-up potential and growing economy.
5. Products are dropped if there are missing values in the construction of the unit values or if there are erratic movements in the unit values.
6. See the Appendix at the end of the chapter for details. Using the same R&D metric for all countries does not allow for the possibility that the technology for even a narrowly defined product category may differ across countries. The assumption is that international competition induces countries to adapt or innovate, though in possibly differing ways. In using a common categorization for all countries, we follow, for example, Rajan and Zingales (1998), who apply the US measure of dependence on external finance to all countries.
7. The term 'developing countries' follows the World Bank classification, with the countries highlighted in bold in Table 15A.1 in the Appendix.
8. It may still be the case – and this analysis does not examine the proposition – that a more ambitious change in production structure (elimination of low-tech products and graduation to new high-tech products) is necessary for increasing world market shares.
9. To calculate the growth rate of trading partners' GDP per capita, we use the GDP per capita (in purchasing power parity terms) of a given country's trading partners in each year. We first take the average of these using the share of each trading partner in that country's exports as weights, and then calculate the annualized growth rate of this trade-weighted average. The alternative is to calculate first the growth rate for each trading partner and then take the trade-weighted average of the growth rates. The values obtained through these two methods are highly correlated, and the regression results are virtually the same.
10. Table 15A.3 in the Appendix provides examples of products in each category.
11. For the European Union, eight-digit trade data are available from the Eurostat database COMEXT, and, for the United States, ten-digit data are available from the US Census Bureau.
12. It came to our attention that the data entries in Comtrade get continuous updates. Therefore, data downloaded at a point in time do not necessarily match data downloaded at a later date. The original data used in this chapter were time-stamped April 2006 and the results obtained were reported in Fabrizio et al. (2007). The data used to obtain the results reported here were time-stamped May 2007.
13. The mapping between the Hatzichronoglou (1997) taxonomy and the HS is based on conversion tables from the UN Statistics Division, and in our judgment for a small number of products left out of the conversion tables.

REFERENCES

Dulleck, U., N. Foster, R. Stehrer and J. Woerz (2005), 'Dimensions of quality upgrading: evidence from CEECS', *Economics of Transition*, **13** (1), 51–76.

Fabrizio, S., D. Igan and A. Mody (2007), 'The dynamics of product quality and international competitiveness', *IMF Working Paper* No. WP/07/97.
Hallak, J.C. (2006), 'Product quality and the direction of trade', *Journal of International Economics*, **68** (1), 238–65.
Hallak, J.C. and P. Schott (2005), 'Estimating cross-country differences in product quality', *Working Paper*, Ann Arbor: University of Michigan.
Hatzichronoglou, T. (1997), 'Revision of the high-technology sector and product classification', *OECD Science, Technology and Industry Working Papers*, No. 1997/2, Paris: OECD, Directorate for Science, Technology and Industry.
Rajan, R. and L. Zingales (1998), 'Financial dependence and growth', *American Economic Review*, **88** (3), 559–86.
Rauch, J.E. (1999), 'Networks versus markets in international trade', *Journal of International Economics*, **48** (1), 959–73.
Shapiro, C. (1983), 'Premiums for high quality products as returns to reputations', *Quarterly Journal of Economics*, **98** (4), 659–80.

16. Structural aspects of competitiveness

Julia Woerz[1]

16.1 INTRODUCTION

In this chapter I will focus on aspects of competitiveness that are not related to exchange rates, namely macroeconomic and structural features of an economy that determine its relative standing in the global economic environment. As pointed out in the influential article by Krugman (1994) and in the discussion by Narula and Wakelin (1995) or Aiginger and Landesmann (2002), to cite just a few, the concept of competitiveness is ill-defined in economics when it comes to the competitiveness of entities other than individual firms, whose objective is to survive and strengthen their market position vis-à-vis their competitors. At all other levels of analysis, be it sectors, regions, or nation states, the objectives of individual agents within these entities may differ, thus making it difficult to define competitiveness unambiguously. For instance, the Organisation for Economic Co-operation and Development (OECD) defines competitiveness as 'the ability of companies, industries, regions, nations or supranational regions to generate, while being exposed to international competition, relatively high factor income and factor employment levels on a sustainable basis' (Hatzichronoglou, 1996).

The EU employs a similar concept when defining competitiveness as output growth and high rates of employment in a sustainable environment. Given their very broad scope, these definitions encompass two – in the short run potentially conflicting – objectives of a nation/region/industry: generating high factor income while keeping employment levels high. Focusing mainly on the country but sometimes also on the industry level in this chapter, we shall make use of the framework offered by Trabold (1995). He defines competitiveness as the strengthening of four abilities: the ability to sell goods and services internationally; the ability to attract resources, in particular foreign direct investment (FDI); the ability to adjust to changing external conditions through structural change and upgrading and finally the ability to earn, which can be measured by GDP and its growth. While being more practicable, this definition of course, neglects concerns about factor employment. Yet the definition is attractive nonetheless, as it focuses on distinct, but highly influential aspects of competitiveness (Hunya, 2007): the external market (ability to sell), thus reflecting the outward orientation of competitiveness; the forward orientation (ability to adjust and ability to earn/grow) and finally, the conditions of the home market (ability to attract), which provide the foundation for being competitive.

In this chapter we shall discuss a range of indicators, spanning the dimensions of competitiveness outlined in the introduction. To set the scene, we will start in the second section with a description of the country sample chosen and describe the relative standing of individual countries and country groups and their ability to grow as indicated by their economic development from 1995 to 2005. In the third section we will look at location factors, describing mainly the ability to attract resources. The fourth section analyses structural and traditional indicators of competitiveness, covering the ability to adjust, to sell and to grow. The fifth investigates the determinants of competitiveness within the service sector for the EU-25 and the final section concludes.

16.2 STRUCTURAL DIFFERENCES AND GLOBAL GROWTH CONVERGENCE

The sample used in this chapter covers a large part of the world, namely the OECD members, the EU and most of Asia. Of special interest is the comparison of the new EU member states to the dynamically evolving countries in East and South-East Asia, in particular their competitiveness on the pre-2004 EU market. With competitiveness being a relative concept, we need to define clearly the reference market beforehand. In our case we will focus on the relative strength of the following countries or country groups in their ability to sell on the market of the pre-2004 EU members: the old members themselves (EU-15), the new members (EU-10), remaining advanced OECD members, catching-up OECD members, the US, Japan, Russia, China, India and two waves of Asian Tiger countries. Table 16.1 lists the countries that fall within these respective groups.

Figure 16.1 reports the levels of GDP and GDP per capita towards the end of our observation period together with the long-run annual average rate of GDP growth between 1995 and 2005. We can clearly see a pattern of strong global convergence[2] with initially poorer regions, which show consistently high growth, especially emerging markets like China and India with almost double-digit rates. GDP per capita is sometimes considered as an indicator of competitiveness, since it can be interpreted as a proxy for a country's overall rate of productivity. In fact, as highlighted by

Table 16.1 Grouping of countries

Advanced Economies	Catching-up Economies
EU-15	EU-10
Austria	Bulgaria
Belgium	Czech Republic
Luxembourg	Estonia
Denmark	Hungary
Finland	Latvia
France	Lithuania
Germany	Poland
Ireland	Romania
Italy	Slovakia
Netherlands	Slovenia
Sweden	
United Kingdom	Catching-up OECD
Greece (cohesion)	Turkey
Portugal (cohesion)	Mexico
Spain (cohesion)	
	1st Tigers
Advanced OECD	Hong Kong, China
Australia	Korea, Rep.
Canada	Singapore
Iceland	
New Zealand	2nd Tigers
Norway	Indonesia
Switzerland	Malaysia
	Philippines
Japan	Thailand
United States	
	China
	India
	Russia

Source: Author's compilation, taken from Landesmann and Woerz (2006).

Figure 16.1, GDP per capita actually reflects a backward-oriented notion of competitiveness, since the most 'competitive' regions according to present GDP per capita levels are the slowly growing advanced regions. As we will see further below, they are also characterized by lower gains in market shares as opposed to the more dynamically growing catching-up regions.

To conclude this section, Table 16.2 reports macroeconomic and export structures in 2005. We see a high dominance of the service sector especially

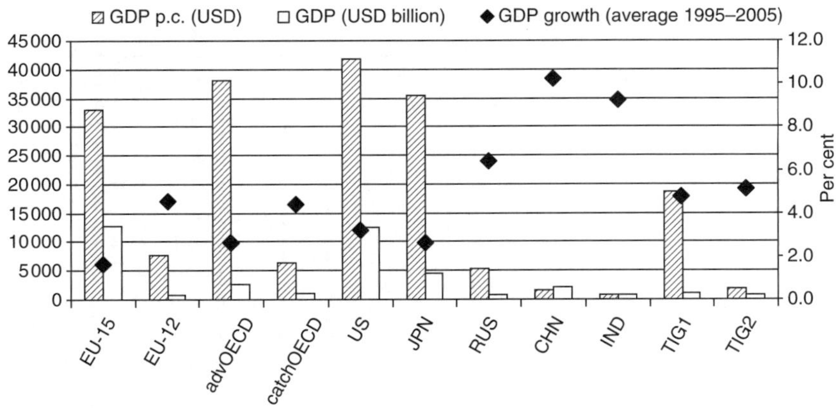

Source: *World Development Indicators*, World Bank (2007).

Figure 16.1 Economic performance of individual regions

in the most advanced regions. We can further distinguish a strong export orientation of the Asian regions (both waves of Tiger economies, the new EU members and, relatively speaking given its size, also China). While the domestic economy is dominated by service sector activities, trade is still concentrated on goods, above all on manufactured products. This pattern is very pronounced for the regions with the highest degree of export orientation. Two of these regions are evidently undergoing a transformation towards leaning more heavily on services in their trade structures. With services exports accounting for close to 20 per cent of total exports, the new EU members and less so the first tier of Asian Tigers show a trade structure that is more typical for the most developed regions. With a trade share of 19.7 per cent in services, India is a clear exception among catching-up economies, reflecting a sound competitive position in services.

16.3 LOCATION FACTORS

Let us now turn to some indicators measuring conditions of the home market conducive to a strong competitive position on export markets. We shall focus here mainly on so-called soft facts affecting the ability to attract resources, in particular FDI. In the following we describe indicators measuring the ease of doing business in a country, drawn from the Investment Climate Surveys of the World Bank carried out in cooperation with the International Finance Corporation. We start first with frequency measures, giving a more or less objective picture of the conditions for private

Table 16.2 Macroeconomic and export structures, 2005

	Economic Structure			Export Structure		
	Agriculture	Manufacturing (in % of gross value added)	Services	Goods and services (in % of GDP)	Manufactured goods (in % of total exports)	Services
EU-15	1.8	17.5	71.7	36.3	61.1	22.9
EU-12	4.9	20.4	61.1	51.2	66.9	17.2
Advanced OECD	2.1	15.8	66.6	34.4	42.8	18.9
Catching-up OECD	6.4	16.6	68.4	29.1	68.3	12.8
United States	1.3	14.2	76.7	10.1	57.6	29.4
Japan	1.7	21.0	68.1	13.4	77.6	15.6
Russia	5.6	17.9	56.4	35.1	17.2	9.2
China	12.6	33.5	39.9	37.5	83.7	8.9
India	18.3	15.7	54.4	20.5	56.4	19.7
1st Tigers	2.5	24.4	62.9	89.7	75.1	16.5
2nd Tigers	11.8	29.6	43.7	62.6	61.2	13.2

Source: *World Development Indicators*, World Bank (2007).

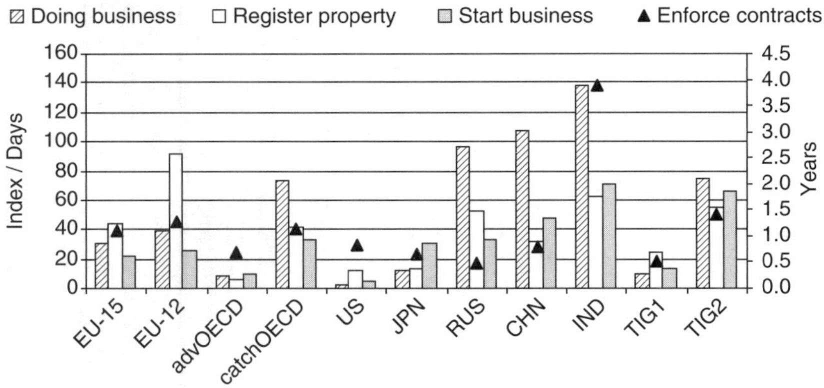

Note: Index (ease of doing business), number of days (register property and start business), number of years (enforce contract); lower values are better.

Source: *World Development Indicators*, World Bank (2007).

Figure 16.2 Ease of doing business (2005)

businesses, and then move to managers' perceptions. Since investment decisions always contain a certain degree of personal judgement, this subjective view is important in judging the conditions of the home market with respect to its international competitiveness.

Figure 16.2 illustrates the strong performance of most advanced OECD members, in particular the US as well as the first tier of Asian Tigers along these indicators. Interestingly, the gaps for the pre-2004 EU members are relatively high in almost all listed sub-dimensions. The position of the more recent EU entrants suggest a great potential for improvement, especially with respect to governance and procedures for registering property rights. The same impression arises from managers' perceptions concerning the functioning of courts, the enforcement of laws, the degree of corruption and general policy uncertainty in the most recent World Bank survey. Along these subjective measures, the old EU members are performing relatively better and closer to other advanced regions, including the first wave of Tiger countries. However, the gap for the new EU members appears to be considerably larger. Figure 16.3 reports another subjective valuation of structural factors, such as the quality of labour skills available in the economy and the appropriateness of tax rates. The picture remains by and large unchanged, with the superior performance of the advanced OECD members (excluding the EU), the US, Japan and the first Asian Tigers, followed with a certain lag by the pre-2004 EU member states. The new EU members' performance is well in the range of the emerging markets (Russia,

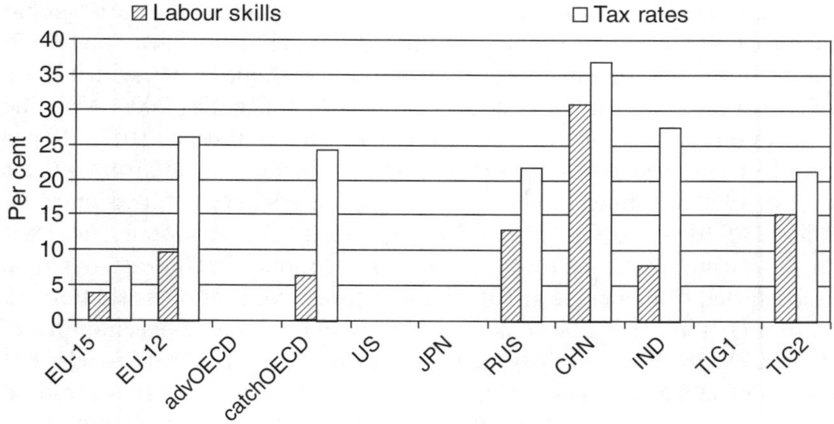

Note: Per cent of managers perceiving this as constraint; lower values are better.

Source: *World Development Indicators*, World Bank (2007).

Figure 16.3 Major business constraints (2005)

India, Turkey and Mexico) and the second tier of Asian Tigers. China is characterized by a considerably worse business environment, which is at odds with the substantial inflows of FDI that it is currently attracting.

The above-mentioned indicators of competitiveness all reflect some common features, which is most strikingly reflected in the ranking of China. These common features include the previous growth performance, but also previous improvements in business environment, thus warranting a backward-oriented judgement of competitiveness. According to these indicators the most competitive regions turn out to be the most advanced economies within the OECD, together with the more recent high-growth performers in East Asia, Hong Kong, Singapore and South Korea. However, this snapshot does not reflect the longer-term developments we observe in global trade flows.

16.4 TRADITIONAL AND STRUCTURAL INDICATORS

Turning now to more output-oriented measures, we will see that they are better suited to reflect current and future ability to sell goods and services on the world market. The geography of global trade flows has undergone dramatic changes since the 1970s. When excluding intra-regional trade flows, the dynamic Asian economies (comprising the first and second wave of Asian Tigers, China and India) have since attained shares in global exports that are similar to those of the old EU member states. The EU-15 has traditionally been by far the most important single trader, with a share of 27 per cent in 1970. This has decreased to 20 per cent by 2006. Also, the relative importance of the US has consequently diminished (from 21 per cent to 13 per cent), while the rising share of Japan (starting from 9.5 per cent in 1970, reaching 17 per cent in 1986) has also been eroded since the mid-1980s (down to 8 per cent in 2006) by rising Asian economies, not least by the opening of China towards the global economy. In contrast, dynamic Asia started from a net share of slightly above 5 per cent of world trade in 1970, thus their rising dominance on the world market has been unprecedented. With roughly 20 per cent of global exports the pre-2004 EU member states and dynamic Asia are now the most important single trading blocks (always excluding all intra-trade flows). When considering intra-trade, the EU-15 are still responsible for the majority of world trade flows, with 35.5 per cent of global exports in 2006, down from roughly 47 per cent in 1970. Dynamic Asia stands at more than 23 per cent of global exports in 2006, which is an impressive increase from its 5 per cent share in 1970.

These long-run developments reflect a strong increase in Asian competitiveness, which is only partially reflected in the soft indicators from the previous section. Also, the new EU entrants exhibit a strong increase in their share in world trade, reaching roughly 4 per cent of world exports in 2006. This is insofar remarkable as their share has been stable around 1 per cent between 1970 and the early 1990s. Thus, their rise in global trade has happened within only one decade.

Figure 16.4 analyses changes in import structures of the world's largest consumer markets. The graphs reveal two important things: first of all, the rising competitiveness of Asian economies becomes highly visible when comparing the years 1990 and 2006. Also, the relative decline of advanced OECD members in overall imports becomes visible. On the EU market this is, above all, caused by the enormous rise of the new members' share in EU-15 imports. On the US and the Japanese market, this is due to strongly rising imports from dynamic Asia. Thus, most regions that emerged as highly competitive according to the soft facts presented in the previous section have lost competitiveness as measured by simple market shares in the major export markets. Second, Figure 16.4 demonstrates nicely that competitiveness is a relative concept. While the new EU members are highly competitive in the EU-15 market, their market share in both other regions is negligible. In contrast, dynamic Asia is selling successfully in all three regions, thus showing global competitiveness.

Next we turn to some structural aspects of this form of competitiveness. Figures 16.5 and 16.6 show import shares of two groups of catching-up

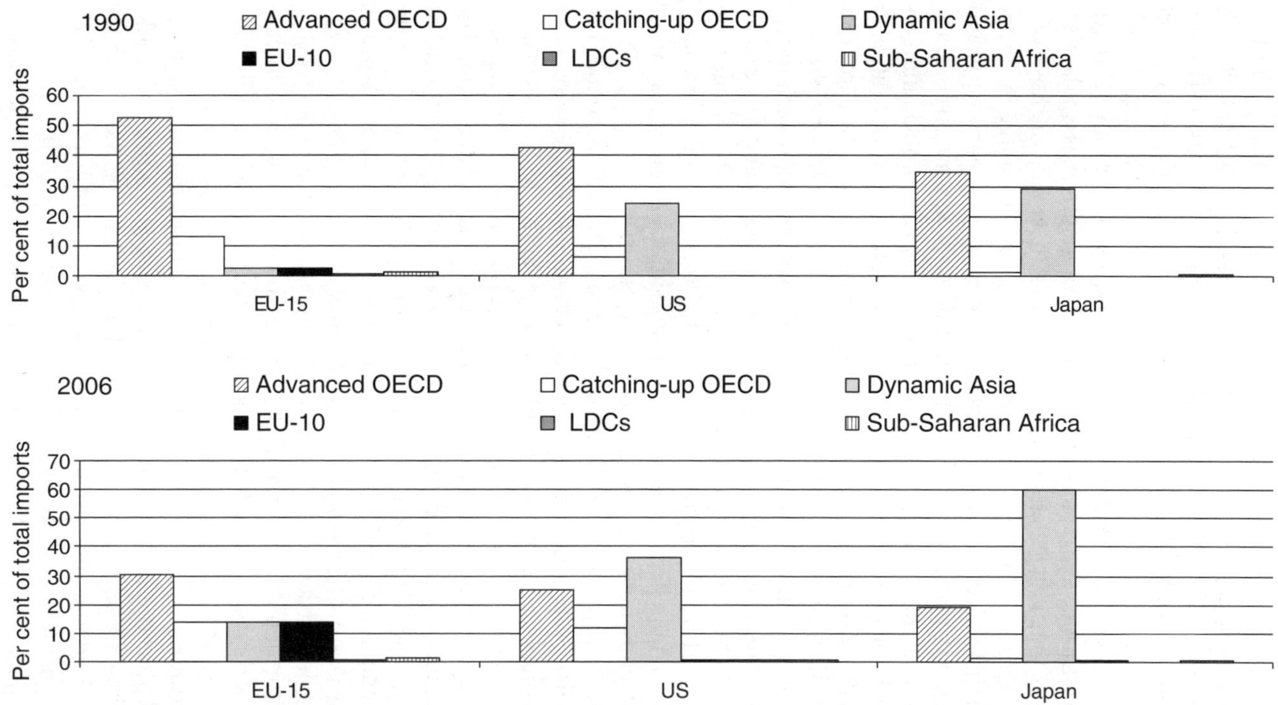

Note: Intra-EU-15 trade is excluded; LDCs = least developed countries.

Source: UN Comtrade.

Figure 16.4 Manufacturing import structure by partners (1990 and 2006) countries in the three major consumer markets, the EU-North (that is, EU-15 without the Southern cohesion countries), the US and Japan. The two groups of catching-up countries are on the one hand the new EU members (EU-10), the cohesion countries and the first wave of Asian Tigers (Figure 16.5) and on the other hand China (Figure 16.6). There are distinct differences between the two graphs, reflecting different competitive positions of the two groups of catching-up countries. The first group (Eastern and Southern Europe and Tigers 1) have gained competitiveness in the EU-North market, but not generally so in the US or in Japan. In those two markets, they managed to expand their market shares only in the medium-high-tech industries (chemicals, electrical and mechanical machinery, and transport equipment) but not in any other technology segment. In contrast, we can observe a universal rise in competitiveness for China on all markets and in all technology segments. The much lower Chinese import ratios in the EU-North as compared with the US and Japan are a statistical artefact arising from the inclusion of intra-EU trade in these calculations. What is striking is not only the sharp increase in import shares in low-tech industries, but the even stronger increase in high-tech industries and, in particular, in office machinery and computing equipment. This dual specialization reflects a successful catching up on the part of China and – despite discussion of potential intellectual property rights violations often heard in this context – a quality upgrading of Chinese production.

Again, the relative meaning of competitiveness becomes pronounced in these two figures. The conclusion as to which regions or countries emerge as being most competitive depends not only on the geographical focus – that is, on which market we observe competition – but also on the sector, industry or industry segment of an economy on which we focus our attention. The new EU member states have gained competitiveness in a clearly defined world region – the EU market – and globally in a clearly defined industry segment – medium-high-tech activities. In contrast, China turns out to be not only globally competitive, but also in all industry segments, especially so in very low-tech industries and in the high-tech intensive electrical industry.

We shall conclude this section with one of the most traditional indicators of competitiveness, namely the trade balance. Table 16.3 reports trade balances by regions and sectors. In goods trade we can observe two regions that run a trade surplus. These are the EU-15 and China. It has to be pointed out that the table includes all trade flows, also intra-EU trade. Excluding these trade flows would still result in a surplus of the EU-15 for manufactured goods, however, it has considerably diminished since 1995. Thus, the highly advanced region of the EU together with the emerging market of China shows the highest competitiveness in goods trade according to trade balances.

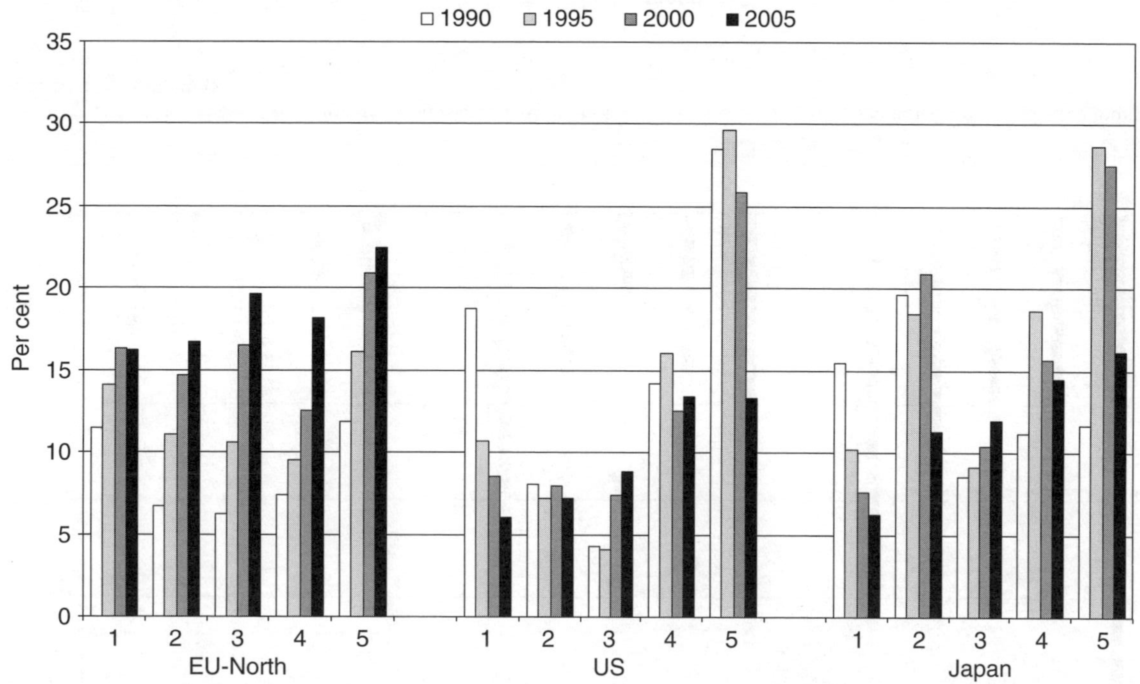

Note: Technology content is indicated by 1: low-tech industries, 2: medium-low industries, 3: medium-high industries, 4: high-tech industries, 5: office machinery and computers.

Source: wiiw.

Figure 16.5 Shares of EU-10, cohesion and Tigers 1 in imports from EU-North, US and Japan

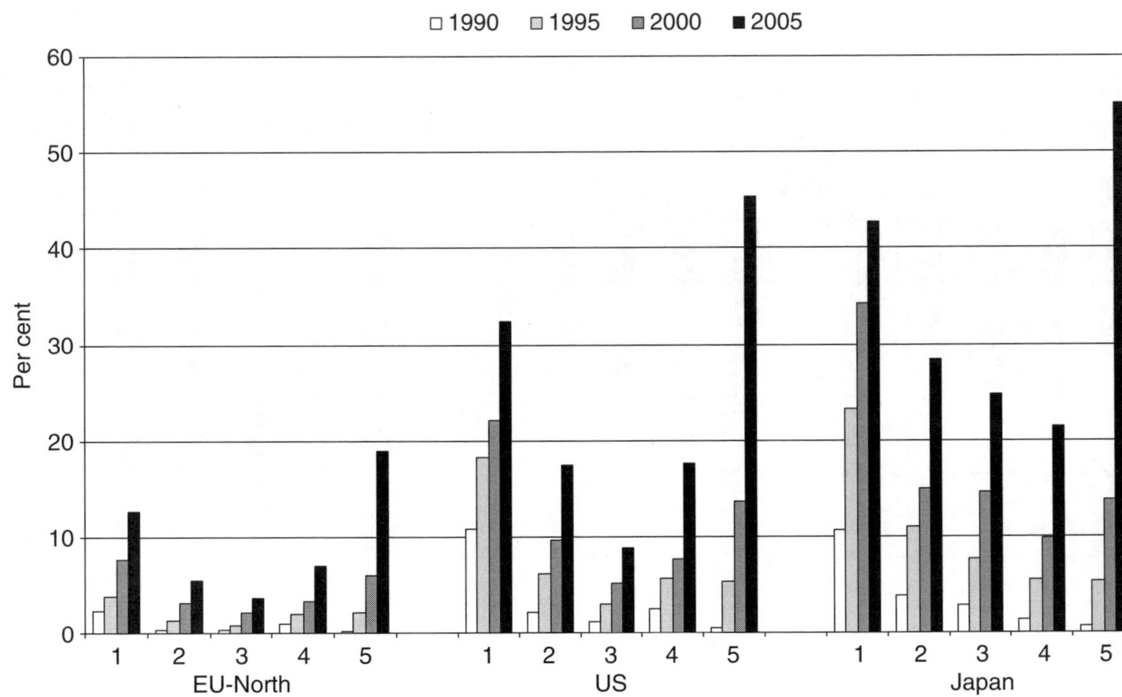

Note: Technology content is indicated by 1: low-tech industries, 2: medium-low industries, 3: medium-high industries, 4: high-tech industries, 5: office machinery and computers.

Source: wiiw.

Figure 16.6 Shares of China in imports from EU-North, US and Japan

Table 16.3 Trade Balance in 2005 (USD million)

	Manufactured goods	Services	Transportation services	Travel services	Other services	Other business
EU-15	297 786	88 117	4 751	−10 812	94 178	25 848
EU-10	−14 900	11 015	5 437	9 402	−3 824	−674
Advanced OECD	−428 561	47 720	−35 319	776	82 314	32 904
Dynamic Asia	−186 069	−37 580	−18 040	−1 738	−17 802	−3 843
China	261 004	−9 391	−13 021	7 537	−3 907	6 996
Emerging Markets	−63 006	−6 088	1 716	7 243	−15 047	−2 100

Source: UN Comtrade, IMF BOP.

Trade in services delivers a different picture: here clearly the most advanced regions (including the new EU members) are characterized by a trade surplus, while all catching-up regions import more services than they export. A closer look into the structure of trade in services reveals that the surplus in the new EU members arises from their strong competitive position in transportation services, as well as their surplus in travel services. However, these two service sectors are characterized by globally falling trade shares, implying that this overall impression of competitiveness may be misleading and the competitive position of the new members in services trade is potentially not sustainable. The advanced OECD members including the old EU members are the only regions to exhibit a stable trade surplus in services, especially so in the most dynamically evolving category of other services. In line with the soft facts reported in Section 16.3, the advanced OECD members (without EU countries) appear to be most competitive in the important area of other business services, which are reported here for comparison purposes as well. This category comprises management, consulting, advertising, real estate and leasing services among others. Due to the UK's outstanding performance in financial services, the EU and the advanced OECD are both performing equally well in financial services (not shown in Table 16.3). Hence, the two economically most advanced regions clearly dominate all other regions in modern, producer-related service sectors.

16.5 COMPETITIVENESS IN THE SERVICE SECTOR

In this section we will investigate in more detail global competitiveness in the service sector, which has come to be the dominant sector in domestic

Table 16.4 Revealed comparative advantages in services (2005)

	Transportation services	Travel services	Other services	Financial services	Other business
EU-15	0.12	−0.17	0.04	−0.15	−0.04
EU-10	0.41	0.30	−0.33	−0.89	−0.25
Advanced OECD	−0.11	−0.12	0.15	0.35	0.13
Dynamic Asia	−0.07	−0.04	−0.18	0.16	−0.08
China	−0.34	0.45	−0.04	−0.03	0.48
Emerging markets	0.36	0.46	−0.43	−0.69	−0.12

Sources: IMF BOP, wiiw calculations.

value-added. Increasingly, services are also traded across international borders, thus deserving more attention when speaking about global competitiveness. Table 16.4 displays revealed comparative advantage indices for individual service sectors. These indices compare a country's net exports in a certain sector to that sector's share in total exports in the sample.[3] Thus, a positive index implies a relative overrepresentation of the sector in the country's trade flows, with the export side being stronger than the import side. This pattern reflects a strong competitive position, while a negative index implies a weak position. The previous results are confirmed at large. However, we observe differences in other business services and financial services concerning the EU-15, using revealed comparative advantages as a measure of competitiveness. It turns out that the old EU members have a revealed comparative disadvantage in financial services and other business services compared with the sample average. Thus, despite running a surplus in these two categories (mainly thanks to the UK) and despite above-average specialization in both exports and imports, imports are relatively more overrepresented, yielding a weak competitive position for the EU-15. The remaining advanced OECD members are representing the most competitive region in this category.

Finally, we investigate the driving factors behind service sector competitiveness within EU members. We employ a simple empirical model to our panel data set, which we reduce here to contain only the 25 EU members over the period 1995–2005. Our estimating equation is given by equation 16.1:

$$RCA_{it}^{k} = \alpha + \beta_1\, LP_{it}^{k} + \beta_2\, ULC_{it}^{k} + \beta_3\, Size_{it}^{k} + \beta_4\, Open_{it}^{k} + \beta_5\, Skills_{it}^{k} + \gamma_i^{k} + \varepsilon_{it}^{k} \qquad (16.1)$$

where *RCA* stands for revealed comparative advantage, *LP* denotes labour productivity growth within the sector, *ULC* are unit labour costs, *Open* mea-

Table 16.5 Determinants of service sector competitiveness in the EU-15 and EU-10

	EU-15	EU-10
Labour productivity growth	0.096	0.062
	0.87	*0.38*
Unit labour costs	0.203***	0.009
	2.91	*0.09*
Size of service sector	−0.090***	−0.052
	−2.41	*−1.08*
Openness	0.335***	0.490***
	11.15	*7.87*
Sector dummies:		
Communication	1.037***	1.136***
	4.4	*4.00*
Construction	1.064***	0.851***
	4.54	*3.16*
Insurance	0.680***	
	2.63	
Computer and information technologies	0.587***	0.659**
	2.29	*2.00*
Tertiary education share	0.011	−0.012
	0.3	*−0.17*
Share of white-collar, high-skill workers	0.033	0.138*
	1.17	*2.65*
Overall R2	0.34	0.57
Observations	720	414
Observations per group	91	76

Note: Dependent variable is the RCA index by industry; *** denotes statistically significant coefficient at the 1% level; ** at the 5% level; * at the 10% level; robust standard errors.

Source: Author's calculations.

sures openness of the service sector through its exports-to-output ratio and *Skills* is a measure of the skill intensity of the sector (we will use two different measures: skills measured by education levels and by occupations). Table 16.5 reports the results of the random effects estimation, pooled across all sectors. We see that the determinants of service sector competitiveness differ between old and new member states, with labour productivity growth and the service sector's size exerting a significant influence on competitiveness in the old member states but not so in the new member states. The positive coefficient on unit labour costs is at first sight surprising.

Unit labour costs in the service sector can, however, be interpreted as measuring the quality of labour inputs, since wages may be related directly with the quality of the service delivered. Seen in this light, the positive ULC coefficient reveals a beneficial impact of higher-quality labour on a country's competitive position. On the other hand, the share of high-skill workers is significant only for the sub-sample of new EU members. Hence, also here quality in terms of high-skill employment boosts competitiveness.

The two sub-samples also share similarities: openness is one of the most important factors; omitting this variable results in a considerable drop in the explanatory power of the model. Second, communication services, construction services and computer and information services emerge as being characterized by above-average competitiveness within each sub-sample.

16.6 CONCLUSIONS

Since the 1970s we have witnessed deep changes in global trade patterns, which in turn reflect fundamental changes of individual regions' competitiveness. In this chapter we confined our attention to a selection of high- and medium-income countries, namely the OECD and most of Asia, to trace and analyse these changes in competitiveness using different indicators. One of the most eye-catching developments is the strong rise in Asia's share in world merchandise trade. With respect to services, the most advanced OECD members are still the major producers and also successful net-exporters of services, in particular of business- and other producer-related services. This indication of the strong gain of Asian competitiveness in goods and advanced OECD competitiveness in services is obtained from using traditional indicators, such as trade balances and revealed comparative advantages.

Also based on structural indicators, Asia (especially China) but also the new EU members (on the EU-15 market) show good structural characteristics and high competitiveness despite relatively low rankings in indicators of business environment. This is not to say that soft facts, business environment, sound governance structures and so on, do not matter. They seem to matter more for post-industrialist countries at higher stages of development, pointing towards competitiveness in service sectors, especially producer-related services. At the same time, good governance structures and a sound business environment may also result from high previous competitiveness in goods.

In general, indicators building on past performance alone may be a weak indicator of future competitiveness. The analysis of structural characteristics and their dynamics gives valuable information, since it comes closer to providing a forward-looking view on a country's performance.

We see a certain distinction between competitiveness in manufacturing and competitiveness in services. While cost factors and general price competitiveness (an aspect not analysed in this chapter) play a greater role in the production of goods, soft factors and hence the general business environment seem to be more influential in determining comparative advantages in the service sector. What follows is a need for analysing a wide range of indicators in order to be able to draw a comprehensive and unbiased picture of a region's competitive position in the world.

All this reflects the general fact that competitiveness is a relative concept in each dimension. It depends on the reference group (that is, the sample chosen) as well as on the unit of analysis (whether we focus on firms, industries, regions or countries), as well as on the industry or service sector under consideration.

NOTES

1. Economist, Foreign Research Division, Oesterreichische Nationalbank. This chapter was written when Julia Woerz was staff economist at the Vienna Institute for International Economic Studies (wiiw).
2. It has to be noted here that the sample excludes Africa (and in particular sub-Saharan Africa) as well as Latin America. The inclusion of these regions would alter the picture.
3. The RCA index is defined as $RCA_k^i = RXA_k^i - R{=}MA_k^i$ where $RXA_k^i = (X_k^i / X_{total}^i) / (X_k^{all} / X_{total}^{all})$ and RMA_k^i is defined analogously, X are exports and M are imports of services in the respective category.

REFERENCES

Aiginger, K. and M. Landesmann (2002), 'Competitive economic performance: USA versus EU', *wiiw Research Reports* No. 291, The Vienna Institute for International Economic Studies.

Hatzichronoglou, Th. (1996), 'Globalisation and competitiveness: relevant indicators', *STI Working Papers* No. 1996/5, OECD.

Hunya, G. (2007), 'EU membership – support and challenges to the competitiveness of the Polish and Romanian economies', *wiiw Monthly report* No. 2/07, The Vienna Institute for International Economic Studies, 9–16.

Krugman, Paul (1994), 'Competitiveness: a dangerous obsession', *Foreign Affairs*, **73** (2), 28–44.

Landesmann, M. and J. Woerz (2006), 'The competitiveness of CEE in a global context', Report Xplicit, Bank Austria Creditanstalt, March 2006 and *wiiw Research Report* No. 328, The Vienna Institute for International Economic Studies.

Narula, R. and K. Wakelin (1995), 'Technological competitiveness, FDI and trade', *MERIT Working Paper Series* No. 95–20.

Trabold, H. (1995), 'Die internationale Wettbewerbsfähigkeit einer Volkswirtschaft', *DIW Vierteljahresheft*, **2**, Berlin, 169–85.

17. Assessing the sustainability of external positions in new EU member states

Enrique Alberola[1] and José María Serena[2]

17.1 INTRODUCTION

One of the main economic concerns for new EU member states (NMS) is external imbalances. Large and, in some cases, widening current account deficits that have accompanied these countries on their path of integration with the European Union represent an important source of economic and financial vulnerability. Their huge current account deficits imply the need for continued foreign inflows to finance domestic growth, causing the net foreign assets position – a stock variable – of the NMS to worsen as inflows accumulate. At the same time, the increasing stock of external liabilities also requires a higher inflow of financial resources to pay for those liabilities, thus exacerbating the deterioration of the current account. In this chapter, we focus on stocks rather than on flows – that is, on the external positions rather than on the external or current account imbalances that have attracted more attention among policy makers and in academic fora.

In Figure 17.1 we observe the parallel – albeit not identical – behaviour of the cumulative current account balances (in terms of GDP) and of the stock of net foreign assets for the two groups of countries generally covered in our analysis for the period 1995–2006, namely the Baltic countries and Bulgaria (denoted by B+B) and the four largest NMS (the Czech Republic, Hungary, Poland and the Slovak Republic – denoted G-4). This comparison shows that the B+B reported higher current accounts deficits in the period than the G-4. In 2006, the B+B's current account imbalance reached 15 per cent of GDP on a weighted average basis and 50 per cent of GDP on a cumulative basis. The G-4 current account deficit in 2006, in contrast, averaged 4 per cent and added up to 30 per cent of GDP in the period considered. This implies a larger stock of net foreign liabilities (64 per cent) for the B+B than for the G-4 (54 per cent).

Basically, there are two conflicting views on the sustainability of external positions in NMS, as well as on the role exchange rates play in this context. The optimistic view stresses the rapid real convergence that the NMS are undertaking, which leads to an appreciation of the equilibrium exchange rate through the Balassa-Samuelson effect. This has indeed happened in the countries under review. In recent years the B+B GDP per capita climbed from one-third of the EU-27 average in 1997 to 54 per cent in 2006. At the same time, the B+B real effective exchange rate appreciated by 39 per cent. In this period, the G-4 real exchange rate appreciated by around 31.5 per cent, yet against the backdrop of slower convergence (from 54 per cent to 63 per cent of the EU average). Under this view, the exchange rate appreciation is a by-product of the process of convergence and helps smooth the adjustments required in such a process. The negative view, in contrast, focuses on the large current account imbalances that most of these countries – in particular the B+B states, which have adopted very rigid pegs – are accumulating, and which translate into a deterioration of the net foreign asset position. Under this view, exchange rate appreciation may have impaired competitiveness, by further deteriorating the trade balance, and it may represent a misalignment from the long-term equilibrium.

The aim of this chapter is to obtain some further insights into the sustainability of the external positions and, in particular, into how exchange rates may impact their sustainability. This requires focusing our attention on the dynamics of external debt, which is heavily influenced by the composition of the net foreign asset position. This framework will allow us to derive the main factors driving the external position, beyond the cumulated trade deficit. Rather, the cost of financing, the impact of exchange rate evolutions through valuation effects and the process of real convergence itself could play a central role in the evolution of the foreign position and, consequently, in the assessment of the external sustainability of these countries.

The conclusions of this analysis are somewhat sobering, contrary to what may be expected, given the concern that external imbalances arise in new EU countries. The main reason for this conclusion is that the convergence process – entailing reduced financing costs, high returns and high growth – mitigates the deterioration of the external positions and improves their sustainability prospects. In this context, the appreciation of the real exchange rate can also be seen as a by-product of convergence, with its impact on the external position through valuation effects being hardly noticeable. This apparently optimistic view on external stocks does not dispel the risks that large current account imbalances – and external flows – convey. On the one hand, this is an aggregate analysis which may blur relevant sectoral weaknesses; on the other hand, to the extent that widening external liabilities deteriorate the current account through the income balance, the evolution of the external liabilities has to be monitored closely as they remain an increasing source of vulnerability.

17.2 THE COMPOSITION OF NET FOREIGN ASSET POSITIONS IN NEW EU MEMBER STATES

As a first step, we have to consider the composition of the foreign asset position. Following the literature on country balance-sheet composition, any rigorous analysis of the sustainability of net foreign assets has to take into account not only the level of net foreign assets (the size of the debt, which affects future net foreign assets and current account dynamics through the income balance), but also the composition of foreign assets and liabilities in terms of instruments. There are at least three reasons why the composition of net foreign assets matters for their prospective evolution. First, the currency denomination of the instrument determines the sensitivity of the external position to exchange rate movements. It is worth recalling that the dramatic deterioration of external positions following

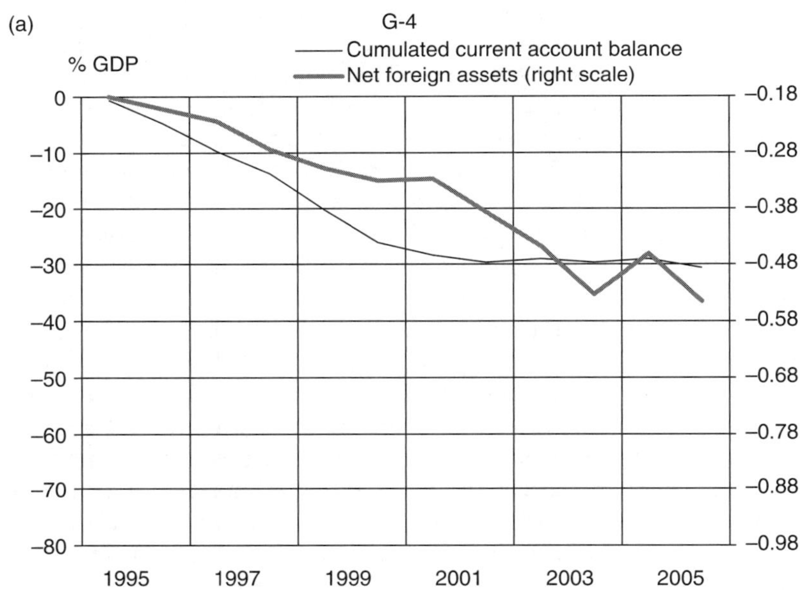

Note: The G-4 includes the Czech Republic, Hungary, Poland and the Slovak Republic.

Sources: IFS-IMF and national statistics.

Figure 17.1 Current account balance and net foreign assets

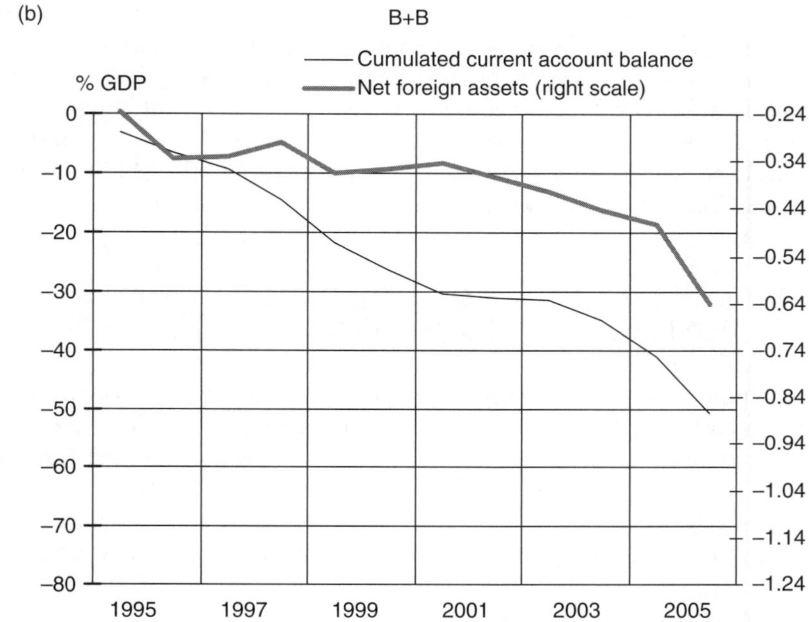

Note: B+B include Bulgaria, Estonia, Latvia and Lithuania.

Sources: IFS-IMF and national statistics.

Figure 17.1 (continued)

exchange rate adjustments has been behind some of the worst emerging market crises in the last 15 years – Mexico, Russia, Brazil, Argentina, and so on. Second, some instruments are expected to be more productivity-enhancing than others, which implies that each type of liability conveys different implications for potential GDP growth. Finally, different instruments provide different profiles and rates returns; this means that the composition of assets and liabilities also shapes the income balance.

We classify assets and liabilities into four groups – reserves, FDI, debt and portfolio equity.[3] This delineates a clear mapping in terms of currency denomination. All assets (of which international reserves account for the bulk) are denominated in foreign currency (euros, by assumption). FDI-related liabilities are denominated in domestic currency, as are portfolio equity holdings. As debt liabilities – in the form of bonds and loans – are mostly denominated in foreign currency, we assume the whole group is in euros.[4]

Figure 17.2 shows a remarkable symmetry between the positions of both G-4 and B+B in foreign currency: assets (mostly reserves) roughly offset debt in foreign currency (debt). There are, however, differences within the groups when it comes to the currency composition of debt, which we explore later. Thus, the overall picture is dominated by FDI inflows, and their properties in terms of productivity enhancement, returns and local currency denomination. This peculiar composition will have important implications for the analysis and conclusions below. The G-4 and the B+B countries basically behave in a similar way, but the level of net foreign liabilities – and the magnitude of its components – is both higher in the B+B group.

17.3 THE DYNAMICS OF THE EXTERNAL POSITION – A MODEL FOR THE ANALYSIS

The dynamics of the net foreign asset position of a country relative to its GDP broadly depend on the evolution of the current account in terms of GDP. Let Δnfa_t be the increase of net foreign assets and cab_t the current

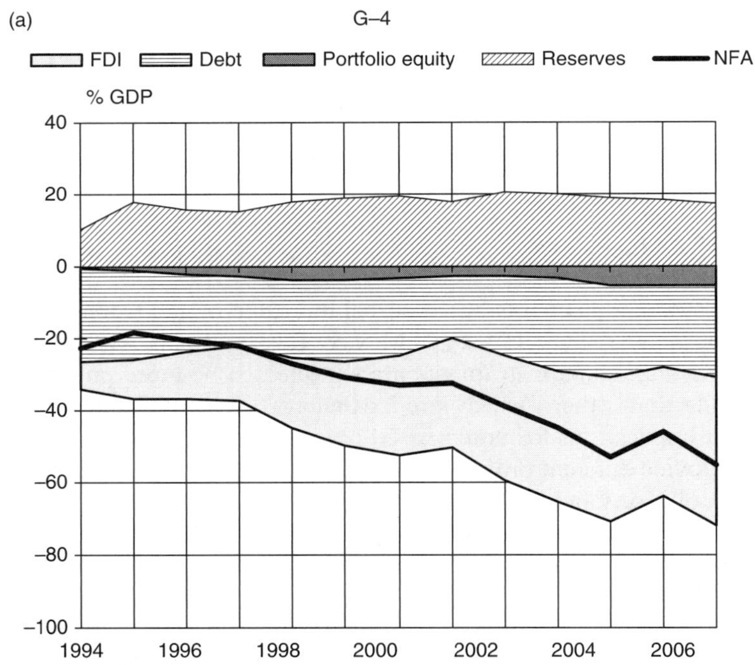

Note: G-4 includes the Czech Republic, Hungary, Poland and the Slovak Republic; NFA = net foreign assets.

Source: IFS-IMF and national statistics.

Figure 17.2 Composition of net foreign assets

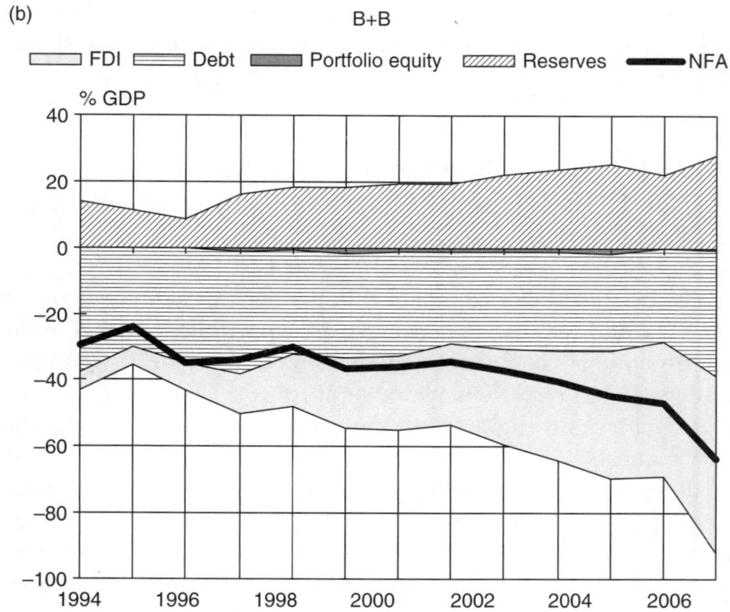

Note: B+B include Bulgaria, Estonia, Latvia and Lithuania; NFA = net foreign assets.

Sources: IFS-IMF and national statistics.

Figure 17.2 (continued)

account balance, both in terms of GDP. Then, the dynamics of the net foreign assets are given by $\Delta nfa_t = (-g/1 + g)\, nfa_{t-1} + cab_t$, where g is the nominal rate of growth. The current account includes the income balance, reflecting net payments – or revenues – derived from the *nfa* (= net foreign assets) position. Thus, it is convenient to define the primary current account balance (*pcab*) as the current account excluding the income balance. This primary balance conveys the trade balance of goods and services and other items, such as current transfers. Performing some simple algebra, the dynamic equation of the external position reads as follows:

$$\Delta nfa_t = \left(\frac{r-g}{1+g}\right) nfa_{t-1} + pcab_t \qquad (17.1)$$

The income balance in this very simplified framework is obtained as the difference between the interest rate or cost of financing r and the rate of growth g – defined either in nominal or in real terms. It is usually assumed that the term in brackets is positive[5] (the cost of financing is higher than growth $r > g$), so that a positive (negative) external position translates into a further improvement (deterioration) of the external position.

17.4 NET FOREIGN ASSET POSITION AND EQUILIBRIUM EXCHANGE RATES – THE PORTFOLIO MODEL

What role does the exchange rate play in the dynamics of the net external position? The main channel is conveyed in the portfolio model of exchange rate determination. The portfolio model is built upon the assumption that a more depreciated real exchange rate improves the competitiveness position of a country and engineers an improvement of the trade and current account balances.

The equilibrium solution to the model implies that the external position of a country cannot grow without bounds. Since an ever-deteriorating *nfa* position is not sustainable in the long run the exchange rate will eventually adjust in order to restore equilibrium. More precisely, the equilibrium condition implies the stabilization of the net foreign asset position. Setting Δnfa_t equal to zero in expression (17.1), this condition establishes that the primary current account balance must equalize the income balance, with an opposite sign: $pcab_t = -(r - g/1 + g)\ nfa_{t-1}$. If *pcab* is lower than the income balance, a depreciation of the real exchange rate will be required to improve the trade balance and attain the equilibrium in the model. Therefore, the real equilibrium exchange rate will appreciate (depreciate) with the improvement (deterioration) of the external position.

How does this model match the data? Analyses of the equilibrium exchange rate for NMS have mushroomed in the last decade – see Égert (2004) for a good survey. Yet they have tended to focus on the Balassa-Samuelson effect, that is, they have emphasized the idea that real convergence engineers a real exchange rate appreciation due to relative gains in productivity. A number of papers have expanded the focus to include also the net foreign position among other additional factors, but few have proceeded in a sequential encompassing way, which is important for the question at hand.

In Alberola and Navia (2008) we started by testing the portfolio model in a co-integration framework. As was to be expected from the diverging evolution of real exchange rates (appreciation) and the net foreign assets position (deterioration), the portfolio model for the main NMS thoroughly fails. However, when we consider the portfolio model jointly with the Balassa-Samuelson effect, that is, when we control for the latter, not only the Balassa-Samuelson hypothesis is validated, but the expected sign of *nfa* on the real exchange rate is recovered.

These results convey a very relevant interpretation in the context of our analysis. On the one hand, we observed in Figure 17.2 that foreign direct investment (FDI) is the dominating factor in the evolution of net foreign asset positions. On the other hand, FDI inflows have been one of the main catalysts of productivity convergence in NMS. Putting all this evidence together leads to two important conclusions: (1) the real convergence process is closely linked to the deterioration of the current account position, which also embodies the flow of financing needs of a country – to the point that it can be stated that they are the two sides of the same coin; (2) this link tends to give support to the idea that large negative external positions are sustainable in NMS. Thus, these two conclusions support an optimistic view of the net foreign external position of these economies.

In this section, we analyse some driving factors of net foreign assets in the countries under review. We consider in the first place the valuation effects derived from the foreign currency composition in the net foreign asset position; second, we focus on the sign and magnitude of the difference between the cost of financing and the rate of growth, which has a large influence on the dynamics of net foreign assets, as the term in brackets in expression (17.1) suggests. Finally, we measure the contribution of the different factors impacting on the evolution of net foreign assets.

17.4.1 Exchange Rate Valuation Effect

The valuation effect is a second channel of impact of the exchange rate movements on *nfa* evolutions, and it is more straightforward than the trade channel. It can be directly introduced into the external dynamics equation. In the previous expression it was implicitly assumed that the assets and liabilities were in domestic currency. By now defining the net foreign assets denominated in foreign currency as nfa^* we can rewrite expression (17.1) as follows after some algebra:

$$\Delta nfa_t = \left(\frac{r-g}{1+g}\right) nfa_{t-1} + \frac{\Delta e_t}{1+g} nfa^*_{t-1} + pcab_t \qquad (17.2)$$

where a positive Δe_t stands for a depreciation of the nominal exchange rate. This expression implies that when the foreign currency-denominated net foreign assets are negative ($nfa^* < 0$) a nominal exchange rate depreciation worsens the external position.

Although these valuation effects could be potentially important for the vulnerability of NMS, note also that, by the same token, a nominal

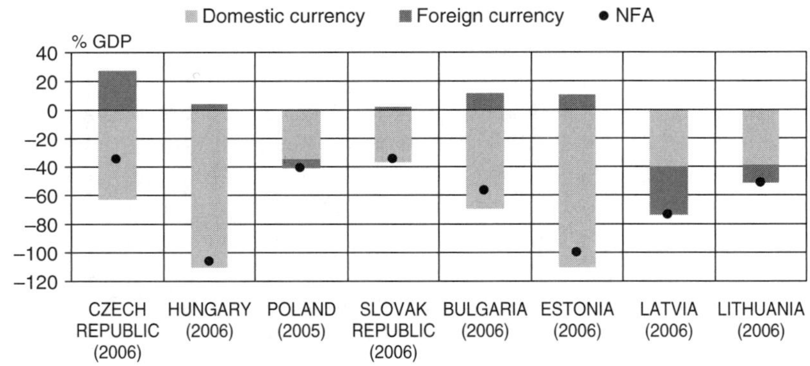

Sources: IFS-IMF and national statistics.

Figure 17.3 Currency composition of net foreign assets

exchange rate depreciation would improve the external position of creditor countries. Using expression (17.2) to test the data we can check whether these effects are relevant.

Figure 17.3 provides the decomposition into domestic and foreign debt, following the criteria outlined above. There are two remarkable features in this decomposition. First, net debt in domestic currency is much larger than net debt in foreign currency for all countries, due to the observed dominance of FDI and the fact that reserve assets offset debt liabilities (see also Figure 17.1). Second, the sign of the *net* positions in foreign currency is split among countries. From expression (17.2), for countries with positive foreign currency positions – creditors in foreign currency (Bulgaria, Czech Republic, Estonia, Hungary, Slovak Republic), an appreciation (depreciation) reduces (increases) the net foreign asset position as a ratio of GDP, thus worsening (improving) the external position. The reverse holds for those countries that have a debtor position in foreign currency (Latvia, Lithuania and Poland): an appreciation (depreciation) of the exchange rate would reduce (increase) the debtor position measured in domestic currency, this way having a positive (negative) effect on *nfa*.

What are the implications of these findings for the actual evolution of net foreign assets? Table 17.1 provides, in the first place, a simulation of the valuation effect resulting from a 10 per cent nominal appreciation of the exchange rate. Note first that *nfa* for most countries is broadly shielded from exchange rate movements because, as seen in Figure 17.3, most of their net debt is in domestic currency. The main exceptions are the Czech Republic and Latvia, which have a large creditor or debtor position in foreign currency, respectively, and are quite exposed to valuation effects

Table 17.1 Valuation effects

	Simulation (% GDP)		Actual 1999–2006	
	Position in foreign currency	10% appreciation	Valuation effect as % GDP[a]	Appreciation (−)/ depreciation (+) %
Czech Republic	Creditor	−2.91	−4.68	−21.90
Hungary	Creditor	−0.63	−0.13	−0.25
Poland	Debtor	0.56	0.79	−6.32
Slovak Republic	Creditor	−0.17	−0.92	−20.31
Bulgaria	Creditor	−1.21	0.02	0.00
Estonia	Creditor	−1.08	0.00	0.54
Lithuania	Debtor	1.16	1.11	−26.02
Latvia	Debtor	3.36	−1.40	4.83

Note: a. >0 reflects an increase / <0 reflects a decrease.

Sources: IFS-IMF, national statistics.

arising from changes in exchange rates. The last columns of Table 17.1 show the actual valuation effects in the period 1999–2006. Indeed, for the Czech Republic, the exchange rate appreciation in the period implied a significant deterioration of its net foreign asset position (close to 5 per cent of GDP). In other countries with substantial exchange rate movements in the period, such as Slovakia or Lithuania, the valuation effects have been scant.

All in all, the low net foreign exchange exposure implies that, contrary to what could be expected, in most countries the net foreign asset position will remain largely unaffected by exchange rate movements through this direct channel. Moreover, as exchange rate revaluations and devaluations are expected to be 'pro-cyclical' (appreciations tend to occur when the economy grows fast), the currency exposure for creditor countries in foreign currency could act as a stabilizing factor. On the contrary, for Latvia especially, which has the largest negative currency exposure, a devaluation of the currency would trigger an increase in foreign debt measured in domestic currency.

To sum up, in these countries balance-sheet currency mismatches do not appear as a source of risks for net foreign asset sustainability. An important caveat is necessary, though. The sectoral currency mismatches can be very relevant in these countries. International reserves are the main assets in foreign currency, and are within the public sector, while liabilities in foreign currency are predominant in the private sector (credit financing for instance). Thus, an exchange rate depreciation would increase, ceteris paribus, reserve holdings in GDP terms, but it could have a negative impact in the private sector, since private sector debts would now be much higher in local currency terms.

17.4.2 Is the Net Cost of Debt Positive?

Equation (17.1), which represents the dynamics of the net foreign assets, underscores that the *nfa* position has a positive impact as long as the cost of financing exceeds the rate of growth, that is, if $r - g > 0$, which is the usual assumption. The fact that all the countries in the sample are net debtors (have negative net foreign assets) implies that their external position will tend to deteriorate – other things being equal – which may entail increasing concerns on their sustainability.

But the question is: does the $r - g > 0$ assumption hold for these countries; that is, do financing costs rise at a stronger pace than the rate of growth? For NMS this is not obvious because, on the one hand, their growth rates are high, and on the other hand, they are probably benefiting from low financing costs thanks to their integration with the European Union and positive risk-return prospects. Both factors put together open the scope for a negative value for $(r - g)$, that is a negative cost of financing after controlling for GDP growth.

How can we measure such a term? Using GDP growth – g – is straightforward, but obtaining the value of financing costs is more complex. The most direct approximation is to use the ratio of the income balance (interest plus dividend payments on the *nfa* position) to the *nfa* position to derive the average cost of financing and use it as a proxy for r. However, the data on the income balance display high volatility, and gross assets and liabilities reflect adjustments typically made by the national statistics offices, since they are subject to severe measurement problems and continued revisions. Also, the composition of assets and liabilities is important in explaining these numbers. For instance, the returns on FDI liabilities can lag on the investments and may spread through a long period of time.[6] Thus, these results have to be taken with lots of caution. To mitigate these problems, we took the average of the financing costs for the period 2002–06. The results are shown in Figure 17.4 and Table 17.2, where the data for the average *nfa* and income balance are also displayed. We observe a large variability in the estimated cost of financing; note also the high value of the Czech Republic and the negative (!) value for Bulgaria (derived from a negative *nfa* position coupled with a positive income balance in the period).

Table 17.2 Assets, liabilities and income balance

	Czech Rep.	Hungary	Poland	Slovak Rep.	Bulgaria	Estonia	Latvia	Lithuania
2001–05 average[a]				In %				
Assets	64.95	48.65	30.05	52.91	64.67	73.20	64.78	34.97
Liabilities	92.24	137.02	74.31	81.95	100.23	158.28	119.72	75.74
Net foreign assets	−27.29	−88.37	−44.26	−29.03	−35.56	−85.08	−54.94	−40.76
Income balance to GDP	−5.22	−5.80	−3.01	−3.08	1.21	−5.03	−1.09	−2.37

Note: a. Income balance to GDP is 2002–06 average.

Sources: IFS-IMF and national statistics.

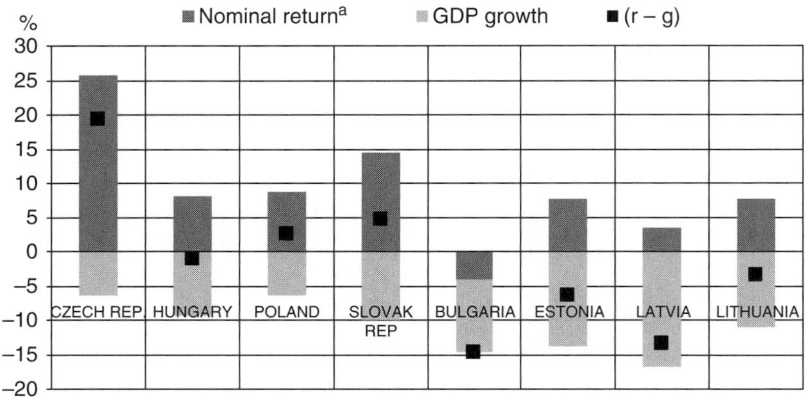

Note: a. Average income balance and nominal GDP growth;
b. Average net foreign assets 2001–05.

Sources: IFS-IMF and national statistics.

Figure 17.4 Net return of net foreign assets[b]

In any case, it is noteworthy that $(r - g)$ is negative when average GDP growth in the period in five of the eight countries in the sample is subtracted (with the Czech Republic being the most notorious exception). With all the caveats, this is a noteworthy result, not only because it reverses the expected dynamics of the *nfa* position, but also – more importantly – because it suggests that the accumulation of net liabilities does not necessarily feed into a dramatic worsening of the external position of NMS.

17.4.3 The Evolution of Net Foreign Assets and Contributing Factors

This final section can be seen as a wrap-up of the discussion above. In Figure 17.5, we computed the contribution of a wide array of factors to the observed evolution of the net foreign asset position (as a ratio of GDP) for the two groups of countries under review here (B+B and G-4). On the one hand, we consider the primary currency balance – distinguishing between the trade and services balance and the current transfer balance – as well as the income balance. On the other hand, we also contemplate other economic factors appearing in equation (17.2): a reduction in *nfa* due to GDP growth and the exchange rate valuation effect. The computation reveals a residual, or non-explained part, which may reflect capital transfers, valuation effects beyond the exchange rates, and statistical and measurement adjustments.

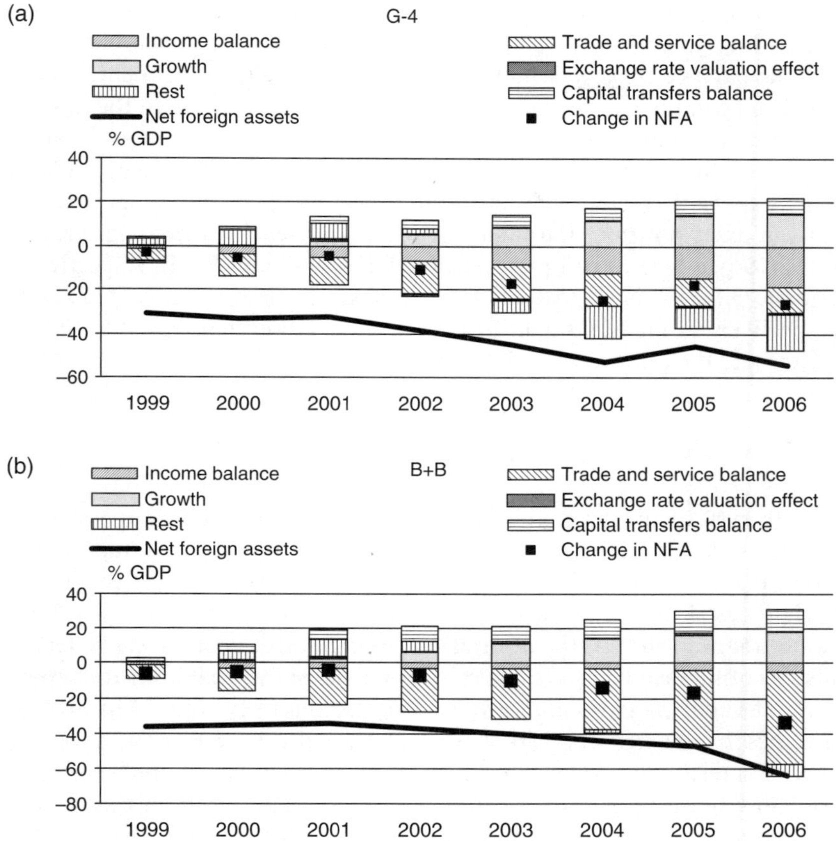

Note: G-4 includes the Czech Republic, Hungary, Poland and the Slovak Republic; B+B includes Bulgaria, Estonia, Latvia and Lithuania.

Sources: IFS-IMF and national statistics.

Figure 17.5 Contribution to change in net foreign assets (cumulative since 1999)

From 1999 to 2006, the net foreign asset position worsened by 27 per cent of GDP for the G-4 group and by 23 percentage points for the B+B group of countries. Note that the behaviour of Poland and Bulgaria greatly influences the outcome for the respective groups, given the large weight of those countries (53 per cent and 44 per cent, respectively). The two main contributors to this deterioration have been the trade balance – with the effect being more pronounced in the B+B group (–52 per cent of GDP) than in the G-4 (–11.9 per cent) – and the income balance. In other words, the net foreign position also broadly reflects the underlying dynamics of the income balance. This is particularly true for the G-4 (–18 per cent), where the decline in the income balance is even more important than the drag of the trade balance. In the case of the B+ B, by contrast, the deteriorating impact of the income balance is rather small (–5 per cent), due mainly to Bulgaria. With regard to factors limiting the deterioration of the net foreign asset position, the main factors have been high nominal growth rates (15 per cent and 18 per cent of GDP in G-4 and B+ B, respectively) and the hefty current transfer balance (6.6 per cent and 12 per cent of GDP, respectively). Finally, note the negligible impact of exchange rate valuation effects and the importance of the residual.

17.5 CONCLUSIONS

The analysis of the external positions of new European Union members is of relevance for different reasons. First, because the research and discussion on external financial vulnerability in these countries has overwhelmingly focused on current account imbalances – in other words, on flows rather than on stocks (the external net foreign asset position). The recent history of financial crises in emerging countries shows that both are important, though, in particular given currency, maturity and sectoral mismatches in the external position. Second, the net foreign asset position is a crucial determinant of the current account through the income balance. A widening negative external position is an increasing drag on the current account; the magnitude of this drag depends on the difference between the cost and return of external financing. Third, the central role of the exchange rate in the debate on NMS ahead of their integration with the euro area and its importance for the external position warrants special attention.

In this chapter we have preliminarily explored these issues; our conclusions tend to be sobering:

1. We have pointed out that the exchange rate real appreciation in these countries does not have a dramatically negative impact on the current account since, overall, these developments are consistent with the process of convergence; in turn, this convergence hinges on external financing and thus, on ample current account deficits and deteriorating external positions.
2. The impact of the exchange rate on the external positions through valuation effects is small, except in some cases, as Latvia. The reason is

that the currency mismatches in the external positions are, in general, small. This is so because of the composition of the external assets – they are mostly reserves, denominated in foreign currency, which offset foreign currency liabilities (debt stocks) – and because of the importance of foreign direct investment, which is denominated in local currency. Nonetheless, sectoral mismatches (corporates and households versus government) may have large negative consequences in the case of large exchange rate depreciations.

3. The negative impact of deteriorating external positions on the current account and on the dynamics of the net foreign position is limited. The reason is the relative low cost of financing that these countries enjoy, relative to the notional return they obtain in the form of high growth, although this result has to be taken with caution due to problems interpreting the data.

All in all, the dynamics of the external positions in NMS and its interaction with the exchange rate are not as perverse as could be feared. Does this mean that we should dismiss our concerns on external sustainability in these countries in the run-up to the economic and monetary union? Not at all. On the one hand, the external positions are indeed negative and widening; this implies that the drag of an increasing deficit in the income balance on the current account is bound to grow; the deterioration of the income balance may exacerbate as foreign direct investment matures and as profits and rents grow; the widening in the income balance deficits translates into a 'structural' deterioration of the current account. On the other hand, all this means is that the needs of capital inflows to cover this 'structural' deficit of the current account also increases. Since the actual problem of external imbalances in emerging markets is that capital flows suffer a sudden stop and this risk increases with the magnitude of the current account deficit, the deterioration of the external position implies, through this channel, an increase in the financial vulnerability of new EU member states.

NOTES

1. Head of International Economics Division, Banco de España.
2. Economist, International Economics Division, Banco de España.
3. The mapping between the standard balance-of-payments (BOP) classification and ours is simple: we just group other investment plus portfolio debt into what we call debt, we constitute a group with portfolio equity and we keep the standard BOP classification FDI and reserves.
4. Although we are aware that in some countries a non-negligible fraction of debt liabilities is denominated in Swiss francs, we make such an assumption because of the difficulties in disentangling the relative importance of euros and Swiss francs.

5. As we will see this assumption can be challenged under certain circumstances, which are reasonable for the countries under study.
6. Note that the reinvestment of profits is not an issue. The accountability convention is to compute all the FDI profits from foreign firms in the income balance. If they are reinvested, they will appear as an additional inflow of FDI.

REFERENCES

Alberola, E. and D. Navia (2008), 'Equilibrium exchange rates in new EU members: external imbalances versus real convergence', *Banco de España Working Paper* No. 0708, in *Review of Development Economics,* **12** (3), 605–19.

Egert, B. (2004), 'Assessing equilibrium exchange rates in CEE acceding countries: can we have DEER with BEER without FEER? A critical survey of the literature', *BOFIT Discussion Papers* No. 1.

PART IV

Policy challenges on the road to and within monetary union

18. Preparing for the euro – perspectives from the monetary policy strategy in Cyprus

Athanasios Orphanides[1]

The purpose of this chapter is to share the experience of Cyprus in preparing for the euro, the lessons learned and the challenges that remain ahead. I will take this opportunity to examine the broader issue of monetary policy strategy on the road to the euro and related challenges for euro aspirants.

Many of these challenges and the appropriate monetary policy strategy required to respond to them are likely to be country-specific – reflecting the historical experience and institutional arrangements in place long before entry into the euro area. Past experience has shown that there is no unique trajectory for a country's entry into a monetary union. For this discussion, I will draw upon the experience of my country's entry into the European Union and preparation for the euro area.

Cyprus has a small, open and services-oriented economy. Real GDP growth has been historically robust, averaging around 6 per cent since the island's independence in 1960 – consistently above the average trend for the euro area as well as for the European Union as a whole (see Figure 18.1).

Consistent with this robust real GDP growth, the unemployment rate has historically been lower and more stable than in the rest of the European Union (see Figure 18.2). Indeed, the remarkable stability is noteworthy. An important exception was the period 1974–75, reflecting the military invasion of Cyprus by Turkey in 1974, which displaced one-third of the population from their homes, making them refugees in their own land. Despite the economic devastation, the Cypriot economy bounced back at an amazing pace.

Though one might expect that high economic growth, in conjunction with low unemployment, would lead to higher inflation, this did not materialize in Cyprus. Inflation remained relatively contained throughout the years, an outcome that could be attributed to the prudent monetary and exchange rate policies that had been followed by the Central Bank of Cyprus ever since its foundation in 1963.

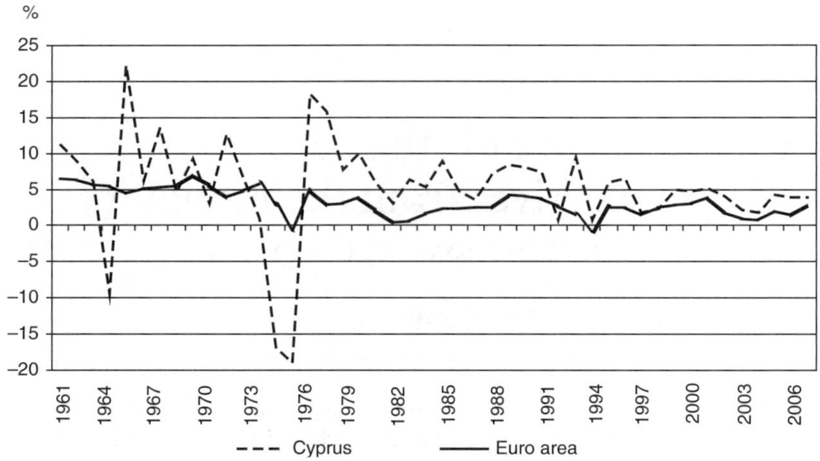

Source: CBC (Central Bank of Cyprus) calculations.

Figure 18.1 Real GDP growth rate

Indeed, against the setting of a small and open economy, it was recognized soon after the establishment of the Central Bank in 1963 that targeting the exchange rate would be an appropriate means for achieving the bank's primary objective of price stability. To the extent that our major trading partners remained committed to price stability, managing the exchange rate by pegging the Cyprus pound to a strong anchor – be it a single currency or a basket of currencies of our main trading partners – could deliver the desired price stability objective. A strong peg would also contribute towards anchoring inflation expectations, thereby alleviating any possible second-round effects of temporary shocks, further facilitating the achievement of price stability.

In 1992 the aspiration to join the European Union led to the unilateral peg of the Cyprus pound to the European currency unit (ECU), with the central rate of ECU 1 = CYP 0.585274 and fluctuation margins of ±2.25 per cent. This was an important step in the policy of linking the economy more closely to the economies of the EU, even though the ECU basket did not reflect very well the composition of trade in Cyprus at the time. Similarly, following the establishment of the European economic and monetary union (EMU) on 1 January 1999, the Central Bank decided to link the Cyprus pound to the euro with a central rate and margins equal to those of the ECU, despite the fact that the UK, our major trading partner, opted to stay out of the euro area.

In view of the introduction of a new monetary policy framework encompassing market-based instruments in 1996, and especially after the abolition

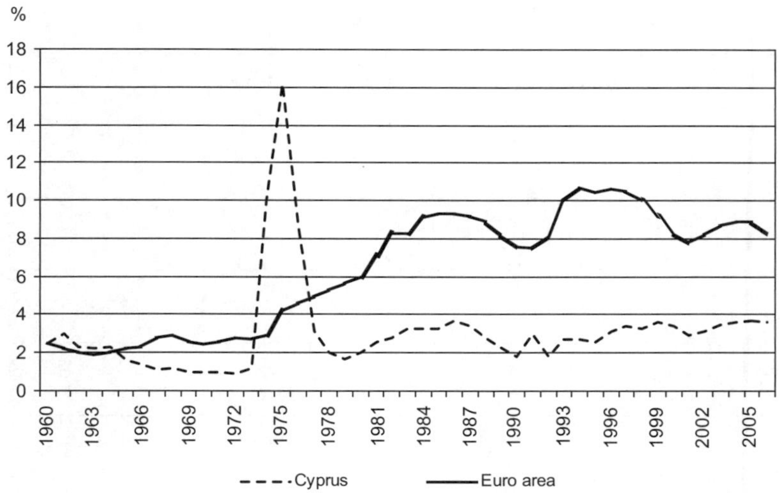

Source: CBC calculations.

Figure 18.2 Unemployment rate

of the statutory interest rate ceiling in 2001, the bank has been implementing this strategy by setting its interest rates so as to steer short-term and long-term market interest rates towards levels consistent with exchange rate stability.

Ultimately, the pursuit of exchange rate stability was seen as equivalent to the pursuit of price stability. The existence of a sound exchange rate regime, the monitoring of the money supply, liquidity of the banking system and credit to the private sector, as well as the pass-through to the current account, have been the key elements of this strategy.

Overall, the monetary policy strategy I have just described has been applied resolutely in a credible and consistent fashion by the Central Bank of Cyprus. The long track record of price stability in Cyprus is the most obvious proof of the success of this strategy.

As can be seen in Figure 18.3, inflation remained in check, averaging between 2–3 per cent over the greatest part of the past 40 years, with the most notable exception being the experience of the 1970s. Even during that decade, however, inflation in Cyprus largely reflected increased inflation faced by the countries of its anchor currencies, rather than loose monetary policy in Cyprus. This favourable comparison, especially for the second half of the 1970s, is even more remarkable in light of the economic destruction of much of the island's economy resulting from the invasion and occupation of over one-third of the island by Turkey. In retrospect, the experience

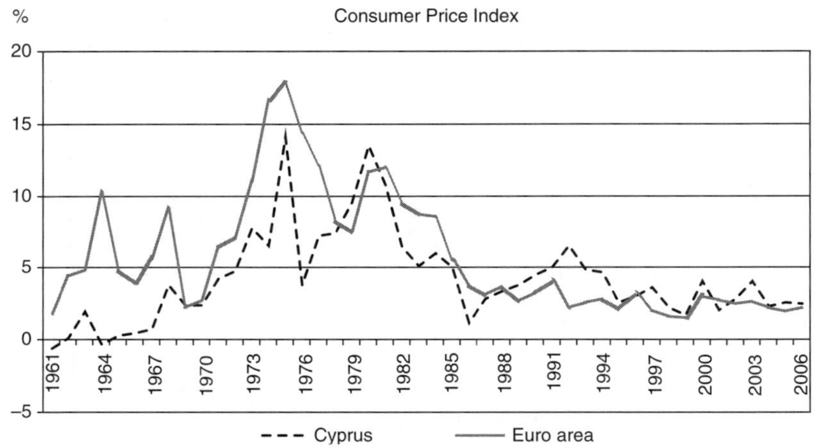

Source: CBC calculations.

Figure 18.3 Inflation

of Cyprus may serve as an instructive example of the long-term benefits of a monetary policy focused on price stability, even in the presence of dislocations that might have been seen as providing cover for looser, less responsible monetary policy in other contexts.

The success of this policy strategy could be attributed to four key elements. The first element was the close monitoring of monetary aggregates and credit, in particular credit to the private sector, with a view towards reigning in excessive rates of expansion that might threaten stability. The second element was the close monitoring of the current account deficit, both as an indicator of inflationary pressures and as a warning signal helping to avoid external imbalances.

The third element contributing to the success of this strategy was the safeguarding of the credibility of policy in maintaining a stable currency – stable against a strong anchor – even during periods of quite adverse economic conditions. For a small open economy, second chances to re-establish credibility following a devaluation may not come by as easily as might be desired. Rather, the loss in credibility resulting from a devaluation might be more costly than the short-term benefits the devaluation might bring.

Apart from credibility, however, other economic conditions prevailing in Cyprus at the time precluded the use of the exchange rate as a means of restoring competitiveness. Given the dependence of the economy on imports, any short-term benefits accruing from a devaluation would have been offset by the higher cost of imports and the subsequent rise in prices due to the prevalence of automatic cost of living adjustments (COLA) in wage contracts. In other words, full employment conditions, the existence of COLA, and low price elasticities for the demand for exports and imports (with the sum estimated to be less than unity), meant that a currency devaluation in Cyprus would have brought a worsening of the balance of payments with the higher demand for exports completely offset by the resulting higher increase in imports' expenditure. Thus, doing what was necessary to maintain external balance and avert the need for devaluation was an important element of the strategy.

In this light, non-traditional policy tools such as capital controls and quantitative credit restraints proved useful supplements to the more traditional tools – and indeed sometimes the crucial main tools – for controlling threats towards imbalances. Hence, the fourth key to success. Non-traditional tools were used with care, however, in order to control and correct imbalances in the short term, and not to obscure and prolong them. Care was needed, of course, because it was well understood that, when improperly used, controls and restraints can easily engender unsustainable imbalances endangering economic collapse at a later stage.

Figure 18.4 illustrates the timing of imposition and relaxation of credit ceilings during periods of hardship. The most significant ones occurred: in 1967, when credit ceilings were relaxed to encourage growth; in 1980, when credit ceilings were imposed to contain inflationary pressures and in 2000, when credit ceilings were imposed to contain an episode of stock market exuberance.

This admirable performance should not obscure the various challenges that tested the efficiency of the policy we had in place. During the 1990s a number of EU accession-induced structural and institutional reforms were among these challenges. The reforms included the welcome liberalization of some prices and, more challenging for the Central Bank, the liberalization of capital movements and the further deepening of financial intermediation. These changes required quick adjustments and an active policy response by the Central Bank to maintain effective monetary stability.

In January 2001, following the abolition of restrictions on medium-term and long-term borrowing by residents, capital inflows rose significantly as private individuals and firms increased their borrowing in foreign currency, mostly euros, taking advantage of the interest rate differential between euro-denominated and pound-denominated loans (see Figure 18.5).

This exerted upward pressure on the exchange rate and it also exposed borrowers to increased exchange rate risks. These developments prompted the Central Bank to abolish the narrow bands of ±2.25 per cent in August 2001, and adopt the wider ±15 per cent margins in line with the exchange rate mechanism (ERM) II (see Figure 18.6).

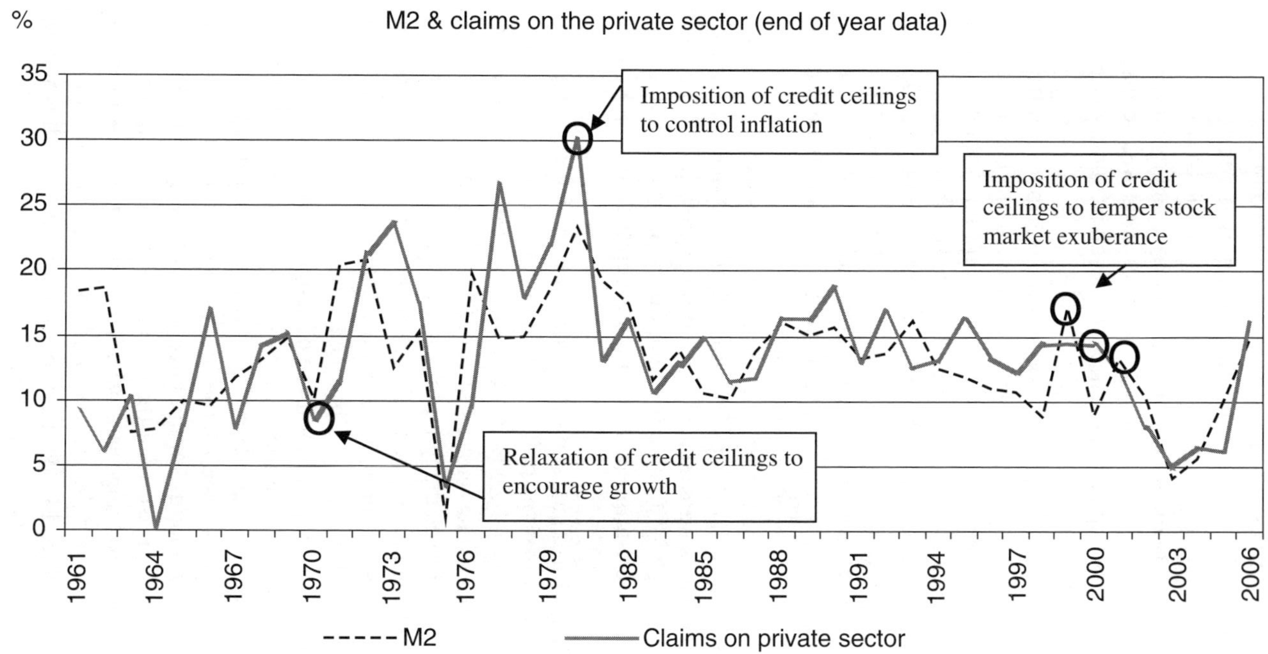

Source: CBC calculations.

Figure 18.4 Money and credit

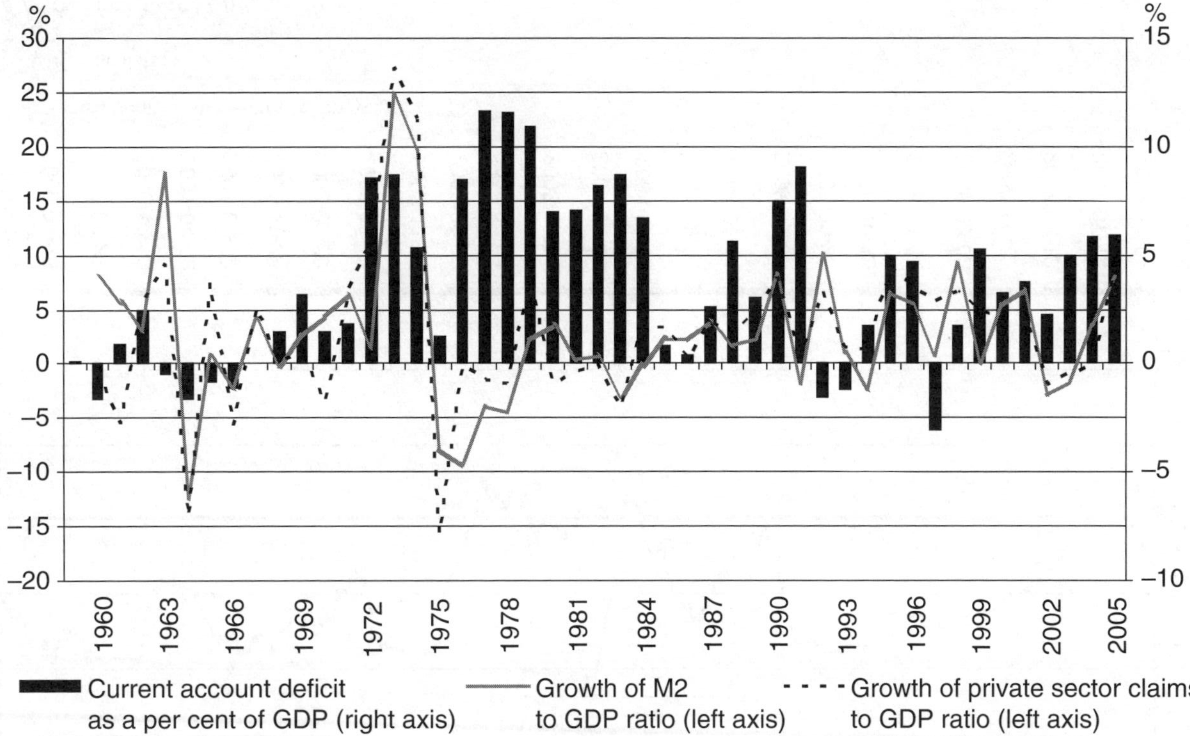

Source: CBC calculations.

Figure 18.5 Credit and current account deficit

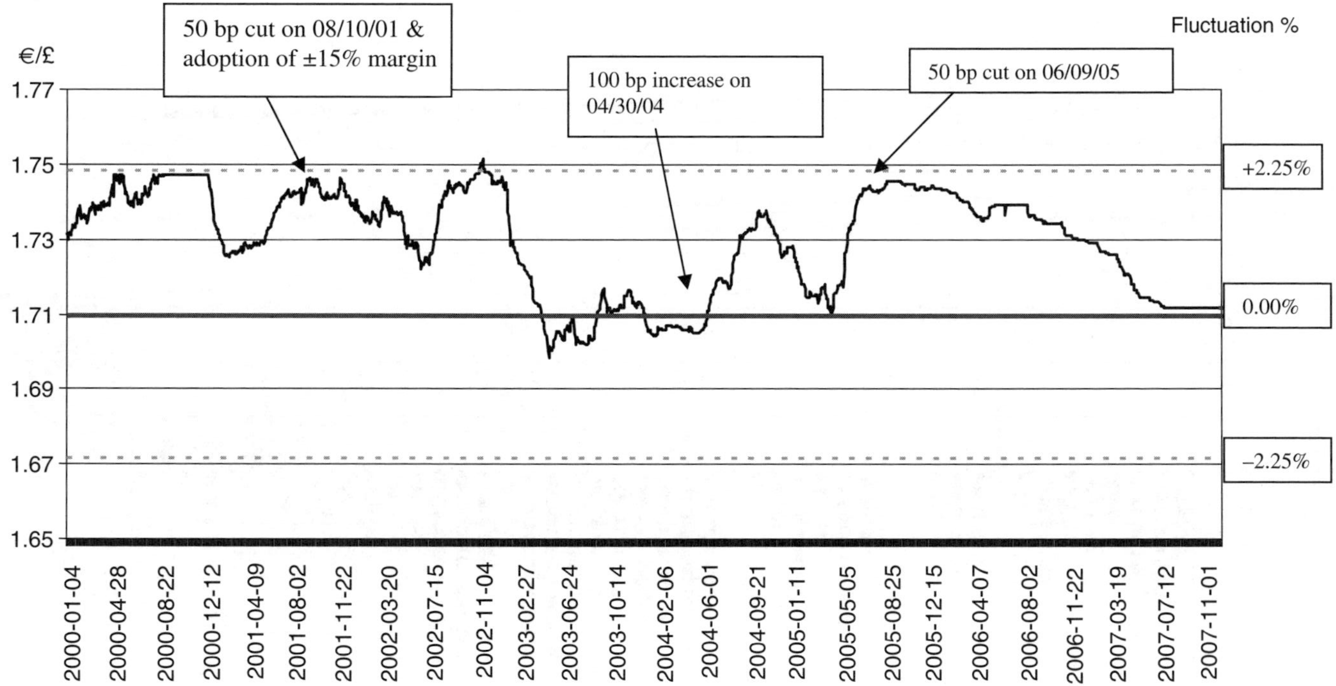

Note: bp = basis point. Dates = month/day/year.

Source: CBC calculations.

Figure 18.6 Exchange rate stability

Concurrently, the bank reduced its interest rates by 50 basis points, a decision that was perceived as being necessary due to the anticipated negative impact of the seemingly prolonged global economic slowdown on the Cyprus economy. The decline in interest rates in Cyprus also reduced the interest rate differential between euro-denominated and pound-denominated loans, which further removed some of the incentive for residents to borrow in foreign currency. Interest rates were subsequently reduced further in September and November 2001 by 50 basis points on each occasion (see Figure 18.7).

Exchange rate flexibility in concert with prudent interest rate decisions proved instrumental in dealing with the aforementioned challenges.

A smooth transition to full financial liberalization by May 2004, when Cyprus joined the EU, would have not been possible without timely strategic changes in bank policy. Three key changes were: (1) the reform of the monetary policy instruments, (2) the abolition of the statutory interest rate ceiling and (3) the phased capital account liberalization. Reference should also be made to the new Banking Laws, which were introduced with a view to reinforcing supervision and enhancing prudential rules.

Overall, the convergence of the financial structures of Cyprus to those prevailing in the EU has been achieved through a carefully planned and gradual reform process. Having in place a well-regulated sound framework proved to be of paramount importance for strengthening the resilience of the banking system and entrenching financial stability against very strong credit expansion, booming asset prices and destabilizing capital flows.

In the run-up to the EU accession, the Central Bank of Cyprus had formulated a comprehensive strategy for the adoption of the euro. The overriding objective of this strategy was to adopt the euro as soon as possible after EU accession. Essentially, this strategy was addressing the issues of when to enter ERM II, what the central parity should be, and how long to stay in the mechanism. After the formation of this strategy, it became evident that the smooth entry and participation in ERM II would be dependent on the prevailing general economic situation and on our success in bringing about the requisite policy adjustments, such as further price liberalization and a credible fiscal consolidation programme.

Unfortunately, public expenditure outruns and the loose implementation of successive fiscal consolidation programmes resulted in major slippages, with the fiscal deficit surging to 6.3 per cent of GDP in 2003. This, in turn, led to increased uncertainty about long-term interest rates. In conjunction with these adverse fiscal conditions, political uncertainty surrounding the prospects for the solution of the Cyprus problem and unfounded rumours concerning imminent devaluation of the Cyprus pound further exacerbated the negative sentiment present at the time. The sizeable capital

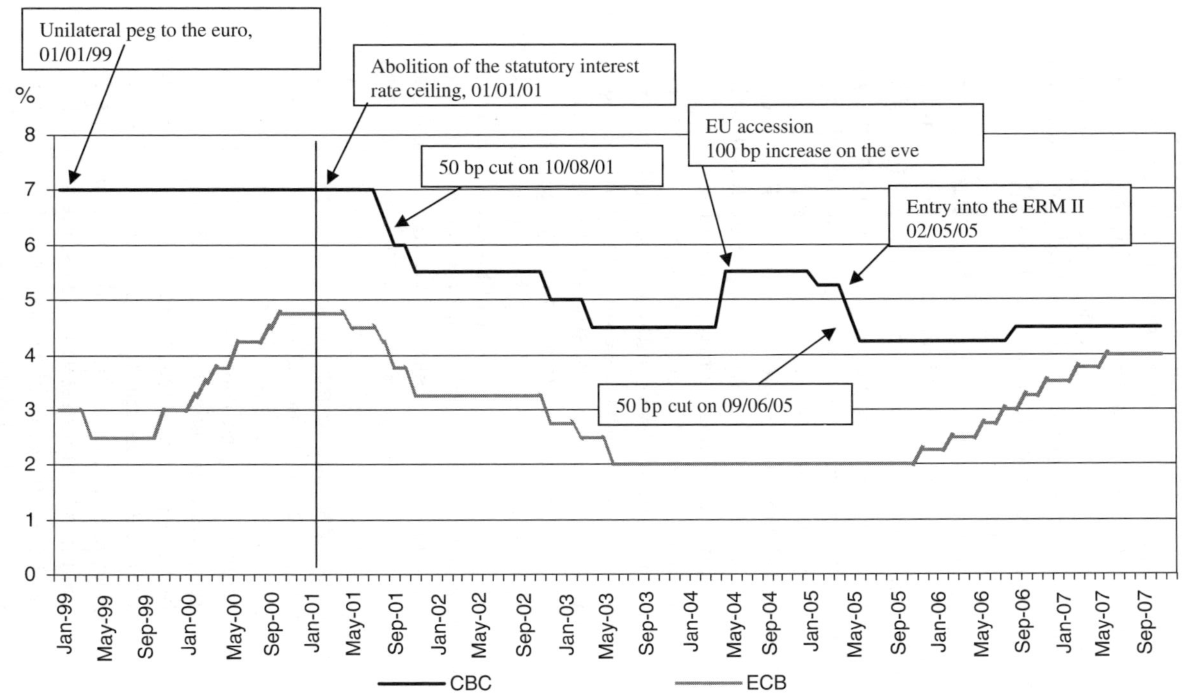

Note: bp = basis point. Dates = day/month/year.

Source: CBC calculations.

Figure 18.7 Policy rates

outflows and the concomitant pressures for currency depreciation in the aftermath of these developments called for increased vigilance by the Central Bank to support the exchange rate. At an extraordinary meeting on the eve of the EU accession day, the Central Bank's Monetary Policy Committee decided to increase its interest rates by 100 basis points and at the same time to send a strong signal supporting the Cyprus pound. Consequently, markets calmed and capital flows returned to their normal seasonal pattern. In this connection, I should emphasize the success of the Central Bank in properly signalling and communicating its readiness to show policy consistency towards achieving the primary objective. This was imperative to stabilize expectations and avoid recurrent shifts in market perceptions.

Notwithstanding the satisfactory degree of real and nominal convergence achieved by the Cypriot economy, and the implementation of a credible fiscal consolidation programme, challenges also emerged during participation in ERM II. Following entry into ERM II, at the same long-standing parity of EUR 1 = CYP 0.585274, sizeable capital inflows were observed, mainly ensuing from enhanced confidence in the Cypriot currency, improved economic outlook and increased residents' borrowing in foreign currency to take advantage of the favourable interest rate differentials. Taking into account subdued inflationary pressures, the bank cut its interest rates by a cumulative 100 basis points at two consecutive Monetary Policy Committee meetings.

Moreover, although the fiscal stance was largely supportive during this period, monetary policy was confronted with the dilemma between price and exchange rate stability once inflationary pressures became evident. These pressures were fuelled by surging oil prices and ample banking liquidity that resulted in the sizeable expansion of credit to the private sector. At the same time, excessive capital inflows owing to residents' increased borrowing in foreign currency were exerting currency appreciation pressures. Reliance on interest rate adjustments on this occasion was not considered as being sufficient to maintain stability. Against this background, the Central Bank embarked on a twofold strategy encompassing both communication and prudential banking supervision measures.

On the communication side, the bank offered frequent reminders to the public of the exchange rate risk associated with borrowing in foreign currency. On the prudential side, the bank issued guidelines reducing the maximum loan-to-value ratio associated with lending in real estate, and delayed decreases of the minimum reserve ratio to euro area standards.

The decision of the ECOFIN Council on 10 July 2007 to accept Cyprus into the euro area and the concurrent setting of the conversion rate, in one sense marked the completion of the island's integration into the European family. But it also served as a reminder that controlling inflationary risks in Cyprus may be harder to tackle going forward without further progress on fiscal consolidation and further structural reforms. The historical differential in policy rates between the Central Bank of Cyprus and the European Central Bank was to be eliminated by the end of 2007, suggesting an easing of monetary conditions at a time when the Cypriot economy is expanding at a brisk pace.

Fast credit expansion, which has been largely directed to the real estate market, continues to be a major concern, particularly because of the increasing exposure of our banks to the real estate sector at the expense of other sectors. With a view towards safeguarding financial stability, the Central Bank called on banks to assess more thoroughly the creditworthiness of loan applicants and further tightened financing conditions by reducing the maximum loan-to-value ratio for real estate loans. With these measures, we believe we are facilitating a smoother transition of the Cypriot economy to the euro.

The spectre of an increase in inflation perceptions is yet another risk. As has been the experience elsewhere in Europe, the adoption of the euro is often accompanied by unjustified fears that producers, distributors and retailers may use the opportunity of the changeover to unjustifiably raise prices. Drawing from the experience of countries that joined the euro before us, we have adopted policies, such as a lengthy period of dual pricing and fair pricing agreements to avert this problem.

The recent increases in energy and food prices, however, have complicated our attempts to allay consumer fears. On the energy side, Cyprus is completely dependent on imported oil for all its energy, leaving us particularly vulnerable to recent oil price increases.

Another complication is the prevalence of cost of living adjustments (COLA) in wage contracts. Twice a year COLA automatically raises wages by an amount equal to the inflation rate in the CPI over the previous six months. This is on top of any other negotiated wage increases. It is unfortunate that the government has not been able to make progress with regard to this distortionary element in the economy even with civil workers. At present, this unfortunate anachronism risks translating a temporary hump in inflation into a more persistent inflationary threat that may be particularly difficult to counter in light of the easing of monetary conditions associated with our entry into the euro area.

Over the longer run, however, I cannot help but be an optimist. The road towards monetary integration can confront policy makers with numerous challenges whose resolution will depend on the historical experience and institutional arrangements in place, prior to entry into the euro. Despite such challenges, the euro can serve as a powerful catalyst for welcome change, ultimately enhancing welfare not only for countries like Cyprus and Malta that are about to join, but for all European citizens.

NOTE

1. Governor, Central Bank of Cyprus.

19. Economic challenges on the path to the euro – the Maltese experience

Michael C. Bonello[1]

The purpose of this presentation is to share some observations about Malta's journey to the euro. Let me commence with some details on the characteristics of Malta. With a geographical area of 316 square km and a population of 400 000, Malta is a very densely populated country with a very small and open economy. In fact within the EU, the Maltese economy is the fourth most open after Luxembourg, Slovakia and Belgium with average imports and exports standing at 85 per cent of gross domestic product (GDP) in 2006. In that same year Malta's GDP amounted to EUR 5 billion.

Notwithstanding these limitations, the Maltese economy was relatively well developed even before the country embarked on its journey to adopt the euro as its currency. For example Malta's income inequality coefficient of 4.1 compares very favourably with that of the euro area, which stands at 4.8. Malta has also achieved a high degree of sophistication in the area of financial intermediation, which goes back to colonial times and has its foundation in British banking practices and institutional structures. Malta also attracts a significant amount of foreign direct investment (FDI). In fact the contribution of FDI to GDP remains relatively large and has been increasing over time (see Figure 19.1). In 2006 Malta ranked second in the EU in terms of FDI inflows as a percentage of gross fixed capital formation.

Here it is relevant to mention that the decision to seek EU membership was an important factor contributing to the establishment of Malta as an attractive investment base. In fact, in recent years, while FDI flows to Malta have continued to rise they have also emanated from non-EU countries like Switzerland and Iceland, which are now taking advantage of Malta's status as an EU member state.

The determination of the authorities to pursue EU membership also became a key element underpinning the structural reform strategy in the

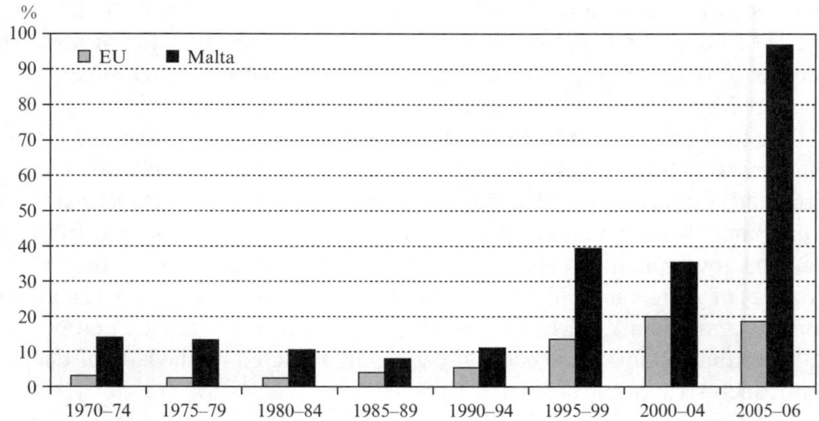

Source: UNCTAD World Investment Report Databases.

Figure 19.1 FDI flows as a percentage of gross fixed capital formation (five-year percentage averages, 1970–2006)

late 1990s. These reforms gained further momentum in the years following EU accession as an early adoption of the euro became the next most urgent national policy objective.

However this does not imply that the economic transition in earlier years always proceeded at a smooth pace. On the political front, after a centre right government submitted an EU membership application in the summer of 1990 and an *avis* was issued by the EU Commission in 1993, this application was subsequently frozen by a new centre left government which was elected to power in 1996 on a political programme that favoured a special relationship with the EU outside full membership. That government collapsed within two years and was then defeated at the polls. The re-elected centre right government immediately reactivated the EU membership application and negotiations with the EU Commission commenced in 1999.

It should be mentioned that the EU Commission's initial response to Malta's EU membership application, contained in the *avis*, was highly critical of the economic structure at that time. It noted that, to modernize the economy, there was a need for a root-and-branch overhaul of the entire regulatory and operational framework. It highlighted the fact that economic development was also being undermined by tight capital controls and a highly regulated financial system. This was also borne out by the relatively low volume of FDI flows in the early 1990s, averaging around 11 per cent of gross fixed capital formation. The government still had a majority shareholding in the two largest banks, while the Central Bank of Malta (CBM) enjoyed little autonomy from the Ministry of Finance and little use was made of interest rate instruments. In a broader perspective, the productive sectors of the economy were still heavily protected while local industry was sheltered by a system of levies and administrative controls.

The task ahead for the Maltese authorities was not an easy one. Some changes were however introduced in the mid-1990s aimed at liberalizing the financial system and gradually easing exchange controls. Thus interest rates were partially deregulated, the Central Bank was granted more autonomy and the government accepted the obligations of Article VIII of the IMF's Articles of Agreement. This notwithstanding, the pace of reform remained uneven and when the EU membership application was reactivated in late 1998, management of the economy was still hindered by the lack of deeply embedded structural reforms.

The commencement of EU membership negotiations in the early part of 1999 paved the way for more meaningful reforms. In fact later that year a first package of liberalization measures was introduced. As trade restrictions were gradually dismantled on the basis of a schedule negotiated with the EU Commission, the vulnerability of the Maltese economy was immediately exposed as the relatively large manufacturing sector faced competitive pressures from emerging economies, particularly those of Asia. More important at that time, however, were the external shocks that severely affected two key sectors of the Maltese economy: tourism and the electronics sub-sector of manufacturing. These two major industries provided employment to 11 per cent of the gainfully occupied. They also directly generated 15 per cent of gross value added and 60 per cent of the country's export earnings. The first shock was the bursting of the dot-com bubble in the early 2000s, which resulted in a mild recession in the developed world, but had a significant negative impact on the local electronics sub-sector. The latter, which in 2000 had accounted for 63 per cent of merchandise exports, saw its share fall to 52 per cent a year later. The second major shock was the 9/11 terrorist attacks on New York that induced an aversion to air travel. This had serious implications for Malta's tourism in 2002, with the number of tourist arrivals down 7 per cent compared to the 2000 level. These external shocks, at a time of ongoing restructuring in various sectors of the economy, contributed to a sharp economic slowdown in the early years of the century. While a slight improvement in the performance of the electronics sub-sector in 2002, mostly because of a base effect, led to some rebound in economic activity, on average the early years of the century prior to EU membership in May 2004 were characterized by stagnant growth.

So what were the challenges facing the authorities at that time? First of all the negative growth trend needed to be reversed and external competitiveness strengthened, given that the current account deficit had widened to

6 per cent of GDP and was on a rising trend. At the same time the fiscal deficit exceeded 3 per cent of GDP, after having peaked in 2003 at 9.8 per cent, albeit that part of this deterioration was due to a one-off transaction, namely, the absorption of the debt obligations of the loss-making shipbuilding sector. Meanwhile the share of public sector employment in the total of the gainfully employed remained at a high level although it had contracted to 34 per cent in 2004 from a peak level of 40 per cent some years earlier. In the financial sector the authorities still had to ensure that the legislative and institutional framework, especially with regard to financial supervision and stability, was upgraded to comply with EU standards and best practices. Furthermore the remaining capital controls had to be removed ahead of the EU accession date.

What were the policy options available at the time? Basically, the authorities had a choice between two options. The first option was to adopt a gradualist approach with the aim of causing as little social disruption as possible. But this of course would have meant delaying much-needed reform measures. Moreover, by following such a course there was also a risk of slippage in the government's commitment to reform and this would have undermined growth prospects in the medium term. It would also have had serious repercussions in the future which would then have necessitated much more painful adjustment at a later stage.

The alternative option was to pursue a plan of immediate policy action based on the premise that the country's commitment to an exchange rate peg in a liberalized capital market, which was well understood by local economic operators, necessitated supporting reforms to ensure currency stability. Thus while recognizing that Malta was already sufficiently integrated with the European economy and well suited to join a monetary union, the successful implementation of structural reforms would ensure rapid entry into EMU. The overall approach was therefore to argue the case that the benefits of this option were so far-reaching that it was worthwhile to embark on a bold reform strategy. In this regard the authorities were persuaded by the sound arguments put forward by the Central Bank of Malta and chose the second option.

This decision of the Maltese authorities to pursue this course was also influenced by the specific features of the Maltese economy, particularly its small size and openness, which, as indicated above, made it very vulnerable to external shocks. Apart from the greater security afforded by membership of the euro area, there were also the intrinsic benefits of having a widely used international currency as the domestic unit. These benefits were bound to be large for small open economies which had achieved a high degree of integration with the euro area – and this was precisely the case with Malta, where the larger euro area member states were among the

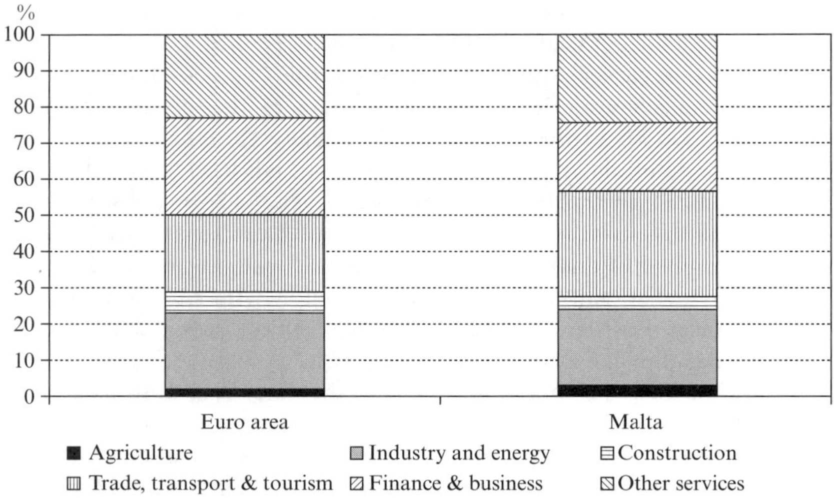

Source: Eurostat.

Figure 19.2 Value-added by activity in the euro area and in Malta (2002–03)

country's major trading partners in terms of both imports and exports. In fact in 2004, the euro area accounted for 54 per cent of Malta's imports of goods and services, and for 35 per cent of its exports. The relatively smaller percentages for exports reflect the fact that a sizeable firm in the electronics sub-sector directs the bulk of its exports to markets outside the EU, mainly in Asia.

Furthermore before EU accession, economic data based on average indicators for the 2002–03 period showed that the economies of Malta and the euro area had very similar structures, with both being heavily oriented towards services (over 70 per cent, as indicated in Figure 19.2). The only two economic sectors where the shares diverged by more than 5 percentage points were the transport, tourism and finance and business sectors. This reflects Malta's heavier dependence on tourism and on transport, the latter largely the function of its insularity and location.

In implementing the chosen strategy, the Central Bank of Malta (CBM) and the government were the main protagonists. The CBM remained committed to pursuing a fixed exchange rate policy consistent with price stability and to contributing to the further development and soundness of the financial sector. The government for its part was committed to a fiscal consolidation programme aimed at containing government expenditures, monitoring and correcting any slippages in revenue collection and lowering the level of public debt as a ratio of GDP. The overall strategy also aimed at containing the current account deficit and ensuring that wage rewards as much as possible reflected developments in productivity. The latter was all the more necessary given the fact that, as in Cyprus, wages in Malta are adjusted for cost of living increases although, in the case of Malta, the adjustments are only partly indexed to the actual inflation rate, which is based on the annual movement in retail prices up to the ninth month of the previous year.

In focusing on the CBM's role in the reform strategy, it is relevant to mention that the bank's commitment on the exchange rate was a reaffirmation of a policy it had been implementing for more than 30 years, that of maintaining a fixed peg to a currency basket. Thus, well in advance of EU accession, Malta had a long history of exchange rate stability. It is true, of course, that an important factor supporting the fixed exchange rate policy was the comprehensive regime of capital controls, which were only eased gradually. However, as capital liberalization started in earnest, from 2000 onwards, in accordance with Malta's prospective obligations under the EC Treaty, it was the bank's active monetary policy stance in ensuring that interest rates in Malta offered an adequate premium to prevent destabilizing capital outflows that was the main factor underpinning the exchange rate. Consequently when the government sought advice on an exchange rate strategy after EU membership the bank quickly recommended entry into the Exchange Rate Mechanism (ERM II) as soon as practicable. It was the bank's declared intention to hasten Malta's participation in EMU so that the country would derive the benefits of the euro as early as possible. It felt confident that with Malta's long track record of exchange rate stability the entry of the Maltese currency into the ERM II would not result in any volatility in the Maltese lira's exchange rate during the anticipated two-year period of participation in the Mechanism. Moreover, the CBM was conscious of the fact that progress was being made in the area of fiscal consolidation and that this was giving a positive signalling effect to market operators.

Eventually the government took the decision to apply for participation in the Mechanism one year after EU accession. Following acceptance at the EU institutional level in late April 2005 Malta joined the ERM II in early May, with a unilateral commitment to maintain the exchange rate at the central parity rate. The decision to eschew flexibility was motivated by the bank's concern that flexibility would have introduced a major element of uncertainty among local economic agents who were always used to a rigidly fixed exchange rate. Thus, there was the possibility that the currency would move erratically within the +/−15 per cent band in a thin foreign exchange market influenced by the transactions of a few operators. Such volatility

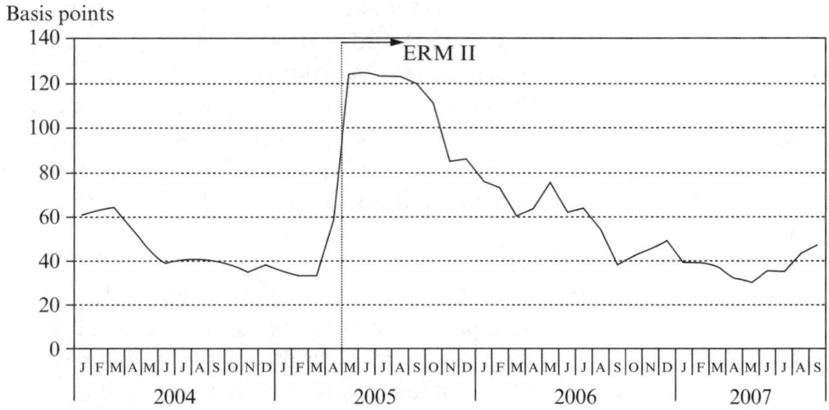

Source: Central Bank of Malta.

Figure 19.3 Three-month interest rate premium in favour of the Maltese lira (synthetic Treasury bill (TB) rate until April 2005, euro TB rate from May 2005)

would have caused needless uncertainty for the business community in Malta who had never experienced severe fluctuations in the currency over the previous 30 years. Moreover, in the months prior to the decision to enter the ERM II, in some local business quarters, speculation was rife that the government would devalue the Maltese currency before establishing the euro–Maltese lira central parity rate in the ERM II. This speculation led to some outflow of capital and a decline in the country's external reserves. Thus to counter this uncertainty and anchor private sector expectations on inflation and interest rates the CBM urged the government to make a clear commitment on the exchange rate, saying that it would maintain it at an unchanged level throughout the ERM II phase. And of course, from the bank's point of view, this commitment would serve as a means of countering any procrastination on the part of the government to implement fiscal and structural reforms, which were long overdue.

During the ERM II phase the CBM pursued an active interest rate policy to support the central parity rate. Thus when interest rates in the euro area started rising thereafter, the bank raised its central intervention rate, but at a more gradual pace. This reduced the risk premium on the Maltese lira (see Figure 19.3). By January 2007, the premium had dropped towards 40 basis points, the lower end of the range observed against the synthetic rate before ERM II.

As I mentioned earlier maintaining a fixed exchange rate in earlier years was facilitated by restrictions on the movement of capital. However despite

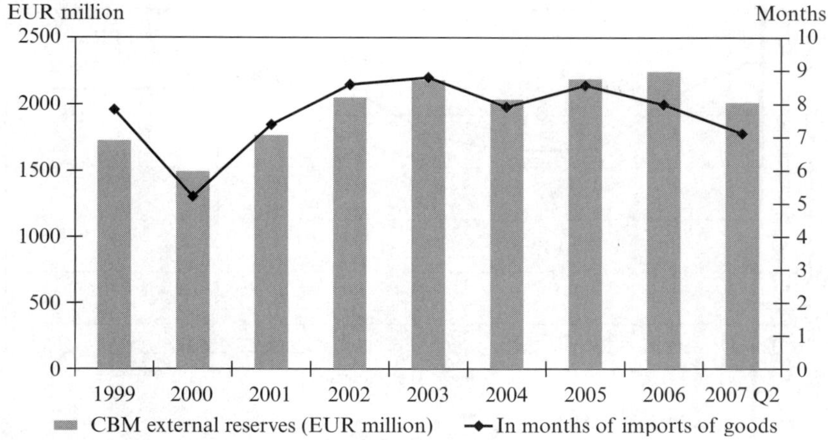

Sources: Central Bank of Malta, National Statistics Office.

Figure 19.4 CBM external reserves

the gradual easing of capital controls from 2000 onwards, the country's external reserves stayed at a relatively high level in terms of months of imports (see Figure 19.4). And this continues to the present day, except that in recent months we began to observe a premature conversion of Maltese currency into euros as the public anticipated a positive response by the EU on Malta's request for euro area membership. This has resulted in a moderate but continuous decline in the external reserves, although they still remain at a comfortable level.

A brief word about Malta's capital liberalization programme. The first measures came into force in the first two years of the new century with the liberalization of outward FDI and investment in real estate. These were followed by a sequence of measures aimed at increasing the overseas portfolio investment allowance of individuals and non-financial companies. The amount was raised gradually every year to ensure that the outward movement was smooth and controllable. Here it should be mentioned that the Maltese had a long tradition of investing in the UK, the former colonial power, more specifically in British government securities. This was the most obvious form of savings for the Maltese and it dated back to the nineteenth century. Tight exchange controls from the late 1960s onwards had limited the amounts that were placed in such investments. Consequently, to manage the anticipated outflow as a result of liberalization, the programme set out a sequenced scheme for portfolio investment. Thus long-term investments were liberalized initially and within set limits. Restrictions on

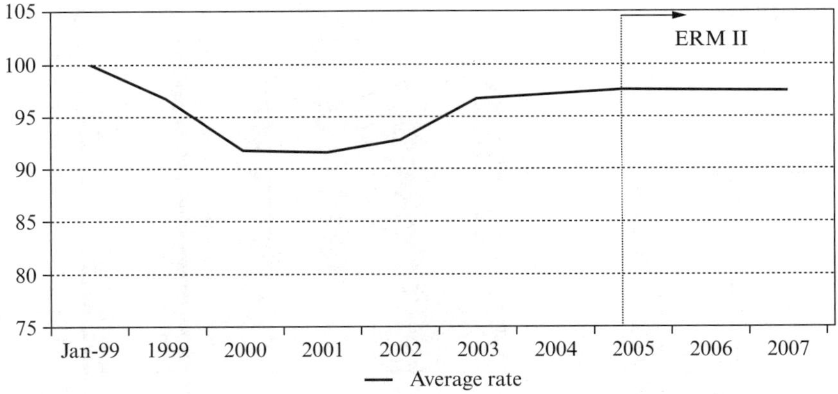

Source: Central Bank of Malta.

Figure 19.5 Maltese lira exchange rate against the euro (index January 1999 = 100)

short-term investments were only liberalized in the first few months of 2004 prior to the EU membership date. This gradual liberalization approach applied not only to portfolio investments but also to a variety of capital transactions between residents and non-residents, such as cash gifts, financial loans and inheritances.

With the completion of the liberalization process all controls disappeared; however there is still an obligation on the part of residents effecting capital transactions with non-residents to report such transactions to the CBM. This is intended solely for statistical purposes related to the preparation of balance-of-payments statements.

Malta's unilateral exchange rate commitment has been maintained throughout the two-year period in the ERM II, as is evident from Figure 19.5. Since Malta joined the EU in May 2005, the exchange rate has remained fixed at the central parity rate, which has now been established as the final conversion rate for euro area participation from January 2008. With regards to the bank's other commitments as part of the reform strategy, we continued to strengthen our preparations for entry into the Eurosystem and to perform all obligations related to our functions as a central bank. We contributed to the drafting of financial legislation in Malta, in particular to give formal independence to the Central Bank in terms of the Treaty. Moreover, when the government transferred responsibility for banking supervision from the bank to the Malta Financial Services Authority (MFSA) in 2002, we committed more of our resources to the development of the financial stability function. Towards this end the CBM signed a number of memoranda of understanding on cooperation and exchange of information with the MFSA and the Ministry of Finance. We have also assisted in the drafting of new legislation to permit new types of financial activities to operate from Malta and to align local practices with those of the EU. We also contributed to the development of the financial infrastructure in terms of payments and settlement systems, improving our data reporting capacity and also introducing modern risk management practices.

For its part, the government has remained committed to fiscal consolidation and in the process introduced other important reforms, including one on pensions. Under the new pension legislation, the retirement age will be raised gradually to 65, and the contributory period for eligibility to a two-thirds pension is raised from 30 to 40 years. Other reforms include public sector downsizing, better monitoring of government expenditure (by a newly set up financial management and monitoring unit), early retirement schemes and retraining. Within the public sector, a collective agreement covering a five-year period from 2006 to 2010 ensures that the cost-of-living adjustment (COLA), granted annually, is subsumed in the pre-announced annual wage increase covered by the agreement. This means that there will be no additional increases in wages to compensate for the COLA. The government has also undertaken income tax reforms aimed at discouraging under-reporting of income, given that a compliance unit set up by the government in 2001 found that 89 per cent of investigated taxpayers had been evading tax. Another investigation was carried out by the unit in 2006, to address welfare abuse. The unit conducted 2000 on-site inspections during this investigation and suspended benefits in 30 per cent of the cases. As a fiscal measure introduced ahead of EU membership, the value-added tax (VAT) rate was increased to 18 per cent from 15 per cent in 2004. Furthermore, cost-based pricing for certain public services took place across a wide range of items. In the area of structural measures it is relevant to mention the liquidation of loss-making companies owned by the state, and the privatization of a number of state-owned entities.

The result of these initiatives and measures is that the deficit-to-GDP ratio has started to decline. It stood at about 2.5 per cent in 2006 and is expected to contract further this year to about 1.6–1.7 per cent. The general government debt ratio, after having peaked in 2004, has started to drop. The European Commission expects it to fall to 59.2 per cent by 2009. So it seems that Malta is heading in the right direction. Here I should mention that the government's commitments have also extended into the area of the Lisbon Agenda targets, and there is a whole range of actual measures taken here such as make-work-pay initiatives, measures to improve labour market participation, retraining and lifelong education. I believe that an area where most progress has been achieved has to do with information and communication technologies. In fact the Economist Intelligence Unit ranked Malta the 24th most technologically prepared country in the world in 2007. And according to Capgemini's seventh annual eGovernment benchmark survey for the EU, Malta scored in second place among EU countries in terms of the provision of online government services, with Austria being the most advanced country in this respect. Moreover, Malta has set up a number of academies in recent years with companies like Microsoft, Cisco and Oracle as major participants.

That, I think, gives you a fairly comprehensive view of the efforts that are being undertaken by the authorities in Malta to modernize the economy. The reforms are ongoing, but implementation is giving some positive results. With the share of services in the economy expanding, real GDP growth in the first half of 2007 is estimated to have increased by 3.6 per cent and is expected to approach 4 per cent by the end of the year. Unemployment has also come down at a steady pace. Likewise, the fiscal balance has improved, and the share of the public sector in employment has fallen notably. Inflation results have been less positive. Based on the HICP the rate of inflation was generally low during the first half of the year but gradually rose thereafter, and is expected to exceed 3 per cent by the end of 2007. It is projected to increase at a faster rate in 2008 given the recent surge in the prices of food and energy. On a positive note, however, productivity growth in Malta has been rising as well.

In concluding I would first have to emphasize that the Maltese experience may have limited relevance for prospective euro area members, mainly because of Malta's unique characteristics. These include the fact that it embarked on the road to euro adoption with a relatively advanced market economy already in place; it also had a long history of fixed exchange rate regimes and its very small size and openness make it markedly different from any of the other new member states.

However an important element, which is of relevance to other aspiring countries, is the active role played by the Central Bank of Malta in the whole euro strategy. The bank was at the forefront of the reform debate highlighting first the long-term benefits of EU membership, and then of early adoption of the euro. It made the point repeatedly that these benefits would only be realized if the authorities addressed internal imbalances and achieved a faster pace of economic convergence with the euro area. Thus to succeed in all this, important structural reforms had to be implemented. The bank also emphasized that the changes that were being advocated were necessary, not only to ensure eligibility for euro area membership, but because they were based on sound economic logic and would at any rate have to be implemented in order to enable the economy to face up to the new competitive pressures that were emerging from globalization.

In retrospect, what was also important was the shared vision between the government and the CBM on policy and objectives and on the need for a holistic approach to achieve them. I have emphasized the government's contribution, which included achieving fiscal consolidation, reducing the public sector and introducing much-needed structural reforms. The CBM on the other hand pursued a monetary policy that continued to emphasize exchange rate and price stability against a background of a sequenced capital account liberalization programme.

Finally, what should also be stressed is that the initial commitment to join ERM II must be credible, particularly when the decision to do so is taken. And of course, it is also very important to have a clear target date for euro adoption since this serves to focus attention and motivate the operators in the economy to reach the desired goal.

NOTE

1. Governor, Central Bank of Malta.

20. Slovakia's road to the euro – lessons learned and challenges ahead

Ivan Šramko[1]

The idea of this chapter is to describe Slovakia's road to the euro – principally, what basic assumptions it took to pave the way successfully for introducing the euro in our country, what kind of measures we have taken, how we are doing in terms of fulfilling the Maastricht criteria, and what are the main challenges connected with the euro adoption.

Let me start with the basic conditions a country must fulfil to be successful in so complex a process like the adoption of the euro. There are two main conditions: first, to have consistent plans and in-depth analyses measuring the possibility of fulfilling the underlying criteria; and second, to have broad political support. Slovakia fulfilled both those conditions when it started with this process in 2003. At that time none of the political parties with significant political power were opposed to adopting the euro, and it was very important that this remained so also after the change of government in 2006. And we started very early with a very consistent plan, which is still effective. We started in 2003, at the time targeting euro area entry by 2008 or 2009. The main problem in 2003 was that Eurostat's position on how to account for the pension reform costs in the budget was not clear yet. That is why, once Eurostat's decision on the fiscal treatment of pension reform costs had become available, we issued a supplementary document specifying Slovakia's euro adoption strategy in 2004, which set the date for euro adoption in 2009.

Furthermore, it was also important that Slovakia made the necessary reforms. In 2004 and 2005 the Slovak government introduced very deep and very complex economic reforms, with sweeping effects on our economy. Among those reforms, two were particularly important from the perspective of euro adoption: the reform of the pension system and the introduction of the flat tax. We now have a three-pillar pension system, with the first pillar constituting the basic state pension, and the second and third pillar based on capitalization of the saving of the public. And our government implemented a tax reform, introducing a flat tax regime among other things. Without these steps it would have been a problem to fulfil completely all plans with regard to euro area entry, which had been approved by that time.

The elections in 2006 brought to power a completely new government. Neither of today's coalition parties belonged to the former government. In this respect it was very important to have broad political support for Slovakia's plans to adopt the euro, and that the elections did not bring about a change in the basic approach to this very important question.

With the approaching date of the planned euro adoption we acquired a more precise view on the overall process. And it enabled us to specify our plans in detail, updating the changeover plans originally designed for euro adoption in 2007.

Turning to the role of the central bank in this process, we contributed in-depth impact analyses in 2006. These analyses confirmed our original results, which stated that euro adoption would be beneficial for Slovakia. Like other countries that have joined the euro area before, the National Bank of Slovakia (NBS) and the Slovak authorities made broad-based analyses about the benefits and costs of the euro adoption. Several impact analyses have been elaborated, assessing the effect of euro adoption on the Slovak economy and its potential effect on the population as well as the business sector in Slovakia. The results of these analyses were broadly in line with impact analyses prepared in current euro area countries. The sweeping analyses confirmed the original broad conclusions of the Slovak authorities that the benefits would outweigh the cost of entering the euro area.

20.1 POTENTIAL EFFECTS OF EURO ADOPTION

I believe that there are some generally accepted benefits from adopting the euro, including direct or immediate and several indirect, long-term benefits. Euro introduction will eliminate the exchange rate risk against the euro, and lower the exchange rate risk against the US dollar. Euro adoption should lead to lower costs of capital. An important direct benefit is the elimination of transaction costs on trades in euros. The euro will bring better resistance to (currency) crises. One of the direct benefits of the euro for consumers will be much easier comparability of prices at home and in the euro area countries. Finally, all the benefits arising from the euro adoption will eventually bring much wider indirect benefits. There is an expectation that foreign direct investment in Slovakia and foreign trade of Slovakia will grow, which will contribute to the faster GDP growth, real convergence and increase of living standards.

Of course there are also the costs of euro adoption, starting with the technical costs of the currency changeover. Immediately before and after the euro changeover the public sector and entrepreneurs will incur costs on the adjustment of information systems, currency exchange, conversion of prices, dual prices, personnel training, and so on. Several facts indicate that the technical costs of euro adoption in Slovakia should be lower than in the original 12 euro area countries. The euro changeover in Slovakia will be made by the 'big bang' scenario. A large number of Slovak enterprises have already been actively trading in euros and owners of many enterprises come from the euro area. We estimate the technical cost of the euro changeover at 0.3 per cent of GDP.

Euro adoption will reduce bank revenues from foreign exchange operations. At the same time, the possible product boom can reverse the expected reduction in revenues.

Loss of independent monetary policy is considered to be the most significant cost of joining the euro area. Euro adoption is connected with further risks or concerns. Consumers are most concerned about increases in prices following price conversion to the euro. In Slovakia the competition within retail trade is very strong and an extensive programme of dual display of prices and other instruments is under preparation.

Based on the assessment procedures implemented in current euro area countries during their euro area entry phase, we plan to ask for convergence reports preparation in spring 2008. We expect the ECB and the European Commission to submit their reports in May 2008. Under the rule of equal treatment, we also expect that fulfilment of Stability and Growth Pact conditions will be followed by acceptance of our sustainability. We believe in a positive assessment that will lead the European Commission to recommend our derogation to be abrogated by the Council.

Following consultations with the European Parliament, the Council's decision on abrogating the derogation and the conversion rate could be known in July 2008. This will allow sufficient time to accomplish the technical preparations and enable us to adopt the euro in 1 January 2009 (see Table 20.1).

20.2 FULFILMENT OF THE MAASTRICHT CRITERIA

At the end of 2007 Slovakia fulfilled the long-term interest rate criterion, the inflation criterion and the exchange rate stability criterion. Inflation had eased substantially in the course of 2007, causing the average 12-month inflation rate to drop below the reference value, so that Slovakia met the

Table 20.1 Timetable of euro adoption

Process	Date
Maastricht criteria fulfilment	Year 2007 to March 2008
Convergence reports of ECB and European Commission	May 2008
European Commission recommendation to the Council on abrogation of derogation	May 2008
Consultation with European Parliament	June 2008
Council abrogates derogation and sets conversion rate	July 2008
Euro area entry	1 January 2009

Note: Based on previous euro area entry examples.

criterion for price stability from August 2007 onward. The average long-term interest rate had been far below the reference value for several years already. The main condition for exchange rate stability – minimum two-year membership in the exchange rate mechanism (ERM II) – was met in November 2007. However, Slovakia did not meet the fiscal criterion, because the general government budget deficit was 3.7 per cent of GDP and thus above the threshold of 3 per cent of GDP.

Yet the perspective of fulfilling the Maastricht criteria in due course was very positive. The 12-month average HICP (Harmonized Index of Consumer Prices) inflation was expected to decline further below the reference value in the following months. According to the NBS's medium-term forecast, average year-on-year inflation as measured by the HICP was estimated at 1.9 per cent in spring 2008. The general government deficit for 2007 was originally budgeted at 2.9 per cent of GDP. The end-2007 estimate was for the deficit to end up at 2.5 per cent.

As regards the exchange rate criterion, the Slovak koruna has been appreciating since ERM II entry. Following agreement with the authorities, we adjusted the central rate of the koruna within ERM II in March 2007, revaluing the koruna by 8.5 per cent against the euro. In this respect it is very important to understand that Slovakia, along with its neighbouring country, operates a free floating regime. This has raised new questions, for instance in our debates with the European Commission and the European Central Bank, on what would be the impact after fixation of the exchange rate, or what was the role of appreciation in the low inflation environment we have in our country.

The inflation target for 2007 and 2008 was set at 2 per cent (Figure 20.1). The target for 2007 was overshot due to external factors and food price increases. Year-on-year HICP inflation reached 2.5 per cent in December

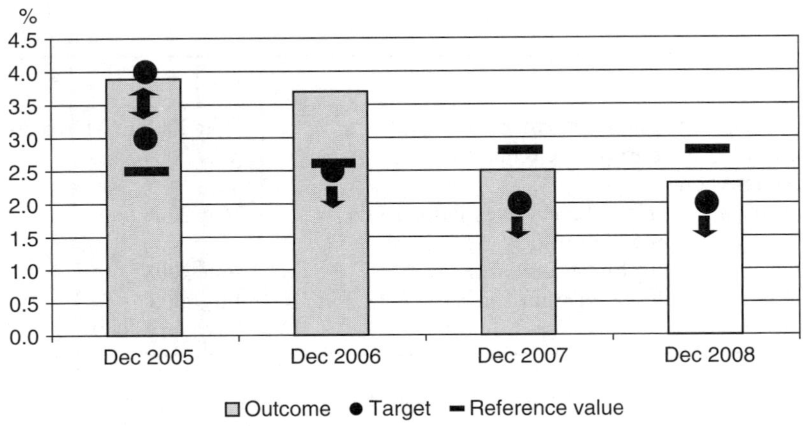

Figure 20.1 The inflation target and its fulfilment

2007. But the 12-month average inflation remained far below the reference value. Based on year-end estimates, the inflation target for 2008 will not be met due to the same factors as in 2007. We expect HICP inflation to rise slightly over the next two years, to 2.3 per cent by the end of 2008 and to 2.8 per cent by the end of 2009. However, inflation is thus expected to remain below the reference value in both 2008 and 2009.

20.3 PUBLIC DEFICIT

In coming years the general government deficit will decline in accordance with the framework set previously (see Figure 20.2). The public government deficit is planned to diminish gradually in the medium term at least 0.5 per cent of GDP per year. It will decline to 2.3 per cent of GDP in 2008, to 1.8 per cent of GDP in 2009 and to 0.8 per cent of GDP in 2010. The budgeted deficit will be lower than the reference value even including full costs of the second pillar.

The development outlook mentioned above confirms that Slovakia will meet all the Maastricht criteria from spring 2008. However, we have observed growing discussion on sustainability of the fulfilment. Probably the most critical criterion for Slovakia is the inflation target. The inflation criterion is expected to stay below the reference value in 2008 and 2009. No artificial measures have taken place. The current inflation was lowered without resorting to regulated price freezes, tax decreases or any other one-off measures. In Slovakia all regulated prices are at cost recovery levels and

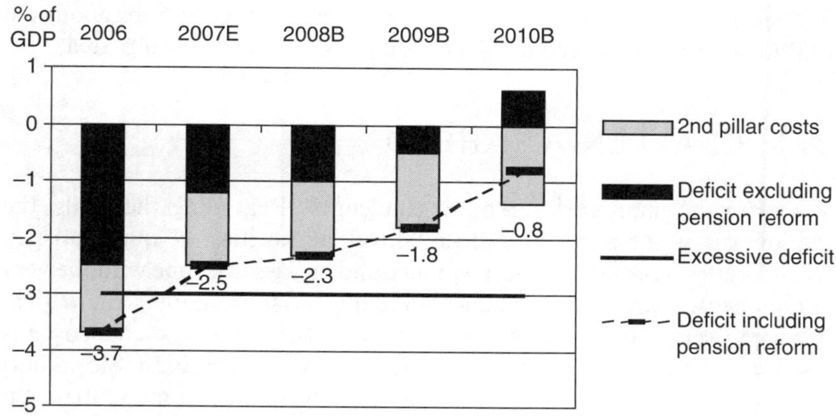

Figure 20.2 General government deficit outlook

most energy prices are at or above European Union average. Here again, I would like to underline that the National Bank of Slovakia is committed not only to reaching the inflation target, but also to put inflation on a sustainable path. And even though the targets will be slightly overshot, inflation will stay below the reference value for at least two years after the assessment of convergence, that is, the inflation criterion will be fulfilled sustainably.

Regarding the public finance sustainability, the implemented public finance reform allows for a sustainable reduction of the public deficit. There was no creation of public–private partnerships or new doubtful state guarantees. We are not resorting to a temporary increase in taxes or intentional postponement of expenditures. The Ministry of Finance maintains a permanent methodology discussion with Eurostat in order to discuss the impact of planned operations in advance. However, the situation is far from being ideal. Methodological changes implemented ex post create a certain amount of uncertainty. Here I would like to note that Slovakia has a very good track record in this area. In the last years the deficit was always lower than budgeted.

Despite the fact that the European Commission considers Slovakia to have a medium risk concerning the long-term sustainability of Slovakia's public finances, I would like to emphasize the authorities' intention to bring the fiscal side to balance over the long-term perspective.

Turning to exchange rate sustainability: like in many other countries in the region, the nominal appreciation was not and is not a result of central bank or government action. It reflects strong economic fundamentals – a high productivity differential vis-à-vis the euro area and a lower inflation differential. This trend is the result of very positive expectations about the outlook of the Slovak economy, including accession to the euro area.

20.4 CHALLENGES AHEAD

What are the main euro adoption challenges? Regarding the goals, the National Bank of Slovakia and the Slovak authorities are quite satisfied with the latest convergence performance and at the same time with the very comprehensive progress in technical preparations for joining the euro area. Yet some very important challenges remain. Meeting these challenges is essential for the sustainability of the Maastricht criteria. First, Slovakia is faced with the so-called 'impossible trinity', meaning that a country with an open capital account cannot control both the exchange rate and inflation. As a result, we opted for the strategy of keeping our participation in ERM II as short as possible. A second challenge is that the inflation criterion is a 'moving target' that we do not know in advance. It often depends on developments in the countries outside of the euro area. For a certain time period we were faced with the paradox that inflation was increasing in the euro area, while the reference value of the inflation criterion was falling. Third, a frequently discussed challenge of the catching-up economies is the Balassa-Samuelson effect, explaining higher price increases in the non-tradable sector that lead to higher overall inflation. Estimates of the value of this effect differ significantly. Based on our analyses, we expect only a 0.7 percentage point contribution to overall inflation in the medium term. The value of our estimate is lower due to several mitigation factors present in our economy. The most important factors are related to recorded wage developments. Wage increases in the tradable sector are lower than the labour productivity growth. Wage increases in the non-tradable sector lag behind the wage increases in the tradable sector. We have also observed some productivity increase in the non-tradable sector based on foreign direct investment inflows.

20.5 CONCLUSION

Given the strong economic fundamentals and equal treatment, it is most probable that Slovakia will meet all Maastricht criteria and that the criteria will be met sustainably. We believe that the thorough realization of consistent plans based on in-depth analyses and supported by political consensus will result in our successful euro area entry by the targeted year, namely 2009. At the same time it is important to point out that Slovakia is the first country adopting the euro from the floating exchange regime within the bounds of ERM II. Our evaluation will probably become the precedent for future assessment, and the sustainability of the exchange rate regimes will be verified.

NOTE

1. Governor, Central Bank of Slovakia.

21. Euro area enlargement: lessons and challenges

Servaas Deroose, Paul Kutos and Massimo Suardi[1]

The process of euro area enlargement is ongoing. Three of the 12 new EU member states (NMS) have already joined the single currency area, and others are set to follow in the foreseeable future. At the same time, some initial expectations about the timing of euro adoption have not been fulfilled, as the achievement of sustainable convergence has proved more difficult than expected. This chapter discusses some of the key challenges facing the NMS on their way to the euro and beyond.

21.1 STYLIZED FACTS ON THE NMS

Most of the new member states are former transition economies that are still undergoing a 'real convergence' process vis-à-vis the euro area, that is, income levels and economic structures are becoming more aligned. Average GDP per capita (expressed in terms of purchasing power standards – PPS) is around 60 per cent of the euro area average, though this masks considerable differences within the group. A robust growth performance, based on successful macroeconomic stabilization strategies and comprehensive structural reform, has led to a narrowing of the income gap vis-à-vis the euro area by more than ten percentage points since the beginning of the 2000s (Figure 21.1). Major progress has thus already been made, accelerated by the EU accession process, but completing real convergence will remain a key task for many years to come.

Among the many economic policies that will bear on this policy challenge, a powerful instrument in the EU tool box is euro adoption. While the NMS are already broadly well placed for euro area participation from an 'optimal currency area' perspective (for an overview see, for example, Darvas and Szapáry, 2008), moving towards the euro under conditions of real convergence and rapid financial deepening – and managing real convergence within monetary union – may pose a number of challenges:

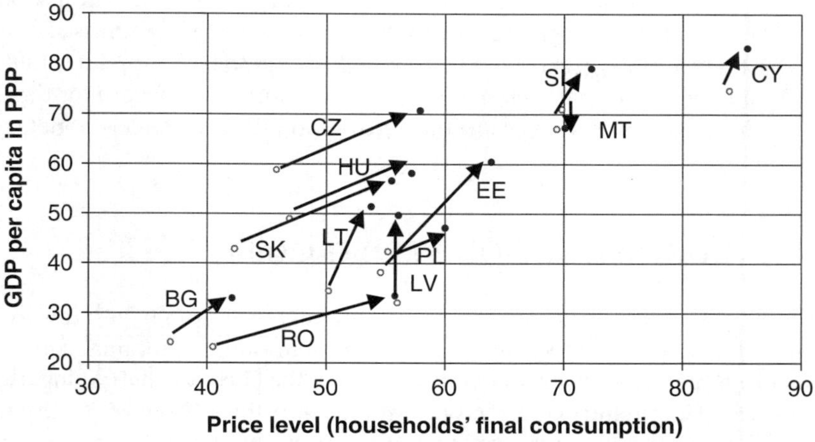

Sources: Eurostat and Commission services.

Figure 21.1 NMS – GDP per capita and price levels (2000 and 2006, EU 15 = 100)

- The NMS receive large capital inflows in a context of high returns and relative scarcity of capital. The loosening of balance-of-payments constraints under economic and monetary union (EMU) (Blanchard and Giavazzi, 2002) would be expected to exacerbate this trend. While the large inflows of capital are in principle a sign of a well-integrated capital market, they also raise absorption challenges. It is important to note that, compared with the member states that have adopted the euro in 1999, the NMS have already been able to expand their external balance sheets vastly, well ahead of euro adoption (for a regional comparison with other emerging markets, see IMF, 2007). To some extent this pre-empts the challenges, as well as the benefits, of euro adoption for a number of NMS.
- The NMS experience a fairly robust convergence of price levels vis-à-vis the euro area (Figure 21.1). This trend, which operates through a number of channels such as the Balassa-Samuelson effect (whose importance in practice is, however, increasingly questioned – see Égert, 2007), increased demand for services, adjustments in administered prices (which are generally still low in the NMS), and improvements in non-price competitiveness of tradables (Égert and Lommatzsch, 2004), may add an 'extra kick' to demand for credit (MacDonald and Wójcik, 2006). While under full capital mobility

this effect would in principle be valid under both fixed and flexible exchange rate regimes, operating either through compressed real interest rates or expected nominal appreciation (see Lipschitz, Lane and Mourmouras, 2005), it is in practice more of a concern for those NMS that operate pegs to the euro – and a fortiori under monetary union.

21.2 EURO ADOPTION STRATEGIES

These considerations suggest that in determining the optimal path towards euro adoption, readiness is more important than timing. Nominal convergence (as defined under the framework of the Treaty establishing the European Community) is an important indicator for a country's ability to contribute to the stability-oriented policy setting of the euro area (as evidence of a shared 'stability culture'). But readiness needs to go beyond that, implying in particular the ability to cope with country-specific adjustment needs.

For the purpose of gauging the NMS' challenges on the way to the euro and beyond, one appealing approach is to group them according to the fixity vs. flexibility of their exchange rate regimes. Under this approach, which maps closely with countries' euro adoption strategies, the NMS can be separated into two rather distinct groups at this juncture (with Slovakia, set to adopt the euro in 2009, as a somewhat intermediate case). As a separate third group, it is also useful to look at the 'forerunners' among the NMS in terms of euro adoption.

21.2.1 What Lessons from the Forerunners?

The experience of Slovenia, Cyprus and Malta in securing early euro area entry can provide some instructive insights for other NMS, though country-specific differences obviously need to be taken into account. Comparing the experience of the three countries, a number of common threads emerge:

- First, in all three countries there was a *strong and sustained political commitment* to adopt the euro and the benefits of participating in the euro area were seen as outweighing the costs. Together with the countries' explicit euro adoption targets, this seems to have been instrumental in successfully focusing policy efforts.
- Second, the *starting position* of the three countries may have been in some respects easier than for others. All three countries are relatively

advanced in terms of their income levels (though Malta's income level is comparable to that of the Czech Republic). Furthermore, Malta and Cyprus did not have to undergo the profound structural change associated with transition, while Slovenia completed this process relatively early.

- However, *policy adjustments* were required in all three countries. Slovenia used participation in the exchange rate mechanism (ERM) II to overcome an inflation bias that had become entrenched through its crawling peg and wage indexation mechanisms. Malta and Cyprus had to undertake sustained fiscal consolidation to end excessive budget deficits and bring down government debt levels.
- In all three countries euro adoption was used as an *anchor for reform*. This concerned primarily policies to achieve nominal convergence, but also included some broader structural policy efforts to maintain, and where necessary strengthen, competitiveness.

Looking ahead, the experience of the 'frontrunners' will be watched closely, to see whether policy discipline can be sustained once euro adoption is secured. Policy challenges include the absorption of interest rate convergence upon euro area entry (which is generally smaller than for previous catching-up euro area members, but differs among the three countries); a realistic management of expectations (which will influence economic agents' behaviour, for instance in terms of wage setting and credit demand) and, crucially, keeping momentum in fiscal and structural policies and avoiding 'reform fatigue'. This will be key to ensure that the benefits of euro adoption can be fully reaped.

21.2.2 The 'Peggers': Victims of Their Own Success?

One group of NMS outside the euro area operates hard pegs vis-à-vis the euro, either through currency board arrangements (Estonia, Lithuania, Bulgaria) or a conventional peg (Latvia). These countries have pursued exchange rate stability already for a prolonged period, which has served to anchor expectations and import credibility. Given their generally small size and high degree of openness, they see the scope for autonomous monetary policy limited, and outweighed by risks of excessive exchange rate volatility amid shallow financial markets. As external anchors, the pegs have contributed to macroeconomic stabilization and underpinned policy discipline, as reflected in comparatively strong fiscal positions (Figure 21.2) and relatively flexible product and labour markets.

That said, country-specific differences remain; for example, Bulgaria lags the Baltics on a number of structural indicators (notably on the business

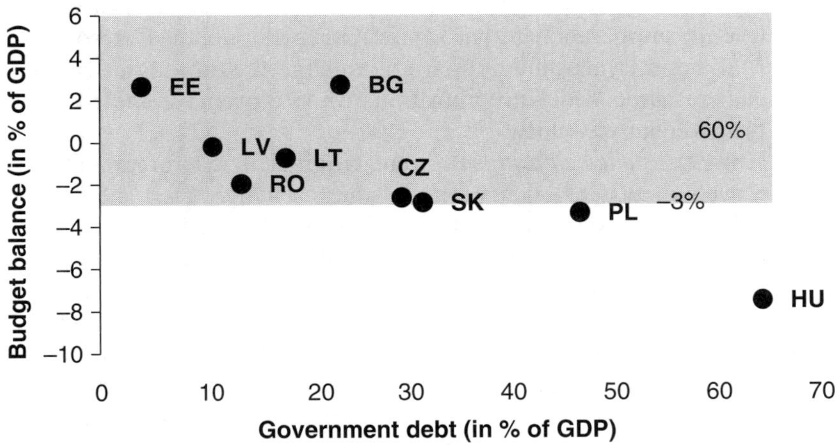

Sources: Eurostat and Commission services.

Figure 21.2 General government balance and government debt (% of GDP, 2006)

environment), while Latvia and Lithuania have pursued a somewhat lesser degree of fiscal policy discipline than the other two countries in the group. With the exception of the latest entrant, Bulgaria, these NMS already participate in ERM II. They aim at euro adoption as soon as conditions permit, though ambitious early adoption plans had to be postponed in view of inflationary pressures, and no firm new dates have been set. When it became clear that euro adoption would be delayed, there was little impact on investor confidence, confirming that credible policy frameworks are more important in shaping investor sentiment than the date of euro adoption itself.

The peggers among the NMS have recorded strong growth over the past years, partly explainable by their comparatively low starting position, but also in the context of a generally high degree of macroeconomic stability and favourable policy settings underpinning investor sentiment (as reflected, for example, in high foreign direct investment – FDI). In most cases, growth has been heavily driven by investment activity, which is in principle consistent with robust catching up (provided that resources are allocated effectively). In a setting of increased financial integration, foreign savings have been mobilized on a large scale to finance investment activity, that is, capital has flowed 'downhill', as opposed to the situation in some other emerging market regions (for a discussion see Abiad, Leigh and Mody, 2007).

Given a high degree of credibility, interest rate convergence with the euro area has advanced, implying strong real interest rate compression in a context of higher trend inflation. Together with buoyant income expectations and increased availability of credit, this has fuelled domestic lending (much of it in euros), which in turn has underpinned a surge in domestic demand and real estate booms. Increasing capacity constraints and overheating pressures have emerged in the recent past, in particular given rapidly tightening labour markets (with emigration adding to strains on labour supply). Large imbalances – such as current account deficits of unprecedented magnitude, high inflation and rapidly rising unit labour costs – will put economic policy frameworks to the test in the coming years. Combined with the recent deterioration in global financial market conditions, the imbalances may lead to a more cautious attitude of foreign investors going forward.

The challenge for these countries is to engineer a 'soft landing' for their economies, that is, an orderly return towards sustainable medium-term growth paths while minimizing vulnerabilities along the way. This will put a premium on efficient and flexible resource allocation in the economy, while prudential policy will need to remain vigilant and the fiscal stance will have to contain demand pressures.

21.2.3 The 'Floaters': Slow, But Steady?

A number of NMS have chosen to maintain a higher degree of flexibility in their exchange rate arrangements for the time being. These countries follow domestic monetary anchors through inflation targeting regimes, with managed or free floats (Czech Republic, Poland, Romania), hybrid inflation/exchange rate targets (Hungary) or inflation targeting under the conditions of ERM II (Slovakia). On average, these countries recorded somewhat slower growth rates, weaker fiscal positions and made less progress in the structural domain than the peggers, but financial imbalances are also smaller. Indeed, in terms of macroeconomic stability they have steadily caught up with the exchange rate 'fixers', while market risk perceptions have improved. Country-specific divergence is clearly larger than among the 'fixers', however, and it is difficult to generalize. For example, Romania, the poorest among the 'floaters', records imbalances comparable to those of the 'fixers', underscoring the importance of initial conditions in framing real convergence-related challenges.

While at first sight it would seem that short-term policy challenges are less pronounced among the 'floating' NMS at this juncture, some caveats are in order. First, the scope for autonomous monetary and exchange rate policy in the NMS is limited by the degree of foreign-currency borrowing (along the lines of the 'fear of floating' literature, following Calvo and Reinhardt, 2000), a consideration that is relevant for example for Hungary. Second, the evidence suggests that in practice, exchange rates act not only as shock absorbers but also as shock amplifiers (see, for example, Borghijs and Kuijs, 2004; Darvas and Szapáry, 2008). Third, if other policies are insufficiently supportive, monetary policy carries a heavy burden to maintain macroeconomic stability, which may have a negative impact on longer-term growth prospects, notably by hampering investment activity, as, for instance, observed in Poland in the early 2000s (see Darnaut and Kutos, 2005).

Thus, while the need for policy discipline may seem somewhat less stringent in the short term for floating currency countries, delaying necessary reforms may have adverse medium-term consequences. For the 'floaters' among the NMS, the challenge is to maintain an orderly convergence path, which is also critical to preserve investor confidence and favourable external financing conditions.[2]

Slovakia stands out as something of a case apart. It has pursued a firm euro adoption strategy (with 2009 specified as the official entry target) and has participated in ERM II since 2005, though it has been the only participant availing itself of the flexibility built into the mechanism. During the time of ERM II participation the koruna recorded a sustained nominal appreciation trend absorbing equilibrium real appreciation pressures related to strong productivity gains in the tradables sector in a context of large FDI inflows. In parallel with its efforts to meet the conditions for euro area entry, Slovakia has also followed a comprehensive structural reform agenda over the last years, including tax reforms and measures to underpin a favourable investment climate (including for FDI).

21.3 POLICY IMPLICATIONS

Based on this brief, and necessarily sketchy, overview, a number of policy challenges emerge. For the purpose of this chapter, four main and interrelated challenges are highlighted that will shape the NMS' policy as they move towards the euro and beyond: (1) absorbing large capital inflows and preserving external sustainability; (2) managing rapid credit growth; (3) securing sound fiscal policies; and (4) enhancing structural channels of adjustment to country-specific developments within the euro area (and even before).

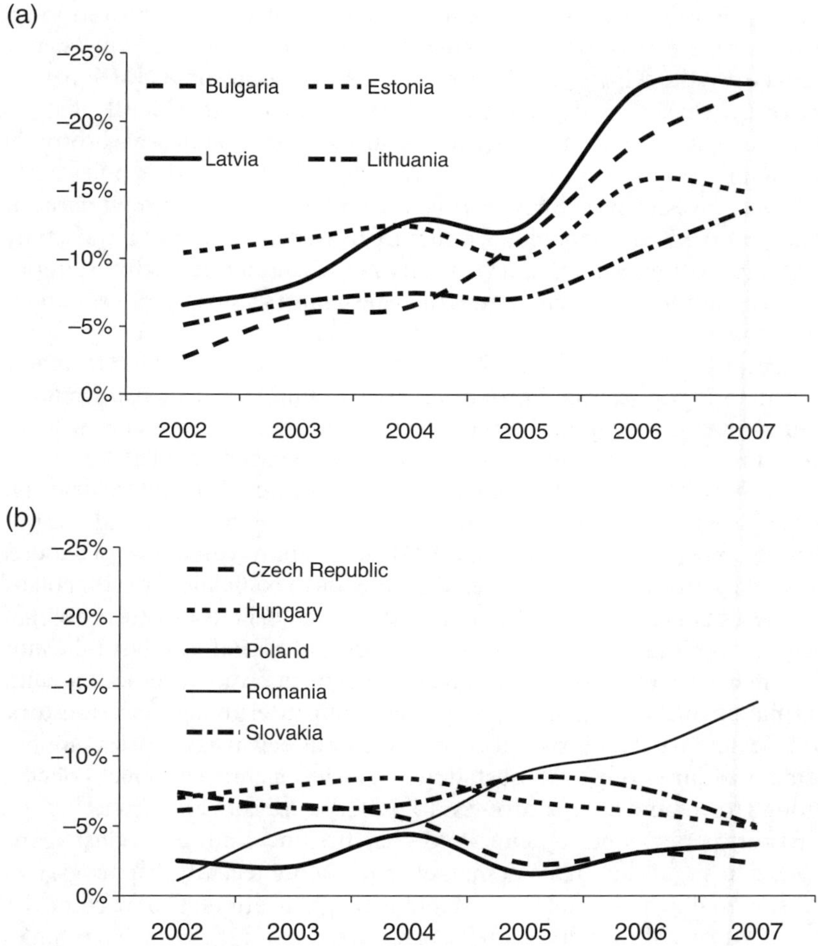

Sources: Eurostat and Commission services.

Figure 21.3 Balance on current transactions with rest of world (% of GDP)

21.3.1 Capital Inflows: Opportunity and Challenge

Many new member states run sizeable current account deficits in the context of their catching-up process (Figure 21.3). This is economically benign insofar as it reflects an efficient inter-temporal allocation of resources by economic agents. Indeed, temporarily high external deficits may be warranted in a context of strong investment activity that is not fully matched by domestic savings. Also, consumers adjust to improved long-term income expectations and release pent-up demand following better access to credit. More recently, external imbalances in some NMS (particularly the 'peggers' within the group) have clearly surpassed levels that are sustainable in the medium term, raising concerns about a disorderly unwinding.

Private investment activity has been the main driver of current account deficits in the NMS, though the structure of investment is not always fully conducive to enhancing export capacity in the medium term (for example, due to a high share of real estate). In some countries (for example, Latvia) private saving rates have also dropped significantly on the back of buoyant consumption. While the public sector has generally not been a major driving force for external imbalances, excessive fiscal deficits contribute to saving–investment gaps in some countries (while in other cases strong fiscal positions have partly compensated for private saving shortfalls).

The NMS' external financing situation appears broadly reassuring, although with some weak spots. The role of FDI has been significant, though sometimes volatile. While FDI flows are not immune to sudden stops, they are generally considered a 'safe' form of financing, with collateral benefits such as knowledge and skills transfers. Short-term foreign credit is significant in some cases (for example, the Baltics), but this indicator may overstate risks as it tends to reflect intra-group transactions with EU parent banks, which are, in principle, long-term strategic investors. Gross external debt has risen to significant levels in some countries, emphasizing the importance of sustaining prudent macroeconomic policies, strong growth and competitiveness to preserve market confidence.

Export performance by most NMS has been robust over the last years, leading to significant gains in market share. More recently, export growth has slowed down in some cases. Rapid real appreciation in some countries points to risks of overvaluation if current very fast wage growth continues against the background of tight labour markets. More generally, slower export growth may indicate that the 'easy gains' of past years are over, and increasing efforts to maintain both price and non-price competitiveness will be necessary in the future (see Fabrizio, Igan and Mody, 2007).

Looking ahead, competitiveness and external sustainability depend on a range of factors, including sectoral export structures (where some countries have made strong progress in advancing to high value-added, fast-growing sectors, while others still rely mainly on low value-added sectors that offer less medium-term prospects), productivity growth in tradables (indicating an efficient use of capital inflows), the efficiency of resource allocation on product and factor markets, and the business environment and investment climate.

21.3.2 Rapid Credit Growth: Risk Management is Key

Domestic credit has accelerated rapidly, albeit from low levels, in many of the NMS in recent years (Figure 21.4). Much of the rapid credit expansion has been denominated in euros or other foreign currencies, particularly in countries with fixed exchange rates vis-à-vis the euro or countries with large interest rate differentials (Hungary). Both demand and supply factors have contributed to buoyant credit dynamics in the new member states. Favourable financing conditions, rising income expectations and structural change in the banking sector – consolidation, increased competition, the entry of foreign players, a broadening of products and services – have been underpinning high domestic credit growth, supported by a strengthening of regulatory and supervisory frameworks in the context of EU accession. Strong interest rate convergence with the euro area, in particular (but not exclusively) for countries with credible pegs (Figure 21.5), has added to credit demand, whose macroeconomic impact will have to be managed through other domestic policies. The overall levels of credit and household indebtedness in the new member states are still considerably lower than in the euro area, though in some cases 'equilibrium' levels of credit relative to fundamentals appear to have been reached, or surpassed (see Backé, Égert and Zumer, 2006). This calls for particular vigilance.

In particular, rapid growth of household lending in the NMS raises the issue of possible 'irrational exuberance' about future income prospects, perhaps coupled with limited risk awareness in an environment of cheap credit. Strong credit growth to sensitive sectors, such as real estate, calls for particular attention with a view to detecting the build-up of asset price bubbles and minimizing risk concentration. Fiscal policy can play a supportive role by eliminating potential distortions (for example, interest subsidies), while the scope for supervisory measures to ensure adequate risk management by both lenders and borrowers (for example, through loan-to-value or loan-to-income ratios) should also be explored, taking, however, into account the limits to domestic prudential intervention in an increasingly integrated financial sector (as recently evidenced by the muted longer-term effect of temporary credit controls in Bulgaria).

The EU regulatory framework provides an important shield for financial stability in the NMS. Financial soundness indicators point to a generally high degree of resilience of financial sectors in the NMS, though some underlying vulnerabilities (such as loan quality or funding risks for subsidiaries) may not be fully picked up in real time during a credit boom. Challenges for financial supervision also include ensuring an efficient supervisory coverage of the non-bank financial sector (for example,

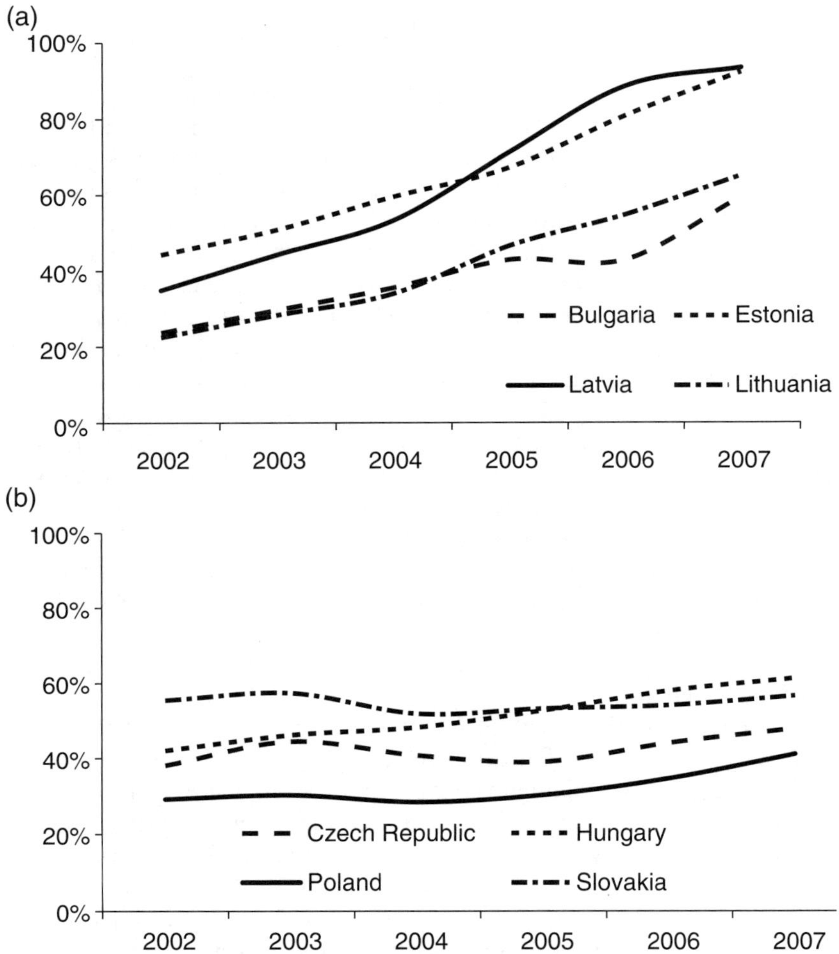

Sources: Reuters EcoWin and central banks.

Figure 21.4 Domestic credit (% of GDP)

leasing), monitoring of direct cross-border lending, and close international cooperation among supervisors, both in a home-host and regional setting.

21.3.3 Fiscal Policy: Steering a Safe Course Amid Multiple Tasks

The NMS' fiscal situation has, overall, recorded a significant improvement since EU accession, with the (unweighted) average general government

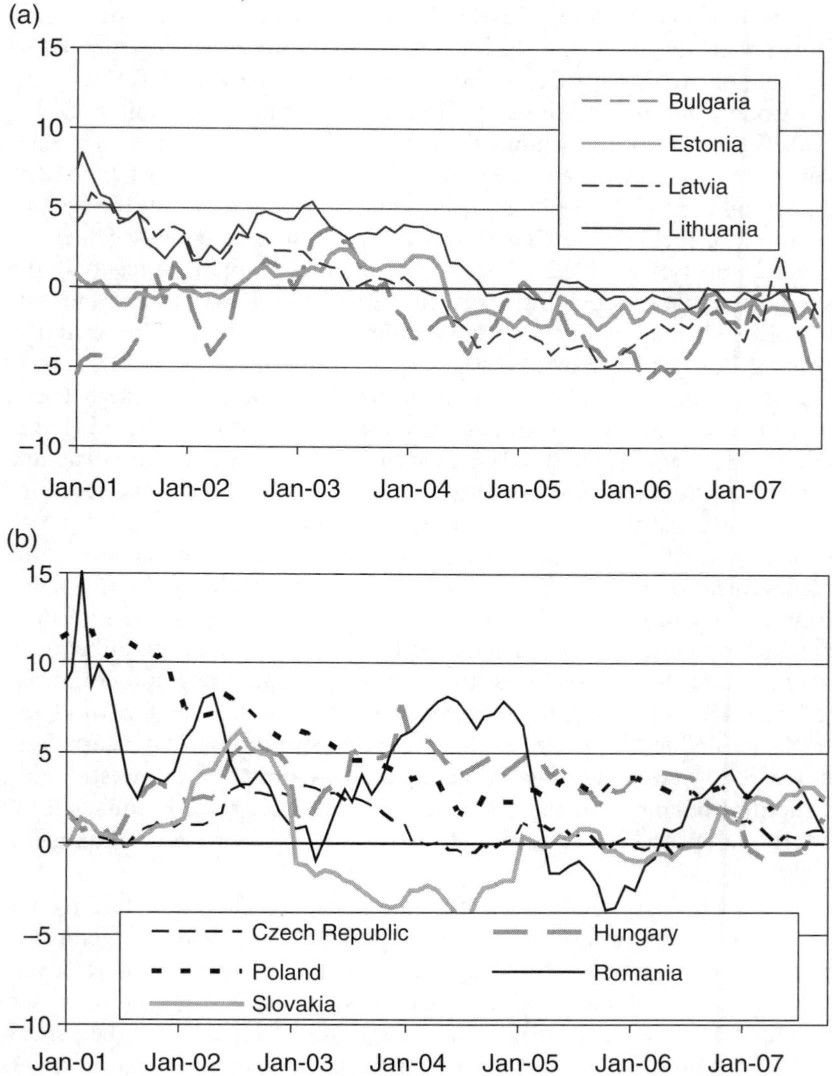

Source: Eurostat.

Figure 21.5 Inflation adjusted three-month interest rates (in per cent)

deficit decreasing from 3.7 per cent to 0.6 per cent of GDP between 2003 and 2007. While half of the NMS became subject to an Excessive Deficit Procedure after accession, they have progressively overcome their excessive deficits since then (with the exception of Hungary). On the other side of the spectrum, some NMS (Bulgaria, Estonia) recorded significant general government surpluses over the last years. The improvement in general government positions has reflected both buoyant revenue growth (on the back of strong cyclical conditions and improvements in tax compliance), but also efforts to restrain spending dynamics. Public debt levels are on average lower than those of the euro area and on a decreasing trend, which reduces vulnerabilities to changes in financing conditions and improves the starting position for tackling the challenges of long-term sustainability, which are acute in most of the NMS. The EU fiscal policy framework has played a supportive role in providing an anchor for fiscal reforms, thus decreasing the risk of fiscal policy-induced asymmetric shocks (see, for example, Darvas, Rose and Szapáry, 2005).

Fiscal policy in the NMS needs to chart a judicious course between multiple challenges (see European Commission, 2005). On the one hand, the need for well-targeted public spending in areas such as infrastructure, education and R&D in the context of catching up may limit the scope for expenditure restraint. On the other hand, however, high revenue growth in the context of strong, tax-rich economic expansion facilitates the achievement of a prudent fiscal stance. This is particularly key in an environment where fiscal policy is the main domestic instrument to rein in demand pressures and overheating risks. To be sure, tackling imbalances may require fiscal positions that go significantly beyond countries' medium-term objectives (MTOs) set under the Stability and Growth Pact; these are defined by reference to long-term sustainability concerns and not with a view to short-term stabilization. Uncertainties in estimating structural balances during strong credit and asset price booms call for additional prudence in setting fiscal targets (Jaeger and Schuknecht, 2004).

The quality of public finances also needs full attention. Redirecting public spending towards pro-growth priorities may require significant reforms of budgetary structures. Public sector employment is relatively large relative to the level of development in a number of countries, and public sector wage setting may have a signalling function for the private sector. A number of countries have enacted tax reforms as part of strategies to improve the business environment. This may be beneficial, but it should not lead to a sustained deterioration in underlying fiscal positions. Fiscal reform should also aim at securing appropriate incentives in the tax/transfer system, aiming at mobilizing labour market resources. The strengthening of the framework for fiscal policy, including fiscal institutions, is an important ingredient in securing the achievement of these multiple objectives.

21.3.4 Structural Policy: The Micro–Macro Link

Effective domestic adjustment mechanisms are a key element for a successful performance under monetary union (see European Commission, 2006). This requires flexible product and labour markets, and a business environment fostering productivity growth and competitiveness. The challenge is particularly pronounced for catching-up economies, which will have to manage underlying structural divergences for some time to come. In the absence of adequate adjustment mechanisms to deal with country-specific developments, catching up within the single currency area can be associated with destabilizing cycles of overheating and overcooling (Deroose, Langedijk and Roeger, 2004).

Concretely, stepping up the pace of structural reforms involves a set of mutually reinforcing policies in many areas: enhancing labour mobility, skill development and wage flexibility (which is relatively high in some of the NMS but lags in others); ensuring that wage setting is in line with productivity gains; fostering innovation and entrepreneurship so as to maintain competitiveness and move up the value-added chain; and maintaining a favourable business environment and investment climate (including for post-privatization FDI).

To be sure, the challenges are strongly country-specific. For example, the Baltics score best among the NMS in the World Bank's Doing Business ranking (with Estonia and Latvia among the top ten EU countries), while most of the other NMS are in the bottom half of the EU-27 (World Bank, 2007). As a crude approximation, the NMS tend to be relatively strong in terms of labour market flexibility (though not always in mobilizing labour supply), while lagging somewhat on product market functioning and the business environment.

Enhancing structural reforms requires a determined policy effort. National Reform Programmes in the context of the Lisbon Strategy are a key instrument in the toolkit of the EU economic policy framework to bring together the various strands of the multi-faceted policy areas in which action is required. National strategies should be geared at mobilizing all stakeholders and creating mutually reinforcing reform dynamics within a concerted overall strategy.

21.4 CONCLUSION

The Treaty establishing the European Community provides a clear framework for the NMS' medium-term path of monetary integration. However, member states have significant leeway to adopt different strategies in terms of timing and policies to achieve the necessary degree of convergence. The Commission does not advocate any particular euro adoption strategy in terms of timing or policy frameworks in the run-up to the euro. Policies need to be attuned to country-specific conditions. The key is to embed euro adoption strategies in a comprehensive policy framework, aimed at promoting longer-term macroeconomic stability and robust real convergence, in an environment of increased financial integration. This will require the mobilization of all domestic instruments in the macroeconomic, structural and prudential domains.

NOTES

1. Economic and Financial Affairs Directorate General (DG ECFIN), European Commission. The views expressed are those of the authors and do not necessarily reflect those of DG ECFIN or the European Commission.
2. Research suggests that already now, the NMS benefit from an 'EU umbrella' effect that reduces yield spreads by some 50–100 basis points relative to comparable economies (Luengnaruemitchai and Schadler, 2007). The 'umbrella effect' has not yet been tested under stress; preliminary evidence from the recent global turbulences suggest that it might be at least partially vulnerable to changes in global risk appetite (that is, act in a pro-cyclical manner).

REFERENCES

Abiad, A., D. Leigh and A. Mody (2007), 'International finance and income convergence: Europe is different', *IMF Working Paper* No. 07/64.

Backé, P., B. Égert and T. Zumer (2006), 'Credit growth in Central and Eastern Europe, new (over)shooting stars?', *Focus on European Economic Integration* No. 1/2006, 112–39.

Blanchard, O. and F. Giavazzi (2002), 'Current account deficits in the euro area: the end of the Feldstein-Horioka puzzle?', *MIT Working Paper* No. 03-05.

Borghijs, A. and L. Kuijs (2004), 'Exchange rates in Central Europe: a blessing or a curse?', *IMF Working Paper* No. 04/2.

Calvo, G. and C. Reinhardt (2000), 'Fear of floating', *NBER Working Paper* No. 7993.

Darnaut, N. and P. Kutos (2005), 'Poland's policy mix: fiscal or monetary leadership?', *ECFIN Country Focus* **2** (1), 2–6.

Darvas, Z. and G. Szapáry (2008), 'Euro area enlargement and euro adoption strategies', forthcoming.

Deroose, S., S. Langedijk and W. Roeger (2004), 'Reviewing adjustment dynamics in EMU: from overheating to overcooling', *European Economy, Economic Papers* No. 198.

Darvas, Z., A. Rose and G. Szapáry (2005), 'Fiscal divergence and business cycle synchronization: irresponsibility is idiosyncratic', *NBER Working Paper* No. 11580.

Égert, B. (2007), 'Real convergence, price level convergence and inflation differentials in Europe', *OeNB Working Paper* No. 138.

Égert, B. and K. Lommatzsch (2004), 'Equilibrium exchange rates in the transition: the tradable price-based real appreciation and estimation uncertainty', *William Davidson Institute Working Paper* No. 676.

European Commission (2005), 'Public finances in EMU', *European Economy* No. 3/2005.

European Commission (2006), 'The EU economy: 2006 review', *European Economy* No. 6/2006.

Fabrizio, S., D. Igan and A. Mody (2007), 'The dynamics of product quality and international competitiveness', *IMF Working Paper* No. 07/97.

IMF (2007), 'Managing large capital inflows', *World Economic Outlook*, October, 105–34.

Jaeger, A. and L. Schuknecht (2004), 'Boom-bust phases in asset prices and fiscal policy behaviour', *IMF Working Paper* No. 04/54.

Lipschitz, L., T. Lane and A. Mourmouras (2005), 'Real convergence, capital flows, and monetary policy: notes on the European transition countries', in S. Schadler (ed.), *Euro Adoption in Central and Eastern Europe: Opportunities and Challenges*, Washington, DC, International Monetary Fund, 61–9.

Luengnaruemitchai, P. and S. Schadler (2007), 'Do economists and financial markets' perspectives on the new members of the EU differ?', *IMF Working Paper* No. 07/65.

MacDonald, R. and C. Wójcik (2006), 'Catching-up, inflation differentials and credit booms in a heterogeneous monetary union: some implications for EMU and new EU member states,' *CESifo Working Paper Series* No. 1761.

World Bank (2007), *Doing Business 2008*, World Bank Publications.

Index